HUMAN STATUE OF LIBERTY
18,000 OFFICERS AND MEN
AT
CAMP DODGE, DES MOINES IA.
COL. WM. NEWMAN, COMMANDING
COL. RUSH S. WELLS, DIRECTING.

*This building holds in trust
the records of our national life
and symbolizes our faith
in the permanency of
our national institutions.*

—INSCRIPTION ON THE NATIONAL ARCHIVES BUILDING

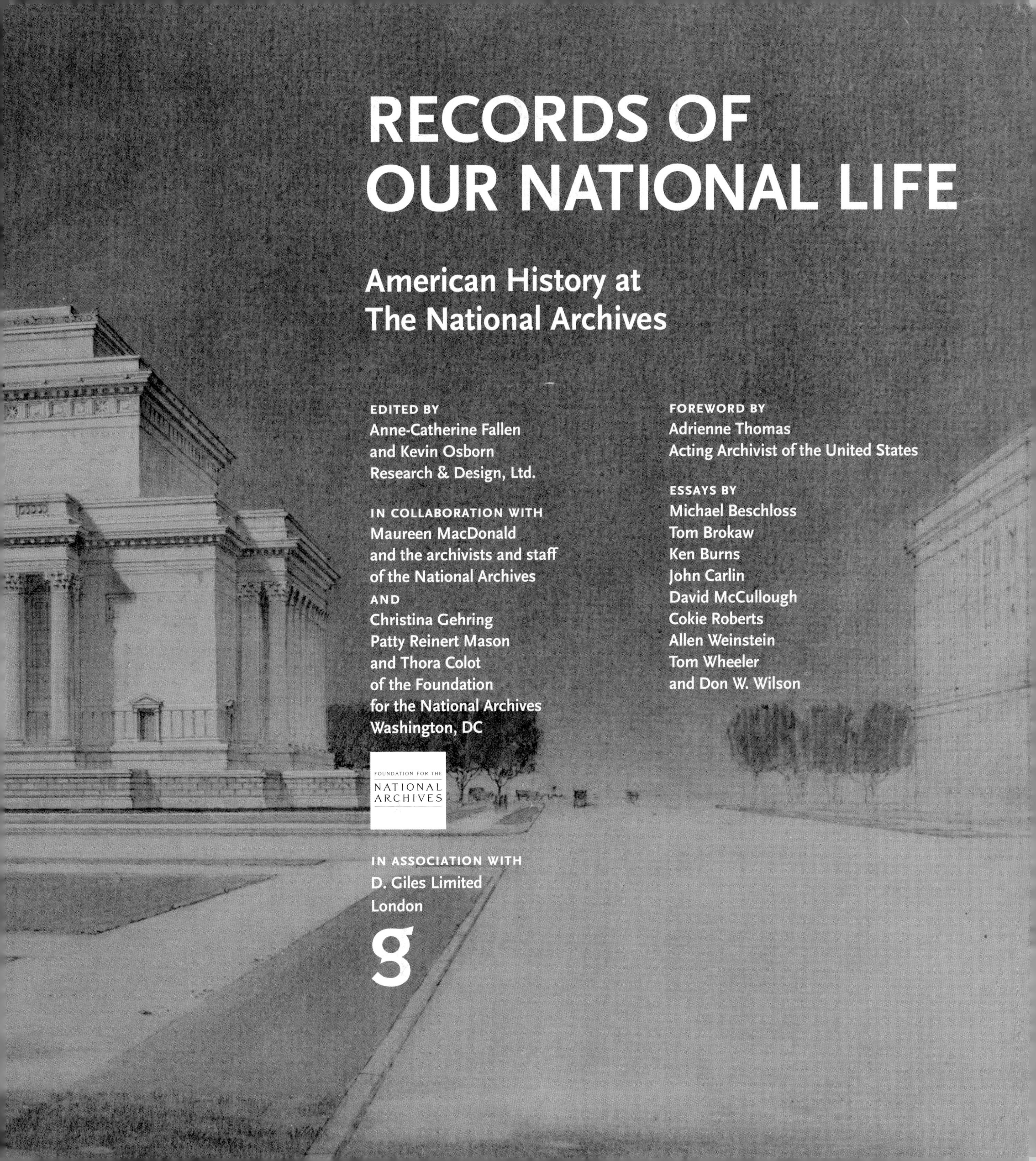

RECORDS OF OUR NATIONAL LIFE

American History at The National Archives

EDITED BY
Anne-Catherine Fallen
and Kevin Osborn
Research & Design, Ltd.

IN COLLABORATION WITH
Maureen MacDonald
and the archivists and staff
of the National Archives
AND
Christina Gehring
Patty Reinert Mason
and Thora Colot
of the Foundation
for the National Archives
Washington, DC

FOREWORD BY
Adrienne Thomas
Acting Archivist of the United States

ESSAYS BY
Michael Beschloss
Tom Brokaw
Ken Burns
John Carlin
David McCullough
Cokie Roberts
Allen Weinstein
Tom Wheeler
and Don W. Wilson

FOUNDATION FOR THE
NATIONAL
ARCHIVES

IN ASSOCIATION WITH
D. Giles Limited
London

g

Records of Our National Life:
American History at The National Archives

Copyright © 2009
The Foundation for the National Archives
Washington, DC

For the Foundation for the National Archives:
Thora S.R. Colot, Executive Director
Christina Gehring, Publications and Research Manager
Patty Reinert Mason, Senior Editor

For the National Archives and Records Administration:
Maureen MacDonald, Project Manager

For Research & Design, Ltd., Arlington, Virginia:
Anne-Catherine Fallen and Kevin Osborn, Editors and Designers

First published in 2009 by GILES
An imprint of D Giles Limited
4 Crescent Stables
139 Upper Richmond Road
London, SW15 2TN, UK
www.gilesltd.com

Library of Congress Cataloging-in-Publication Data

Records of our national life : American history at the National Archives /
edited by Anne-Catherine Fallen and Kevin Osborn ; in colloboration with
Maureen MacDonald and the archivists and staff of theNational Archives ; and
Christina Gehring, Patty Reinert Mason, and Thora Colot ; foreword by Adrienne Thomas.
     p. cm.
     ISBN 978-1-904832-71-3 (hardcover : alk. paper) —
     ISBN978-0-9841033-0-0 (softcover : alk. paper)
1. United States--History--Sources--Bibliography--Catalogs. 2. United States.
National Archives--Catalogs. I. Fallen, Anne-Catherine. II. Osborn,
Kevin. III. MacDonald, Maureen. IV. Foundation for the National
Archives.
     Z1236.R436 2009
     [E178]
     016.973--dc22
          2009031920

ISBN 978-1-904832-71-3 (hardback)
ISBN 978-0-9841033-0-0 (paperback)
All rights reserved.

Printed and bound in Hong Kong

Front cover:
Selected images from
Records of Our National Life

Back cover and pages 2–3:
Perspective View of National Archives Building
Constitution Avenue Side, 1931.
RG 121, Records of the Public Buildings Service

Frontispiece:
Human Statue of Liberty. 18,000 Officers
and Men at Camp Dodge, Des Moines, Iowa.
Col. William Newman, Commanding.
Col. Rush S. Wells, Directing. Mole & Thomas,
September 1918. [165-WW-521B(1)]

This book celebrating the 75th anniversary of the National Archives would not have been possible had it not been for the extraordinary contributions of time and talent by the staff of the National Archives and Records Administration and the Foundation for the National Archives.

In particular, we would like to recognize the tireless efforts of two individuals, without whom this book could not have moved forward. Our sincere gratitude to Maureen MacDonald, a veteran of the National Archives whose knowledge of the records, positive spirit, and dedication to the project made all the difference. We also thank Christina Gehring, Publications and Research Manager for the Foundation, who managed the book project and worked indefatigably along with Maureen to bring it to completion, demonstrating the true value of the ongoing partnership between the Archives and the Foundation.

We would also like to thank the editors, Anne-Catherine Fallen and Kevin Osborn of Research & Design, Ltd., for bringing their knowledge and experience to this project. After extensive research, they developed the concept for the book and collaborated with National Archives and Foundation staff to create this innovative and beautiful volume.

The outstanding quality of images in this book is due to the professionalism and expertise of the Archives' Digital Lab. Their willingness to make this book a priority and give it their best effort is much appreciated. In particular, we would like to thank: Doris Hamburg, Martin Jacobson, Michelle Farnsworth, Sheri Hill, Michael Horsley, Steve Puglia, Jeff Reed, and Jennifer Seitz.

Records are important, and this book is about the records. But it is the people behind the records who bring them to life every day at the National Archives. The stunning array of records highlighted in this commemorative book is a tribute to the National Archives staff and their intimate knowledge of the holdings. We thank Acting Archivist Adrienne Thomas and Michael Kurtz, Assistant Archivist for Records Services–Washington, DC, whose support of the project and willingness to make their staff, especially Chief of Staff Debra Wall, available, made this book possible. We would like to thank the following individuals for lending their expertise:

From the Washington, DC, area: Pat Anderson, Juliette Arai, Brian Barth, Rick Blondo, Richard Boylan, Greg Bradsher, Peter Brauer, Ashley Bucciferro, Bruce Bustard, Cynthia Campbell, Rachael Carter, Rebecca Collier, Jim Collins, Robin Cookson, Katherine Coram, Rebecca Crawford, Daniel Dancis, Dorothy Dougherty, Bob Ellis, Annie Farrar, Jane Fitzgerald, Kate Flaherty, Cynthia Fox, Matt Fulgham, Sandra Glasser, Martha Grove, Paul Harrison, Rania Hassan, James Hastings, Kenneth Heger, Jim Hemphill, Richard Hunt, Mary Ilario, Charlie Joholske, Miriam Kleiman, Christina Kovac, Jessie Kratz, Tab Lewis, Tina Ligon, Ed McCarter, Darlene McClurkin, Earl McDonald, Mark Mollan, Gene Morris, Nancy Mottershaw, Martha Murphy, Nick Natanson, Catherine Nicholson, Rick Peuser, David Pfeiffer, Trevor Plante, Connie Potter, Holly Reed, Mary Lynn Ritzenthaler, Mary Frances Ronan, Lisa Royse, Mary Ryan, Richard Schneider, George Shaner, Rebecca Sharp, Katherine Vollen, Les Waffen, Reginald Washington, Kris Wilhelm, Kelly Wisch, Mitch Yockelson and James Zeender.

From the Presidential libraries: Olivia Anastasiadis, Kelly Barton, Brian Blake, Patricia Burchfield, Robert Clark, Tony Clark, Barbara Cline, Janice Davis, Stacy Davis, Susan Donius, James Draper, Sheila Drumheller, Mary Finch, Steve Green, Kenneth Hafelim, Margaret Harman, James Herring, Don Holloway, Spencer Howard, John Keller, Michelle Kopfer, Clifford Laube, Tim Naftali, Polly Nodine, Stephen Plotkin, Ed Quick, Timothy Rives, Emily Robison, Samuel Rushay, Sara Saunders, Pauline Testerman, James Wagner, and Caitlin White.

From NARA's regional facilities: Douglas Bicknese, Priscilla Foley, Scott Forsythe, Joan Gearin, William Greene, Meg Hacker, Guy Hall, Walter Hickey, Donald Jackanicz, Melinda Johnson, Susan Karren, Glenn Longacre, Jenny McMillen, Dan Nealand, Jennifer Nelson, Greg Plunges, Aaron Prah, Rich Rayburn, Kimberlee Ried, Arlene Royer, Leslie Simon, Mary Evelyn Tomlin, Martin Tuohy, and Paul Wormser.

The **Foundation for the National Archives** also deserves our thanks. Senior Editor Patty Reinert Mason helped research, write, and edit text for the book, and Kristy Gibson provided valuable administrative support. We also want to recognize and thank the rest of the Foundation staff and its Board of Directors who continue to work to raise funds to support important projects, such as this commemorative book.

Happy 75th Anniversary, National Archives! This publication celebrates the importance of the documents, pictures, film, and more—the *Records of Our National Life*—which you preserve and protect for all of us.

Thora S.R. Colot
Executive Director
Foundation for the National Archives

TABLE OF CONTENTS

TABLE OF CONTENTS

Adrienne Thomas
Acting Archivist of the United States

Three-quarters of a century ago, the National Archives was created to safeguard our nation's most treasured records and to preserve them for future generations. Without benefit of modern technology or preservation techniques, with little data on how records would survive exposure to light, temperature, or humidity, and amid much disagreement over where the Archives should be built and what exactly it should contain, our predecessors forged ahead. Their goal was to protect the nation's most important official records, but also to share them with their fellow citizens, so they could carry out their democratic duty to hold their Government accountable.

Even before the National Archives Building in downtown Washington was completed, it was clear the amount of records generated by the growing Federal bureaucracy would require more space. An interior courtyard to the building intended for future expansion was converted to stacks much sooner than planned. And as the Government continued to grow, so did the National Archives.

Today, the National Archives' original building in the heart of the nation's capital draws more than a million visitors and researchers each year who come to study their own family histories and to discover the incredible stories of our nation. The Archives remains the proud home of the official Charters of Freedom—the Declaration of Independence, the U.S. Constitution, and the Bill of Rights—as well as the Treaty of Paris that ended the Revolutionary War, President Abraham Lincoln's Emancipation Proclamation, the Homestead Act, and many other seminal documents of our shared history.

Its original building also is home to the National Archives Experience with its award-winning "Public Vaults" educational exhibition; the Boeing Learning Center, flagship of the National Archives' educational programs in the Washington area for teachers and students; the Lawrence F. O'Brien Gallery, which showcases temporary and traveling exhibitions; and the William G. McGowan Theater, Washington's premier venue for documentary films, author lectures, and panel discussions.

But the National Archives encompasses so much more. It includes the National Archives at College Park, a modern, 1.8 million square foot facility in suburban Maryland, as well as a vast network of Federal record centers, regional archives, and Presidential libraries and museums around the country. It includes the *Federal Register*, the daily record of the official actions of the Executive Branch, and the Information Security Oversight Office, which is responsible for developing policies for classifying, declassifying, and safeguarding information vital to our national security.

Today, more than ever, the National Archives lives up to the inscription on its historic building on the National Mall. "This building," it reads, "holds in trust the records of our national life and symbolizes our faith in the permanency of our national institutions."

This book, produced in partnership with the Foundation for the National Archives, takes the reader on an incredible journey through the momentous events of American history. Inviting close-up inspection of documents, photographs, and maps arranged in chronological order, it provides a unique opportunity to explore and appreciate some of the billions of records held by the National Archives.

I hope it will inspire you to begin your own journey through the National Archives on your next visit to Washington or to one of our facilities closer to your home. These records are safeguarded by the National Archives, but they belong to every American and they are yours to discover.

H. R. 8910

(PUBLIC No. 432 73d CONGRESS)

Seventy-third Congress of the United States of America;

At the Second Session,

Begun and held at the City of Washington on Wednesday, the third
day of January, one thousand nine hundred and thirty-four.

AN ACT

To establish a National Archives of the United States Government,
and for other purposes.

*Be it enacted by the Senate and House of Representatives of the
United States of America in Congress assembled,* That there is
hereby created the Office of Archivist of the United States, the
Archivist to be appointed by the President of the United States,
by and with the advice and consent of the Senate.

SEC. 2. The salary of the Archivist shall be $10,000 annually. All
persons to be employed in the National Archives Establishment
shall be appointed by the Archivist solely with reference to their
fitness for their particular duties and without regard to civil-service
law; and the Archivist shall make rules and regulations for the
government of the National Archives; but any official or employee
with salary of $5,000 or over shall be appointed by the President
by and with the advice and consent of the Senate.

SEC. 3. All archives or records belonging to the Government of
the United States (legislative, executive, judicial, and other) shall
be under the charge and superintendence of the Archivist to this
extent: He shall have full power to inspect personally or by deputy
the records of any agency of the United States Government whatsoever and wheresoever located, and shall have the full cooperation
of any and all persons in charge of such records in such inspections,
and to requisition for transfer to the National Archives Establishment such archives, or records as the National Archives Council,
hereafter provided shall approve for such transfer, and he shall
have authority to make regulations for the arrangement, custody,
use, and withdrawal of material deposited in the National Archives
Building: *Provided,* That any head of an executive department,
independent office, or other agency of the Government may, for
limited periods, not exceeding in duration his tenure of that office,
exempt from examination and consultation by officials, private individuals, or any other persons such confidential matter transferred
from his department or office, as he may deem wise.

SEC. 4. The immediate custody and control of the National
Archives Building and such other buildings, grounds, and equipment as may from time to time become a part of the National

Act to establish a National Archives
of the United States Government,
June 19, 1934.
RG 11, General Records
of the U.S. Government

H. R. 8910—3

SEC. 9. That the Archivist shall make to Congress, at the beginning of each regular session, a report for the preceding fiscal year as
to the National Archives, the said report including a detailed statement of all accessions and of all receipts and expenditures on account
of the said establishment. He shall also transmit to Congress the
recommendations of the Commission on National Historical Publications, and, on January 1 of each year, with the approval of the
Council, a list or description of the papers, documents, and so forth
(among the archives and records of the Government), which appear
to have no permanent value or historical interest, and which, with
the concurrence of the Government agency concerned, and subject
to the approval of Congress, shall be destroyed or otherwise effectively disposed of.

SEC. 10. That there are hereby authorized such appropriations
as may be necessary for the maintenance of the National Archives
Building and the administration of the collections, the expenses, and
work of the Commission on National Historical Publications, the
supply of necessary equipment and expenses incidental to the operations aforesaid, including transfer of records to the Archives Building; printing and binding; personal services in the District of
Columbia and elsewhere; travel and subsistence and per diem in lieu
of subsistence, notwithstanding the provisions of any other Acts;
stenographic services by contract or otherwise as may be deemed
necessary; purchases and exchange of books and maps; purchase,
exchange, and operation of motor vehicles; and all absolutely necessary contingent expenses, all to be expended under the direction of
the Archivist, who shall annually submit to Congress estimates there-
for in the manner prescribed by law.

SEC. 11. All Acts or parts of Acts relating to the charge and
custody, preservation, and disposition of official
papers and documents of executive departments and other governmental agencies inconsistent with the provisions of this Act are
hereby repealed.

Henry T. Rainey
Speaker of the House of Representatives.

Jno N Garner
Vice President of the United States and
President of the Senate.

Approved
June 19 - 1934

Franklin D Roosevelt

Michael Beschloss
Presidential Historian and Author

When President Kennedy was assassinated, I was a seven-year-old fourth grader at Western Avenue School outside Chicago. I wrote a letter on wide-ruled grammar school paper to the new President Johnson, suggesting that he "get some large carving firm" to add the late President's head to Mount Rushmore. Soon I got back a typed letter on White House stationery signed in blue ink by LBJ's secretary, Juanita Roberts, saying that her boss had asked her to thank me for sharing my idea to honor his predecessor. I took the letter down to our local skating rink, where my friends immediately denounced it as a forgery, insisting that no President's secretary would bother to reply to some kid out in Illinois.

Fourteen years passed. By then, I had graduated from Williams College and was turning my senior honors thesis, on the relationship between Joseph Kennedy and Franklin Roosevelt, into a book. Just before Christmas 1977, I made my first visit to the Lyndon Johnson Presidential Library in Austin, Texas, to see the papers of both LBJ and the columnist Drew Pearson, who had both been involved with both of my main characters. Loudspeakers on the library's main floor were playing the "Hallelujah" chorus (whether in honor of LBJ or the impending holiday, I wasn't certain).

Presiding over the library's research room was the able Nancy Kegan Smith. I told her about the letter I sent President Johnson in 1963. I, of course, had Ms. Roberts's reply but not my original letter, since I wasn't exactly in the habit of keeping copies of my correspondence at the age of seven. I said, "It's a long shot, since my guess is that you don't keep routine letters to the President from unknown kids, but is there any chance you could take a look?" She did—and in 20 minutes, with a flourish, she produced my old letter, exquisitely preserved in an acid-free National Archives folder. She reminded me that I had to handle it under the same rules that applied to more august state documents—wearing white gloves and with no ink pens anywhere in proximity. I obeyed.

More than 30 years later, Nancy is now the Director of the Presidential Materials Staff in Washington, DC. And as I've told her more than once, the story of that first meeting of ours encapsulates for me one of the glories of the institution. Most people know that the Archives houses the documents and other materials created by our Presidents and other leaders. What they sometimes forget is that, in much greater measure, it preserves the records of all the American people—fourth-graders in Illinois and everyone else—who not only come to choose those leaders but whose lives are so transformed by them.

Our Founders conceived of America as a constant dialogue between leaders and citizens. What better symbol is there of this principle than the National Archives? It is a steady reminder to all of us that, whenever we are tempted to look at our history as the product of famous leaders, we should remember that when our democracy works, the most powerful title available to an American is that of citizen. I think the Founders would be chagrined that it took Americans a full century and a half to realize how much we needed a National Archives!

Tom Brokaw
Special Correspondent, NBC News

As a young man living hard by the Missouri River in a sparsely populated corner of south central South Dakota, I was endlessly fascinated by the history all around me in the form of Sioux Indian artifacts—stools fashioned from bison bones, arrow heads, and hide scrapers chiseled out of sweet water agate stones. As I turned over in my hands these reminders of the past, I felt an almost spiritual connection to the resourceful native Americans who had roamed this vast prairie not that many years earlier.

I was reminded of those formative experiences when I visited the National Archives and the staff took me deep into the vaults of this priceless collection of Americana to examine documents reflecting some of my personal interests.

When they produced the original February 19, 1880, application of Charles Phillip Ingalls in Dakota Territory for a homestead near the village of DeSmet, I looked at his signature and wondered where his daughter, Laura, may have been that day. Was she with him when he filed the claim at the land office in Brookings, or was she with her mother back at Section 3, Township 110 N., Range 56 W. in Kingsbury County, walking the frozen ground, trying to imagine how the spring would bring a new barn that would dwarf their little house on the prairie? A house that measured 14 by 20 feet—smaller than many modern bedrooms—but grew to legendary proportions in Laura's timeless prose. I purchased copies of the Ingalls homestead application and sent them to my book-loving grandchildren for Christmas.

The National Archives also has a copy of the application of a young man from Ohio for admission to the U.S. Military Academy at West Point. He was not yet 18 when he applied so his parents had to sign for him. It occurred to me that those who rode with him to Little Bighorn may have wished his parents had other career ideas for their son, George Armstrong Custer.

The Ingalls and Custer documents, of course, are not on a par with copies of the Declaration of Independence or the Emancipation Proclamation, but I am always as intrigued by the small strokes of history as well as the bolder events. As a journalist and author of popular history, what appeals is the caulking of the seams of great events. The Civil War comes alive in the journals of the enlisted men as well as their generals.

The National Archives is nothing less than our national DNA, the genetic code of our history as it has played out in large ways and small, in triumph and tragedy, through the years. Any visit to this vibrant place is an exhilarating experience, an instructive and enduring reminder of who we are and how this nation is in a constant state of renewal.

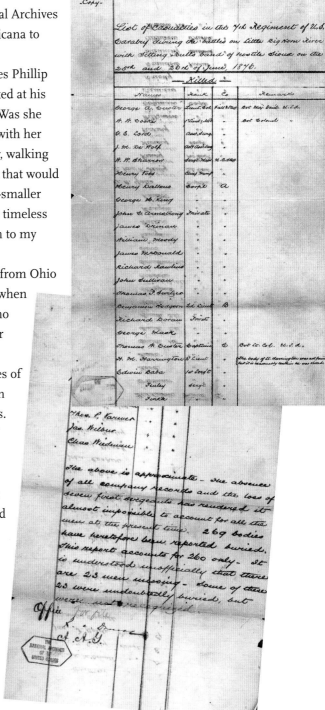

List of casualties from the Battle of Little Bighorn, June 25–26, 1876. RG 94, Records of the Adjutant General's Office

Ken Burns
Documentary Filmmaker

We are a fortunate people. Unlike every other country on Earth, we did not come together because of our common race, religion, language, or geography. We did not unite because of economics or as a result of conquest.

Instead, different as we are, we *choose* to cohere as a people because of our commitment to the words and ideas that founded our nation—words and ideas preserved in our Declaration of Independence, our Constitution, and our Bill of Rights, but also in the billions of other records, large and small, held in trust for us by the National Archives.

We prove, with every collective breath we take, that words and ideas matter. They stitch us together as a people, and they remind us why, against all odds, despite our many disagreements, and contrary to the general impulses of human nature, we decide to stand together.

In the vast vault of the National Archives are preserved our words and our ideas at our worst—the Alien and Sedition Acts, President Jackson's message to Congress on Indian removal, the Supreme Court's decisions in *Dred Scott* and *Plessy* v. *Ferguson*.

But here also are words that reflect our best ideas: Our Constitution, drafted at the end of the 18th century but still a reliable rulebook for adjudicating the most complicated problems of the 21st century, our Declaration of Independence, and our Bill of Rights. Our Homestead Act is here too, as is the Emancipation Proclamation, and the act establishing Yellowstone National Park. Our 19th Amendment is here, acknowledging women's right to vote, and so are the Marshall Plan and Lincoln's Inaugural Addresses and other messages to Congress about the importance of holding ourselves together as a nation.

In the midst of Civil War, Abraham Lincoln, our great poet President, urged us: "Fellow citizens, we cannot escape history...The fiery trial through which we pass will light us down, in honor or dishonor, to the latest generation...We shall nobly save, or meanly lose, the last best hope of earth."

Even today, we cannot escape history. And the very existence of the National Archives, which preserves the hard evidence on which our country was built—without regard to partisanship or the condemnation or adulation that future generations might heap upon it—reminds us in every generation to reintroduce ourselves to the words and ideas of our Founders.

For while the Archives is the safe house for our words and ideas, it is up to us to live up to their meaning—to renew our bonds, to hold our Government accountable, to preserve our freedoms, and to nobly save our country for our children—and theirs. When we ask ourselves, what finally does endure of our civilization, we find the answer at the National Archives: The great gift of our accumulated memory—our good words as well as our terrible ideas—is here. It is the evidence of the people and the nation that we were and that we are still becoming.

John Carlin
Eighth Archivist of the United States

I had the honor of serving as the Eighth Archivist of the United States from 1995 to 2005, overseeing an agency that is critically important to our citizens, our democracy, and our history. For three-quarters of a century, the National Archives has served as our national record keeper, preserving as a national trust the records on which we, as a democratic people, depend: to document our rights, to ensure the accountability of our Government, and to understand our nation's past so we can better plan for our future. The fulfillment of these responsibilities was the motivating force behind my service as Archivist.

The accountability of the Government to its people and the protection of their rights is the very cornerstone of the democracy in which we live. The dedicated efforts of Archives staff to preserve and make available the records of the three branches of our Government enable us to claim our rights and entitlements. Through these efforts, we are able to hold our Government officials accountable as well as understand our past and the breadth of our national experience. For our history is found not only in the Charters of Freedom, constitutional amendments and Presidential proclamations, but also in census records that enumerate each individual of our population, in veterans records that detail the service of the courageous men and women who have fought for our rights, and in immigration records that tell the compelling story of men and women who risked everything to pursue their dream of freedom and opportunity in the new country they chose to call their own.

Upon becoming Archivist, I soon realized that for all the importance of the National Archives, few people appreciated its role in our society and how its records could affect their lives. One reporter commented that most people came to the National Archives for the "religious" experience of seeing the Charters of Freedom. While it's true we hold the Charters sacred, too many visitors were leaving with little knowledge of the scope of the collection of records we held in trust for them or of the work involved in preserving and providing access to those records. It was that realization that gave rise to the idea of the National Archives Experience and to the creation of a robust partnership with the Foundation for the National Archives, designed to make the pantheon of the National Archives records collection more completely and readily available to the American citizen.

The importance of the National Archives in telling our stories was made very real to me throughout my tenure, but one of the most poignant times was shortly after the terrorist attacks of September 11, 2001. We had planned to open our "American Originals" traveling exhibit at the New York Public Library on October 5. In the wake of the 9/11 tragedies, we considered postponing the tour. At the urging of our partners, we held the event and were very glad we did. It is at times of crisis we most need to be reminded of our shared history as Americans. The documents in that exhibit, like all the records preserved by the Archives, testify to the spirit of our nation and its ability to endure through hardship and tragedy as well as prosperity.

To maintain citizen confidence in the integrity of the recordkeeping mission of the National Archives, it is essential that it remain a truly independent agency both by law and in the beliefs of the people. The agency and the Archivist must be free from any hint of partisan interference. That was the clear intent of its establishing act, and that was how I performed my duties as Archivist. Support for a strong and independent National Archives must never be compromised.

In a lifetime of public service, it is the opportunity I had to lead the National Archives and Records Administration and to work with its many dedicated employees in Washington and throughout the country for which I am most grateful. I am very proud to have served for 10 years as the guardian of the records of America. Records matter...the National Archives matters...for us, for our future, for the future of our democracy.

David McCullough
Author

The building is colossal, imposing, even by the standards of monumental Washington. From Constitution Avenue, a sweep of granite steps leads to a huge Corinthian portico, over which rises a massive stone attic. There are no windows to be seen, not a glimpse inside, only the main entrance with its tremendous, sliding bronze doors.

The architect was John Russell Pope, who designed the National Gallery of Art and the Jefferson Memorial, and his intention, plainly enough, was to convey feelings of permanence and grandeur. Yet the effect is more than a little forbidding. It might be the temple of some august secret order. Only those privy to the mysteries and privileges of Scholarship need enter here, you might conclude, and that would be mistaken and a shame. For the great collection of the National Archives is one of the wonders of our country, the richest, most enthralling documentation we have as a nation of who we are, what we have achieved, our adventures, and what we stand for. Everything within is about us, all of us, all the way back for more than 200 years, in good times and bad. It is a momentous, inexhaustible story, on paper—no one knows how much paper— and on microfilm and electromagnetic tape, in big leather-bound ledgers and albums, in maps, drawings, and something over 20 million photographs.

The three incomparable founding documents are the best known treasures. The Declaration of Independence, the Constitution, and the Bill of Rights are enshrined here, in heavy display cases in the marble Rotunda inside the main entrance, and they remain, year after year, among Washington's principal tourist attractions. But here, too, is housed the Louisiana Purchase Treaty of 1803, that piece of paper by which, with a stroke of a pen, Napoleon Bonaparte signed over a territory larger than that of all the original 13 colonies. Lincoln's Emancipation Proclamation is here. So is the Homestead Act. So is the instrument of surrender of the forces of Japan signed on board the battleship *Missouri* in 1945.

Officially, the Archives is the storehouse for those Federal papers and records judged to be of permanent value. With few exceptions there is no treaty or proclamation, no ordinance, act of Congress or amendment to the Constitution, no Government document of importance that is not here. And to hold one of them in your own hands can be an experience you never forget.

I once made a special visit to the Archives, to the Records of the Department of State, to see the original Hay-Bunau-Varilla Treaty of 1903, the treaty that cleared the way for the building of the Panama Canal and that remained a bone of contention between Panama and the United States for another 75 years. There was no practical need to see the original— I knew what the treaty said—but I was writing about the peculiar circumstances under which it was signed, and it was not until I actually held those neatly typed, very official looking pages, and studied the two signatures, of John Hay, the Secretary of State, and Philippe Bunau-Varilla, the Frenchman who had made himself Panama's envoy, that I felt a direct personal contact with that distant turning point. The sensation is not easy to describe and one that historians and researchers experience often in the Archives.

I am told that the majority of those who use the Archives are people doing genealogical research, personal family history. But it might also be said that everybody who comes here, whether briefly to look at the great documents enshrined beneath glass, or to work with the collections, is somebody who feels the kinship in all our history as a people. The collection is of us and it is for us. "This building holds in trust the records of our national life..." reads an inscription carved in one wall, and it is that feeling of *life* that draws us here. That, above all. We can never know enough about those in whose footsteps we follow. We will never tire of their stories. As much as has already been found in the records of our past there is still more to be found, much more.

Excerpted from: *The National Archives of the United States*, with permission from Mr. McCullough.

Louisiana Purchase Treaty, Agreement to pay France, April 3, 1803.
RG 11, General Records of the U.S. Government

Cokie Roberts
Political Analyst for ABC News and NPR; Author

The Rotunda of the National Archives Building serves as something of an American shrine. Church-like in its darkness and its hush, even schoolchildren instinctively whisper inside its circumference. And then there's the arrangement of the documents in altar-like casings. As a Catholic, I'm struck by the ecclesiastical similarities—the Constitution presides as the main altar, the Declaration of Independence occupies St. Joseph's place, and the Bill of Rights fills Our Lady's spot.

It's appropriate that we should so revere what we've come to call the "Charters of Freedom." They are the very stuff of our nationhood. Think about it: We have no common religion, ethnicity, history, or even language. What binds us together as a country are the ideas represented by those documents and the institutions they created.

That's why it's so important to keep those institutions honest. And one of the ways we do that is through records. The Congress, the courts, and the cabinet must keep accounts of their activities, so that we the people can know what our elected representatives and the people they appoint are up to. We need to know and we need to remember. Without records, history is simply an argument. When we can look at the written word or hear the oral argument, we have the ability to actually understand not only what happened but why.

What seems like dry stuff—census reports, immigration papers, military commissions, congressional debates—actually bring the past alive. They tell the stories of dreams realized, in patents and petitions, and dreams dashed. Take the remarkable document researchers unearthed when they were preparing an exhibit on woman suffrage. Missing from the history books was "A Petition for Universal Suffrage" filed with Congress as the lawmakers were amending the Constitution to protect the rights and ensure the enfranchisement of freed slaves following the Civil War.

In requesting an amendment that would also prohibit states from disenfranchising "any of their citizens on the ground of sex" the petitioners argue: "The Constitution classes us as 'free people' and counts us as *whole* persons in the basis of representation; and yet we are governed without our consent, compelled to pay taxes without appeal, and punished for violation of law without choice of judge or juror."

Imagine the surprise of the document detectives as they stared at the handwritten signatures: "E. Cady Stanton," "Susan B. Anthony," "Lucy Stone," and others. Here were the great women of the suffrage movement taking their cause to Congress only to see their petition politically discarded. Reading through their brief but powerful arguments makes it all the more outrageous that it would take more than 30 years—after the signers were dead—for Congress to recognize women's most basic right as citizens.

If a dusty document can make you mad almost 150 years after it was written, there's nothing dry about it. Our history isn't always pretty, but it's often provocative. And only with records can we know it accurately. We can read through the struggles and sacrifices over the centuries and continuing today to perfect our union, making the realization of the ideals of the Charters of Freedom worthy of a shrine.

Petition for Universal Suffrage, January 1866.
RG 233, Records of the U.S. House of Representatives

Allen Weinstein
Ninth Archivist of the United States

One of my earliest memories of the Archives was as a graduate student and young instructor seeking access to sensitive, recently declassified World War II intelligence records overseen by the even-then-legendary archivist, John Taylor, who died only recently after a half-century's service to the National Archives and Records Administration (NARA). For young historians, Mr. Taylor served as our personal Virgil, steering us toward treasured documents that could lead to important career-shaping discoveries.

I went from "user" to "defender" of the National Archives somewhat later when, as a *Washington Post* editorial writer, I became passionately outraged that NARA had been placed under the General Services Administration's control. I wrote an editorial, "Free the Archives," published on July 4, 1981, urging the restoration of the agency's independence. A half-decade later, in 1986, I found myself working closely with the Commission led by then-Chief Justice Warren Burger, which was preparing the national component of the Constitution's bicentennial. We launched the effort with a magnificent reception and educational event at the National Archives. In the years that followed I took part in a variety of lectures, panel discussions, and other events at NARA.

In February 2005, however, my occasional involvement with the National Archives changed into my central commitment when I was sworn in by Supreme Court Justice Ruth Bader Ginsburg as the Ninth Archivist of the United States. The 44 months as Archivist that followed were among the greatest of my entire life. How could I fail to be suitably impressed by the confident professionalism of the Archives' 3,000 employees? Whether they are reviewing standards for declassifying complex records, preparing the day's *Federal Register*, developing policies adequate for defense in court testimony, explaining constitutional concepts to high school students, or preparing public exhibits for schools and civic groups, archivists budget for the unexpected and are rarely disappointed.

Archivists of the United States may change from time to time, but the work continues and the job description remains constant. As the designated custodian of America's records for the three branches of Government, the Archivist of the United States must work for the American people, impervious to partisanship. Scrupulous independence is necessary to perform this work because the Archivist serves to assure the timeliest and greatest measure of access to the documents of Government, access essential to preserving our democracy.

Tom Wheeler
Managing Director, Core Capital Partners

For half a dozen years, I had the privilege of being the president of the Foundation for the National Archives. One day, while showing some of the Archives' amazing holdings to a potential donor, military archivist Rick Peuser pulled out a book of glassine pages, each containing a telegraph message handwritten by Abraham Lincoln. I turned to the Archivist of the United States, John Carlin, and commented, "These are Mr. Lincoln's T-Mails." My book *Mr. Lincoln's T-Mails* grew from that moment.

Thanks to the new technology of telegraphy, Abraham Lincoln was the first online President. Thanks to the National Archives, Lincoln's original messages speak to us with a rare insight to his top-of-the-head thinking. The original records allow us to see what the printed word obscures: the scratch-outs and insertions that reflect Lincoln's real-time thinking. The original documents permit us to get as close as will ever be possible to a transcript of Abraham Lincoln's thought process.

When you see in Lincoln's own hand the telegram to Gen. George McClellan, "Can you please tell me what the horses of your army have done since the Battle of Antietam that would fatigue anything?" his frustration that the army had not pursued the rebels in September/October 1862 is palpable.

When we read the terse and to the point telegram to Gen. Ulysses Grant in the dark month of August 1864, "Hold on with a bull-dog grip and chew and choke as much as possible," we, too, respond as Grant did with a chuckle. And like Grant, we can sense the President's resolve.

But my favorite of all the Lincoln telegrams is one to a traveling Mary Lincoln responding to their 11-year-old son Tad's query about his pet goats: "Tell Tad the goats and father are very well— especially the goats." There, in his own hand, is Abraham Lincoln speaking to us about the burdens he felt and demonstrating the refuge he found in wit.

Documents such as these are the original text of the American Story, told in the hand of those who made that story. That the Government has preserved and protected these seminal shreds of history allows the records to speak to us today.

We simply would not know the fullness of our national story without these documents. In previous ages history was undocumented; tales passed from person-to-person. I first began to love history as my grandfather continued that oral tradition. When it became time to learn more, however, the hard copy at the National Archives preserved the facts and created the ability to dive deeper and discover even more.

That our nation holds these records sacred distinguishes it from despots and dictators who destroy records because of the truths they tell. But perhaps the greatest gift of the National Archives is the documents' ever-present reminder that someday our actions will be judged; just as we look at the records of those who preceded us and make our own assessments. It is a sobering reminder that we are custodians of our legacy—a legacy we know because of the documents that tell its story; a legacy we continue through our own actions and our own documents that will be preserved for future generations.

Telegrams from President Abraham Lincoln to Lt. Gen. Ulysses S. Grant (top)
and to Mrs. Mary Todd Lincoln (bottom).
RG 107, Records of the Office of the Secretary of War

Don W. Wilson, Ph.D.
Seventh Archivist of the United States

I had the great honor of serving the National Archives as the Seventh Archivist of the United States from 1985 until 1993. It was a period of great change for an institution seeking to define itself as a new independent agency in the Executive branch of the Federal Government. Many predicted that such a small agency was doomed to fail in the face of the many difficult issues that had to be addressed: the explosion in the number of new Federal records being created, especially in electronic form; the lack of space and resources to maintain the nation's most valuable historical records; mounting preservation issues for all types of Federal records; and the great need for adequate research facilities in its regional archives and Federal records centers across the country. After assuming the office, I was particularly struck by the need to upgrade the field operations. Regional archives and record centers had long been tucked away in General Services Administration warehouse facilities and industrial parks that made research access to original documents very difficult for most constituents. That issue along with educational outreach throughout the agency became priorities during my tenure.

Some of the same issues remain as challenges to the National Archives to this day, namely how to deal with the issues of electronic records. However, thanks to an extremely talented and strongly committed group of National Archives employees, often unrecognized national treasures in their own right, much headway has been made since becoming an independent agency. For example, during a very narrow window of opportunity in 1989, some creative thinking and timely action by several key senior managers, along with strong support from a few members of Congress, allowed the National Archives to put into process the building of the National Archives at College Park—Archives II. That accomplishment alone, I believe, assured the success of the National Archives as an independent agency.

Subsequent remodeling with an emphasis on education and public outreach at the original National Archives Building in Washington, DC, accompanied by strong outreach efforts in the regional archives and Presidential libraries, has enabled the agency to take its place as one of the nation's cultural and educational icons. Its importance as the place that houses the records that document the greatest democratic form of Government in the world is recognized by a history-minded public more than at any time in our country's history. The National Archives serves as an essential foundation of our society. The original records housed throughout its more than 30 facilities around the country help document our culture, identify our successes and failures as a form of Government, and perhaps most importantly, provide our citizens complete and equal access to any Federal record that personally impacts their lives or the lives of their families. A strong National Archives, I firmly believe, is an essential part of a strong nation. May our National Archives continue to grow stronger in its next 75 years of service to the American people.

RECORDS OF OUR NATIONAL LIFE

Our nation started from scratch—the scratch of quill on parchment. With indelible words, a group of determined and visionary citizens recorded the ideals of freedom and justice that gave birth to a new form of government. Parchment, paper, and ink allowed the Founders to preserve their revolutionary propositions and create a common understanding of the objectives for which they were willing to fight and die. The enduring documents they crafted out of their own hopes and sacrifices became the first "records of our national life."

Now in its third century, this experiment in self-government has grown into a diverse democracy. When our forbears created the Constitution, they could never have imagined the societal and technological changes that would follow, yet the Government they established "in Order to form a more perfect Union" continues to evolve in response to the needs of its citizens. The Founders believed in the power of words shaped through deliberation and debate, and the documents they created laid a solid foundation for the structure of government. Known collectively as the Charters of Freedom, these founding documents preserve the unalterable words and enduring spirit of our nation's birth. They provide the legal foundation and inspirational ideas for perfecting what the Founders began.

On display in the National Archives in Washington, DC, the Charters of Freedom are only the most visible of the records of national life held in trust for all citizens. When it was established in 1934, the National Archives assumed the recordkeeping responsibility for the Federal Government and inherited the accumulated records of departments and agencies. Since then, many more records have been added. Maintained in facilities throughout the United States, the numbers and types of materials are staggering—approximately 10 billion pages of textual records; 20 million photographs; 365,000 reels of film and 110,000 videotapes; 7 million maps, charts, and technical drawings; thousands of artifacts; and billions of machine-readable data sets. Yet these represent a tiny fraction of all the records generated by the Government since its beginning. Only the most important and useful records are preserved for posterity.

Records retained by the National Archives demonstrate the Government's responsibility to its citizens and provide evidence of its actions on their behalf—from collecting taxes to paying Social Security benefits; from processing immigrants to administering health studies; from building highways to defending borders. Records reveal the inner workings of all three branches of Government—

legislative, executive, and judicial. Records reflect the hopes and struggles of every generation of Americans—settlers on new soil, refugees from repression, veterans of wars, and victims of disasters. From parchment to pixels, the records register the successes and failures of Government as it responds to its citizens, proving, above all, that the process of perfecting the Union is imperfect and perpetual.

Discovering the Records

The hundreds of records collected in this book give a glimpse into the extensive holdings waiting to be discovered at the National Archives. They are arranged in chronological order, sweeping from the struggle for independence to the 2009 Tally of Electoral Votes. All facets of the American story emerge here, from the noble to the ignoble, the monumental to the mundane. The overriding themes of the nation's history are covered—territorial exploration and expansion, immigration and migration, political life, the rights of women and minorities, and the growth of industry and technology.

These records are proof that the life of our nation is the life of its citizens. Whether they feature the famous or the unknown, records reveal the human face of history—the shock of a militiaman when the British fire at Lexington; the anguish of a wife whose husband is held by Barbary pirates; the relief of immigrants passing through Ellis Island; the pride and defiance of parents whose teenagers integrate a Little Rock high school; the poignancy as Lady Bird Johnson describes events in Dallas.

The records are presented straightforwardly, with a minimum of description, so the reader can experience the thrill of encountering materials as if doing primary research at the National Archives. Some pages feature a single document, while others cover a subject through multiple records. The date appears on the outside corner of each page to maintain the chronology. The title introduces the record or its subject, and when the record is a written document, a quote from the page on display is included. Where there is more than one record on the page, each item is identified in a brief caption. A more extensive description of each record or topic is included with citation information in a special section beginning on page 271. This section is also organized in chronological order; dates and record titles are clearly identified.

To discover thousands more records or to begin in-depth research on a particular subject, please visit the National Archives web site: *www.archives.gov.*

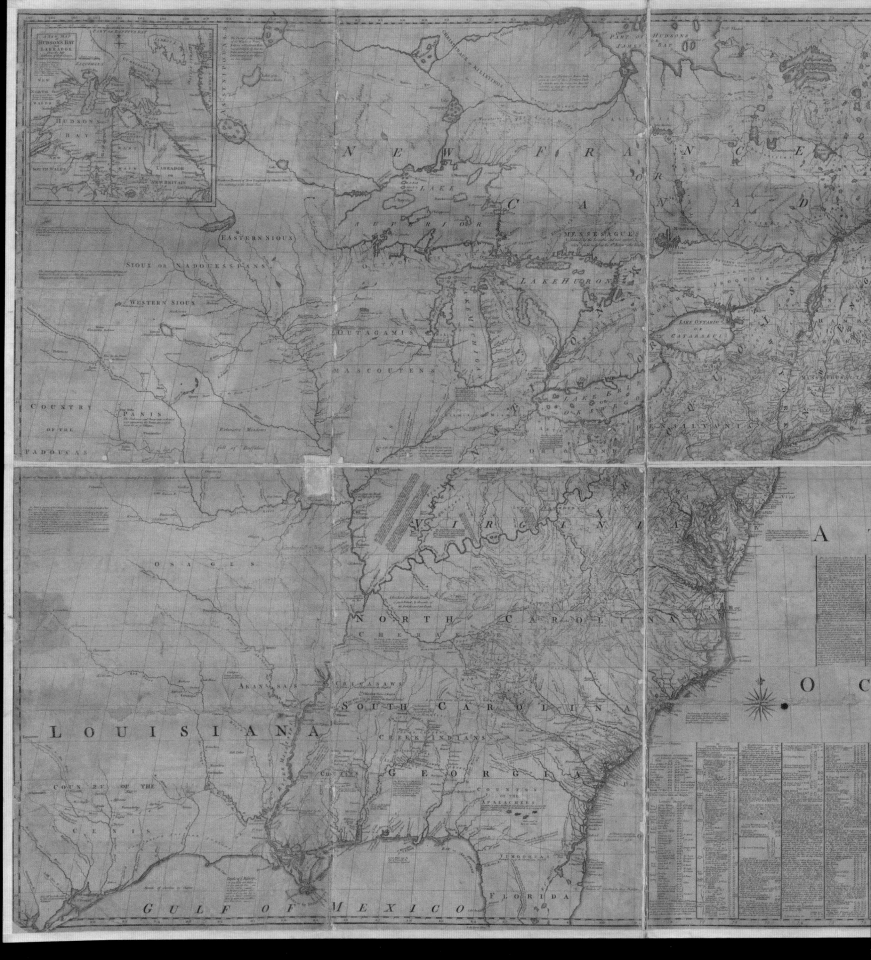

Annotated Map of the British Colonies in North America
"...with the Roads, Distances, Limits, and Extent of the Settlements..."
ca. 1762

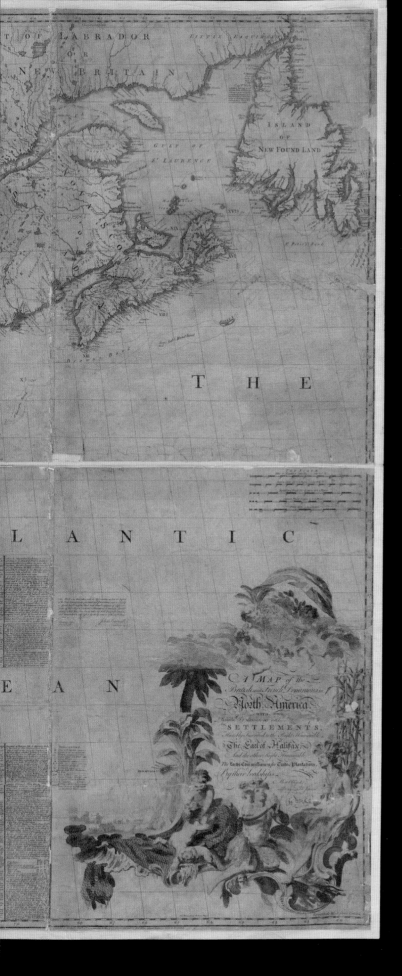

Lexington April 24th 1775

J John Robins being of lawfull age, do Testifye & Say that on the Nineteenth Inst. the Company under the Command of Capt. John Parker, being drawn up, (sometime before sun Rise) on the Green or Common, And I being in the front Rank, there suddenly appeared a Number of the Kings Troops About a Thousand as I thought, at the distance of about 60. or 70 Yards from us Huzzaing and on a quick pace towards us, with three Officers in their front, on Horse Back and on full Gallop towards us, the foremost of which cryed, throw down your Arms ye Villains, ye Rebels, upon which said Company Dispersing. The foremost of the three Officers orderd their Men, saying fire, by God fire, at which Moment we Received a very heavy & close fire from them, at which Instant, being wounded J fell, & Several of our men were shot Dead by one, Capt. Parkers men, J beleive had not then fired a Gun and further the Deponant saith, Not —————

John Robins.

Middlesex ss. April

J John Robins within named appeard and being duely cautioned to Testifye the truth & Nothing but the truth made Solemn Oath to the truth of this within Deposition subscribed by his special order, he being so maim'd & Wounded, that he thought he could neither Write his Name nor Make his Mark

Coram

Wm Reed
Josiah Johnson
} Just. Pacis

BY THE

K I N G,

A

PROCLAMATION,

For Suppressing Rebellion and Sedition.

GEORGE *R.*

HEREAS many of Our Subjects in divers Parts of Our Colonies and Plantations in *North America*, misled by dangerous and ill-designing Men, and forgetting the Allegiance which they owe to the Power that has protected and sustained them, after various disorderly Acts committed in Disturbance of the Public Peace, to the Obstruction of lawful Commerce, and to the Oppression of Our loyal Subjects carrying on the same, have at length proceeded to an open and avowed Rebellion, by arraying themselves in hostile Manner to withstand the Execution of the Law, and traitorously preparing, ordering, and levying War against Us.

AND whereas there is Reason to apprehend that such Rebellion hath been much promoted and encouraged by the traitorous Correspondence, Counsels, and Comfort of divers wicked and desperate Persons within this Realm: To the End therefore, that none of Our Subjects may neglect or violate their Duty through Ignorance thereof, or through any Doubt of the Protection which the Law will afford to their Loyalty and Zeal; We have thought fit, by and with the Advice of Our Privy Council, to issue this Our Royal Proclamation, hereby declaring that not only all Our Officers, Civil and Military, are obliged to exert their utmost Endeavours

vours

The Agreement of Secrecy
"...every member of this Congress considers himself under the ties of virtue, honor & love of his Country..."

1775

In Congress Nov: 9: 1775

Resolved That every member of this Congress considers himself under the ties of virtue, honor & love of his Country, & not to divulge directly or indirectly any matter or thing agitated or debated in Congress before the same shall have been determined, without leave of the Congress; nor any matter or thing determined in Congress which a majority of the Congress shall order to be kept secret, and that if any member shall violate this agreement he shall be expelled this Congress & damed an enemy to the liberties of America & liable to be treated as such & that every member signify his consent to this agreement by signing the same.

Ja.º Duane
Lewis Morris
Fran.º Lewis
W.m Floyd
Rob.t R Livingston jun.r
Henry Wisner
Steph.n Crane
Will.m Livingston
Tho.s Willing
And.w Allen
C. Humphreys
James Wilson
Rob.t Morris

John Hancock
Josiah Bartlett
John Langdon
Thomas Cushing
Sam.l Adams
John Adams
Rob.t Treat Paine
E. Gerry
Sam.l Ward
Eliph.t Dyer
Roger Sherman
Sil.s Deane

B. Franklin
George Ross
Ed. Biddle

the Com:ee of the whole Congress to whom was referred the resolution and the Declaration respecting independence. — 17

Resolved   That these united colonies are and of right

ought to be free and independant States;

that they are absolved from all allegiance

to the british crown and that all political

connection between them and the state of

great Britain is and ought to be totally

dissolved

Report & July 2. 1776
No 3 the resolution for
independancy
agreed to July 2. 1776

90
81
96
96
383

64

In CONGRESS. July 4, 1776.

The unanimous Declaration of the thirteen united States of America.

1778

Oaths of Allegiance

"...I...will serve the said United States in the office of...which I now hold, with fidelity, according to the best of my skill and understanding."

I the Marquis de la Fayette Major General in the Continental army do acknowledge the UNITED STATES of AMERICA to be Free, Independent and Sovereign States, and declare that the people thereof owe no allegiance or obedience to George the Third, King of Great-Britain; and I renounce, refuse and abjure any allegiance or obedience to him; and I do *Swear* that I will, to the utmost of my power, support, maintain and defend the said United States against the said King George the Third, his heirs and successors, and his or their abettors, assistants and adherents, and will serve the said United States in the office of *Major General* which I now hold, with fidelity, according to the best of my skill and understanding.

Sworn before me this 9th day June 1778

Marquis de Lafayette, June 9, 1778.

I Benedict Arnold Major General do acknowledge the UNITED STATES of AMERICA to be Free, Independent and Sovereign States, and declare that the people thereof owe no allegiance or obedience to George the Third, King of Great-Britain; and I renounce, refuse and abjure any allegiance or obedience to him; and I do *Swear* that I will, to the utmost of my power, support, maintain and defend the said United States against the said King George the Third, his heirs and successors, and his or their abettors, assistants and adherents, and will serve the said United States in the office of *Major General* which I now hold, with fidelity, according to the best of my skill and understanding.

Sworn before me this 30th May 1778 at the Artillery Park Valley Forge

Benedict Arnold, May 30, 1778.

I Alexander Hamilton Lieutenant Colonel and Aide De Camp to His Excellency The Commander in Chief do acknowledge the UNITED STATES of AMERICA, to be Free, Independent and Sovereign States, and declare that the people thereof owe no allegiance or obedience to George the Third, King of Great-Britain; and I renounce, refuse and abjure any allegiance or obedience to him; and I do *Swear* that I will to the utmost of my power, support, maintain and defend the said United States, against the said King George the Third, his heirs and successors and his or their abettors, assistants and adherents, and will serve the said United States in the office of ———— *Aide De Camp* which I now hold, with fidelity, according to the best of my skill and understanding. ————

Sworn before me, Camp Valley Forge May 12th 1778 —

Stirling Major Gen'l

Alexander Hamilton, May 12, 1778.

I George Washington Commander in chief of the armies of the United States of America do acknowledge the UNITED STATES of AMERICA, to be Free, Independent and Sovereign States, and declare that the people thereof owe no allegiance or obedience to George the Third, King of Great-Britain; and I renounce, refuse and abjure any allegiance or obedience to him; and I do *Swear* — that I will to the utmost of my power, support, maintain and defend the said United States, against the said King George the Third, his heirs and successors and his or their abettors, assistants and adherents, and will serve the said United States in the office of Commander in chief as aforesaid which I now hold, with fidelity, according to the best of my skill and understanding.

Sworn before me Camp at Valley Forge. May 12th 1778

Stirling Major Gen'l

George Washington, May 12, 1778.

To all to whom

these Presents shall come, we the undersigned Delegates of the States affixed to our Names send greeting. Whereas the Delegates of the United States of America in Congress assembled did on the fifteenth day of November in the Year of our Lord One Thousand Seven Hundred and Seventy seven, and in the Second Year of the Independence of America agree to certain articles of Confederation and perpetual Union between the States of New hampshire, Massachusetts bay, Rhode island and Providence Plantations, Connecticut, New York, New Jersey, Pennsylvania, Delaware, Maryland, Virginia, North Carolina, South Carolina and Georgia in the Words following, viz. Articles of Confederation and perpetual Union between the states of Newhampshire, Massachusetts bay, Rhode island and Providence Plantations, Connecticut, New York, New Jersey, Pennsylvania, Delaware, Maryland, Virginia, North Carolina, South Carolina and Georgia.

Article I. The Stile of this confederacy shall be "The United States of America".

Article II. Each state retains its sovereignty, freedom and independence, and every Power, Jurisdiction and right, which is not by this confederation expressly delegated to the United States, in Congress assembled.

Article III. The said states hereby severally enter into a firm league of friendship with each other, for their common defence, the security of their Liberties, and their mutual and general welfare, binding themselves to assist each other, against all force offered to, or attacks made upon them, or any of them, on account of religion, sovereignty, trade, or any other pretence whatever.

Article IV. The better to secure and perpetuate mutual friendship and intercourse among the people of the different states in this union, the free inhabitants of each of these states, paupers, vagabonds and fugitives from Justice excepted, shall be entitled to all privileges and immunities of free citizens in the several states; and the people of each state shall have free ingress and regress to and from any other state, and shall enjoy therein all the privileges of trade and commerce, subject to the same duties, impositions and restrictions as the inhabitants thereof respectively, provided that such restriction shall not extend so far as to prevent the removal of property imported into any state, to any other state of which the Owner is an inhabitant; provided also that no imposition, duties or restriction shall be laid by any state, on the property of the united states, or either of them.

If any Person guilty of, or charged with treason, felony, or other high misdemeanor in any state, shall flee from Justice, and be found in any of the united states, he shall upon demand of the Governor or executive power, of the state from which he fled, be delivered up and removed to the state having jurisdiction of his offence.

Full faith and credit shall be given in each of these states to the records, acts and judicial

Plan of the Attacks of York in Virginia
by the Allied Armies of America and France
Commanded by his Excellency General Washington
his Excellency the Count Rochambeau commanding
the french Army.

Note. the Enemys works are Coloured with red — Those of the Allied
Army with yellow

The 28th September the Allied Army arrived before york and
found the Enemy in possession of the Works marked A.
the night of the 29th to the 30th the Enemy evacuated those posts
the opening of the trenches was made from the 6th to the 7th
the first parallel with its Communications begun as above
and Completed the night following — the Batteries of this parallel
were Commenced from the 7th to the 8th
the 9th in the afternoon some Batteries were able to f
morning of the 10th they were all opened
The night of the 11th 12th the Second parallel with its Communication K
in the was undertaken, and finished in the Course of the
succeeding day and night.
the 13th the Batteries of the Second parallel were Commenced
the Batteries E.F. of the 1st parallel continued to fire upon the two Works G.H.
the Night of the 14th to the 15th the two Works G.H. were Carried
Sword in hand. the lodgement effected and the Second parallel
Continued as far as those Works. and the Communications I. were made
the 17th Some of the Batteries of the Second parallel Commenced
their
The Same day Lord Cornwallis Sent to offer terms

Cornwallis gave out the 29th 1781

Gouvion
Lt. Col. of Engineers

600 yards

York Town

Road from

Williamsburg

34

"She replied 'no, the bullets would not cheat the gallows...'"

she met Gen'l Washington, who asked her if she 'was not afraid of the Cannon balls.' She replied 'no, the bullets would not cheat the gallows...'"

Yorktown – Deponent was on foot, and
the other females above named, and her
said husband still on the Commissary's
guard – Deponent's attention was arrested
by the appearance of a large plain
between them and Yorktown and an
entrenchment thrown up – She also
saw a number of dead negroes lying
round their encampment whom she
understood the british had driven
out of the town and left to starve,
or were first starved and then
thrown out – Deponent took her stand
just in the rear of the american tents, say about a mile from the town,
and busied herself washing, mending and
cooking for the soldiers, in which she
was assisted by the other females,
some men washed their own
clothing – She heard the roar of
the artillery for a number of days,
and the last night the americans
threw up entrenchments it was a
misty, foggy night, rather wet but
not rainy – Every soldier threw up
for himself as she understood and
she afterwards saw and went into
the entrenchments – Deponent's said
husband was there throwing up
entrenchments and deponent cooked
and carried in beef and bread, and
coffee (in a gallon pot) to the soldiers
in the entrenchment – On one occasion when deponent was thus employed carrying in provisions she met
Gen'l Washington, who asked her if she

"was not afraid of the Cannon balls."
She replied "no, the bullets would
not cheat the gallows – that it would
[...] ue to fight and
they dug entrenchments
at Yorktown [...] or two
[...] every night till
[...]e digging that, the enemy
[...] till about nine
[...] morning – then stopped
[...] from the enemy
Deponent was a little
[...] or the officers'
New Schurch's marque
[...] of officers were present
[...]as Captain Gregg,
[...] of infirmities did
[...] to do duty –
[...]ined beating, and all
[...]ficers hurra'd and
[...], and deponent asked
[...] the matter now –
[...]lied "are you not
[...] to know what the
[...]" deponent replied
[...] replied "the British
[...]ed" Deponent, having
[...], carried the same
[...] entrenchments that
[...] four of the soldiers
[...] in the habit of cook-
[...]eir breakfasts –
[...] on one side of the road
[...]an officers upon the
[...] the British officers
[...] town and rode up
[...] officers and deliv-

From the Revolutionary War pension file of John Peter Miller.

From the Revolutionary War pension file of Jacob Esser.

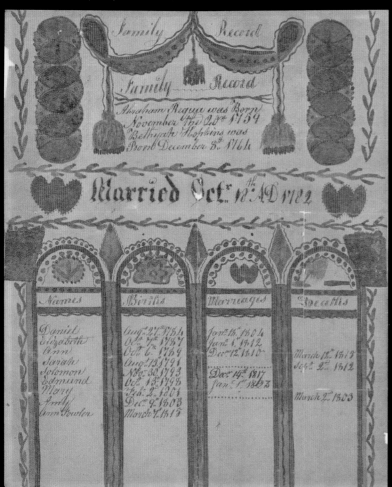

From the Revolutionary War pension file of Abraham Requa.

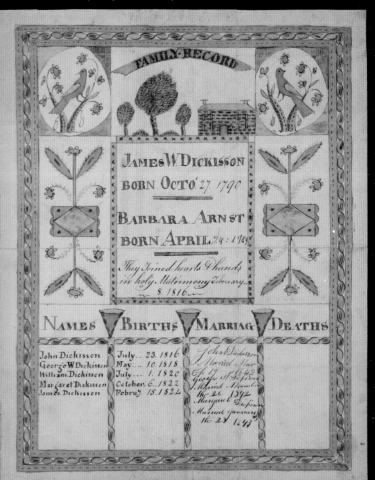

From the Revolutionary War pension file of Isaac Dickisson.

From the Revolutionary War pension file of John Moyer.

From the Revolutionary War pension file of John Engelhaupt.

From the Revolutionary War pension file of Christian Nichols.

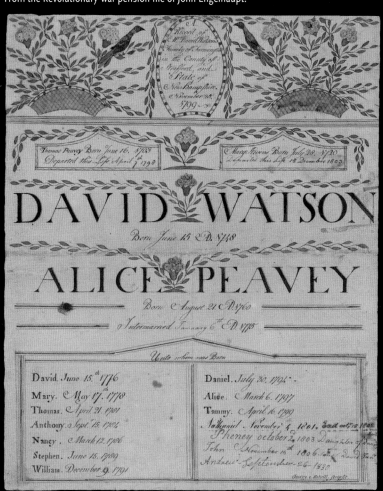

From the Revolutionary War pension file of David Watson.

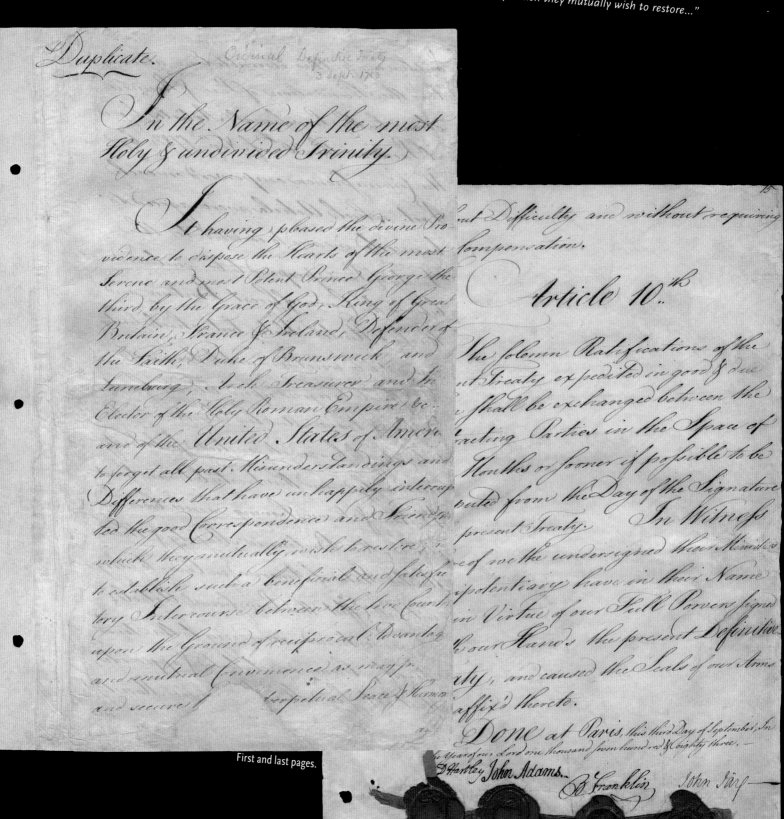

Duplicate.

Original Definitive Treaty
3 Sept. 1783

In the Name of the most Holy & undivided Trinity.

It having pleased the divine Providence to dispose the Hearts of the most Serene and most Potent Prince George the third by the Grace of God, King of Great Britain, France & Ireland, Defender of the Faith, Duke of Brunswick and Luneburg, Arch Treasurer and Prince Elector of the Holy Roman Empire &c... and of the United States of America to forget all past Misunderstandings and Differences that have unhappily interrupted the good Correspondence and Friendship which they mutually wish to restore; and to establish such a beneficial and satisfactory Intercourse between the two Countries upon the Ground of reciprocal Advantages and mutual Convenience as may promote and secure ... perpetual Peace & Harmony ...

...out Difficulty and without requiring ... Compensation.

Article 10th.

The solemn Ratifications of the ...nt Treaty expedited in good & due ... shall be exchanged between the ... racting Parties in the Space of ... Months or sooner if possible to be ... puted from the Day of the Signature ... present Treaty. In Witness ... we the undersigned their Ministers ... ipotentiary have in their Name ... in Virtue of our Full Powers signed ... our Hands the present Definitive ... aty, and caused the Seals of our Arms ... affix'd thereto.

DONE at Paris, this third Day of September, In ... Year of our Lord one thousand seven hundred & eighty three.

D Hartley   John Adams.   B Franklin   John Jay

First and last pages.

Letter from John Adams, Minister to Britain, to John Jay, Secretary of State, Reporting on His Audience with King George III

"...the Door was shut and I was left with his Majesty and the Secretary of State alone."

1785

479

Room very full of Ministers of State, Bishops & all other sorts of Courtiers, as well as the next Room which is the King's bed Chamber, you may well suppose that I was the Focus of all Eyes. I was relieved however from the Embarassment of it by the Swedish and Dutch Ministers, who came to me & entertained me in a very agreeable Conversation during the whole Time. Some other Gentlemen whom I had seen before, came to make their Compliments to me, until the Marquis of Carmarthen returned & desired me to go with him to his Majesty. I went with his Lordship thro' the Levee Room into the King's Closet, — the Door was shut and I was left with his Majesty and the Secretary of State alone. I made the three Reveren= =ces, one at the Door, another about half Way & the third before the Presence, according to the Usage established at this and all the Northern Courts of Europe; and then addressed myself to his Majesty in the following Words —

"Sir, The United States of America have appointed me "their Minister Plenipotentiary to your Majesty, and have directed "me to deliver to your Majesty this Letter which contains the Evidence "of it. It is in Obedience to their express Commands that I have the "Honor to assure your Majesty of their unanimous Disposition and

/ Desire

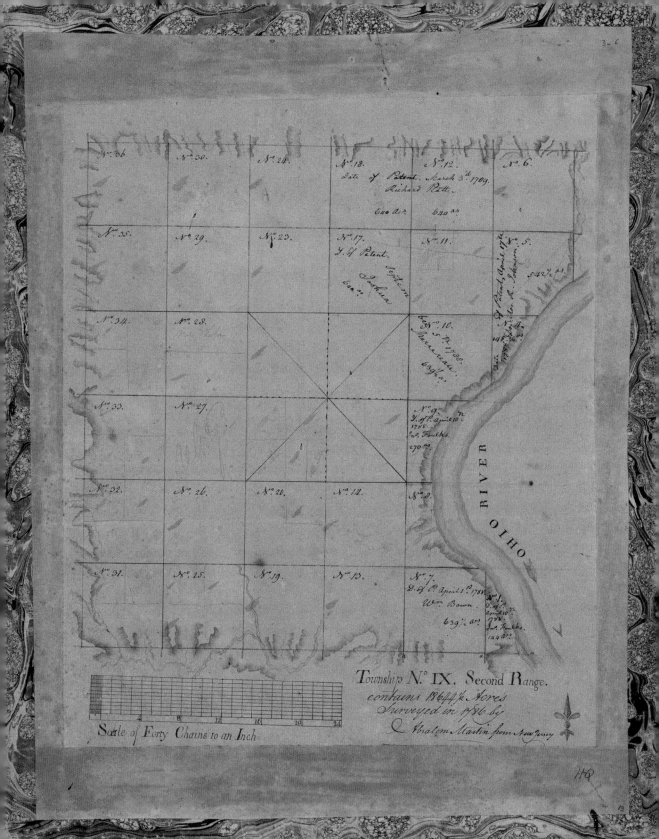

No. 36.   No. 30.   No. 24.   No. 18.   No. 12.   No. 6.
Date of Patent. March 3d 1789.
Richard Ratt.

640 as.   640 as.

No. 35.   No. 29.   No. 23.   No. 17.   No. 11.   Date of Patent April 17th
                              D. of Patent.   5.
                              Joshua   542½ as.

No. 34.   No. 28.   No. 10.   145.
                                          Jeremiah   No. 4.
                                          639 as.

No. 33.   No. 27.   No. 9.
                                          D. of P. april 10
                                          1788
                                          270 as.

No. 32.   No. 26.   No. 20.   No. 14.   No. 8.

No. 31.   No. 25.   No. 19.   No. 13.   No. 7.
                                          D. of P. April 1st 1788   No. 1.
                                          Wm. Bown.
                                          639½ as.

RIVER   OIHO

Township No. IX. Second Range.
contains 18644½ Acres
Surveyed in 1786 by
Absalom Martin from New Jersey

Scale of Forty Chains to an Inch

An Ordinance for the Government of the Territory of the United States, North-West of the River Ohio.

BE IT ORDAINED by the United States in Congress assembled, That the said territory, for the purposes of temporary government, be one district; subject, however, to be divided into two districts, as future circumstances may, in the opinion of Congress, make it expedient.

Be it ordained by the authority aforesaid, That the estates both of resident and non-resident proprietors in the said territory, dying intestate, shall descend to, and be distributed among their children, and the descendants of a deceased child in equal parts; the descendants of a deceased child or grand-child, to take the share of their deceased parent in equal parts among them: And where there shall be no children or descendants, then in equal parts to the next of kin, in equal degree; and among collaterals, the children of a deceased brother or sister of the intestate, shall have in equal parts among them their deceased parents share; and there shall in no case be a distinction between kindred of the whole and half blood; saving in all cases to the widow of the intestate, her third part of the real estate for life, and one third part of the personal estate; and this law relative to descents and dower, shall remain in full force until altered by the legislature of the district. ———— And until the governor and judges shall adopt laws as herein after mentioned, estates in the said territory may be devised or bequeathed by wills in writing, signed and sealed by him or her, in whom the estate may be, (being of full age) and attested by three witnesses; —— and real estates may be conveyed by lease and release, or bargain and sale, signed, sealed, and delivered by the person being of full age, in whom the estate may be, and attested by two witnesses, provided such wills be duly proved, and such conveyances be acknowledged, or the execution thereof duly proved, and be recorded within one year after proper magistrates, courts, and registers shall be appointed for that purpose; and personal property may be transferred by delivery, saving, however, to the French and Canadian inhabitants, and other settlers of the Kaskaskies, Saint Vincent's, and the neighbouring villages, who have heretofore professed themselves citizens of Virginia, their laws and customs now in force among them, relative to the descent and conveyance of property.

Be it ordained by the authority aforesaid, That there shall be appointed from time to time, by Congress, a governor, whose commission shall continue in force for the term of three years, unless sooner revoked by Congress; he shall reside in the district, and have a freehold estate therein, in one thousand acres of land, while in the exercise of his office.

There shall be appointed from time to time, by Congress, a secretary, whose commission shall continue in force for four years, unless sooner revoked, he shall reside in the district, and have a freehold estate therein, in five hundred acres of land, while in the exercise of his office; it shall be his duty to keep and preserve the acts and laws passed by the legislature, and the public records of the district, and the proceedings of the governor in his executive department; and transmit authentic copies of such acts and proceedings, every six months, to the secretary of Congress: There shall also be appointed a court to consist of three judges, any two of whom to form a court, who shall have a common law jurisdiction, and reside in the district, and have each therein a freehold estate in five hundred acres of land, while in the exercise of their offices; and their commissions shall continue in force during good behaviour.

The governor and judges, or a majority of them, shall adopt and publish in the district, such laws of the original states, criminal and civil, as may be necessary, and best suited to the circumstances of the district, and report them to Congress, from time to time, which laws shall be in force in the district until the organization of the general assembly therein, unless disapproved of by Congress; but afterwards the legislature shall have authority to alter them as they shall think fit.

The governor for the time being, shall be commander in chief of the militia, appoint and commission all officers in the same, below the rank of general officers; all general officers shall be appointed and commissioned by Congress.

Previous to the organization of the general assembly, the governor shall appoint such magistrates and other civil officers, in each county or township, as he shall find necessary for the preservation of the peace and good order in the same: After the general assembly shall be organized, the powers and duties of magistrates and other civil officers shall be regulated and defined by the said assembly; but all magistrates and other civil officers, not herein otherwise directed, shall, during the continuance of this temporary government, be appointed by the governor.

For the prevention of crimes and injuries, the laws to be adopted or made shall have force in all parts of the district, and for the execution of process, criminal and civil, the governor shall make proper divisions thereof——and he shall proceed from time to time, as circumstances may require, to lay out the parts of the district in which the Indian titles shall have been extinguished, into counties and townships, subject, however, to such alterations as may thereafter be made by the legislature.

So soon as there shall be five thousand free male inhabitants, of full age, in the district, upon giving proof thereof to the governor, they shall receive authority, with time and place, to elect representatives from their counties or townships, to represent them in the general assembly; provided that for every five hundred free male inhabitants there shall be one representative, and so on progressively with the number of free male inhabitants, shall the right of representation increase, until the number of representatives shall amount to twenty-five, after which the number and proportion of representatives shall be regulated by the legislature; provided that no person be eligible or qualified to act as a representative, unless he shall have been a citizen of one of the United States three years and be a resident in the district, or unless he shall have resided in the district three years, and in either case shall likewise hold in his own right, in fee simple, two hundred acres of land within the same:——Provided also, that a freehold in fifty acres of land in the district, having been a citizen of one of the states; and being resident in the district; or the like freehold and two years residence in the district shall be necessary to qualify a man as an elector of a representative.

The representatives thus elected, shall serve for the term of two years, and in case of the death of a representative, or removal from office, the governor shall issue a writ to the county or township for which he was a member, to elect another in his stead, to serve for the residue of the term.

The general assembly, or legislature, shall consist of the governor, legislative council, and a house of representatives. The legislative council shall consist of five members, to continue in office five years, unless sooner removed by Congress, any three of whom to be a quorum, and the members of the council shall be nominated and appointed in the following manner, to wit: As soon as representatives shall be elected, the governor shall appoint a time and place for them to meet together, and, when met, they shall nominate ten persons, residents in the district, and each possessed of a freehold in five hundred acres of land, and return their names to Congress; five of whom Congress shall appoint and commission to serve as aforesaid; and whenever a vacancy shall happen in the council, by death or removal from office, the house of representatives shall nominate two persons, qualified as aforesaid, for each vacancy, and return their names to Congress; one of whom Congress shall appoint and commission for the residue of the term; and every five years, four months at least before the expiration of the time of service of the members of council, the said house shall nominate ten persons, qualified as aforesaid, and return their names to Congress, five of whom Congress shall appoint and commission to serve as members of the council five years, unless sooner removed. And the governor, legislative council, and house of re-

WE the People of the States of New-Hampſhire, Maſſachuſetts, Rhode-Iſland and Providence Plantations, Connecticut, New-York, New-Jerſey, Pennſylvania, Delaware, Maryland, Virginia, North-Carolina, South-Carolina, and Georgia, do ordain, declare and eſtabliſh the following Conſtitution for the Government of Ourſelves and our Poſterity.

ARTICLE I.

The ſtile of this Government ſhall be, " The United States of America."

II.

The Government ſhall conſiſt of ſupreme legiſlative, executive and judicial powers.

III.

The legiſlative power ſhall be veſted in a Congreſs, to conſiſt of two ſeparate and diſtinct bodies of men, a Houſe of Repreſentatives, and a Senate ; ~~each of which ſhall, in all caſes, have a negative on the other. The Legiſlature ſhall meet on the firſt Monday in December in every year.~~

The Legiſlature ſhall meet at leaſt once in every year and that meeting ſhall be on the firſt Monday in December unleſs a different day ſhall be appointed by law.

IV.

Sect. 1. The Members of the Houſe of Repreſentatives ſhall be choſen every ſecond year, by the people of the ſeveral States comprehended within this Union. The qualifications of the electors ſhall be the ſame, from time to time, as thoſe of the electors in the ſeveral States, of the moſt numerous branch of their own legiſlatures.

Sect. 2. Every Member of the Houſe of Repreſentatives ſhall be of the age of twenty-five years at leaſt ; ſhall have been a citizen in the United States for at leaſt ____ years before his election ; and ſhall be, at the time of his election, ____ of the State in which he ſhall be choſen.

Sect. 3. The Houſe of Repreſentatives ſhall, at its firſt formation, and until the number of citizens and inhabitants ſhall be taken in the manner herein after deſcribed, conſiſt of ſixty-five Members, of whom three ſhall be choſen in New-Hampſhire, eight in Maſſachuſetts, one in Rhode-Iſland and Providence Plantations, five in Connecticut, ſix in New-York, four in New-Jerſey, eight in Pennſylvania, one in Delaware, ſix in Maryland, ten in Virginia, five in North-Carolina, five in South-Carolina, and three in Georgia.

Sect. 4. As the proportions of numbers in the different States will alter from time to time ; as ſome of the States may hereafter be divided ; as others may be enlarged by addition of territory ; as two or more States may be united ; as new States will be erected within the limits of the United States, the Legiſlature ſhall, in each of theſe caſes, regulate the number of repreſentatives by the number of inhabitants, according to the ____ the rate of one for every forty thouſand. *Provided that every State ſhall have at leaſt one repreſentative.*

Sect. 5. All bills for raiſing or appropriating money, and for fixing the ſalaries of the officers of government, ſhall originate in the Houſe of Repreſentatives, and ſhall not be altered or amended by the Senate. No money ſhall be drawn from the public Treaſury, but in purſuance of appropriations that ſhall originate in the Houſe of Repreſentatives.

Sect. 6. The Houſe of Repreſentatives ſhall have the ſole power of impeachment. It ſhall chooſe its Speaker and other officers.

Sect. 7. Vacancies in the Houſe of Repreſentatives ſhall be ſupplied by writs of election from the executive authority of the State, in the repreſentation from which they ſhall happen.   V.

We the People

of the United States, in order to form a more perfect Union, establish Justice, insure domestic Tranquility, provide for the common defence, promote the general Welfare, and secure the Blessings of Liberty to ourselves and our Posterity, do ordain and establish this Constitution for the United States of America.

Article. 1.

Section. 1. All legislative Powers herein granted shall be vested in a Congress of the United States, which shall consist of a Senate and House of Representatives.

Section. 2. The House of Representatives shall be composed of Members chosen every second Year by the People of the several States, and the Electors in each State shall have the Qualifications requisite for Electors of the most numerous Branch of the State Legislature.

No Person shall be a Representative who shall not have attained to the Age of twenty five Years, and been seven Years a Citizen of the United States, and who shall not, when elected, be an Inhabitant of that State in which he shall be chosen.

Representatives and direct Taxes shall be apportioned among the several States which may be included within this Union, according to their respective Numbers, which shall be determined by adding to the whole Number of free Persons, including those bound to Service for a Term of Years, and excluding Indians not taxed, three fifths of all other Persons. The actual Enumeration shall be made within three Years after the first Meeting of the Congress of the United States, and within every subsequent Term of ten Years, in such Manner as they shall by Law direct. The Number of Representatives shall not exceed one for every thirty Thousand, but each State shall have at Least one Representative; and until such enumeration shall be made, the State of New Hampshire shall be entitled to chuse three, Massachusetts eight, Rhode-Island and Providence Plantations one, Connecticut five, New York six, New Jersey four, Pennsylvania eight, Delaware one, Maryland six, Virginia ten, North Carolina five, South Carolina five, and Georgia three.

When vacancies happen in the Representation from any State, the Executive Authority thereof shall issue Writs of Election to fill such Vacancies.

The House of Representatives shall chuse their Speaker and other Officers; and shall have the sole Power of Impeachment.

Section. 3. The Senate of the United States shall be composed of two Senators from each State, chosen by the Legislature thereof, for six Years; and each Senator shall have one Vote.

Immediately after they shall be assembled in Consequence of the first Election, they shall be divided as equally as may be into three Classes. The Seats of the Senators of the first Class shall be vacated at the Expiration of the second Year, of the second Class at the Expiration of the fourth Year, and of the third Class at the Expiration of the sixth Year, so that one third may be chosen every second Year; and if Vacancies happen by Resignation, or otherwise, during the Recess of the Legislature of any State, the Executive thereof may make temporary Appointments until the next Meeting of the Legislature, which shall then fill such Vacancies.

No Person shall be a Senator who shall not have attained to the Age of thirty Years, and been nine Years a Citizen of the United States, and who shall not, when elected, be an Inhabitant of that State for which he shall be chosen.

The Vice President of the United States shall be President of the Senate, but shall have no Vote, unless they be equally divided.

The Senate shall chuse their other Officers, and also a President pro tempore, in the Absence of the Vice President, or when he shall exercise the Office of President of the United States.

The Senate shall have the sole Power to try all Impeachments. When sitting for that Purpose, they shall be on Oath or Affirmation. When the President of the United States is tried, the Chief Justice shall preside: And no Person shall be convicted without the Concurrence of two thirds of the Members present.

Judgment in Cases of Impeachment shall not extend further than to removal from Office, and disqualification to hold and enjoy any Office of honor, Trust or Profit under the United States: but the Party convicted shall nevertheless be liable and subject to Indictment, Trial, Judgment and Punishment, according to Law.

Section. 4. The Times, Places and Manner of holding Elections for Senators and Representatives, shall be prescribed in each State by the Legislature thereof; but the Congress may at any time by Law make or alter such Regulations, except as to the Places of chusing Senators.

The Congress shall assemble at least once in every Year, and such Meeting shall be on the first Monday in December, unless they shall by Law appoint a different Day.

Section. 5. Each House shall be the Judge of the Elections, Returns and Qualifications of its own Members, and a Majority of each shall constitute a Quorum to do Business; but a smaller Number may adjourn from day to day, and may be authorized to compel the Attendance of absent Members, in such Manner, and under such Penalties as each House may provide.

Each House may determine the Rules of its Proceedings, punish its Members for disorderly Behaviour, and, with the Concurrence of two thirds, expel a Member.

Each House shall keep a Journal of its Proceedings, and from time to time publish the same, excepting such Parts as may in their Judgment require Secrecy; and the Yeas and Nays of the Members of either House on any question shall, at the Desire of one fifth of those Present, be entered on the Journal.

Neither House, during the Session of Congress, shall, without the Consent of the other, adjourn for more than three days, nor to any other Place than that in which the two Houses shall be sitting.

Section. 6. The Senators and Representatives shall receive a Compensation for their Services, to be ascertained by Law, and paid out of the Treasury of the United States. They shall in all Cases, except Treason, Felony and Breach of the Peace, be privileged from Arrest during their Attendance at the Session of their respective Houses, and in going to and returning from the same; and for any Speech or Debate in either House, they shall not be questioned in any other Place.

No Senator or Representative shall, during the Time for which he was elected, be appointed to any civil Office under the Authority of the United States, which shall have been created, or the Emoluments whereof shall have been increased during such time; and no Person holding any Office under the United States, shall be a Member of either House during his Continuance in Office.

Section. 7. All Bills for raising Revenue shall originate in the House of Representatives; but the Senate may propose or concur with Amendments as on other Bills.

Every Bill which shall have passed the House of Representatives and the Senate, shall, before it become a Law, be presented to the President of

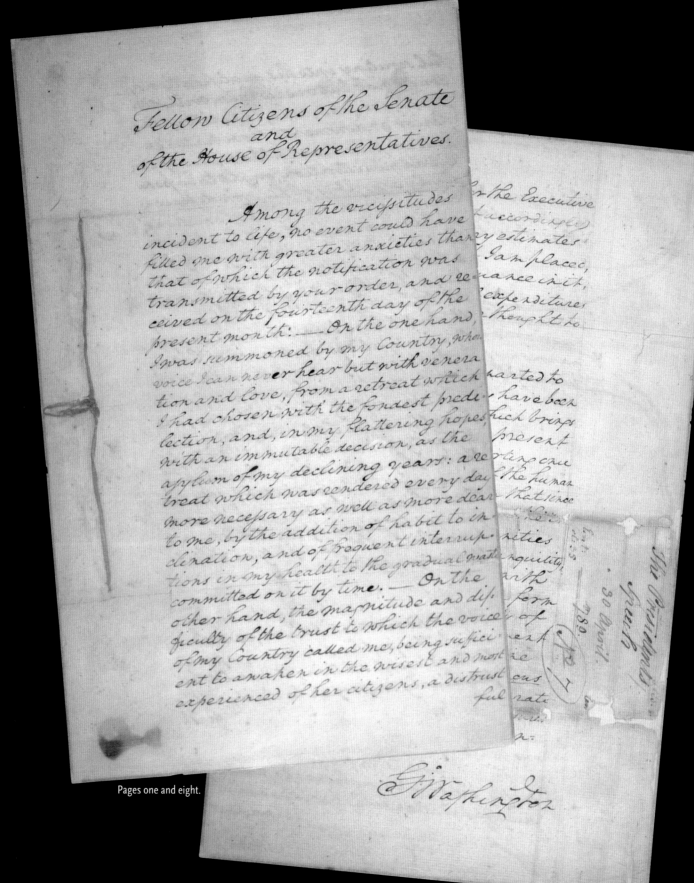

Pages one and eight.

The Bill of Rights As Passed by the Senate | **1789**

"The Conventions of a Number of the States...expressed a Desire...that further declaratory and restrictive Clauses should be added..."

The Conventions of a Number of the States having, at the Time of their adopting the Constitution, expressed a Desire, in Order to prevent misconstruction or abuse of its Powers, that further declaratory and restrictive Clauses should be added: And as extending the Ground of public Confidence in the Government, will best insure the beneficent ends of its Institution—

RESOLVED, by the Senate and House of Representatives of the United States of America in Congress assembled, two thirds of both Houses concurring, That the following articles be proposed to the Legislatures of the several States, as amendments to the Constitution of the United States, all or any of which articles, when ratified by three fourths of the said Legislatures, to be valid to all intents and purposes, as part of the said Constitution—Viz.

Articles in addition to, and amendment of, the Constitution of the United States of America, proposed by Congress, and ratified by the Legislatures of the several States, pursuant to the fifth Article of the original Constitution.

ARTICLE the FIRST.

After the first enumeration, required by the first article of the Constitution, there shall be one Representative for every thirty thousand, until the number shall amount to one hundred; to which number one Representative shall be added for every subsequent increase of forty thousand, until the Representatives shall amount to two hundred, to which ... ty thou-sentative shall be added ...
perso...

ARTICLE the SECOND.

No law, varying the compensation for the services of the Senators and Representatives, shall take effect, until an election of Representatives shall have intervened.

ARTICLE the THIRD.

Congress shall make no law establishing articles of faith, or a mode of worship, or prohibiting the free exercise of religion, or abridging the freedom of speech, or of the press, or the right of the people peaceably to assemble, and to petition to the government for a redress of grievances.

ARTICLE the FOURTH.

A well regulated militia, being necessary to the security of a free State, the right of the people to keep and bear arms, shall not be infringed.

ARTICLE the FIFTH.

No soldier shall, in time of peace, be quartered in any house, without the consent of the owner, nor in time of war, but in a manner to be prescribed by law.

ARTICLE the SIXTH.

The right of the people to be secure in their persons, houses, papers, and effects, against unreasonable searches and seizures, shall not be violated, and no warrants shall issue, but upon probable cause, supported by oath or affirmation, and particularly describing the place to be searched, and the persons or things to be seized.

[2]

ARTICLE the SEVENTH.

No person shall be held to answer for a capital, or otherwise infamous crime, unless on a presentment or indictment of a Grand Jury, except in cases arising in the land or naval forces, or in the militia, when in actual service in time of war or public danger; nor shall any person be subject for the same offence to be twice put in jeopardy of life or limb; nor shall be compelled in any criminal case, to be a witness against himself, nor be deprived of life, liberty or property, without due process of law; nor shall private property be taken for public use without just compensation.

ARTICLE the EIGHTH.

In all criminal prosecutions, the accused shall enjoy the right to a speedy public trial, to be informed of the nature and cause of the accusation, be confronted with the witnesses against him, to have compulsory process for obtaining witnesses in his favour, and to have the assistance of counsel for his defence.

ARTICLE the NINTH.

In suits at common law, where the value in controversy shall exceed twenty dollars, the right of trial by Jury shall be preserved, and no fact tried by a Jury, shall be otherwise re-examined in any court of the United States, than according to the rules of the common law.

ARTICLE the TENTH.

Excessive bail shall not be required, nor excessive fines imposed, nor cruel and unusual punishments inflicted.

ARTICLE the ELEVENTH.

... any or disparage others retained by the people. ... shall not be con-

ARTICLE the TWELFTH.

... not delegated to the United States by the Constitution, nor ... it to the States, are reserved to the States respectively, or ...

... K, PRINTED BY THOMAS GREENLEAF.]

1790

Petition from the Pennsylvania Society for Promoting the Abolition of Slavery, Signed by Benjamin Franklin, President of the Society

"...that you will devise means for removing this Inconsistency from the Character of the American People..."

To the Senate & House of Representatives of the United States,

    The Memorial of the Pennsylvania Society for promoting the Abolition of Slavery, the relief of free Negroes unlawfully held in bondage, & the Improvement of the Condition of the African Race—

    Respectfully Sheweth,

      That from a regard for the happiness of Mankind an Association was formed several years since in this State by a number of her Citizens of various religious denominations for promoting the Abolition of Slavery & for the relief of those unlawfully held in bondage. A just & accurate Conception of the true Principles of liberty, as it spread through the land, produced accessions to their numbers, many friends to their Cause, & a legislative Co-operation with their views, which, by the blessing of Divine Providence, have been successfully directed to the relieving from bondage a large number of their fellow creatures of the African Race. They have also the Satisfaction to observe, that in consequence of that Spirit of Philanthropy & genuine liberty which is generally diffusing its beneficial Influence, similar Institutions are gradually forming at home & abroad.

      That mankind are all formed by the same Almighty being, alike objects of his Care & equally assigned for the Enjoyment of Happiness the Christian Religion teaches us to believe, & the Political Creed of America fully coincides with the Position. Your Memorialists, particularly engaged in attending to the Distresses arising from Slavery, believe it their indispensible Duty to present this Subject to your notice— They have observed with great Satisfaction that many important & salutary Powers are vested in you for promoting the Welfare & securing the blessings of liberty to the People of the United States. And as they conceive, that these blessings ought rightfully to be administered, without distinction of Colour, to all descriptions of People, so they indulge themselves in the pleasing expectation, that nothing, which can be done for the relief of the unhappy objects of their care, will be either omitted or delayed—

      From a persuasion that equal liberty was originally the Portion, & is still the birthright of all men, & influenced by the strong ties of Humanity & the Principles of their Institution, your Memorialists conceive themselves bound

bound to use all justifiable endeavours to loosen the bands of Slavery and promote a general Enjoyment of the blessings of Freedom. Under these Impressions they earnestly intreat your serious attention to the Subject of Slavery, that you will be pleased to countenance the Restoration of liberty to those unhappy Men, who alone in this land of Freedom, are degraded into perpetual Bondage, and who amidst the general Joy of surrounding Freemen, are groaning in Servile Subjection, that you will devise means for removing this Inconsistency from the Character of the American People, that you will promote mercy and justice towards this distressed Race, & that you will Step to the very verge of the Powers vested in you for discouraging every Species of Traffick in the Persons of our fellow Men:

hia feb 3. 1790

B Franklin
Presid. of the Society

Memorial from Hannah Stephens Requesting the Release of Her Husband from Prison in Algiers

"The Sufferings of your Memorialist and of her Children become insupportable when added to the Distress she feels for her husband..."

1791

To the President, Senate, and House of Representatives of the United States of America in Congress assembled.——

The memorial of Hannah Stephens of Concord in the County of Middlesex and Commonwealth of Massachusetts, wife of Isaac Stephens now a prisoner in Algiers: Humbly sheweth that her husband sailed from the Port of Boston in said Commonwealth on the twenty fourth day of June Anno Domini 1785, in the Schooner Nancy of which he was Commander bound to Cadiz, and was taken on the twenty fourth day of July in the same year by the Algerines, and has ever since remained a prisoner among them, deprived of his liberties & of every mean of providing for himself, his wife or children. Said Stephens left three children the eldest of which is a daughter fourteen years old, sickly and not able to support herself, and the other two still remain a great expense to their mother. Said Stephens several years previous to his last sailing from Boston, bought a house and & small piece of land in said Concord for his wife and family, that they might have a certain home, whilst he pursued the Business of a Mariner, and paid part of the purchase money; but by means of his great misfortune in being made a prisoner, he has been unable to complete the purchase, and the money that has been paid is lost by reason of the failure of the payment of the remainder: therefore your Memorialist has been turned out of

Doors,

Doors, and driven to the cruel necessity of doing the lowest duties of a servant to prevent herself, and her helpless children from suffering hunger, and nakedness. The Sufferings of your Memorialist and of her Children become insupportable when added to the Distress she feels for her husband, who ___ually representing by his Letters his melancholy ___ and praying for the interposition of the United ___ behalf.——— Your Memorialist in this her ___ forsaken condition, humbly begs the interposition ___ States for her husband, that they would devise some ___ he may be freed from his present state of Captivity ___ her helpless children may once more enjoy the ___ of seeing their long lost friend, at liberty and in this ___. Your Memorialist is likewise under the ne-___, and she now does in the most humble ___ Legislature of the United States would also take ___ circumstances into their wise Consideration, ___ for the subsistence of herself and her Children, ___ may have some Alleviation of her accumulated ___ ___ as in Duty bound shall ever

pray Hannah Stephens

___ ___ the facts stated in the above Memorial ___ Merrick Justice of the peace.

___ the Facts stated in the above Memorial ___ ___ley Pastor of the Church in Concord.

___ ___ Selectmen of said Town of Concord ___ memorial are true.——

Ephraim Wood
Jacob Brown
Asa Brooks

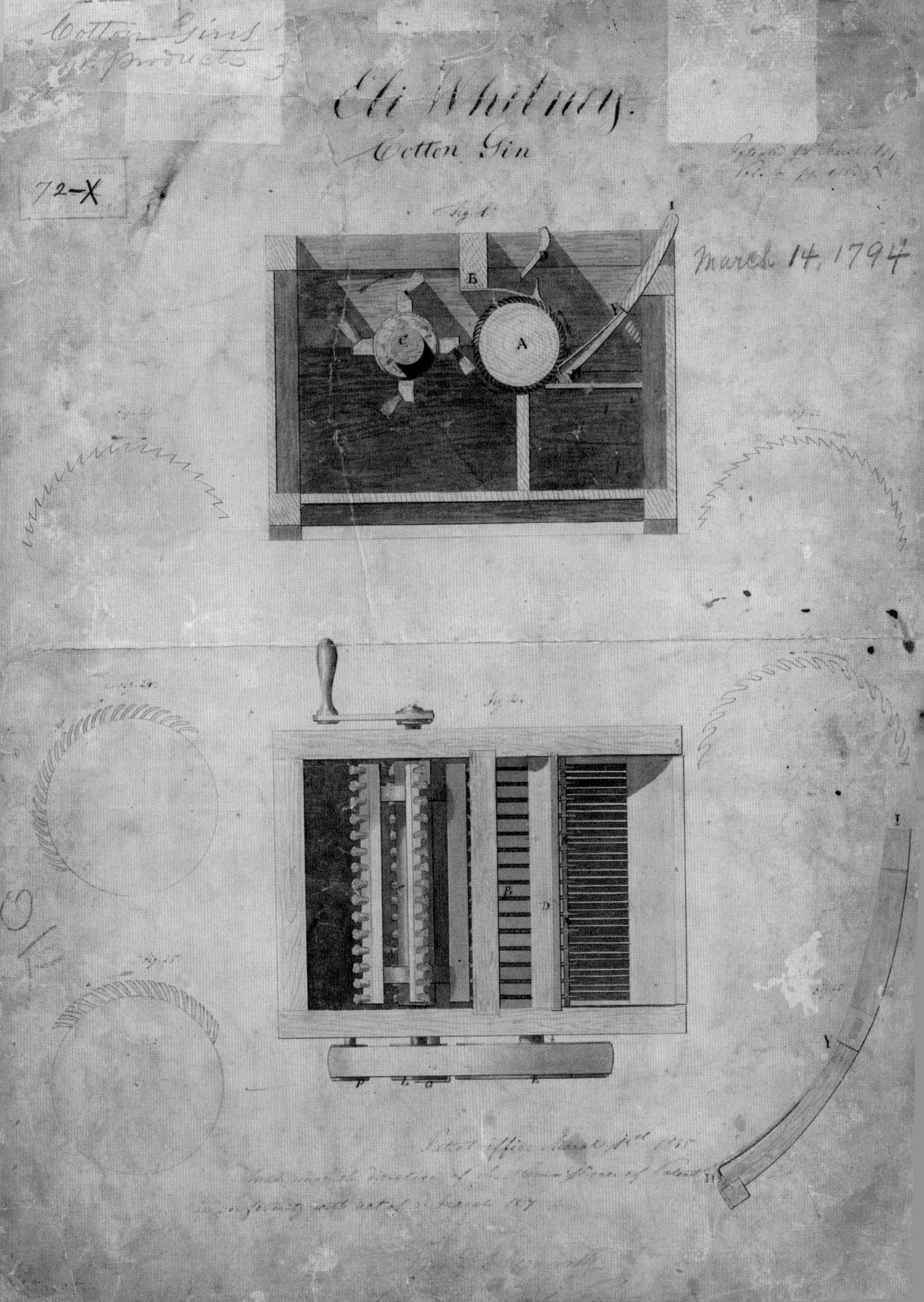

Eli Whitney.

Cotton Gin

March 14, 1794

Fig 1.

B

C   A

Fig 2.

B   D

P   Q

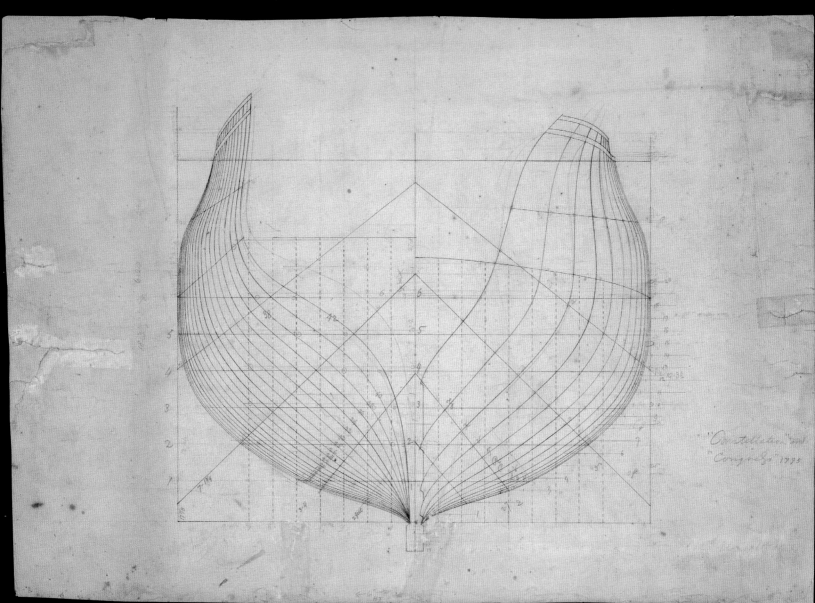

"Constellation" and
"Congress" 1795

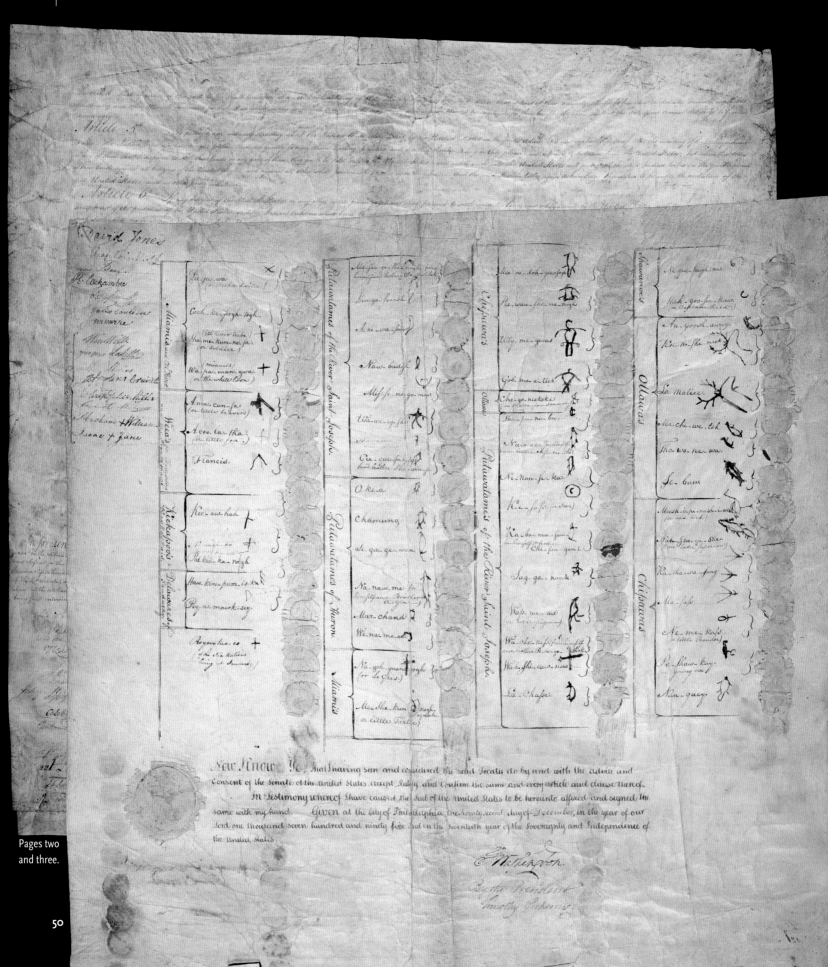

Pages two
and three.

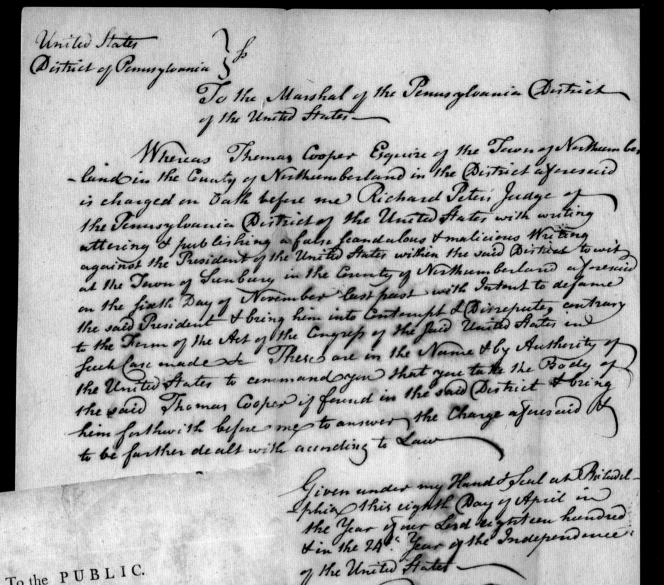

Judge Richard Peter's letter to the U.S. Marshal, November 5, 1799.

Newspaper broadside filed in the
United States v. Thomas Cooper,
November 5, 1799.

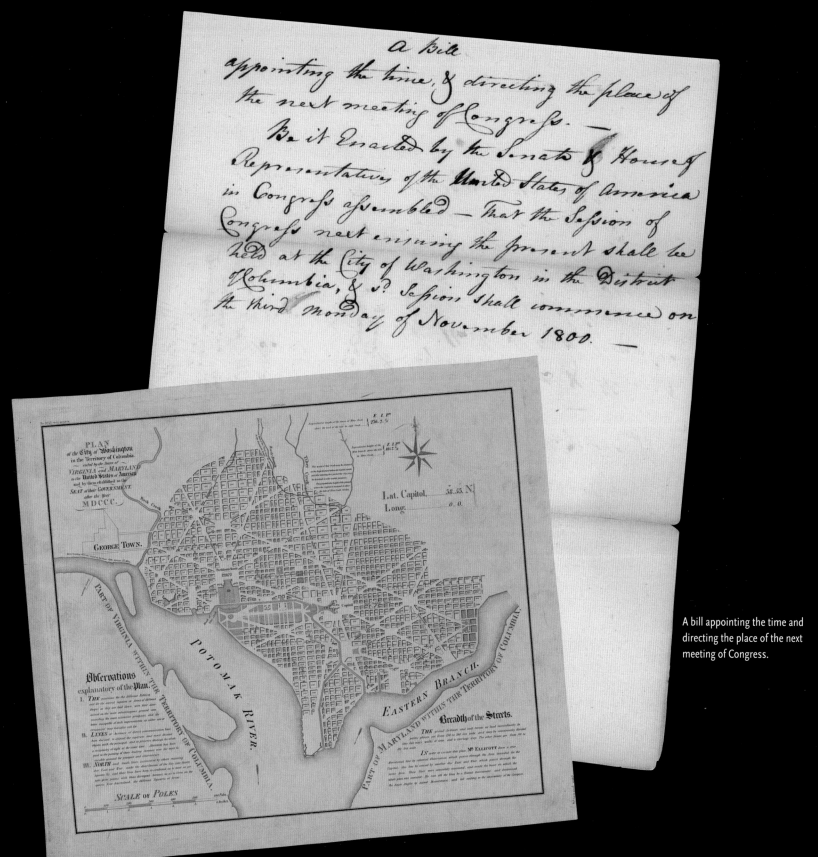

A bill appointing the time and directing the place of the next meeting of Congress.

Plan of the City of Washington in the Territory of Columbia ceded by the states of Virginia and Maryland, 1800.

	Thomas Jefferson of Virginia	Aaron Burr of New York	John Adams of Massachusetts	Charles Cotesworth Pinkney of South Carolina	John Jay of New York
New Hampshire			6	6	
Massachusetts			16	16	
Rhode Island			4	3	1
Connecticut			9	9	
Vermont			4	4	
New York	12	12			
New Jersey			7	7	
Pennsylvania	8	8	7	7	
Delaware			3	3	
Maryland	5	5	5	5	
Virginia	21	21			
Kentucky	4	4			
North Carolina	8	8	4	4	
Tennessee	3	3			
South Carolina	8	8			
Georgia	4	4			
	73	73	65	64	1

182   2.

To the Senate and House of Representatives of the United States.

In my communication to you, of the 17th instant, I informed you that Conventions had been entered into with the government of France for the cession of Louisiana to the United States. These, with the advice and consent of the Senate, have now been ratified, & my ratification exchanged for that of the First Consul of France in due form, they are communicated to you for consideration in your legislative capacity. you will observe that some important conditions cannot be carried into execution but with the aid of the legislature; & that time presses a decision on them without delay.

The ulterior provisions, also suggested in the same communication, for the occupation & government of the country, will call for early attention. such information, relative to it's government, as the time & distance have permitted me to obtain, will be ready to be laid before you within a few days. but as permanent arrangements for this object may require time & deliberation, it is for your consideration whether you will not forthwith make such temporary provisions for the preservation, in the mean while, of order & tranquility in the country, as the case may require.

Th Jefferson

Oct. 21. 1803.

PROCLAMATION.

By his Excellency
WILLIAM C. C. CLAIBORNE,
Governor of the Mississippi Territory, exercising the powers of Governor General and Intendant of the Province of Louisiana.

Par son Excellence
Guillaume C. C. Claiborne,
Gouverneur du Territoire du Mississippi, exerçant les Pouvoirs de Gouverneur Général, et Intendant de la Province de la Louisiane.

Por el Señor,
Don Guillermo C. C. Claiborne,
Gobernador del Territorio del Mississippi, exerciendo los Poderes de Gobernador General é Intendente de la Provincia de la Luisiana.

54

"An intelligent officer with ten or twelve chosen men...might explore the whole line, even to the Western ocean..."

While the extension of the public commerce among the Indian tribes may deprive of that source of profit such of our citizens as are engaged in it, it might be worthy the attention of Congress, in their care of individual as well as of the general interest to point in another direction the enterprise of these citizens, as profitably for themselves, and more usefully for the public. the river Missouri, & the Indians inhabiting it, are not as well known as is rendered desireable by their connection with the Missisipi, & consequently with us. it is however understood that the country on that river is inhabited by numerous tribes, who furnish great supplies of furs & peltry to the trade of another nation carried on in a high latitude, through an infinite number of portages and lakes, shut up by ice through a long season. the commerce on that line could bear no competition with that of the Missouri, traversing a moderate climate, offering according to the best accounts, a continued navigation from it's source, and, possibly with a single portage, from the Western ocean, and finding to the Atlantic a choice of channels through the Illinois or Wabash, the lakes and Hudson, through the Ohio and Susquehanna or Potomac or James rivers, and through the Tennissee and Savanna rivers. an intelligent officer with ten or twelve chosen men, fit for the enterprize and willing to undertake it, taken from our posts, where they may be spared without inconvenience, might explore the whole line, even to the Western ocean, have conferences with the natives on the subject of commercial intercourse, get a[dmission for our traders as] others are admitted, agree on convenien[t...] and return with the information acquire[d...] arms & accoutrements, some instruments of [...] -dians, would be all the apparatus they co[uld...] souldier's portion of land on their retur[n...] pay would be going on, whether here or [...] encountered great expence to enlarge [...] voiages of discovery, & for other literary [...]

President Jefferson's confidential message to Congress concerning Indian relations and western exploration, page three, January 18, 1803.

List of Indian presents purchased by Meriwether Lewis in preparation for the expedition to the West, 1803.

804

Mediterranean Passport Guaranteeing Safe Passage for the Vessel _Mount Hope_

"Suffer the Ship called the Mount Hope...To Pass with her Company, Passengers, Goods and Merchandize, without any hinderance, seizure or molestatio"

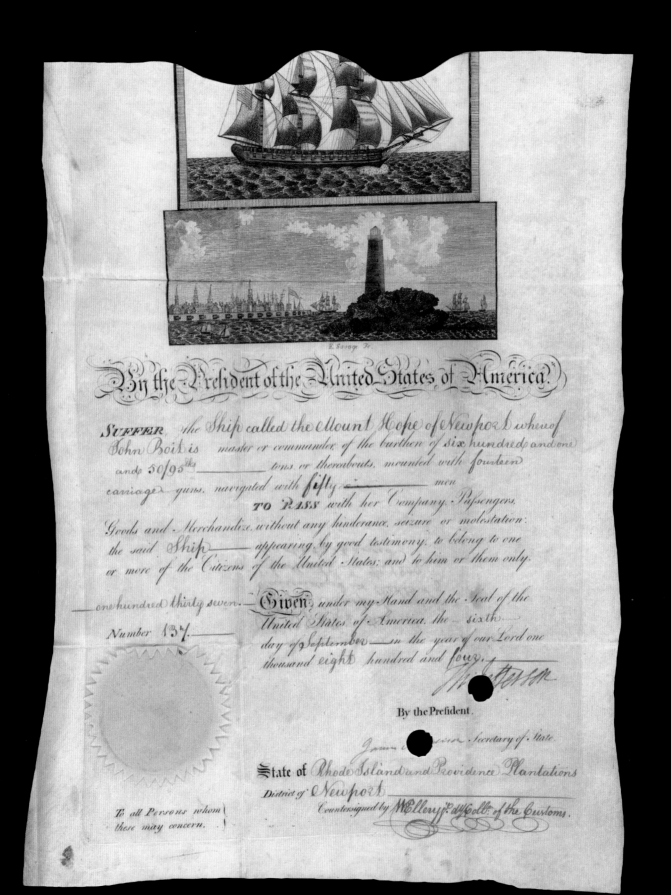

By the President of the United States of America.

SUFFER, the Ship called the Mount Hope of Newport whereof John Boit is master or commander, of the burthen of six hundred and one and 50/95 ths tons or thereabouts, mounted with fourteen carriage guns, navigated with fifty men TO PASS with her Company, Passengers, Goods and Merchandize, without any hinderance, seizure or molestation: the said Ship appearing, by good testimony, to belong to one or more of the Citizens of the United States: and to him or them only.

one hundred thirty seven. Given under my Hand and the Seal of the United States of America, the sixth day of September in the year of our Lord one thousand eight hundred and four.

Number 137.

By the President.

_____ Secretary of State.

State of Rhode Island and Providence Plantations
District of Newport

Countersigned by Wm Ellery Jr 44 Collr of the Customs.

To all Persons whom these may concern.

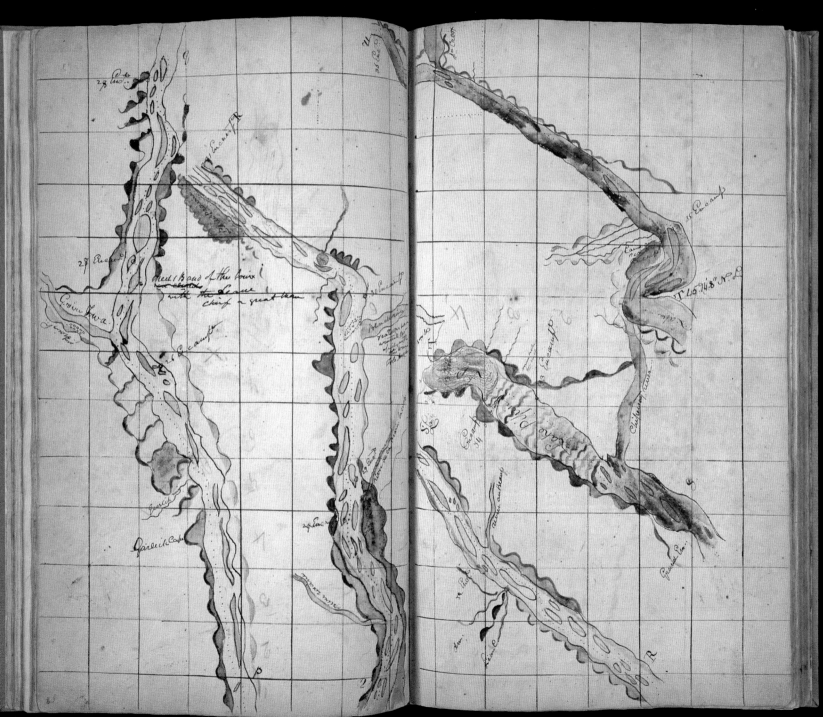

1

Fort McHenry 24th September 1814

Sir

A severe indisposition, the effect of great fatigue and
exposure, has prevented me heretofore from presenting you with an accou
nt of the Attack on this Post — On the night of Saturday the 10th inst.
the British Fleet consisting of Ships of the line, heavy Frigates, and Bomb vessel
amounting in the whole to 30 Sail, appeard at the mouth of the River Patap
sco, with every indication of an attempt on the City of Baltimore, my
own Force consisted of one Company of U. S. Artillery under Capt. Evans,
and two Companies of Sea Fencibles under Captains Bunbury and Addison,
of these three Companies 35 Men were unfortunately on the Sick list and
unfit for duty — I had been furnished with two Companies of Volunteer
artillery from the City of Baltimore under Capt. Berry and Lieut Command.
Pennington, — to these I must add another very fine Company of Volunteer
Artillerists under Judge Nicholson, who had profferd their Services to aid
in the defence of this Post whenever an attack might be apprehended,
and also a Detatchment from Commodore Barney's (under Lt. Rodman) flotilla: — Brigadier Genl.
Winder had also furnished me with about Six hundred Infantry under
the Command of Lt Col. Steuart & Major Lane, consisting of detatchments
from the 12th. 14th. 36th & 38th Regt. of U. S. troops, the total amounting to about
one thousand effective Men — On Monday Morning very early,

Report of Lt. Col. George Armistead on the defense of Fort McHenry, page one, September 24, 1814.

Map of Baltimore, 1815.

9. BOATS.
[13] Rafting & Booming.

Vol. 4. pg. 113.

CLASSIFICATION
2912.+
DIVISION.

David Gordon

Raft.

Patented February 16th 1818.

References
a the platform of timbers.
b.b.b.the spring poles. c the row block
d the stir block

Patent Office December 3d 1839

Made under the direction of the Commissioner of
Patents in Conformity with Act of 3d March 1837.

Commissioner of Patents.

The committee of Conference of the Senate and of the House of Representatives, on the subject of the disagreeing votes of the Two Houses, upon the Bill entitled an "Act for the admission of the State of Maine into the Union";

Report the following Resolution.

Resolved.

1.st That they recommend to the Senate to recede from their amendments to the said Bill

2.d That they recommend to the two Houses to agree to strike out of the fourth Section of the Bill from the House of Representatives, now pending in the Senate, entitled an "Act to authorize the people of the Missouri Territory to form a Constitution and State Government, and for the admission of such State into the Union upon an equal footing with the original States." The following proviso in the following words. — and shall ordain and establish, that there shall be neither Slavery nor involuntary servitude otherwise than in the

830 Congressman Davy Crockett's Resolutions to Abolish West Point

"...if the bounty of the government is to be at all bestowed, the destitute poor and not the rich & influential are the objects who most claim it

1. Resolved that if the bounty of the Government is to be at all bestowed the destitute poor and not the rich & influential are the objects who most Claim it and to whome the voice of Humanity most loudly Calls the attention of Congress

2. Resolved that no one Class of the Citizens of these united States has an exclusive right to demand or recieve for purposes of education or for other purposes more than an equal & ratable proportion of the funds of the national treasury which is replenished by a Common Contribution and in Some instances more at the Cost of the poor man who has but little to defend than that of the rich man who Seldom fights to defend himself or his — property —

3. Resolved that each and every institution Calculated at public expence and under the patronage and Sanction of the Government to grant exclusive priviledges except in — Consideration of public Services is not only aristocratic but a down right invasion of the rights of the Citizen and a violation of the Civil Compact Called the Constitu = tion,

4. Resolved further that the Military — academy at west point is Subject to the foregoing objections — in as much as those who are educated there, recieve their instruction at the public expense and are Generally the Sons of the rich and — influential who are able to educate their own Children — while the Sons of the — poor for want of active friends are often — neglected — or if educated even at the —

The court being duly sworn in the presence of the prisoner, proceeded to the trial of Cadet E. A. Poe of the U.S. Military Academy, who being previously asked if he had any objections to being tried by either of the members named in the order, and replying in the negative, was arraigned on the following charges and specifications:

Charge 1... Gross neglect of Duty.

Specification 1... In this, that he the said Cadet Poe did absent himself from the following parades and roll ca... 27 January... evening para... 24 and 25 j...

Trial of Cadet E. A. Poe.

reveillie roll call on the 8, 16, 17, 19, 21, 25 and 26 January 1831; absent from class parade on the 17, 18, 19, 20, 24 and 25 January 1831; absent from guard mounting on the 10 January 1831; and absent from church parade on the 23 of January 1831: all of which at West Point New York.

Specification 2... In this, that he the said Cadet Poe did absent himself from all his academical duties between the 15 and 27 January 1831: viz, absent from Mathematical recitation on the 17, 18, 19, 20, 21, 22, 24, 25 and 26 January 1831: all of which at West Point, New York.

Cover page and pages four and five.

REGISTER of *Cherokee* INDIANS *who have emigrated to the West of the Mississippi*

Names of Heads of Families.	Numbers and Ages of INDIANS.								Number of Slaves.		Total No. of each Family.	Date of Arrival in the New Country.	How, and by whom Removed.	REMARKS. Shewing the Mode of Subsistence—the Increase and decrease by Births, Deaths, &c.
	MALES.				FEMALES.									
	Under 10.	Of 10, & under 25.	Of 25, & under 50.	Over 50.	Under 10.	Of 10, & under 25.	Of 25, & under 50.	Over 50.	Males.	Females.				
Black Fox			1		2						3	1834 May 16	In Steam Boat	Supplied with Corn, Beef &c in boat. One died 13 Novem 1834
James McGhey	2				3	1	1				7		Moved by List	two
William England	2	2				3					7		J. W. Harris	
Alexander McGhey	1	1			1		1				4			
David Ross	3	1	1				1				6			
William Wooly Russell	3	1	1		1		1				7			reb'd west of the Miss: one birth 10 Aug 1834
Samuel Simons	3	1	1		2						7			
Elijah Sevenjohn		1									1			
Hosea Morgan Sen		2	2		1	1	1				7			deserted in June 1834
Hosea Morgan Jun		1									1			
Bryant Ward	1	1	1		2		1				6			
Anny Sevenjohn	1				1	1					3			reb'd west of the Mississippe
Harman Bolin			1								1			
Polly Ward	1				1	1	1				4			one birth 16 Nov 1834
Samuel Downing		1									1			
William Griffin's wife							1				1			
Betsy Bone & husband	1				1	1	1				4			
Jack Sanders & wife Molly		1					1				2			Jack makes returns west of the Miss:
James McDaniel & wife	1		1		2	1	1				7			one died 15 May 1834
Samuel Ward			1				1				2			Sam' Born this 7 Oct
George W. Ward	1		1		2	1					5			
Charles Ward			1								1			reb'd west of the Mississippi
Bears Foot	1		1		2		1				6			one birth 12 August 3 died 1 June 3 died 1 Oct 1834
Tea-nu-tee			1			1					2			
Tim Carey					1	1	1				3			Supplied with Corn in boat. All dead in July 1834
James Reynolds	1	1	1				1				4			Supplied with Corn, Beef, Salt in boat. James Reynolds reb'd east.
Stephen Spaniard			1							140		2			
John Woodard	1	1	1		3	1	1				8			Both died Oct Feb 1834
Maria Spaniard	3	3					1				7			Polly died 20 Sept 1834
Polly Spaniard					1	1					2			
Green Rogers		1									1			died
Mistaken Watts			1								1			one increase
Moses Watts			1								1			
Francis Johns	2	2	3					1			8			
Jack Spaniard	2		1		4	1					8			3 died 27 Aug 1834
											140			

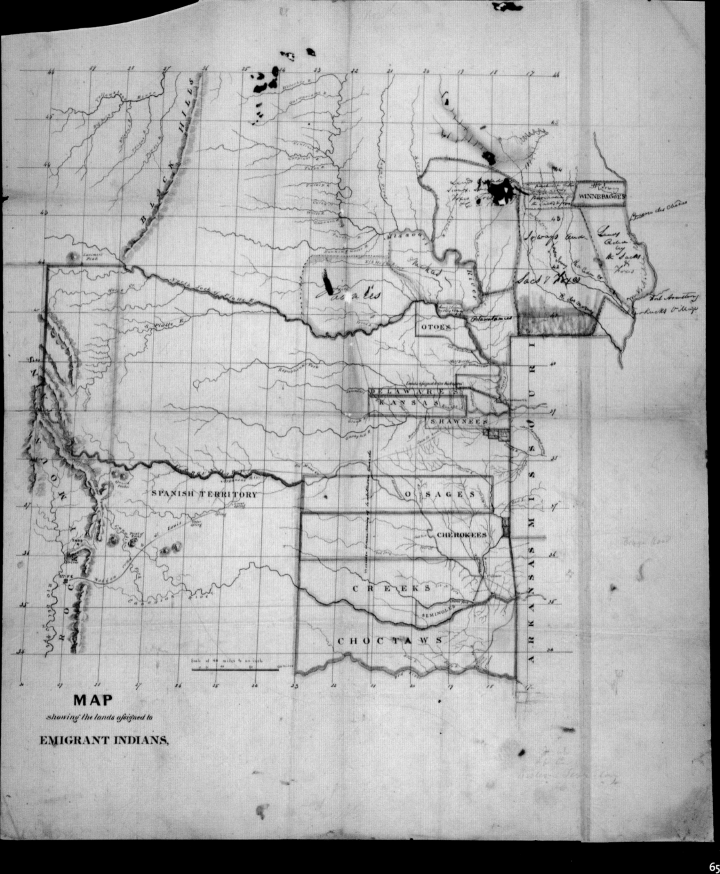

MAP

showing the lands assigned to

EMIGRANT INDIANS,

1830

1837

Gag Rule

"Resolved, that all petitions...touching the abolition of slavery or the buying, selling, or transferring of slaves...be laid upon the table without being debated

Upon the name of John Quincy Adams being called in taking the yeas & nays on special this resolution ~ ~~answered~~

I hold the Resolution to be in direct violation of the Constitution of the United States, of the Rules of this House, and of the rights of my constituents. ~ and gave his answer in writing to the Chair.

John Quincy Adams's resolution denouncing the gag rule against antislavery petitions as unconstitutional, May 27, 1836.

Resolved, that all petitions, memorials, and papers Touching the abolition of slavery or the buying, selling, or transferring of slaves in any state, district or Territory of the United States, be laid upon the table without being debated, printed, read or referred and that no further action whatever shall be had thereon —

The gag rule resolution, December 21, 1837.

To the Honorable the House of Representatives of the United States.

The undersigned *Women* of *Brookline* in the Commonwealth of Massachusetts, have learned with astonishment and alarm, that your honorable body did, on the 21st of December last, adopt a resolution in the words following, to wit:

'Resolved, That all memorials, petitions, and papers, touching the abolition of slavery, or the buying, selling, or transfer of slaves in any State, territory, or district of the United States, shall be laid on the table, without reading, or reference, or printing, and that no further action whatever shall be had thereon.' *being debated printed read or referred, & that no further action whatever shall be had thereon*

Your memorialists 'consider this resolution a violation of the Constitution of the United States—of the right of the people of the United States to petition—and of the right of their Representatives to freedom of speech as members of your honorable body:' They further regard it as an assumption of authority, at once dangerous and destructive to the fundamental principles of republican government, to the rights of minorities, to the sovereignty of the People, and TO THE UNION OF THESE UNITED STATES: They therefore present this their solemn and earnest remonstrance against said resolution, and respectfully ask your honorable body to IMMEDIATELY RESCIND IT.

Sarah M. Grimké

Angelina E. Grimké

Eliza Philbrick

Fanny Bell

Sarah Celfe

Hepzibah Celfe

Chloe H. Whitney

Rebecca Gerry

Rebecca S. Perry

Rosyra Jaquith   10

Ann A. Ogden

Abigail Tolman

Mary F. R. Tolman

Elizabeth Whyte

Susan G. Whyte

Ellen S. Whyte

Eliza Aspinwall

Semantha B. Higgins

Mehitable Stone

Mary H. Stone   20

Annie Powell Philbrick

Catherine Lopez

838

Gen. Winfield Scott's General Order No. 25

"All strong men, women, boys & girls, will be made to march under proper escorts. For the feeble, Indian horses and ponies will furnish a ready resource"

ORDERS. No. 25.

Head Quarters, Eastern Division.
Cherokee Agency, Ten. May 17, 1838.

MAJOR GENERAL SCOTT, of the United States' Army, announces to the troops assembled and assembling in this country, that, with them, he has been charged by the President to cause the Cherokee Indians yet remaining in North Carolina, Georgia, Tennessee and Alabama, to remove to the West, according to the terms of the Treaty of 1835. His Staff will be as follows:

LIEUTENANT COLONEL W. J. WORTH, acting Adjutant General, Chief of the Staff.

MAJOR M. M. PAYNE, acting Inspector General.

LIEUTENANTS R. ANDERSON, & E. D. KEYES, regular Aids-de-camp.

COLONEL A. H. KENAN & LIEUTENANT H. B. SHAW, volunteer Aids-de-camp.

Any order given orally, or in writing, by either of those officers, in the name of the Major General, will be respected and obeyed as if given by himself.

The Chiefs of Ordnance, of the Quarter-Master's Department and of the Commissariat, as also the Medical Director of this Army, will, as soon as they can be ascertained, be announced in orders.

To carry out the general object with the greatest promptitude and certainty, and with the least possible distress to the Indians, the country they are to evacuate is divided into three principal Military Districts, under as many officers of high rank, to command the troops serving therein, subject to the instructions of the Major General.

Eastern District, to be commanded by BRIGADIER GENERAL EUSTIS, of the United States' Army, or the highest officer in rank, serving therein:—North Carolina, the part of Tennessee lying north of Gilmer county, Georgia, and the counties of Gilmer, Union, and Lumpkin, in Georgia. Head Quarters, in the first instance, say, at Fort Butler.

Western District, to be commanded by COLONEL LINDSAY, of the United States' Army, or the highest officer in rank serving therein:—Alabama, the residue of Tennessee and Dade county, in Georgia. Head quarters, in the first instance, say, at Ross' Landing.

Middle District, to be commanded by BRIGADIER GENERAL ARMISTEAD of the United States' Army, or the highest officer in rank, serving therein:—All that part of the Cherokee country, lying within the State of Georgia, and which is not comprised in the two other districts. Head Quarters, in the first instance, say, at New Echota.

It is not intended that the foregoing boundaries between the principal commanders shall be strictly observed. Either, when carried near the district of another, will not hesitate to extend his operations, according to the necessities of the case, but with all practicable harmony, into the adjoining district. And, among his principal objects, in case of actual or apprehended hostilities, will be that of affording adequate protection to our white people in and around the Cherokee country.

The senior officer actually present in each district will receive instructions from the Major General as to the time of commencing the removal, and every thing that may occur interesting to the service, in the district, will be promptly reported to the same source. The Major General will endeavour to visit in a short time all parts of the Cherokee country occupied by the troops.

The duties devolved on the army, through the orders of the Major General & those of the commanders of districts, under him, are of a highly important and critical nature.

The Cherokees, by the advances which they have made in christianity and civilization, are by far the most interesting tribe of Indians in the territorial limits of the United States. Of the 15,000 of those people who are now to be removed—(and the time within which a voluntary emigration was stipulated, will expire on the 23rd instant—) it is understood that about four fifths are opposed, or have become averse to a distant emigration; and altho' none are in actual hostilities with the United States, or threaten a resistance by arms, yet the troops will probably be obliged to cover the whole country they inhabit, in order to make prisoners and to march or to transport the prisoners, by families, either to this place, to Ross' Landing or Gunter's Landing, where they are to be finally delivered over to the Superintendant of Cherokee Emigration.

Considering the number and temper of the mass to be removed, together with the extent and fastnesses of the country occupied, it will readily occur, that simple indiscretions—acts of harshness and cruelty, on the part of our troops, may lead, step by step, to delays, to impatience and exasperation, and in the end, to a general war and carnage—a result, in the case of those particular Indians, utterly abhorrent to the generous sympathies of the whole American people. Every possible kindness, compatible with the necessity of removal, must, therefore, be shown by the troops, and, if, in the ranks, a despicable individual should be found, capable of inflicting a wanton injury or insult on any Cherokee man, woman or child, it is hereby made the special duty of the nearest good officer or man, instantly to interpose, and to seize and consign the guilty wretch to the severest penalty of the laws. The Major General is fully persuaded that this injunction will not be neglected by the brave men under his command, who cannot be otherwise than jealous of their own honor and that of their country.

By early and persevering acts of kindness and humanity, it is impossible to doubt that the Indians may soon be induced to confide in the Army, and instead of fleeing to mountains and forests, flock to us for food and clothing. If, however, through false apprehensions, individuals, or a party, here and there, should seek to hide themselves, they must be pursued and invited to surrender, but not fired upon unless they should make a stand to resist. Even in such cases, mild remedies may sometimes better succeed than violence; and it cannot be doubted that if we get possession of the women and children first, or first capture the men, that, in either case, the outstanding members of the same families will readily come in on the assurance of forgiveness and kind treatment.

Every captured man, as well as all who surrender themselves, must be disarmed, with the assurance that their weapons will be carefully preserved and restored at, or beyond the Mississippi. In either case, the men will be guarded and escorted, except it may be, where their women and children are safely secured as hostages; but, in general, families, in our possession, will not be separated, unless it be to send men, as runners, to invite others to come in.

It may happen that Indians will be found too sick, in the opinion of the nearest Surgeon, to be removed to one of the depots indicated above. In every such case, one or more of the family, or the friends of the sick person, will be left in attendance, with ample subsistence and remedies, and the remainder of the family removed by the troops. Infants, superannuated persons, lunatics and women in a helpless condition, will all, in the removal, require peculiar attention, which the brave and humane will seek to adapt to the necessities of the several cases.

All strong men, women, boys & girls, will be made to march under proper escorts. For the feeble, Indian horses and ponies will furnish a ready resource, as well as for bedding and light cooking utensils—all of which, as intimated in the Treaty, will be necessary to the emigrants both in going to, and after arrival at, their new homes. Such, and all other light articles of property, the Indians will be allowed to collect and to take with them, as also their slaves, who will be treated in like manner with the Indians themselves.

If the horses and ponies be not adequate to the above purposes, wagons must be supplied.

Corn, oats, fodder and other forage, also beef cattle, belonging to the Indians to be removed, will be taken possession of by the proper departments of the Staff, as wanted, for the regular consumption of the Army, and certificates given to the owners, specifying in every case, the amount of forage and the weight of beef, so taken, in order that the owners may be paid for the same on their arrival at one of the depots mentioned above.

All other moveable or personal property, left or abandoned by the Indians, will be collected by agents appointed for the purpose, by the Superintendant of Cherokee Emigration, under a system of accountability, for the benefit of the Indian owners, which he will devise. The Army will give to those agents, in their operations, all reasonable countenance, aid and support.

White men and widows, citizens of the United States, who are, or have been intermarried with Indians, and thence commonly termed, *Indian countrymen*; also such Indians as have been made denizens of particular States by special legislation, together with the families and property of all such persons, will not be molested or removed by the troops until a decision, on the principles involved, can be obtained from the War Department.

A like indulgence, but only for a limited time, and until further orders, is extended to the families and property of certain Chiefs and head-men of the two great Indian parties, (on the subject of emigration) now understood to be absent in the direction of Washington on the business of their respective parties.

This order will be carefully read at the head of every company in the Army.

Winfield Scott

By Command:

W. I. Worth &c.
Adj. of the Staff

1838
1841

Financial Account of John Ross for Transporting a Detachment of Emigrant Cherokee by Steamboat to Indian Territory in Late 1838 and 1839

"Provisions for Emigrants from the 5th Dec. 1838 up to the 18th March 1839…"

A rough estimate of the probable cost of the Water Detachment of Emigrant Cherokees, conducted by Capt. John Drew —

Conductors pay from the 7th Nov. to the 4th Dec. 1838 inclusive being for the time detained unavoidably by low water, at the Agency pre- vious to embarkation for the $140.00

The Asst. Conductor's pay at the sam...

The Attending Physician's pay —

"   "   Interpreter...

"   Commissary's pay...

"   4 flat bottomed boats for transp... grants down the Hiwasee & Ten... Services for Boat hands, and pil... the Suck and the Muscle Sho... including ... tollage the round ... ... Canal, supposed to... for about 40 or 45 days

1 Steam Boat Cost /bough... 1 Keel boat purchased at... Capt Steam Boats Captains p... or 18th Jany 1839 to 18th of Mar... Capt. Mate's pay   same Principal Engineers pay Asst.   do —   " Carpenter's   — "
Carried...

Pages one and two.

Amount brought Over ————————	$ 1304.00
Cook, Steward and 6 boat hands @ 30 p mo. for 2 months	480.00
Pilot from Tuscumbia to Paduca ————	100.00
ditto — " Paduca to Montgomery's Point —	100.00
ditto — " Montgomery's Point to Fort Gibson —	150.00
Wood for Steam Boat averaging about 8 Cords p day for say 60 days, ... 480 Cords @ $3 p...	1440.00
Provisions for Steam Boats Crew of 14 persons for 60 days making 840 rations @ 16 cts	134.40
Conductors Pay from the 5th Dec 1838 to 18th March 1839 making 104 days ——————— @ 5 p	520.00
Asst. Conductors pay 104 days ———— " 3.00	312.00
Attending Physicians pay 104 days — " 5.00	520.00
Interpreter to Ditto — " — 104 ——— " 2.50	260.00
Commissary's pay — " 104 ——— " 2.50	260.00
Provisions for Emigrants from the 5th Dec. 1838 up to the 18th March 1839 inclusive 24024 rations 16 cts	3843.84
3 lb Soap to every 100 rations making 720 3/4 lbs @ 15 cts	108.11¼
	$ 21242.35¼
For the employment of Waggons teams & teamsters, going to the mouth of the Illinois river and transporting the emi- grants from the Steam Boat there Stoped, (in consequence of low waters) and haul- ing them out about 40 miles, to the Camp Ground on the same river, where the Detachment was dissolved, and the people were ... subsisted by the U.S. Contractors &c	422.00
	$ 21664.35¼

1839
1841

The *Amistad* Case

"...the said Slaves rose upon the Captain & Crew of said Schooner & Killed & murdered the Captain & one of said Crew..."

" 28th Day of June AD 1839 from the Port of Havanna
bound to a port in the Province of Principe
both in said Island of Cuba under the Command
of Raymen Ferrer as master th... —said
Schooner had on board and
a large & valuable Cargo Con
as the libellants believe to b
pieces 1 Crate 11 boxes Crocker
vermicelli. 15 ps linen Stuff
Beans. 25 Boxes Raisins. 50 c
Morocco Skins. 5 Dz Calf
200 feet Rods. 20 Sides Sole L
Warehouse. 8 Crowns 1 B
Kettles. 14 packages Common
linen. 4 dz parasols or um.
yds each. 2 dz ps Hose 3 c
Lilisia 2 ps Victoria 2 ps
54 ps Calicoes 5 ps Laces
24 ps Stripes 148 ps Ribbon
Glazed Linen 4 ps Rouen
Hans. Gloves. Shirts. Taf
29 Muslin Dress patter
15 Rugs Buttons Sadd
30 ps Long lawn 1 ps C
8 Dz Linen Cambric
Robbins 2 ps Ribbon
linen Cambric 800
30 Dress patterns 6 M
Blankets 1 box Hard
linen 60 Vols B

of Cohpen. Hardware 50 Demijohns Olive Oil 20 Boxes
vermicelli 20 Quintals Jerked Beef 15 Sides Sole Leather
6 Kegs Olives 2 Quintals Hams 190 ps Muslins 26 ps
Stripes 3 ps Brown Drilling 4 ps linens 21 ps Colored fine
linens 11 dz Ladies Hose 2 Doz Belts 10 doz linen
Cambric Hdkffs 12 Common La and a large quantity
of Silks Linens Hardware & provisions to the Amount
in all of $40,000 Dollars — And also fifty four
Slaves to wit fifty one male Slaves and three young
female Slaves who were worth Twenty five thousand
Dollars. and while on said voyage from Havanna
to Principe the said Slaves rose upon the Captain
& Crew of said Schooner & Killed & murdered the
Captain & one of said Crew & two more of said Crew
escaped & got away from said Schooner. that the
two Spaniards on board. to wit Pedro Montes and
Jose Ruis.— remained alive on board said Schooner
after the murder of the Captain and after the said
Negroes had taken possession of said vessel & Cargo
that their lives were spared to assist in the sailing
of said vessel & it was directed by said negroes
that said Schooner should be navigated for the
Coast of Africa & said Pedro Montes & Jose Ruis
did accordingly steer as thus directed & compelled
by said Negroes at the peril of their lives in the
day time & in the night altered their Course & Steer
for the American Shore. but after more than two
months on the Ocean they succeeded in coming round
Montauk Point. then they were discovered and

Libel of Lt. Thomas R. Gedney,
U.S. brig *Washington*, pages three
and four, August 29, 1839.

70

"...each of them are natives of Africa and were born free, and ever since have been and still of right are and ought to be free, and not slaves..."

42.

The United States. Appt. vs The Libellants & Claimants of the Schooner Amistad, her tackle apparel and furniture, together with her Cargo, and the Africans mentioned and described in the several Libels and Claims.

On appeal from the Circuit Court of the United States for the District of Connecticut. This Cause came on to be heard on the transcript of the record from the Circuit Court of the United States for the District of Connecticut and was argued by counsel. On consideration whereof, It is the opinion of this Court, that there is error in that part of the decree of the Circuit Court affirming the decree of the District Court which ordered the said Negroes to be delivered to the President of the United States to be transported to Africa in pursuance of the Act of Congress of the 3d of March 1819; and that as to that part it ought to be reversed; and in all other respects that the said decree of the Circuit Court ought to be affirmed. It is therefore adjudged and decreed by this Court that the decree of the said Circuit Court be and the same is hereby affirmed except as to the part aforesaid and as to that part that it be reversed; and that the cause be remanded to the Circuit Court with directions to enter in lieu of that part a decree that the said Negroes be and are hereby declared to be free and that they be dismissed from the custody of the Court and be discharged from the suit and go thereof quit without day.

March 9. 1841.

Opinion of the Supreme Court in the *United States* v. *the Schooner* Amistad, page one, March 9, 1841.

said libel: and also under process of this Honorable Court issued and served at Hartford on the 18th day of September 1839 while the Respondents were in custody of the Marshall of said District as aforesaid viz at Hartford within the body of the State and District of Connecticut, on the libel and claim of William S. Hollabird Esqr. United States District Attorney for said District of Connecticut and the libels respectively of Pedro Montes & Jose Ruiz; and also under process of this Honorable Court issued at Hartford aforesaid on the 19th day of November 1839 on the claim and representation of the said District Attorney then and there made and filed.

The said respondents severally by protestation not admitting or acknowledging that the Government of the United States, or any department, Court, or officer thereof hath jurisdiction over the persons of these Respondents, or any of them, by reason of any of the allegations & proceedings aforesaid, & not confessing or acknowledging any of the matters & things in the libellants said several libels & claims to be true in manner and form as the same are therein and thereby alledged, appear before this Honorable Court, and for answer to the several libels, claims & representations aforesaid severally say.

That they and each of them are natives of Africa and were born free, and ever since have been and still of right are and ought to be free and not slaves, as is in said several libels or claims pretended or surmised; that they were never domiciled in the Island of Cuba, or in the dominions of the Queen of Spain, or subject to the laws thereof; that on or about the 15th day of April 1839 they and each of them were in the

Answer of the Proctors for the *Amistad* Africans, page two, January 7, 1840.

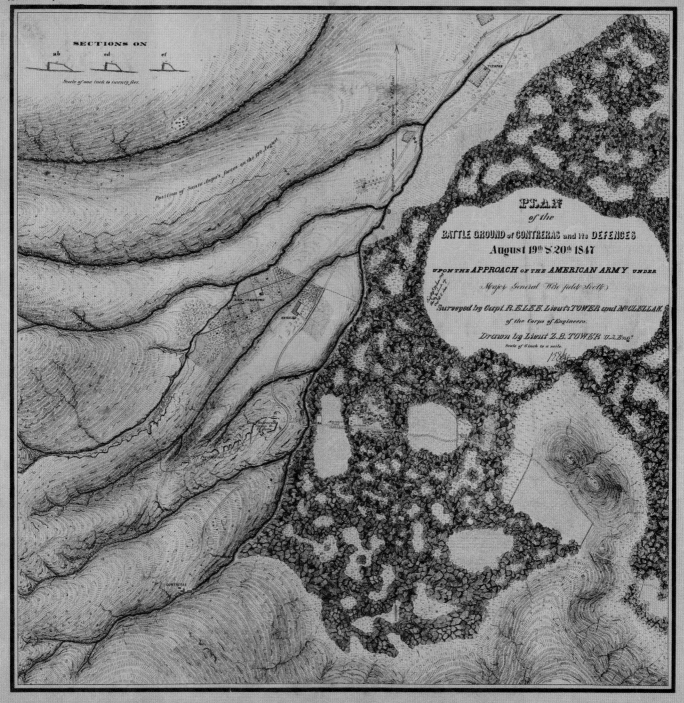

SECTIONS ON

ab   cd   ef

Scale of one inch to twenty feet.

Position of Santa Anna's forces on the 19e August

TITAPAN

SAN JERONIMO

AMSALED

CONTRERAS

PLAN
of the
BATTLE GROUND of CONTRERAS and its DEFENCES
August 19th & 20th 1847
UPON THE APPROACH OF THE AMERICAN ARMY UNDER
Major General Win field Scott)
Surveyed by Capt. R. E. LEE. Lieuts TOWER and McCLELLAN.
of the Corps of Engineers.
Drawn by Lieut Z. B. TOWER U. S. Engr
Scale of 6 inch to a mile.

1848 Electromagnetic Telegraph Patent

"Fifth. A signal Lever, which breaks and connects the circuit of conductors."

Samuel F.B. Morse, ca. 1860–1865.

U.S Patent #1647, Reissue #117, June 13, 1848.

To All Persons whom it may concern.

Be it known, That I the undersigned, Samuel F.B. Morse, of

have invented a new and

THE U. STATES **PATENT OFFICE.**

TO ALL PERSONS TO WHOM THESE PRESENTS SHALL COME, GREETING:

THIS IS TO CERTIFY, That the annexed is a true copy from the files of this Office of the Specification of Letters Patent of Samuel F. B. Morse for an Electro-Magnetic Telegraph (said Letters Patent being dated June 20th 1840) said specification which the Patent was issued having various marks, interlineations in blue ink & pencil which (except the words "not represented") are believed to have been made by Professor Morse himself in his own handwriting & which are expressed in this copy, those in blue ink likewise by blue ink and the pencil ones by red ink; the words "with one corner bevelled" opposite the note on the fifth page of this copy, are in the original, written on an erasure, as is attempted to be indicated in this said copy

In testimony whereof, I Edmund Burke Commissioner of Patents, have caused the seal of the Patent Office to be hereunto affixed this twentieth day of October in the year of our Lord one thousand eight hundred and forty-eight and of the Independence of the United States the seventy-third

Edmund Burke

use, and also that of the signal lever.
Fifth. A signal Lever, which breaks and connects the circuit of conductors.

U.S. Patent Office certificate issued to Samuel F.B. Morse for an electromagnetic telegraph, 1848.

Map of Sutter's Mill, Coloma, California, July 20, 1848.

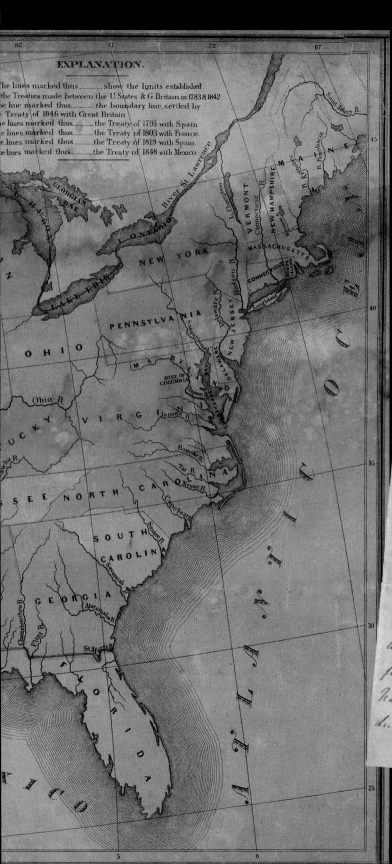

EXPLANATION.

The lines marked thus _____ show the limits established
the Treaties made between the U.States & G.Britain in 1783 & 1842
he line marked thus _____ the boundary line, settled by
Treaty of 1846 with Great Britain
e lines marked thus _____ the Treaty of 1795 with Spain
e lines marked thus _____ the Treaty of 1803 with France.
e lines marked thus _____ the Treaty of 1819 with Spain.
e lines marked thus _____ the Treaty of 1848 with Mexico.

Map of the United States, including Western Territories, December 1848.

Senator Henry Clay's resolutions proposing the
Compromise of 1850, page one, January 29, 1850.

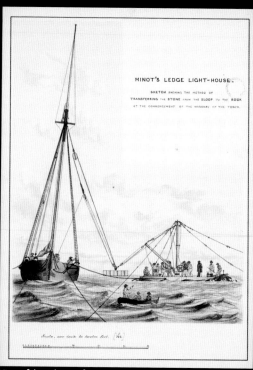

View of derrick transferring stone.

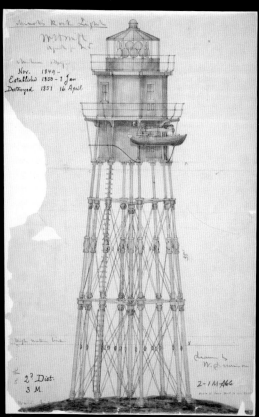

Elevation plan with boat, by Dennison, 1851.

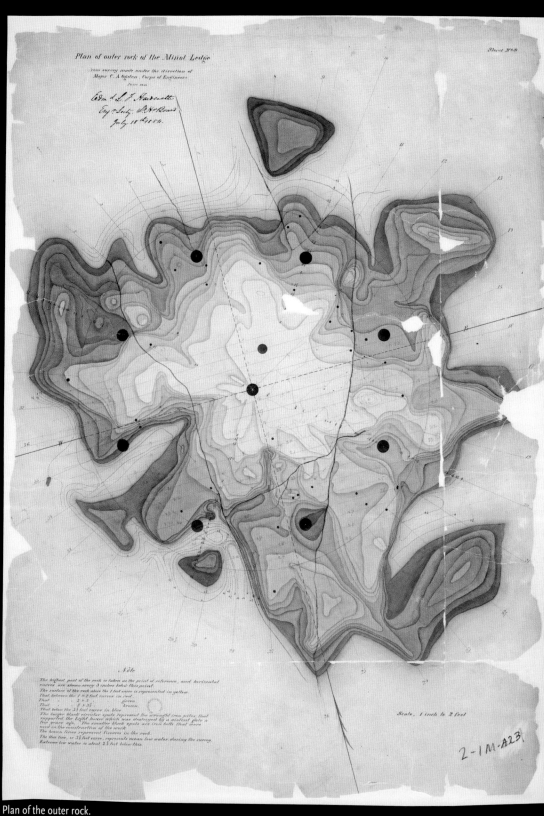

Plan of the outer rock.

Elevation plan with figure, boat, and flag.

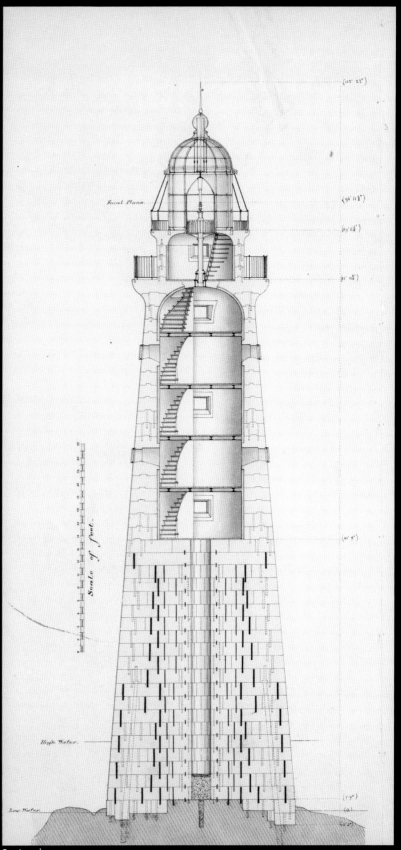

Section plan.

Esquimalt Harbor, from the summit of "Mill Mountain."

Active Passage. Saturna Group, looking west.

Straits of Haro, Stewart's Island in the center.

Straits of Rosario. Cypress Island and Strawberry Harbor on the right.

Semiahmoo Bay, from Bluff near entrance of "Mud Bay."

View from hill on San Juan Island.

Mrs. Mundelle.

Miss M. McDaunt.

Mrs. H. J. Rogers.

Agnes Robinson.

Miss Pruyn.

Miss Waugh.

Miss Bateman.

Mrs. C. P. Roberts.

Miss Alice Harrison.

Miss Ida Williams.

Miss L. C. Miris.

Mrs. Abraham Lincoln.

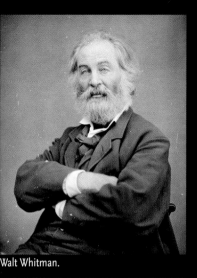

Walt Whitman.

Sioux Chief Hole-In-The-Day.

Constantino Brumidi, detail.

Japanese man, detail.

Mathew Brady.

Lucien Anatole Prévost-Paradol.

Sam Houston.

Master J. Callahan.

Jefferson Davis.

Benjamin S. Turner.

Horace Greeley, detail.

Abraham Lincoln.

Fort Sumter

"...defended Fort Sumter for thirty Four hours until the quarters were entirely burned..."

Interior view of Fort Sumter after its evacuation by Union Maj. Robert Anderson, 1st Artillery, April 1861.

View of Fort Sumter in the distance from Fort Johnson, South Carolina.

S.S.BALTIC.OFF SANDY HOOK APR.EIGHTEENTH.TEN THIRTY A.M. .VIA NEW YORK. . HON.S.CAMERON. SECY.WAR. WASHN. HAVING DEFENDED FORT SUMTER FOR THIRTY FOUR HOURS. UNTIL THE QUARTERS WERE ENTIRELY BURNED THE MAIN GATES DESTROYED BY FIRE.THE GORGE WALLS SERIOUSLY INJURED.THE MAGAZINE SURROUNDED BY FLAMES AND ITS DOOR CLOSED FROM THE EFFECTS OF HEAT .FOUR BARRELLS AND THREE CARTRIDGES OF POWDER ONLY BEING AVAILABLE AND NO PROVISIONS REMAINING BUT PORK.I ACCEPTED TERMS OF EVACUATION OFFERED BY GENERAL BEAUREGARD BEING ON SAME OFFERED BY HIM ON THE ELEVENTH INST.PRIOR TO THE COMMENGEMENT OF .HOSTILITIES AND MARCHED OUT OF THE FORT SUNDAY AFTERNOON THE FOURTEENTH INST.WITH COLORS FLYING AND DRUMS BEATING.BRINGING AWAY COMPANY AND PRIVATE PROPERTY AND SALUTING MY FLAG WITH FIFTY GUNS. ROBERT ANDERSON.MAJOR FIRST ARTILLERY.COMMANDING.

Telegram announcing the surrender
of Fort Sumter, April 18, 1861.

"...we, the People of Virginia do declare and ordain...that said Constitution of the United States of America is no longer binding..."

An Ordinance to Repeal the Ratification of the Constitution of the United States of America by the State of Virginia, and to resume all the rights and powers granted under said Constitution.

THE PEOPLE OF VIRGINIA in their ratification of the Constitution of the United States of America adopted by them in Convention on the twenty fifth day of June in the year of our Lord one thousand, seven hundred and eighty eight having declared that the powers granted under the said Constitution were derived from the people of the United States, and might be resumed whensoever the same should be perverted to their injury and oppression; and the Federal Government having perverted said powers not only to the injury of the people of Virginia, but to the oppression of the Southern slaveholding States:

Now, therefore, we, the People of Virginia do declare and ordain that the Ordinance adopted by the people of this State in Convention, on the twenty fifth day of June, in the year of our Lord one thousand seven hundred and eighty eight whereby the Constitution of the United States of America was ratified, and all acts of the General Assembly of this State ratifying or adopting amendments to said Constitution are hereby repealed and abrogated; that the Union between the State of Virginia and the other States under the Constitution aforesaid is hereby dissolved; and that the State of Virginia is in the full possession and exercise of all the rights of sovereignty which belong and appertain to a free and independent State. And they do further declare that said Constitution of the United States of America is no longer binding on any of the citizens of this State.

This ordinance shall take effect, and be an act of this day when ratified by a majority of the votes of the people of this State cast at a poll to be taken thereon on the fourth Thursday in May next, in pursuance of a schedule hereafter to be enacted.

Done in Convention in the City of Richmond on the seventeenth day of April, in the year of our Lord one thousand eight hundred and sixty one, and in the eighty fifth year of the Commonwealth of Virginia. Angus R. Blakey

Wm H Bulany.   John Rand Tchamblep   John Tyanny - President
John T. Thornton Geo. W. the Newlyk   Geo. W. Taylor   W B Cecil   James W. Holley
Mr. Echols James P. Holcombe   P 1313 ord   Geo. Blower Addison Hall
Williams Carter Wickham   Samuel G Staples John L Campbell Jeremiah Morton
R.H. Cox George W. Richardson.   Wm A Coffman   Wood Bouldin
John Tyler. B.F. Grant Wm J. Neblett   M. Tabscbrd Virginia
John Goode Jr.   Josh E Seawell   Edward S Stace
Edm F Morris   Miers W. Fisher. Walter D. Leake William W Forbes
Wm W Boyd   Manitus Chapman   Lewis D Isbell
James H Cox   W. G. Fulkalson J B Mallo Benj F Wysor
John L Marye   George Wm Brent   James C Bruce
Sam C Williams   James M. Strange   James Gustavus Holladay
Marmaduke Johnson   Kindor G Moffett   Lewis E Harvie
James Boisseau   Hugh M. Nelson   Franklin P Turner
P B Mosby   John Richardson Kilby   Wm Ballard Preston

Detail.

85

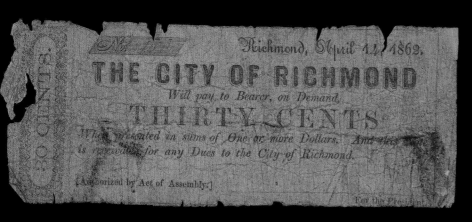

Confederate

UNITED STATES OF AMERICA,
SOUTHERN DISTRICT OF ALABAMA.

So. Div.

Be it Remembered, That Benjamin C. Burritt personally appeared before me *Confederate* ~~Clerk of the District~~ Court of the ~~United~~ *Confederate* States for the District aforesaid, on this 12th day of September in the year of our Lord one thousand eight hundred and ~~fifty~~ sixty one, who upon his solemn oath, doth depose and say, that he is a native of of New York,

now residing in the State of Alabama—that he has been in the ~~United~~ States years—that he is aged years or thereabouts—that it is *bona fide* his intention to become a citizen of the ~~United~~ *Confederate* States, and absolutely and entirely to renounce and abjure all allegiance and fidelity to every foreign Prince, Potentate, State or Sovereignty and particularly to the State of New York, & the government of the United States; & that he doth acknowledge the authority of the government of the Confederate States.

IN TESTIMONY WHEREOF, I have hereunto set my hand and affixed the seal of said Court at Mobile, this day and date above written.

John A. Cuthbert

Clerk.

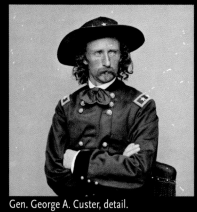

Gen. George A. Custer, detail.

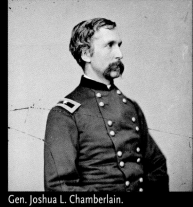

Gen. Joshua L. Chamberlain.

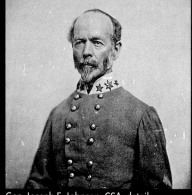

Gen. Joseph E. Johnson, CSA, detail.

Gen. P.G.T. Beauregard, CSA, detail.

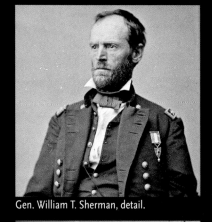

Gen. William T. Sherman, detail.

Gen. William Mahone, CSA, detail.

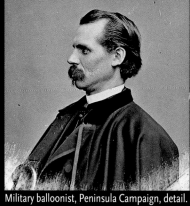

Military balloonist, Peninsula Campaign, detail.

Gen. Thomas "Stonewall" Jackson, CSA, detail.

Gen. John B. Gordon, CSA, detail.

Gen. Joseph Hooker, detail.

Gen. John B. Hood, CSA, detail.

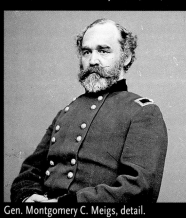

Gen. Montgomery C. Meigs, detail.

Gen. Philip H. Sheridan, detail.

Lt. Gen. Joseph Wheeler, CSA, detail.

Gen. George B. McClellan, detail.

W. Black, wounded boy, detail.

Confederate ram, *Atlanta*, on the James River after capture.

Battery on drill.

Mortar mounted on railroad car, U.S. Military railroad, Petersburg, Virginia.

Military bridge over the Tennessee River built in 1863–1864.

Infantry regiment in camp.

Gen. Ulysses S. Grant's baggage wagon.

A Company of the 6th Maine Infantry on parade after the battle of Fredericksburg, Virginia, 1862.

Confederate dead behind a stone wall at Fredericksburg, Virginia, 1862.

1863

Emancipation Proclamation, Presidential Proclamation 95

"...all persons held as slaves within any State...in rebellion against the United States, shall be...forever free..."

Pages one and five.

one thousand eight hundred and sixty three; and of the Independence of the United States of America the eighty-seventh.

Abraham Lincoln

By the President:

William H. Seward
Secretary of State.

By the President of the United States of America:

A Proclamation.

Whereas, on the twenty-second day of September, in the year of our Lord one thousand eight hundred and sixty-two, a proclamation was issued by the President of the United States, containing, among other things, the following, to wit:

"That on the first day of January, in the year of our Lord one thousand eight hundred and sixty-three, all persons held as slaves within any State or designated part of a State, the people whereof shall then be in rebellion against the United States, shall be then, thenceforward, and forever free; and the Executive Government of the United States, including the military and naval authority thereof, will recognize and maintain the freedom of such persons, and will do no act or acts to repress such persons, or any of them, in any efforts they may make for their actual freedom.

"That the Executive will, on the first day

Contraband school, ca. 1860–ca. 1865.

Freedmans Village near Arlington Heights,
Virginia, July 10, 1865.

Pvt. Hubbard Pryor before and after his enlistment in the 44th U.S. Colored Infantry, 1864.

Military service record of Louis F. Douglass, wounded in the assault on Fort Wagner, South Carolina, 1863.

Recruitment poster, July 13, 1863.

TO COLORED MEN!

FREEDOM,

Protection, Pay, and a Call to Military Duty!

On the 1st day of January, 1863, the President of the United States proclaimed FREE-DOM to over THREE MILLIONS OF SLAVES. This decree is to be enforced by all the power of the Nation. On the 21st of July last he issued the following order:

PROTECTION OF COLORED TROOPS.

"WAR DEPARTMENT, ADJUTANT GENERAL'S OFFICE,
WASHINGTON, July 21.

"General Order, No. 233.

"The following order of the President is published for the information and government of all concerned:—

EXECUTIVE MANSION, WASHINGTON, July 30.

"It is the duty of every Government to give protection to its citizens, of whatever class, color, or condition, and especially to those who are duly organized as soldiers in the public service. The law of nations, and the usages and customs of war, as carried on by civilized powers, permit no distinction as to color in the treatment of prisoners of war as public enemies. To sell or enslave any captured person on account of his color, is a relapse into barbarism, and a crime against the civilization of the age.

"The Government of the United States will give the same protection to all its soldiers, and if the enemy shall sell or enslave any one because of his color, the offense shall be punished by retaliation upon the enemy's prisoners in our possession. It is, therefore, ordered, for every soldier of the United States, killed in violation of the laws of war, a rebel soldier shall be executed; and for every one enslaved by the enemy, or sold into slavery, a rebel soldier shall be placed at hard labor on the public works, and continued at such labor until the other shall be released and receive the treatment due to prisoners of war.

"'ABRAHAM LINCOLN.'

"By order of the Secretary of War.
"E. D. TOWNSEND, Assistant Adjutant General.'

the rebels soon began to find out, as witness the follow-

List of the Names of the Enlisted Men of the
54th Regiment Mass. Vols.
Missing after the assault on Ft. Wagner July 18th 1863.

Co.	Names	Rank	Co	Names	Rank
A.	1 Andrew Benton	Sergeant	9	67 Charles Body	Private
"	2 Ralph Gardner	Corporal	"	68 William H Meyers	"
"	3 Henry Abbot	Private	"	69 Harrison Nichols	"
"	4 James M. Allen	"	"	70 Charles Steanborn	"
"	5 Henry F. Burghardt	"	"	71 John Stewart	"
"	6 George W Duncan	"	"	72 William Tyler	"
"	7 George F Ellis	"	"	73 William Underwood	"
"	8 Joseph Ford	"	H	74 Walter A. Jeffries	Sergeant
"	9 Edward Hines	"	"	75 Amsted Williams	Corporal
"	10 Sanford Jackson	"	"	76 James Caldwell	Private
"	11 Marshall Lamb	"	"	77 James A Williams	"
"	12 Harrison Pierce	"	"	78 J. W. Dickenson	"
"	13 Joseph Brown	"	"	79 Wm. N. Harrison	"
"	13 John Smith	"	"	80 Henry Kirk	"
"	14 George F. Waterman	"	"	81 Enos Smith	"
"	14 Cornelius Watson	"	"	82 Frederick Wallace	"
"	14 William F. Hill	"	5	83 H. W. Worthington	
B	15 Robert J Simons	Sergeant	5	84 Alfred Whitbie	Sergeant
"	16 Charles Hardy	Corporal	"	85 Charles Augustus	Corporal
"	17 S. E Anderson	Private	"	86 Robert L Jones	"
"	18 George Allison	"	"	87 Randolph Brady	"
"	19 Jesse H Brunn	"	"	88 J. M. Freeman	Private
"	20 David Baily	"	"	89 Noah Gaines	"
"	21 Morris Brunn	"	"	90 William Pillow	"
"	22 John H Brooks	"	"	91 Thomas Stone	"
"	23 James Elatts	"	"	92 B. H. Williams	"
"	24 George Grant	"	"	93 Ezekel Williams	"
"	25 Lueden Glascow	"	"	94 J. Williamson	"
"	26 Alfred Green	"	"	95 B Smith	"
"	27 Wm. Kesby	"	"	96 L. W. Woods	"
"	28 John A Sisewllen	"	"	97 H. C. Charleston	"
"	29 Daniel State	"	K	98 Jesse Mahan	Sergeant
"	30 Charles Williams	"	"	99 John H Wilson	Corporal
"	31 Samuel R Wilson	"	"	100 Colonel Morgan	Private
C	32 Joseph H Campbell	Corporal	"	101 Samuel Ford	"
"	33 Abram G Turner	Private	"	102 Henry Craig	"
"	34 Joseph L Hall	"	"	103 William Brady	"
"	35 Cornelius Henson	"	"	104 Joseph Bayard	"
"	36 Ira Hulsy	"	"	105 Thomas R Ampey	"
"	37 Samuel Johnson	"	"	106 Allen W Stevenson	"
"	38 John Lott	"			
"	39 Tradwell Turner	"			
"	40 George Rea	"			
D	41 Andrew Clark	"			
"	42 George E Coxswell	"			
"	43 William Edgerly	"			
"	44 Albert Evarts	"			
"	45 Benj Hoggins	"			
"	46 Thomas Lloyd	"			
"	47 William Lloyd	"			
"	48 Stephen Swan	"			
"	49 George F Proctor	"			
E	50 Thomas P Riggs	"		Missing on James Is	
"	51 Joseph J Proctor	"		July 16 1863	
"	52 Morris Butler	"			
"	53 William Grover	"	B	1 Alfred Grace	Private
"	54 Nathaniel Hurley	"	"	2 Samuel Blakes	
"	55 Charles W Lopeman	"	"	3 George Allison	
"	56 John Weeks	"			
"	57 William Anderson	"			
F	58 Jefferson Ellis	"			
"	59 John P Gray	"			
"	60 Daniel Kelley	"			
"	61 Francis Howe	"			
"	62 George W Mashoe	"			
"	63 David Roper	"			
"	64 Sheldon Thomas	"			
"	65 George K. Thomas	"			
"	66 Edward Williams				

List of the enlisted men of the 54th Massachusetts Regiment missing after the assault on Fort Wagner, South Carolina, July 18, 1863.

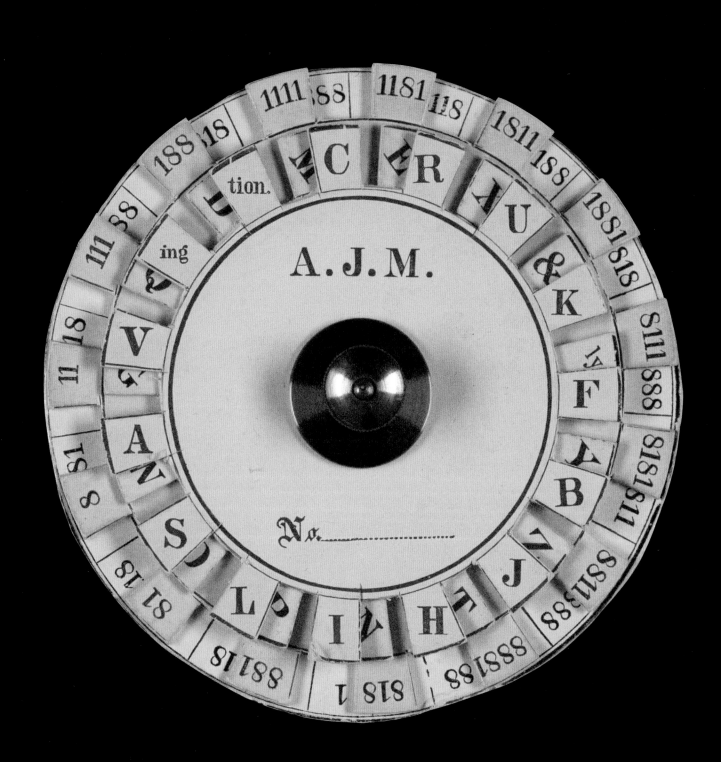

Telegram from President Lincoln to Lt. Gen. Ulysses Grant
at City Point, Virginia, August 17, 1864.

Executive Mansion,

Washington, August 17, 1864.

"Cypher"

Lieut. Gen. Grant
City Point, Va.

I have seen your despatch expressing your unwillingness to break your hold where you are. Neither am I willing. Hold on with a bull-dog grip, and chew & choke, as much as possible.

A. Lincoln

Telegram from President Lincoln to
Lt. Gen. Ulysses Grant, February 1, 1865.

Office U. S. Military Telegraph,
WAR DEPARTMENT,
Washington, D. C. February 1. 1865

"Cypher"

Lieut. Genl. Grant
City. Point.

Let nothing which is transpiring, change, hinder, or delay your Military Movements, or plans.

A. Lincoln

Office U. S. Military Telegraph,
WAR DEPARTMENT,
Washington, D. C. August 14 1864.

Time
"Cypher"
1.30 Pm
Sutton

Lieut. Genl. Grant
City. Point, Va.

The Secretary of War and I concur that you better confer with Gen. Lee and stipulate for a mutual discontinuance of house-burning and other destruction of private property. The time for and manner of conference, and particulars of stipulation we leave, on our part, to your convenience and judgment.

A. Lincoln

Field telegraph battery wagon, Petersburg, Virginia, September 1864.

Telegram from President Lincoln to
Lt. Gen. Ulysses Grant, August 14, 1864.

Lt. Gen. Ulysses Grant, Cold Harbor, Virginia, ca. June 1864.

Gen. Robert E. Lee, ca. 1865.

The Assassination of President Abraham Lincoln
"I have always endeavored to be a good and dutiful son..."

Telegram from John Wilkes Booth to
Michael O'Laughlin, March 19, 1865.

John Wilkes Booth.

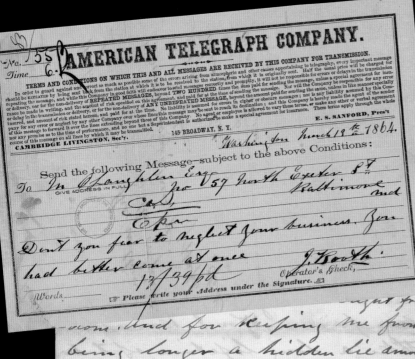

Letter from John Wilkes Booth to his mother,
ca. 1865.

Reward poster for
John Wilkes Booth,
April 1865.

$30,000 REWARD

DESCRIPTION
OF

JOHN WILKES BOOTH!

Who Assassinated the PRESIDENT on the Evening
of April 14th, 1865.

Height 5 feet 8 inches; weight 160 pounds; compact built; hair jet black, inclined to
curl, medium length, parted behind; eyes black, and heavy dark eye-brows; wears a large seal
ring on little finger; when talking inclines his head forward; looks down.

Description of the Person who Attempted to Assassinate Hon. W. H. Seward, Secretary of State.

Height 6 feet 1 inch; hair black, thick, full and straight; no beard, nor appearance of
beard; cheeks red on the jaws; face moderately full; 22 or 23 years of age; eyes, color not
known—large eyes, not prominent; brows not heavy, but dark; face not large, but rather
round; complexion healthy; nose straight and well formed, medium size; mouth small; lips
thin; upper lip protruded when he talked; chin pointed and prominent; head medium size;
neck short, and of medium length; hands soft and small; fingers tapering; shows no signs of
hard labor; broad shoulders; taper waist; straight figure; strong looking man; manner not
gentlemanly, but vulgar; Overcoat double-breasted, color mixed of pink and grey spots, small

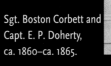

Sgt. Boston Corbett and
Capt. E. P. Doherty,
ca. 1860–ca. 1865.

Testimony of Dr. Robert King Stone, President Lincoln's doctor, pages one and two, May 16, 1865.

43 a

Dr. Robert King Stone,

a witness called for the prosecution, being duly sworn, testified as follows:

By the Judge Advocate

2. State to the Court if you are a practising physician in this city?

A. I am.

2. Were you, or not, the physician the late President of the United Stat

A. I was his family physician.

2. State whether or not you wer called to see him on the evening of assassination, and the examinat made, and the result?

was sent for by Mrs Linc tely after the assassina there in a very few moments d that the President had

44a

been removed from the theatre to the house of a gentleman living directly opposite the theatre, had been carried into the back room of the residence, and was there placed upon a bed. I found a number of gentlemen, citizens, around him, and among others two Assistant Surgeons of the army who had brought him over from the theatre and had attended to him. They immediately gave over the case to my care, knowing my relations to the family. I proceeded then to examine him, and instantly found that the President had received a gun shot wound in the back part of the left side of his head, into which I carried immediately my finger. I at once informed those around that the case was a hopeless one; that the President would die; that there was no positive limit to the duration of his life; that his

767

22 **23**

Register of Marriages among Freedmen in Dist Arkadelphia during year 1865

Date 1865	Name of Male	Place of Residence	Name of Female	Place of Residence	Age	Color			Lived with another woman years	Separated by	No. of children by previous	Age	Color			Lived with another man years	No. of children by previous	Separated by	No. of children united	Name of Officiating Minister
August 9	Edward Tate	Clark Co.	Margaret Tate	Clark Co.	25	Dark		Black	4 yrs	adultery	3	28	Black		Light	5 yrs	2	banished		P. M. Carmichael J.P.
" 12	George Heard	"	Lish Ann Shackleford	"	26	do.	Dark	Dark	2	"		16	Yellow	White	dark		1	—		" " "
" 6	Miles Faswick	"	Caroline Stuart	"	25	"	"	"	1½ "	increment	1	25	dark	—	—			—		" " "
Sept. 3	Washington Gillet	"	Harriet Townsend	"	61	"	"	"	40 yrs	Death	8	40	Copper	White	dark	9	4	no cause		" " "
" "	John Sanders	Pike Co	Mary Mobley	Pike Co	42	White	White	White				30	dark	dark	dark				7	J. W. Kirkham J.P.
" "	Burrell Mobley	"	Fanny Buck	"	45	Dark	Dark	Dark		Sale		26	"	"	"				4	" " "
" 10	John Barter	"	Rachel Ece	"	80	"	"	"	2	"	3	52	"	Mulat	black	3	3	Sale	6	" " "
" 11	Peter Conway	"	Anna Evans	"	38	"	"	"	1	"		25	Copper	dark	dark				2	" " "
" 12	Jerry Jackson	"	Susan Davis	"	25	"	"	"				16	Dark							" " "
" 13	Isaac Brewer	"	Mary Brewer	"	65	"	"	Black				50	Yellow	Mulat	Light				11	" " "
" 18	Cloven Newbern	Dallas Co	Jenny Glen	Dallas Co	45	Yellow	Mulat	Black	21	Death	8	26	Black	Black	black	6	5	disagreement		Jesse R. Harris J.P.
" 21	Isaac Harrington	Clark Co	Maria Overton	Clark Co	50	dark	dark	dark	3 from	Removed		58	Copper	White	copper	15	7	death		P. M. Carmichael J.P.
Oct. 1	Haywood Bangs	"	Caroline Barkman	"	36	"	"	"	3 yrs	Death	2	16	dark	dark	dark					" " "
" 8	Thos. Dickinson	"	Sina J. Bangs	"	32	"	"	"	5	"	2	25	copper	white	copper	4		leaving		" " "
" 19	Cyrus Smith	"	Mary Ann Golden	"	31	"	"	"				25	dark	dark	dark	3	1	adultery		" " "
" 29	Andrew Williams	"	Harriet Cole	"	47	copper	dark	dark		Sale	6	20	"				1	bad conduct		S. Stephenson, Rev.
Nov. 10	Green Reynolds	Dallas Co	Betty Rigden	Dallas Co	20	dark	"	light				18	light	orphan		—		—	—	P. M. Carmichael J.P.
" 12	Louis Hardage	Clark	Harriet Maken	Clark	27	"	"	dark	7	leaving	2	23	copper	copper	copper	3	2	death		" " "
" "	Louis Mitchell	"	Ardelia Hardage	"	24	copper	copper	copper				22	"	"	"		3			" " "
" 20	Judge Mitchell	"	Mary Ann E. Langley	"	50							40								" " "
" 26	Noah Spencer	"	Harriet Hardage	"	21							21								" " "
" "	Simon Johnson	"	Betty Ann Davis	"	26							26								" " "
" "	Berry Ewing	"	Lucy Johnson	"	24							17								" " "
Dec. 3	William Curtis	"	Catharine Rogers	"	24							25								S. C. Coffman J.P.
Nov. 3	Lewis Lee	"	Mary Lee	"	23							23								A. Mizell, Revd.
Dec. 24	Ralph McLure	"	Mary Stuart	"	32							37								P. M. Carmichael J.P.
" 31	Geo. Ewing	"	Dora Maddox	"	26							21								F. M. J. E. Caldwell
" 24	Burton Ridton	"	Thursday Barkman	"	23							23								P. M. Carmichael Jr.
" 14	Chas. Marberry	"	Lucinda Hardy	"	28							18								
" 31	Henry Ross	"	Violet Ewing	"	19							21								S. S. Williams Rev.
" "	Stuart Andrew	"	Adaline Smith	"	30							20								John W. Norton J.P.
" 30	Nero Williams	Hot Spring Co.	Milly Porter	Hot Spring Co	45							40								P. M. Carmichael J.P.
Jan. 7 1866	Jacob Copitt	Clark Co	Hannah Copitt	Clark Co	36							26								" " "
" "	Albert Johnston	"	Frances Peeples	"	26							26								" " "
" "	John Hearn	"	Tempy Spence	"	21							21								" " "
" "	Jordan Ball	"	Harriet Cargile	"	47							30								" " "

Register of marriages among freedmen during 1865, selected pages, August 9, 1865.

Marriage certificate of Reuten Bunrel and Ester Seurs of Virginia, n.d.

Marriage certificate of Peter Thompson and Maria Hall of Louisiana, March 3, 1865.

Marriage certificate of Joseph and Mary Provines, Nashville, Tennessee, February 26, 1866.

1866

A Petition for Universal Suffrage

"...we would call your attention to the fact that we represent...one half the entire population of the country—intelligent, virtuous, native-born American citizens..."

A PETITION

FOR

UNIVERSAL SUFFRAGE.

To the Senate and House of Representatives:

The undersigned, Women of the United States, respectfully ask an amendment of the Constitution that shall prohibit the several States from disfranchising any of their citizens on the ground of sex.

In making our demand for Suffrage, we would call your attention to the fact that we represent fifteen million people—one half the entire population of the country—intelligent, virtuous, native-born American citizens; and yet stand outside the pale of political recognition.

The Constitution classes us as "free people," and counts us *whole* persons in the basis of representation; and yet are we governed without our consent, compelled to pay taxes without appeal, and punished for violations of law without choice of judge or juror.

The experience of all ages, the Declarations of the Fathers, the Statute Laws of our own day, and the fearful revolution through which we have just passed, all prove the uncertain tenure of life, liberty and property so long as the ballot—the only weapon of self-protection—is not in the hand of every citizen.

Therefore, as you are now amending the Constitution, and, in harmony with advancing civilization, placing new safeguards round the individual rights of four millions of emancipated slaves, we ask that you extend the right of Suffrage to Woman—the only remaining class of disfranchised citizens—and thus fulfil your Constitutional obligation "to Guarantee to every State in the Union a Republican form of Government."

As all partial application of Republican principles must ever breed a complicated legislation as well as a discontented people, we would pray your Honorable Body, in order to simplify the machinery of government and ensure domestic tranquillity, that you legislate hereafter for persons, citizens, tax-payers, and not for class or caste.

For justice and equality your petitioners will ever pray.

NAMES.	RESIDENCE.
Elizabeth Stanton	New York
Susan B. Anthony	Rochester — N.Y.
Antoinette Brown Blackwell	New York
Lucy Stone	Newark N. Jersey
Joanna S. Morse	48 Livingston. Brooklyn
Ernestine L. Rose	New York.
Harriet E. Eaton	6, West. 14th Street N Y
Catharine C. Wilkeson	83 Clinton Place New York
Elizabeth R. Tilton	48 Livingston St. Brooklyn
Mary Fowler Gilbert	295 W. 19" St New York
Mary E. Gilbet	New York
M. Griffith	

H.J. Res. 127. Joint Resolution Proposing an Amendment to the Constitution of the United States

"No State shall make or enforce any law which shall abridge the privileges or immunities of citizens of the United States..."

1866

39TH CONGRESS,
1ST SESSION.

H. R. 127.

IN THE SENATE OF THE UNITED STATES.

MAY 10, 1866.

Read twice, by unanimous consent.

JOINT RESOLUTION

Proposing an amendment to the Constitution of the United States.

1   *Resolved by the Senate and House of Representatives*

2   *of the United States of America in Congress assembled,*

3   (two-thirds of both Houses concurring,) That the following

4   article be proposed to the legislatures of the several States

5   as an amendment to the Constitution of the United States,

6   which, when ratified by three-fourths of said legislatures,

7   shall be valid as part of the Constitution, namely :

8   ARTICLE —.

9   SECTION 1. No State shall make or enforce any law

10   which shall abridge the privileges or immunities of citizens

11   of the United States; nor shall any State deprive any per-

12   son of life, liberty, or property, without due process of law;

13   nor deny to any person within its jurisdiction the equal pro-

14   tection of the laws.

15   SECTION 2. Representatives shall be apportioned among

16   the several States which may be included within the Union,

Howard to insert - see [handwritten marginal note]

am [handwritten marginal note]

Timothy O'Sullivan, Photographs for the 40th Parallel Survey

Timothy O'Sullivan's portable darkroom, Carson Desert, Nevada, 1867.

Geyser Pool, Ruby Valley, Nevada, ca. 1868.

Shoshone Falls, Idaho, ca. 1868.

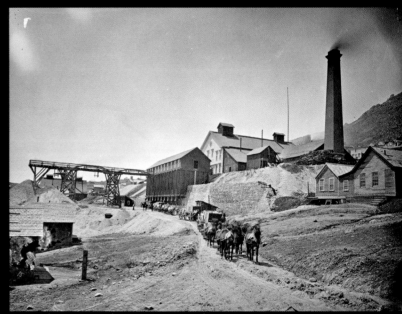

Savage Silver Mining Works, Virginia City, Nevada, ca. 1867–ca. 1868.

Witches' Rocks, Echo, Utah, ca. 1869.

Witches' Rocks, Echo, Utah, ca. 1869.

Witches' Rocks, Echo, Utah, ca. 1869.

Witches' Rocks, Echo, Utah, ca. 1869.

Tufa Domes and Steamboat Rock, Pyramid Lake, 1867.

Virginia City, Nevada, 1867.

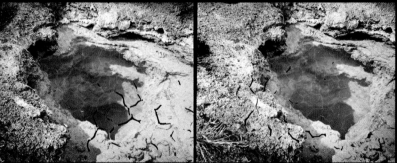

Miners at work underground, Virginia City, Nevada, 1867.

Mine interior, Virginia City, Nevada, 1867.

Hot Spring, Ruby Valley, Nevada, 1868.

Hot Springs Cone, Provo Valley, Utah, 1869.

Devil's Slide, Utah, 1869.

Railroad, near Devil's Slide, Utah, 1869.

Article XI

YEAS.	May 16. 1868.	NAYS.
Guilty	Anthony	
	Bayard	not guilty
	Buckalew	not guilty
Guilty	Cameron	
Guilty	Cattell	
Guilty	Chandler	
Guilty	Cole	
Guilty	Conkling	
Guilty	Conness	
Guilty	Corbett	
Guilty	Cragin	
	Davis	not guilty
	Dixon	not guilty
	Doolittle	not guilty
Guilty	Drake	
Guilty	Edmunds	
Guilty	Ferry	
	Fessenden	not guilty
	Fowler	not guilty
Guilty	Frelinghuysen	
	Grimes	not guilty
Guilty	Harlan	
	Henderson	not guilty
	Hendricks	not guilty
Guilty	Howard	
Guilty	Howe	
	Johnson	not guilty
	McCreery	not guilty
Guilty	Morgan	
Guilty	Morrill, of Maine	
Guilty	Morrill, of Vt.	
Guilty	Morton	
	Norton	not guilty
Guilty	Nye	
Guilty	Patterson, of N. H.	
	Patterson, of Tenn.	not guilty
Guilty	Pomeroy	
Guilty	Ramsey	
	Ross	not guilty
	Saulsbury	not guilty
Guilty	Sherman	
Guilty	Sprague	
Guilty	Stewart	
Guilty	Sumner	
Guilty	Thayer	
Guilty	Tipton	
	Trumbull	not guilty
	Van Winkle	not guilty
	Vickers	not guilty
Guilty	Wade	
Guilty	Willey	
Guilty	Williams	
Guilty	Wilson	
Guilty	Yates	

35   19

MAY 11, 1868.

Impeachment ballot for
Andrew Johnson, 1868.

The Impeachment
Committee, ca. 1868.
Seated (left to right):
Benjamin F. Butler,
Thaddeus Stevens,
Thomas Williams,
John A. Bingham.
Standing: James F. Wilson,
George S. Boutwell,
John A. Logan.

Resolved, That Andrew Johnson, President of the United States, be impeached of high crimes and misdemeanors.

Resolution of Impeachment for
President Andrew Johnson,
February 21, 1868.

Order to Senate Sergeant of Arms George
Brown to serve a "Writ of Summons" on
Andrew Johnson, signed by Chief Justice
Salmon P. Chase, March 7, 1868.

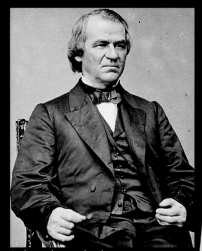

Andrew Johnson, detail, ca. 1860–ca. 1865.

The United States Of America, s.s:

The Senate of the United States to George T. Brown, Sergeant at Arms of the Senate. Greeting: You are hereby commanded to deliver to, and leave with Andrew Johnson, President of the United States, if conveniently to be found, or if not, to leave at his usual place of abode, in some conspicuous place, a true and attested Copy of the within Writ of Summons, together with a like Copy of this precept, and in whichsoever way you perform the service let it be done at least five days before the appearance day mentioned in said Writ of Summons.

Fail not, and make return of this Writ of Summons and precept with your proceedings thereon indorsed on or before the appearance day mentioned in the said Writ of Summons.

Witness Salmon P. Chase, Chief Justice of the United States and President of said Senate sitting on the trial of the said impeachment, at the City of Washington this Seventh day of March in the year of Our Lord One thousand eight hundred and sixty-eight and of the independence of the United States the ninety-second.

Salmon P. Chase
Chief Justice of the United States

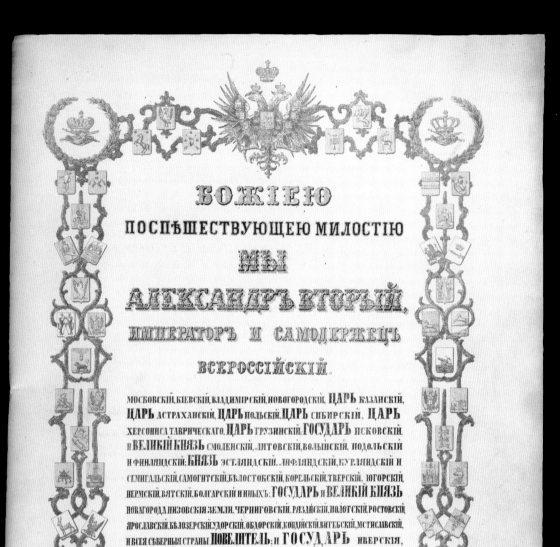

Secretary of State William H. Seward, ca. 1860–ca. 1865.

Russian ratification of the Treaty
of Cession of Alaska, Treaty Series
301 Exchange Copy, May 1867.

Treasury warrant for the purchase of Alaska, August 1, 1868.

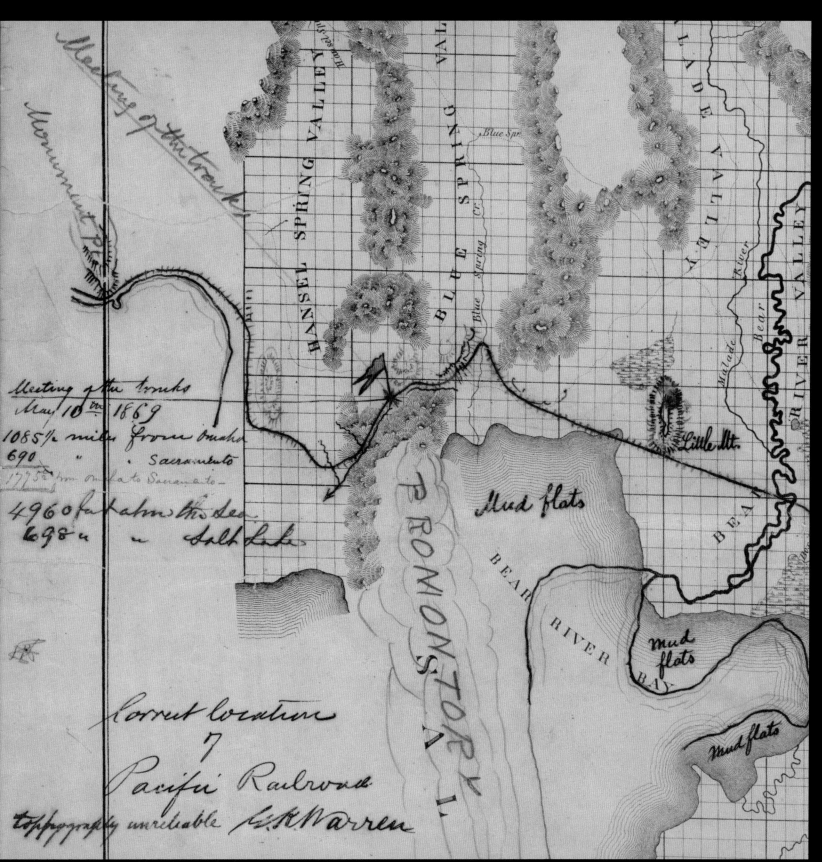

Map showing the meeting point of the tracks, near Salt Lake, map by Gen. G. K. Warren, May 10, 1869.

Timothy O'Sullivan, Photographs for the Wheeler Survey

Group of Zuni Indians at their pueblo, or town, New Mexico, 1873.

Indian pueblo of Zuni, New Mexico, view from the interior, 1873.

San Xavier del Bac Mission near Tucson, Arizona, 1871.

Store at the Mexican village of Conejos, New Mexico, 1874.

Soldiers and women in front of house, 1871.

Fort Garland, Colorado, 1874.

Historic Spanish record of the conquest, south side of Inscription Rock, New Mexico, 1873 (inscription dated 1526).

1876 | **Battle of Little Bighorn**

"It is my painful duty to report that day before yesterday...a great disaster overtook Genl Custer & the troops under his command..."

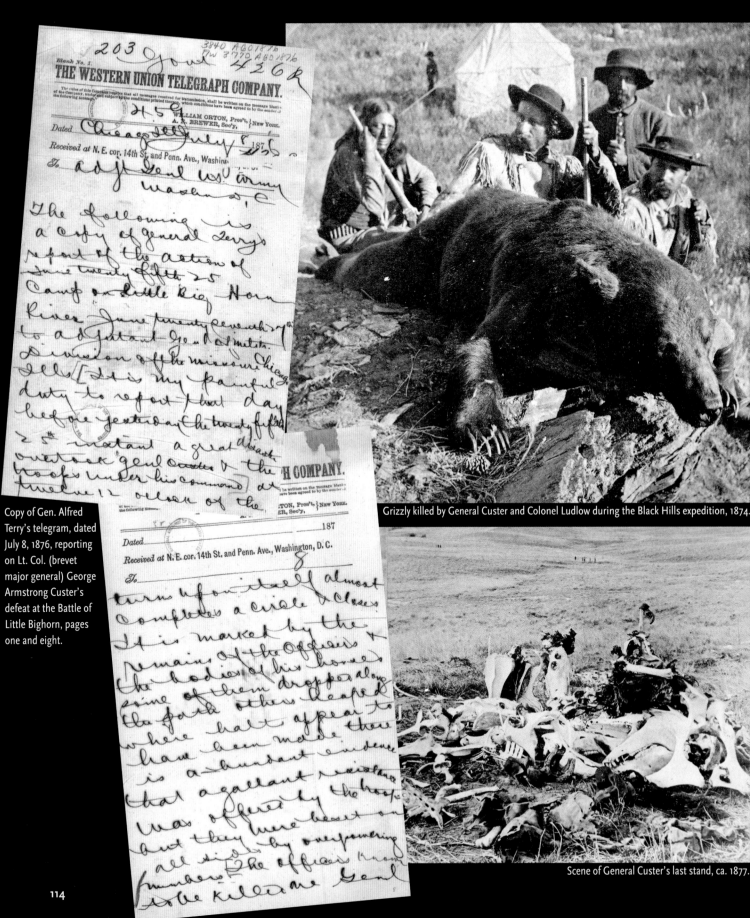

Copy of Gen. Alfred Terry's telegram, dated July 8, 1876, reporting on Lt. Col. (brevet major general) George Armstrong Custer's defeat at the Battle of Little Bighorn, pages one and eight.

Grizzly killed by General Custer and Colonel Ludlow during the Black Hills expedition, 1874.

Scene of General Custer's last stand, ca. 1877.

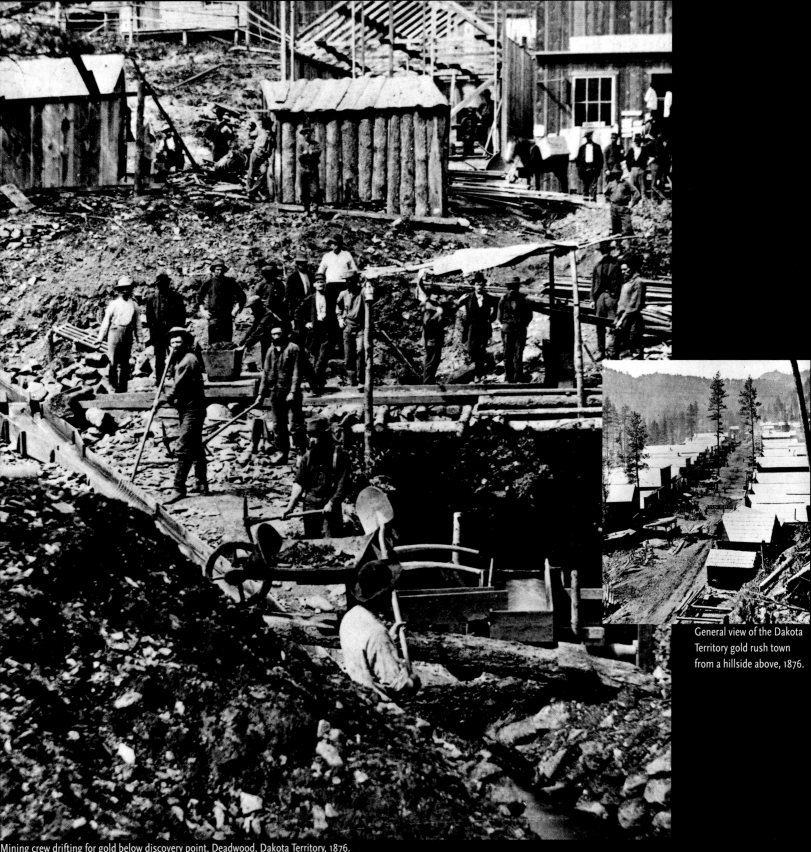

General view of the Dakota Territory gold rush town from a hillside above, 1876.

Mining crew drifting for gold below discovery point, Deadwood, Dakota Territory, 1876.

1490.

It is hereby certified That, pursuant to the provisions of Section No. 2291, Revised Statutes of the United States, _Almanzo J. Wilder_ has made payment in full for _the North East quarter_

of Section No. _21_, in Township No. _111 North_, of Range No. _56 West_, of the _5th_ Principal Meridian _Dakota_, containing _160_ 100 acres.

Now, therefore, be it known, That on presentation of this Certificate to the COMMISSIONER OF THE GENERAL LAND OFFICE, the said _Almanzo J. Wilder._ shall be entitled to a Patent for the Tract of Land above described.

_____ Register.

[12391—30 M.]

Homestead Final Certificate for Almanzo Wilder, September 16, 1884.

HOMESTEAD.

Land Office at _Yankton Dak Terr._

August 21", 1879.

I, _Eliza J. Wilder_, of _Kingsbury County Dakota Territory_, do hereby apply to enter, under Section 2289, Revised Statutes of the United States, the _North West ¼_ of Section _28_, in Township _111_ of Range _56_, containing _160_ acres.

Eliza J. Wilder

Land Office at _Yankton, Dak_

August 21st 1879

I, _G A Wetter_, REGISTER OF THE LAND OFFICE, do hereby certify that the above application is for Surveyed Lands of the class which the applicant is legally entitled to enter under Section 2289, Revised Statutes of the United States, and that there is no prior valid adverse right to the same.

G A Wetter Register.

Eliza Wilder's Homestead Application, August 21, 1879.

Oklahoma City, Indian Territory, 1889.

Panoramic view of Oklahoma Territory flatlands, January 1894.

The nine booths at Orlando, detail, September 15, 1893.

First train and wagons leaving the line north of Orlando for Perry, September 16, 1893.

In line at the Land Office, Perry, September 23, 1893.

Looking for a town lot, Guthrie, ca. 1889.

Close-up view of Broadway Street, Round Pond, January 1894.

– 4 –

a certain area around our lands, was proclaimed
to be for our use, but the extent of this area is
unknown to us, nor has any Agent, ever been able
to point it out, for its boundaries have never
been measured. We most earnestly desire to have
one continuous boundary ring enclosing all the
Tewa and all the Hopi lands, and that it shall
be large enough to afford sustenance for our
increasing flocks and herds. If such a scope can
be confirmed to us by a paper from your hands,
securing us forever against intrusion, all our
people will be satisfied:

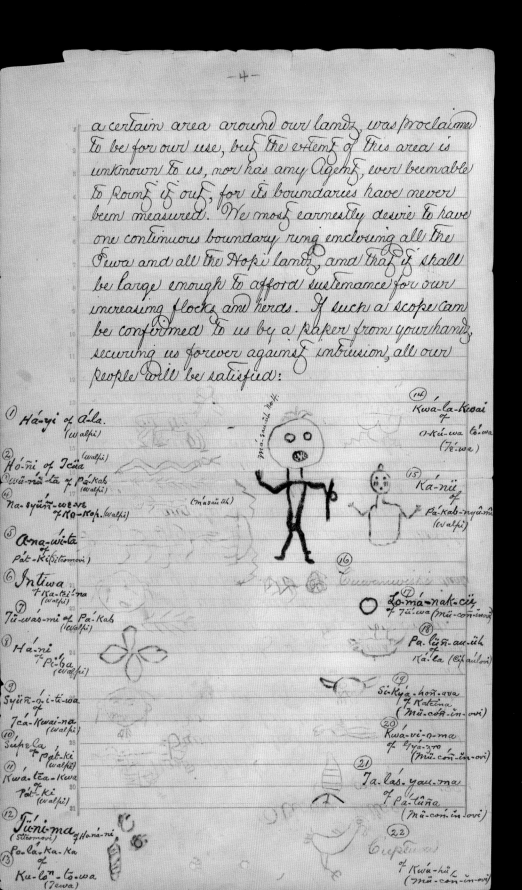

(1) Há-yi of A-la.
(Walpi)

(2) Hó-ñi of Tcúa
(Walpi)

(3) Wü-nú-la of Pá'Kab
(Walpi)

(4) Na-syün-we-ve
of Kọ-Kop. (Walpi)

(5) Ona-wi-ta
of
Pát-Ki (Sitcomovi)

(6) Intiwa
of Ka-tci-na
(Walpi)

(7) Tü-was-mi of Pa'Kab
(Walpi)

(8) Há-ni
of
Pi-ba
(Walpi)

(9) Syün-o-i-ti-wa
of
Tca-Kwai-na
(Walpi)

(10) Sùpela
of pat-ki
(Walpi)

(11) Kwa-tca-Kwa
of
Pát-Ki
(Walpi)

(12) Tüni-ma of Hona-ni
(Sitcomovi)

(13) Po-la-Ka-Ka
of
Ku-lọn-tó-wa
(Tewa)

(ma-saü üh)

(ma-saü üh)

(14) Kwá-la-Kwai
of
O-Kú-wa tó-wa
(Tewa)

(15) Ka-nü
of
Pá-Kab-nyüm
(Walpi)

(16) Tuwanwishi

(17) Lo-má-nak-cü
of Tü-wa (mü-con-inovi)

(18) Pa-lü ñ-au-üh
of
Ka-la (Cifaulovi)

(19) Si-Kyá-hoñ-ava
of Katcina
(Mü-con-in-ovi)

(20) Kwa-vi-o-ma
of Lya-zro
(Mü-con-in-ovi)

(21) Ta-las-yau-ma
of Pa-tüña
(Mü-con-in-ovi)

(22) Cüp...
of Kwa-hü
(Mü-con-in-ovi)

Légation de ...
Washington le 28 Mai, 1895

Monsieur le sous-Secrétaire d'État

J'ai eu l'honneur de recevoir la note que Votre Excellence m'a fait l'honneur de m'adresser, communiquant la triste nouvelle du trépas de Son Excellence Monsieur le Secrétaire d'État, Walter Quinton Gresham, et je me fais un devoir de présenter a Votre Excellence l'expression du profond regret que j'ai éprouvé.

En accomplissant le pénible devoir d'envoyer à Votre Excellence mes condoléances, je dois ajouter qu'il "vraiement douloureux pour moi

Hon. Edwin F. Uhl
etc.   etc.   etc.

Death mask of Secretary of State Gresham.

CABLE MESSAGE.
THE WESTERN UNION TELEGRAPH COMPANY.
INCORPORATED

All CABLE MESSAGES received for transmission must be written on the Message Blanks provided by this Company for that purpose, under and subject to the conditions printed thereon, and on the back hereof, which conditions have been agreed to by the sender of the following message.

THOS. T. ECKERT, President and General Manager.

TWO AMERICAN CABLES FROM NEW YORK TO GREAT BRITAIN.
CONNECTS ALSO WITH FOUR ANGLO-AMERICAN AND ONE DIRECT U. S. ATLANTIC CABLES.
DIRECT CABLE COMMUNICATION WITH GERMANY AND FRANCE.
CABLE CONNECTION WITH CUBA, WEST INDIES, MEXICO AND CENTRAL AND SOUTH AMERICA.
MESSAGES SENT TO, AND RECEIVED FROM, ALL PARTS OF THE WORLD.

OFFICES IN AMERICA:
All Offices (21,000) of the Western Union Telegraph Company and its Connections.

JUN 3 1895
Department of State.

OFFICES IN GREAT BRITAIN:
LONDON: No. 21 Royal Exchange, E.C.   LIVERPOOL: A5 Exchange Buildings.
No. 109 Fenchurch Street, E.C.   GLASGOW: No. 29 Gordon Street.
BRISTOL: Backhall Chambers.

NUMBER	SENT BY	REC'D BY	No. OF WORDS.	FROM
	Ny	Of	Jm 28	San Joe CR

RECEIVED at   504   June 2   1895

Uhl
Acting Secretary of State Washn

Your Cable announcing death of Secretary Gresham was delayed in transmission flags of all nations here draped at half mast

Baker   Copied

Costa Rica

Telegrams from Portugal, Costa Rica, and Mexico on the death of Secretary Walter Q. Gresham.

Mexican Legation.
Washington, May 28th, 1895.

The Minister of Mexico has received the note of the Acting Secretary of State, informing him that the funeral of the Honorable Walter Q. Gresham, late Secretary of State, will take place to-morrow (Wednesday) at ten o'clock A. M. in the East Room of the Executive Mansion, and that places have been reserved for the members of the diplomatic corps and the ladies of their families, which may be occupied at a quarter before ten.

The Minister of Mexico, the members of the Mexican Legation, and the ladies of their families will have the honor to attend the funeral at the hour above named.

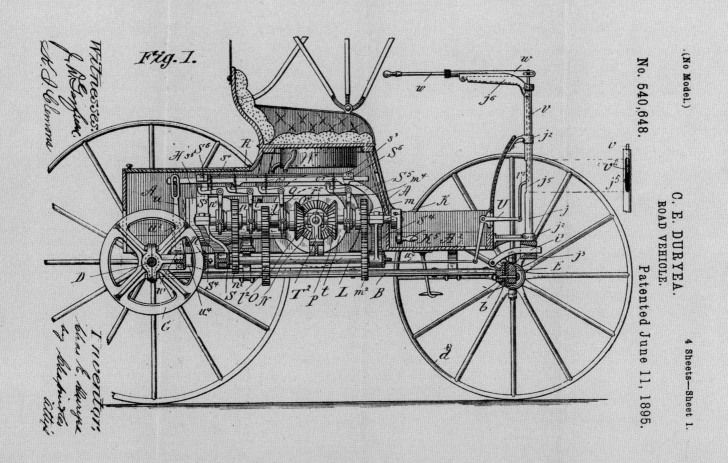

(No Model.)

No. 540,648.

C. E. DURYEA.
ROAD VEHICLE.

Patented June 11, 1895.

4 Sheets—Sheet 1.

Fig.1.

Witnesses:

Inventor:

IN THE DISTRICT COURT OF THE UNITED STATES, IN AND FOR THE

NORTHERN DISTRICT OF CALIFORNIA.

-------oOo-----

In the Matter of

WONG KIM ARK   No.11,198.

On Habeas Corpus.

OPINION

rendered January 3rd, 1896.

Petition for a Writ of Habeas Corpus. Petition granted and petitioner, Wong Kim Ark, discharged.

Thos.D.Riordan, Esq., and Napthaly, Fredenrich & Ackerman, Attorneys for Petitioner.

H.S.Foote, Esq., U.S.District Attorney, and Geo.D.Collins Esq., as Amicus curiae, appearing for the United States.

MORROW, District Judge:-

A petition for a writ of habeas corpus was filed on behalf of Wong Kim Ark, alleging that said Wong Kim Ark is unlawfully confined and restrained of his liberty on board of the steamship "Coptic", and prevented from landing into the United States, by John H.Wise, Collector of Customs at the port of San Francisco, and D.B.Stubbs, General Manager of the Occidental and Oriental Steamship Company, acting under his authority

-1-

Opinion rendered in the matter of Wong Kim Ark on habeas corpus, pages one and twenty-four, January 3, 1896.

Identification photo from immigration papers of Wong Kim Ark, 1894.

it to be the law against controlling judicial authority. It may be that the Executive Departments of the government are at liberty to follow this international rule in dealing with questions of citizenship, which arise between this and other countries, but that fact does not establish the law for the Courts in dealing with persons within our own territory. In this case, the question to be determined is as to the political status and rights of Wong Kim Ark under the law in this country. No foreign power has intervened or appears to be concerned in the matter. From the law as announced and the facts as stipulated, I am of opinion that Wong Kim Ark is a citizen of the United States within the meaning of the citizenship clause of the 14th Amendment. He has not forfeited his right to return to this country. His detention, therefore, is illegal. He should be discharged from custody and permitted, by the Collector of the Port, to land; and it is so ordered.

“We, the undersigned, native Hawaiian women...earnestly protest against the annexation...”

Petition Against the Annexation of Hawaii

1897

PALAPALA HOOPII KUE HOOHUIAINA.

I ka Mea Mahaloia WILLIAM McKINLEY, Peresidena,
a me ka Aha Senate, o Amerika Huipuia.

ME KA MAHALO :—

No ka Mea, ua waihoia aku imua o ka Aha Senate
o Amerika Huipuia he Kuikahi no ka Hoohui aku ia
Hawaii nei ia Amerika Huipuia i oleloia, no ka noonooia
ma kona kau mau iloko o Dekemaba, M. H. 1897; nolaila,

O MAKOU, na poe no lakou na inoa malalo iho, he
poe makaainana a poe noho oiwi Hawaii hoi no ka
Apana o Honolulu Kona , Mokupuni o
Oahu , he poe lala no ka
AHAHUI HAWAII ALOHA AINA O KO HAWAII PAE-
AINA, a me na poe e ae i like ka manao makee me ko
ka Ahahui i oleloia, ke kue aku nei me ka manao ikaika
loa i ka hoohuiia aku o ko Hawaii Paeaina i oleloia ia
Amerika Huipuia i oleloia ma kekahi ano a loina paha.

IKEA—ATTEST:

Enoch Johnson
Kakauolelo — Secretary.

Sept. 1, 1897

PETITION AGAINST ANNEXATION.

To His Excellency WILLIAM McKINLEY, President,
and the Senate, of the United States of America.

GREETING :—

WHEREAS, there has been submitted to the Senate of
the United States of America a Treaty for the Annexation
of the Hawaiian Islands to the said United States of
America, for consideration at its regular session in December,
A. D. 1897; therefore,

WE, the undersigned, native Hawaiian citizens and
residents of the District of Honolulu Kona ,
Island of Oahu , who are members
of the HAWAIIAN PATRIOTIC LEAGUE OF THE HAWAII-
AN ISLANDS, and others who are in sympathy with the
said League, earnestly protest against the annexation of
the said Hawaiian Islands to the said United States of
America in any form or shape.

James Keauiluna Kaylia
Peresidena — President.

	INOA—NAME.	AGE.
1	Keaniani	30
2	Kaululehua	42
3	Phillip Naone	17
4	J. H. Naone	31
5	Kealakai	30
6	L. Naone	32
7	P. L. Stephens	58
8	Kealoha Kanekoa	62
9	Lui Kamaua	47
10	J. A. Lawlor	31
11	Achi Apana	28
12	Thomas Unea	14
13	Alona Apana	34
14	John Keahi	23
15	Kalahaeha	44
16	Kaula	45
17	Keaupuni	20
18	Sam. Kaili	48
19	Thomas Johnson	29
20	Hailele Maulahili	45
21	Pahukila	48
22	Manua	32
23	Joseph Kaui	32
24	P. J. Heleao	62
25	Maikai William	28

		AGE.
26	S. B.	
27	Joar	
28	H. Z.	
29	Ha.	
30	Kah	
31	So.	
32	Jar	
33	K.	
34	K.	
35	Ki	
36	K.	
37	R.	
38	E.	
39	M.	

PALAPALA HOOPII KUE HOOHUIAINA.

I ka Mea Mahaloia WILLIAM McKINLEY, Peresidena,
a me ka Aha Senate, o Amerika Huipuia.

ME KA MAHALO :—

NO KA MEA, ua waihoia aku imua o ka Aha Senate
o Amerika Huipuia he Kuikahi no ka Hoohui aku ia
Hawaii nei ia Amerika Huipuia i oleloia, no ka noonooia
ma kona kau mau iloko o Dekemaba, M. H. 1897; nolaila,

O MAKOU, na poe no lakou na inoa malalo iho, na
wahine Hawaii oiwi, he poe makaainana a poe noho hoi
no ka Apana o Kona Honolulu , Mokupuni o
Oahu , he poe lala no ka AHAHUI
ALOHA AINA HAWAII O NA WAHINE O KO HAWAII PAE-
AINA, a me na wahine e ae i like ka manao makee me ko
ka Ahahui i oleloia, ke kue aku nei me ka manao ikaika
loa i ka hoohuiia aku o ko Hawaii Paeaina i oleloia ia
Amerika Huipuia i oleloia ma kekahi ano a loina paha.

IKEA—ATTEST:

Mrs. Lilia Aholo
Kakauolelo — Secretary.

PETITION AGAINST ANNEXATION.

To His Excellency WILLIAM McKINLEY, President,
and the Senate, of the United States of America.

GREETING :—

WHEREAS, there has been submitted to the Senate of
the United States of America a Treaty for the Annexation
of the Hawaiian Islands to the said United States of
America, for consideration at its regular session in December, A. D. 1897; therefore,

WE, the undersigned, native Hawaiian women, citi-
zens and residents of the District of Kona Honolul ,
Island of Oahu , who are members of the
WOMEN'S HAWAIIAN PATRIOTIC LEAGUE OF THE HAWAII-
AN ISLANDS, and other women who are in sympathy with
the said League, earnestly protest against the annexation
of the said Hawaiian Islands to the said United States of
America in any form or shape.

Mrs. Kuaihulani Campbell
Peresidena — President.

INOA—NAME.	AGE.
Hannah Wahine	29
Amie Naone 18	29
Mrs. Melina Baker W.	30
mrs Lelulina Honan W	35
Lale W	
Mrs. Harrison	18
Cammie Parker	49
W. R. Woodrig	43
H. W. Parker	19
Hattie Purdy W	23
Clara L. Low	14
Mrs. Lewis W.	30
Kamu Kumakuilui W	20
mrs A. M. Hewett	49
Mrs. R. Andrew	32
Grace Kahalewai	36
Mrs. Grace Chapman	45
Mrs. Hattie Jaeger	17
Julia W	42
Mary Silva	33
Kaliko Silva	18
Mrs.	14

INOA—NAME.	AGE.
Mrs. S. M. Parmenter	42
Mrs. C. A. Long	
Mrs. W. R. Buchanan	20
Grace Buchanan	49
Kahaleohai	18
Kahilahila W	28
Manoha W	23
Kilihoohanohano W	14
Hanola W	60
Kaulahiwa W	30
Lizzie	31
Mrs. Ale	17
Mrs. Mele makekau	15
Keahi W	80
Malie makekau	24
A. Keola Aylett	16
Kahaakiki	36
Kaleo Aylett	20
M. Keola Aylett	18
ane	19
	37

LIST OR MANIFEST OF ALIEN IMMIGRANTS FOR THE COMMISSIONER OF IMMIGRATION

Required by the regulations of the Secretary of the Treasury of the United States, under Act of Congress approved March 3, 1893, to be delivered to the Commissioner of Immigration by the Commanding officer of any vessel having such passengers on board upon arrival at a port in the United States.

S.S. *Brasilia* sailing from *Hamburg 15 Januar* 1899 Arriving at Port of *New York 31th January 1899* 267

No. on List	NAME IN FULL	Age Yrs. Mos.	Sex	Married or Single	Calling or Occupation	Read. Write	Nationality	Last Residence	Seaport for landing in the United States	Final destination in the United States	Whether having a ticket	By whom was passage paid	Whether in possession of money	Whether ever before in the United States	Whether going to join a relative	Ever in Prison or Almshouse	Whether a Polygamist	Whether under contract to labor	Condition of Health	Deformed or Crippled
1	Stanislaw Grzyb	29	m	m	labour	yes yes	Austrian	Nagorzyn	New York	Chicago Ill	yes	self	8			near Michel Wanker 729				good	no
2	Stanislaw Zorulla	22	m	m									2			Stephen Bien Lukowski 616 Northwestern Av					
3	Mihály Bacik	23	m		farmer		Hungarian Pardrukops		Trenton N.J.			6			near Johann Feith					
4	Ladislaw Rybski	30	m	m			Austrian Pivdler		New York N.J.	yes		20			no					
5	Andreas Kemenaik	17	m				Hungarian Saros		Cleveland Ohio	yes		26			near Peter Lemak 1938 St Clair St					
6	János Szerno	38	m	m									110			brother 1472 Race St					
7	Valentin Jacobek	29	m	m				Bucoma		Woodstock			20							
8	Johann Mendela	36	m	m			Austrian Behwinoch		New York	yes		20	Przem	Josef Stakewsky					
9	Anton Troxniak	27	m	m				Piatkowa		Chicopee Mass	no		12							
10	Jacob Kruper	29	m	m				Mendorouch		Derberiotol			852			brother Paul Summamy					
11	György Ramera	27	m	m												uncle Anton Ulorosky 515 Col Ave					
12	Maria —"—	22	f	m	wife		Hungarian Peppros		New Kensington Pa			50			father in law Valenti Sprosk					
13	Lucia	40	f		child																
14	Anna Haydus	16	f		none	yes yes	Lipra Bela		New York	yes		5			sister					
15	Jonas Singer	29	m	s	labourer	yes yes	Roumanian Josey					m			uncle Salom Siber					
16	Lesser Einsthof	25	m	s	harness	yes yes	Roumania								cousin Shiffe Mund					
17	Soter Gaula	35	m	s	labr		Austrian Modarka		Shenandoah	m		142			brother Jambron Kruk					
18	Itte Zinomen	60	f	widow	wife			Bielitz		New York	yes	son	4			son Shaul Zinomen					Israelite
19	Jan Hasskiewik	28	m	s	labourer			Malin				brother	5			brother Wojech Hankiewz 78 Bay St Greenpoint					
20	Bronislaw Robacunarky	16	m	s				Sfranow		Nanticoke			7			" Wladislaw Robacwy					
21	Davis Schermann	19	m	s	tailor			Walfowmos		Philadelphia	father		m			father Itihan Schermann 312 Lo 5 St					
22	Franziska Nomborska	20	f	s				Judroge		Maspeth Lis	no	brother	3			brother Josel Koroszy					
23	Hirsch Bilchig	30	m	m	tailor			Pronitz		New York	yes	father	37			father Jankel Bilchig					
24	Abram Lipkowsky	30	m	m		Russian	Poboin				brother	5			brother Starke Kote					
25	Jan Kisholewsky	29	m	s	labour			Sreba		Barry Island	no	self	2			" " Camen Misuzky					
26	Franz Ruschowsky	19	m					Lomza					2			uncle Alex Stopowny					
27	Adam Milschefsky	25	m										7			friend Felix Katzfke					
28	Falk Finkelstein	34	m	m	cap maker			Grajewo		New York	yes		7			brother Leib Finkelstein					
29	Berl Perlmutter	28	m	s	smith			Biemirt					250			brother Leib Finkelstein					
30	Estha Perwoska	17	f	s	none			Lomza		Lackawanna			25			brother Mann Brown Jersey Pa					

132

Boch

Immigrants on a ferry boat near Ellis Island, n.d.

U.S. Immigrant Building, Ellis Island, 1900.

Immigrants buying railroad tickets on Ellis Island, n.d.

Immigrants standing outside a building on Ellis Island, n.d.

Immigrants landing at Ellis Island, ca. 1900.

Immigrants walking with luggage on Ellis Island, n.d.

Russian soldiers recruiting Chinese peasants by force to serve in the Russian Army.

The Chinese Army attacking and capturing a Russian city on the shores of the Amur River.

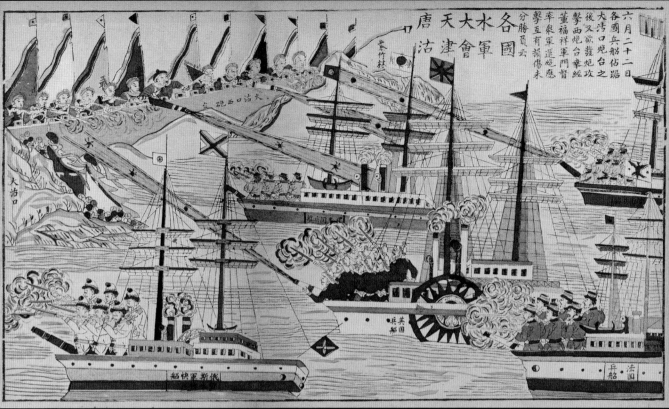

The assemblage of Allied naval forces at Taku Forts and Tientsin.

Allied forces engaged in a massive land battle with the Boxers that ended in a stalemate.

COPYRIGHT 1900, By Thos. A. Edison.

U. S. Circuit Court
S. D. of New York

Thomas A. Edison
vs
American Mutoscope Co., et al

In Equity
No. 69 28

Complainant's Exhibit

Kayser Photograph

Thomas Edison filed these exhibits in his court case, *Thomas A. Edison* v.
American Mutoscope Co. and Benjamin F. Keith, on December 15, 1900,
to show why he claimed to be the inventor of the motion picture camera.

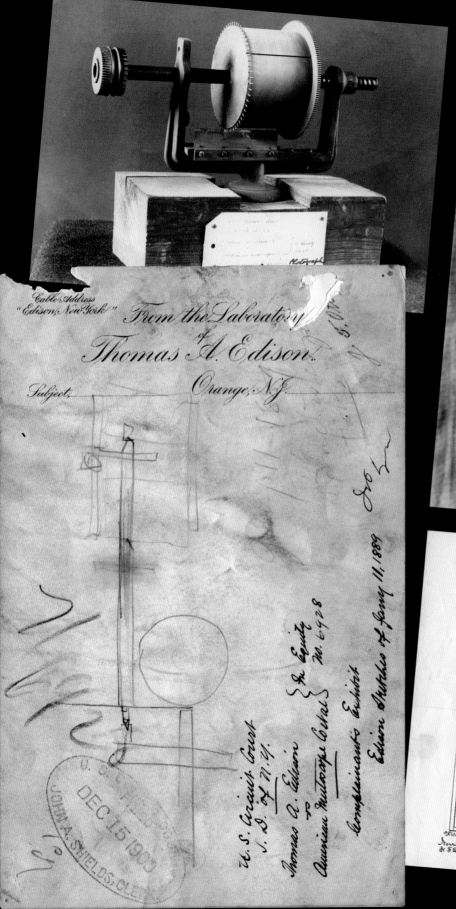

U.S. Circuit Court
S.D. of N.Y.

In Equity
No. 6928

Thomas A. Edison
v.
American Mutoscope Co et al

Complainants Exhibit

Edison Sketches of Jany 11, 1889

U.S. [CIRCUIT COURT] FILED
DEC 15 1903
JOHN A. SHIELDS CLERK

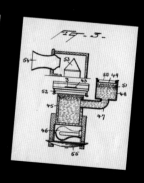

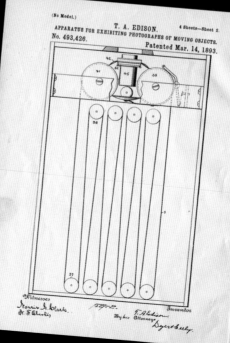

(No Model.)   T. A. EDISON.   4 Sheets—Sheet 2.
APPARATUS FOR EXHIBITING PHOTOGRAPHS OF MOVING OBJECTS.
No. 493,426.   Patented Mar. 14, 1893.

Witnesses   Inventor
Norris I. Clark,   T. A. Edison
N. F. Ambler   By his Attorneys
                                                  Dyer & Seely.

SS America, trapped in ice, October 28, 1901.

"The moon, rising over the glacier on Hall Island. Oct. 25, 1901. 3 p.m."

Walking past cairn with flag at base, May 1902.

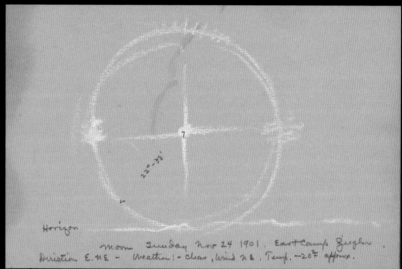

"Moon, Sunday Nov 24 1901. East Camp Ziegler. Direction E. NE
–Weather: - clear, wind NE. Temp. -20 F approx."

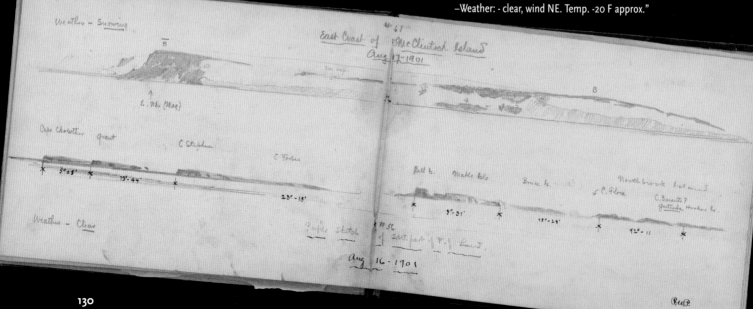

Sketch of East Coast
of McClintock Island,
August 17, 1901.

Slumbering Giant, North Island, October 1901.

Walruses in a Water Pool, August 1901.

Salt Water Leads and Fresh Water Pools, August 8, 1901.

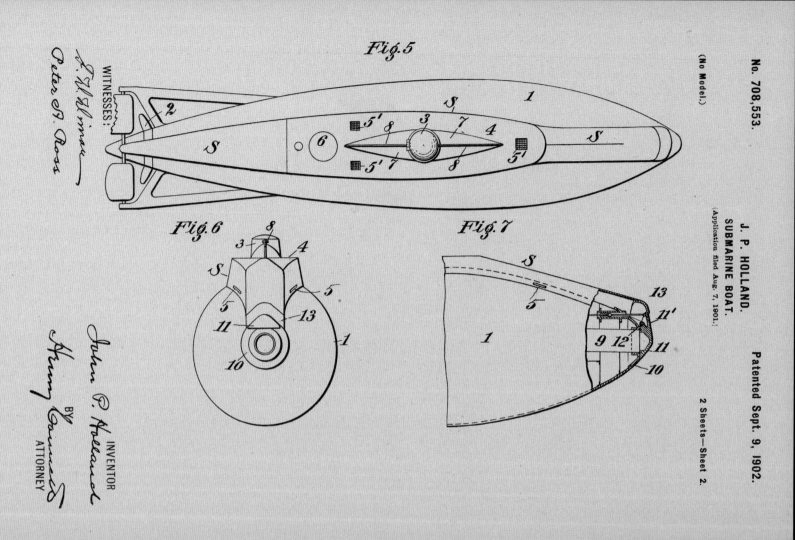

No. 708,553.

(No Model.)

Fig.5

J. P. HOLLAND.
SUBMARINE BOAT.
(Application filed Aug. 7, 1901.)

Patented Sept. 9, 1902.

2 Sheets—Sheet 2.

Fig.6

Fig.7

WITNESSES:

INVENTOR
BY
ATTORNEY

Patent drawing for a submarine boat, September 9, 1902.

Plunger (SS2), renamed *A1*, 1902.

First successful flight, original Wright Brothers Aeroplane, Kitty Hawk, North Carolina, December 17, 1903.

Wilbur and Orville Wright's oath to accompany patent # 821,393, an "Improvement in Flying Machines," March 19, 1903.

133

Probably Fulton Street, this was the edge of the fire district.

California Street looking north from Battery Street, 1906.

Souvenir hunters after the earthquake, 1906.

A camp in Golden Gate Park under military control after the earthquake, 1906.

Refugee camp, possibly in the Presidio of San Francisco, April 18, 1906.

Storage shed, one of the many relief stations in San Francisco, ca. 1906.

Map of San Francisco showing limits of the burned area destroyed by the fire, 1906.

The Jungle Publishing Co.

"The Jungle," a Story of
Packingtown.
The "Uncle Tom's Cabin" of
wage slavery.—JACK LONDON.
The greatest novel written in
America in fifty years.
—DAVID GRAHAM PHILLIPS.

Publishers of the books of Upton Sinclair.
P. O. Box 2064, New York City.
(Letters intended for Upton Sinclair personally should be addressed to Princeton, N. J.)

King Midas: A Romance.
The Journal of Arthur Stirling.
Prince Hagen: A Phantasy.
Manassas: A Novel of the War.

March 10, 1906.

President Theodore Roosevelt,
Washington, D. C.

My dear President Roosevelt:

I have just returned from some exploring in the Jersey glass factories and find your kind note. I am glad to learn that the Department of Agriculture has taken up the matter of inspection, or lack of it, but I am exceedingly dubious as to what they will discover. I have seen so many people go out there and be put off with smooth pretences. A man has to be something of a detective, or else intimate with the working-men, as I was, before he can really see what is going on. And it is becoming a great deal more difficult since the publication of "The Jungle." I have received to-day a letter from an employe of Armour & Company, in response to my request to him to take Ray Stannard Baker in hand and show him what he showed me a year and a half ago. He says: "He will have to be well disguised, for 'the lid is on' in Packingtown; he will find two detectives in places where before there was only one." You must understand that the thing which I have called the "condemned meat industry," is a matter of hundreds of thousands of dollars a month. I see in to-day's "Saturday Evening Post" that Mr. Armour declares in his article (which I happen to know is written by George Horace Lorimer) that "In Armour and Company's business not one atom of any

Letter from Upton Sinclair to President Theodore Roosevelt, page one, March 10, 1906.

Message from President Theodore Roosevelt to the House of Representatives and the Senate, page three, June 4, 1906.

873-4

3

I call special attention to the fact that this report is preliminary, and that the investigation is still unfinished. It is not yet possible to report on the alleged abuses in the use of deleterious chemical compounds in connection with canning and preserving meat products, nor on the alleged doctoring in this fashion of tainted meat and of products returned to the packers as having grown unsalable or unusable from age or from other reasons. Grave allegations are made in reference to abuses of this nature.

Let me repeat that under the present law there is practically no method of stopping these abuses if they should be discovered to exist. Legislation is needed in order to prevent the possibility of all abuses in the future. If no legislation is passed, then the excellent results accomplished by the work of this special committee will endure only so long as the memory of the committee's work is fresh, and a recrudescence of the abuses is absolutely certain.

I urge the immediate enactment into law of provisions which will enable the Department of Agriculture adequately to inspect the meat and meat-food products entering into interstate commerce and to supervise the methods of preparing the same, and to prescribe the sanitary conditions under which the work shall be performed. I therefore commend to your favorable consideration and urge the enactment of substantially the provisions known as Senate amendment No.29 to the act making appropriations for the Department of Agriculture for the fiscal year ending June 30,1907, as passed by the Senate, this amendment being commonly known as the Beveridge amendment.

Theodore Roosevelt

The White House,
June 4, 1906.

Cudahy Packing Co., Omaha, Nebraska, 1910

Lewis Hine, Photographs for the National Child Labor Committee

Spinner, Whitnel Cotton Mill, Whitnel, North Carolina, December 22, 1908.

Young driver in mine, detail, September 1908.

Rob Kidd, glass factory worker, Alexandria, Virginia, detail, June 23, 1911.

Little spinner, Globe Cotton Mill, Augusta, Georgia, detail, January 15, 1909.

Small newsie downtown, Saturday afternoon, St. Louis, Missouri, detail, May 7, 1910.

Boys of the dumps, South Boston, Massachusetts, detail, October 1909.

The Ewen Breaker of the Pennsylvania Coal Company, South Pittston, Pennsylvania, January 10, 1911.

Two lifeboats carrying *Titanic* survivors, April 15, 1912.

HYDROGRAPHIC OFFICE,
WASHINGTON, D. C.

DAILY MEMORANDUM

N-8

April 15, 1912.

No. 1013.

NORTH ATLANTIC OCEAN

OBSTRUCTIONS OFF THE AMERICAN COAST.

Mar. 28 - Lat 24° 20', lon 80° 02', passed a broken spar projecting about 3 feet out of water, apparently attached to sunken wreckage.--EVELYN (SS) Wright.

OBSTRUCTIONS ALONG THE OVER-SEA ROUTES.

Apr 7 - Lat 35° 20', lon 59° 40', saw a lowermast cover with marine growth.--ADRIATICO (It. ss), Cevascu.

ICE REPORTS.

Apr 7 - Lat 45° 10', lon 56° 40', ran into a strip of field ice about 3 or 4 miles wide extending north and south as far as could be seen. Some very heavy pans were seen.--ROSALIND (Br ss), Williams.

Apr 10 - Lat 41° 50', lon 50° 25', passed a large ice field a few hundred feet wide and 15 miles long extending in a NNE direction.--EXCELSIOR (Ger ss). (New York Herald)

COLLISION WITH ICEBERG - Apr 14 - Lat 41° 46', lon 50° 14', the British steamer TITANIC collided with an iceberg seriously damaging her bow; extent not definitely known.

Apr 14 - The German steamer AMERIKA reported by radio telegraph passing two large icebergs in lat 41° 27', lon 50° 08',--TITANIC (Br ss).

Apr 14 - Lat 42° 06', lon 49° 43', encountered extensive field ice and saw seven icebergs of considerable size.--PISA (Ger ss).

J. J. KNAPP

Captain, U. S. Navy,
Hydrographer.

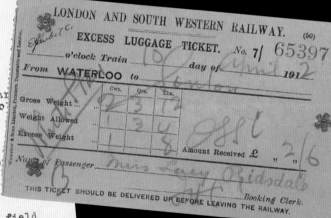

LONDON AND SOUTH WESTERN RAILWAY. (50)
EXCESS LUGGAGE TICKET. No. 7/ 65397
o'clock Train ... day of ... 1912

From WATERLOO to

	Cwt.	Qrs.	Lbs.
Gross Weight			
Weight Allowed			
Excess Weight			

Amount Received £ "/6

Name of Passenger

THIS TICKET SHOULD BE DELIVERED UP BEFORE LEAVING THE RAILWAY.

Booking Clerk.

Excess luggage ticket from a
Titanic passenger, April 10, 1912.

Daily Memorandum from the Hydrographic Office
reporting *Titanic* disaster, April 15, 1912.

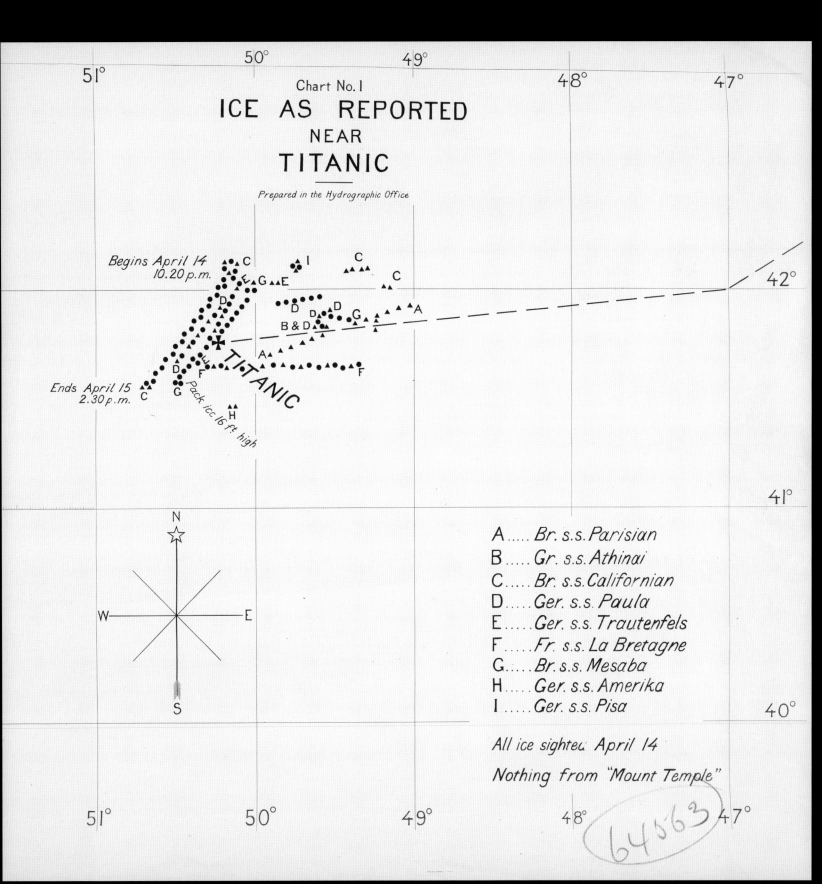

Chart No. I
ICE AS REPORTED
NEAR
TITANIC

Prepared in the Hydrographic Office

Begins April 14
10.20 p.m.

Ends April 15
2.30 p.m.

Pack ice 16 ft. high

TITANIC

A .....*Br. s.s. Parisian*
B .....*Gr. s.s. Athinai*
C .....*Br. s.s. Californian*
D .....*Ger. s.s. Paula*
E .....*Ger. s.s. Trautenfels*
F .....*Fr. s.s. La Bretagne*
G .....*Br. s.s. Mesaba*
H .....*Ger. s.s. Amerika*
I .....*Ger. s.s. Pisa*

All ice sighted April 14

Nothing from "Mount Temple"

Chart showing ice as reported near *Titanic*.

Form 1040.

INCOME TAX.

List No. ....

THE PENALTY
FOR FAILURE TO HAVE THIS RETURN IN
THE HANDS OF THE COLLECTOR OF
INTERNAL REVENUE ON OR BEFORE
MARCH 1 IS $20 TO $1,000.
(SEE INSTRUCTIONS ON PAGE 4.)

File No. ....

.... District of ....

Assessment List ....

Date received ....

Page .... Line ....

UNITED STATES INTERNAL REVENUE.

RETURN OF ANNUAL NET INCOME OF INDIVIDUALS.

(As provided by Act of Congress, approved October 3, 1913.)

RETURN OF NET INCOME RECEIVED OR ACCRUED DURING THE YEAR ENDED DECEMBER 31, 191....

(FOR THE YEAR 1913, FROM MARCH 1, TO DECEMBER 31.)

Filed by (or for) .... *of* ....
(Full name of individual.)   (Street and No.)

in the City, Town, or Post Office of .... *State of* ....

(Fill in pages 2 and 3 before making entries below.)

1. GROSS INCOME (see page 2, line 12)	$	
2. GENERAL DEDUCTIONS (see page 3, line 7)	$	
3. NET INCOME	$	

Deductions and exemptions allowed in computing income subject to the normal tax of 1 per cent.

4. Dividends and net earnings received or accrued, of corporations, etc., subject to like tax. (See page 2, line 11)	$	
5. Amount of income on which the normal tax has been deducted and withheld at the source. (See page 2, line 9, column A) ...		
6. Specific exemption of $3,000 or $4,000, as the case may be. (See Instructions 3 and 19)		
Total deductions and exemptions. (Items 4, 5, and 6)	$	
7. TAXABLE INCOME on which the normal tax of 1 per cent is to be calculated. (See Instruction 3)	$	

8. When the net income shown above on line 3 exceeds $20,000, the additional tax thereon must be calculated as per schedule below:

	INCOME.	TAX.
1 per cent on amount over $20,000 and not exceeding $50,000....	$	$
2 " " 50,000 " " 75,000.........		
3 " " 75,000 " " 100,000........		
4 " " 100,000 " " 250,000.......		
5 " " 250,000 " " 500,000.......		
6 " " 500,000		
Total additional or super tax		$
Total normal tax (1 per cent of amount entered on line 7)		$
Total tax liability		$

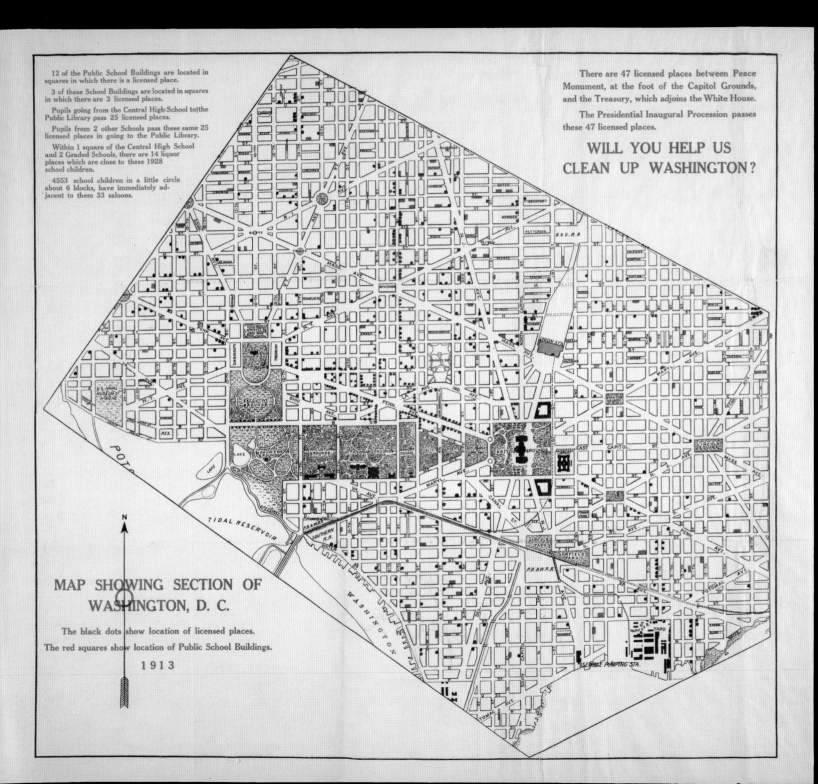

12 of the Public School Buildings are located in squares in which there is a licensed place.

3 of these School Buildings are located in squares in which there are 3 licensed places.

Pupils going from the Central High School to the Public Library pass 25 licensed places.

Pupils from 2 other Schools pass these same 25 licensed places in going to the Public Library.

Within 1 square of the Central High School and 2 Graded Schools, there are 14 liquor places which are close to these 1928 school children.

4553 school children in a little circle about 6 blocks, have immediately adjacent to them 33 saloons.

There are 47 licensed places between Peace Monument, at the foot of the Capitol Grounds, and the Treasury, which adjoins the White House.

The Presidential Inaugural Procession passes these 47 licensed places.

WILL YOU HELP US CLEAN UP WASHINGTON?

MAP SHOWING SECTION OF WASHINGTON, D. C.

The black dots show location of licensed places.

The red squares show location of Public School Buildings.

1913

Retail curb market, Wilmington, Delaware, 1914.

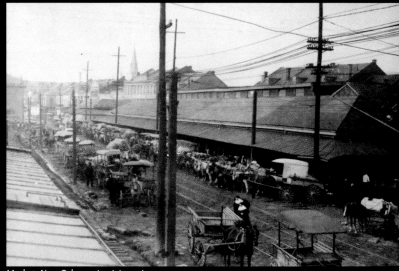

Market, New Orleans, Louisiana, January 1915.

South Water Street, Chicago, Illinois, April 1915.

Elk Street Market, Buffalo, New York, 1915.

Retail public market, privately owned, Cleveland, Ohio, 1915.

Farmers' retail curb market, Dubuque, Iowa, 1916.

Young boy tending fruit and vegetable stand in Center Market, Washington, DC, February 18, 1915.

Frank Augustin, John Augustin, Clara Augustin.

James Brennan.

Cyril H.E. Bretherton.

Mary Chamberlain.

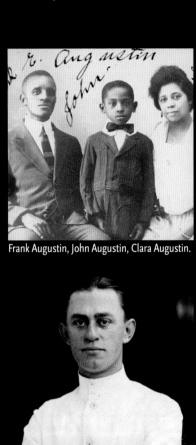

Louis Joseph de Saules.

William E.B. Du Bois.

Langston Hughes.

John Tucker.

Chancy W. Frees.

Anatole Gould.

Margaret Hauberg.

Annie M. Hernandez and Carmen Hernandez.

George Louis Koehler.

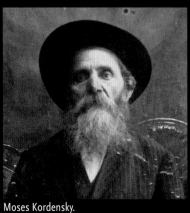

Moses Kordensky.

Guy B. Magley.

Irene Magley.

Denis A. Moloney.

Gerda Quietmeyer and Allen Quietmeyer.

Carroll G. Riggs.

Leon Rosen.

Albert L. Strauss.

Amy B. Strauss.

Lee J. Strauss.

Margaret P. Strauss.

Mary Swallow.

Henrietta Szold.

Storer Preble Ware.

Ware Family.

Jerome Wertheim.

White Antelope.

Martha A. Wolff.

Florence E. Youngs.

REGISTRATION CARD No. 23

Form 1 247   29

1. Name in full   Chester Springer
2. Home address   Box 263 — Block Island, R.I.
3. Date of birth   August   19   1887
4. Are you (1) a natural-born citizen, (2) an naturalized citizen, (3) an alien, (4) or have you declared your intention (specify which)?   Natural Born
5. Where were you born?   Fall River, Mass, USA
6. If not a citizen, of what country are you a citizen or subject?   General Prisoner
7. What is your present trade, occupation, or office?   United States
8. By whom employed?   Alcatraz, Cal.
9. Have you a father, mother, wife, child under 12, or a sister or brother under 12, solely dependent on you for support (specify which)?   No
10. Married or single (which)?   Single   Race (specify which)?   Caucasian
11. What military service have you had? Rank   Pvt. 1ˢᵗ Cl.   branch   Q.M.C.   years   1½   Nation or State   U.S.A.
12. Do you claim exemption from draft (specify grounds)?   No

I affirm that I have verified above answers and that they are true.   Chester Springer

---

REGISTRATION CARD No. 157

Form 2 2894   688   Age in yrs. 30

1. Name in full   Marcus Garvey
2. Home address   235 W 131 N.Y. N.Y.
3. Date of birth   Aug. 17 1887
4. Are you (1) a natural-born citizen (2) a naturalized citizen, (3) an alien, (4) or have you declared your intention (specify which)?   Alien
5. Where were you born?   Jamaica British W.I.
6. If not a citizen, of what country are you a citizen or subject?   British
7. What is your present trade, occupation, or office?   Journalist
8. By whom employed?   Universal Negro Ass.
Where employed?   Jamaica, Brit. W.I.
9. Have you a father, mother, wife, child under 12, or a sister or brother under 12, solely dependent on you for support (specify which)?   Father
10. Married or single (which)?   Single   Race (specify which)?   Colored
11. What military service have you had? Rank   No   branch   —   years   Nation or State
12. Do you claim exemption from draft (specify grounds)?   Physically Unfit

I affirm that I have verified above answers and that they are true.   Marcus Garvey
(Signature or mark)

REGISTRATION CARD

4693   ORDER NUMBER 18

1. Name in full   George Swinhoe (known as Moon)
2. Permanent home address   W. 79ᵗʰ St. New York City
3. Date of birth   Aug. 23 188_
RACE   [U.S. CITIZEN] / [ALIEN]
If not a citizen of the U.S. of what nation are you a citizen or subject?   England
PRESENT OCCUPATION   Vaudeville Artist   EMPLOYER'S NAME   United Booking Office
PLACE OF EMPLOYMENT OR BUSINESS: New York City
Name   Mrs. G. Swinhoe (wife)
Address   39_ W. 79 St. New York

I affirm that I have verified above answers and that they are true.   George Swinhoe
(Registrant's signature or mark)

P.M.G.O. No. 1 (Red)

REGISTRATION CARD

Form 1 235-4

1. Name in full   Angelo Reo
2. Home address   Esmond
3. Date of birth   Sept. 2
4. Are you (1) a natural-born citizen, (2) a naturalized citizen, (3) an alien, (4) or have you declared your intention (specify which)?   Alien
5. Where were you born?   Dopino, Ita...
6. If not a citizen, of what country are you a citizen or subject?   Ita...
7. What is your present trade, occupation, or office?   Weaver
8. By whom employed?   Esmond M...
Where employed?   Esmond, R...
9. Have you a father, mother, wife, child under 12, or a sister or brother under 12, solely dependent on you for support (specify which)?   Wife works...
10. Married or single (which)?   Married   Race (specify which)?   Ca...
11. What military service have you had?   Nation or State
12. Do you claim exemption from draft (specify grounds)?

I affirm that I have verified above answers and that they...

REGISTRATION CARD No. 1063

Form 434

1. Name in full   Abdul Hasan   Age in yrs. 14
2. 169 Elizabeth   Det. Mich.
3. Date of birth   Mar. 1894
4. Are you (1) a natural-born citizen, (2) a naturalized citizen, (3) an alien, (4) or have you declared your intention?   Alien
5. Where were you born?   Corda, Albania
6. If not a citizen, of what country are you a citizen or subject?   Albania
7. What is your present trade, occupation, or office?   Shoe shine
8. By whom employed?   Majestic Building   Det. Mich.
9. Have you a father, mother, wife, child under 12, or a sister or brother under 12, solely dependent on you?   No
10. Married or single (which)?   No   Race (specify which)?   Cau...
11. What military service have you had? Rank   No   branch   years   Nation or State

---

REGISTRATION CARD

SERIAL NUMBER 928   ORDER NUMBER 4177

1.   Lewis Armstrong
2. PERMANENT HOME ADDRESS: 1233 Perdido St. N.O. La.
3. Age in Years   18   Date of Birth   July 4th 1900

RACE: White / Negro / Oriental / Indian (Citizen / Noncitizen)

U.S. CITIZEN: Native Born / Naturalized / Citizen by Father's Naturalization Before Registrant's Majority

ALIEN: Declarant / Nondeclarant

15. If not a citizen of the U.S., of what nation are you a citizen or subject?

16. PRESENT OCCUPATION   Musician   17. EMPLOYER'S NAME   Peter Lala
18. PLACE OF EMPLOYMENT OR BUSINESS: 1500 Conti St. N.O. La.

20. NEAREST RELATIVE   May Armstrong   Address   1233 Perdido St. N.O. La.

I AFFIRM THAT I HAVE VERIFIED ABOVE ANSWERS AND THAT THEY ARE TRUE
P.M.G.O. Form No. 1 (Red)   Louis Armstrong
(Registrant's signature or mark)

REGISTRATION CARD

SERIAL NUMBER 2940   ORDER NUMBER 18

1.   Jacob Pomerantz
2. PERMANENT HOME ADDRESS: 202 East 103 St. NY
3. Age in Years   41   Date of Birth   ? ? 1877

RACE: White   X   Negro / Oriental / Indian

U.S. CITIZEN: No   Native Born / Naturalized / Citizen by Father's Naturalization Before Registrant's Majority   ALIEN: Declarant / Nondeclarant   X

15. If not a citizen of the U.S., of what nation are you a citizen or subject?   Russia

16. PRESENT OCCUPATION   Presser   17. EMPLOYER'S NAME   Weinstein Bros.
18. PLACE OF EMPLOYMENT OR BUSINESS: 30/32-21st St. NY

Wife   Annie Pomerantz
20. NEAREST RELATIVE   Address   202 East 103 St. — NY

I AFFIRM THAT I HAVE VERIFIED ABOVE ANSWERS AND THAT THEY ARE TRUE.

Duplicate

REGISTRATION CARD

SERIAL NUMBER 5776   ORDER NUMBER 5

1.   Francesco Gentile
2. PERMANENT HOME ADDRESS: 911 Southern Boulevard N...
3. Age in Years   38   Date of Birth   June 5

RACE: White   yes   Negro / Oriental / Indian   Citizen

U.S. CITIZEN: Native Born / Naturalized / Citizen by Father's Naturalization Before Registrant's Majority   ALIEN: Declarant / Nondeclarant

15. If not a citizen of the U.S., of what nation are you a citizen or subject?   Italy

16. PRESENT OCCUPATION   soldier Italian Army   17. Italian Min... shipping
18. PLACE OF EMPLOYMENT OR BUSINESS: 291 Broadway   New York

Name   Linda Cortine
20. NEAREST RELATIVE   Address   911 Southern Boulevard...

I AFFIRM THAT I HAVE VERIFIED ABOVE ANSWERS AND...
P.M.G.O. Form No. 1 (Red)   Francesco Gentile
(Registrant's signature or mark)

mail to Italian Ministry of Shipping
Barretto St...

REGISTRATION CARD

Serial No. 14   Registration No. 35

1. Name in full   Silas Fire Cloud   21
2. Home address   Little Eagle S.D.
3. Date of birth   Aug 1896
4. Where were you born?   Standing Rock Ind. Res. S.D.
5. I am (1) a natural born citizen (2) ... (3) ... (4) ...
7. Father's birthplace   Standing Rock Ind. Res.
8. Name of employer   Self   Place of employment   Little Eagle S.D.
9. Name of nearest relative   Alfred Fire Cloud   Address of nearest relative   Little Eagle S.D.
10. Race—White / Negro / Oriental / Indian / Citizen / Noncitizen

I affirm that I have verified above answers and that they are true.
P.M.G.O. Form 1 (blue)   Silas Fire Cloud
(Signature or Mark of Registrant)

REGISTRATION CARD

6   ORDER NUMBER

1.   Amos Afraid Of Horses
2. PERMANENT HOME ADDRESS   Oglala Shannon S.D.
3. Age in Years   Date of Birth   1876

RACE: White / Negro / Oriental / Indian

U.S. CITIZEN / ALIEN

16. PRESENT OCCUPATION   Laborer   17. EMPLOYER'S NAME   None
18. PLACE OF EMPLOYMENT OR BUSINESS:

Name   Naomi Afraid Of Horses   wife
20. NEAREST RELATIVE   Address   Oglala Shannon S.D.

I AFFIRM THAT I HAVE VERIFIED ABOVE ANSWERS AND THAT THEY ARE TRUE
P.M.G.O. Form I (Red)   Amos Afraid Of Horse (OVER)

REGISTRATION CARD

1221   ORDER NUMBER 35

SERIAL NUMBER 1221

1.   Haching Arzoomanian
2. PERMANENT HOME ADDRESS: 195 Solvay Detroit Wayne Mi...
3. Age in Years   33   Date of Birth   March 28 1885

RACE: White   ✓   Negro / Oriental / Indian

U.S. CITIZEN: Native Born / Naturalized / Citizen by Father's Naturalization Before Registrant's Majority   ALIEN: Declarant / Nondeclarant

15. If not a citizen of the U.S., of what nation are you a citizen or subject?   Armenian Tur...

16. PRESENT OCCUPATION   Carpenter   17. EMPLOYER'S NAME   Own Boss
18. PLACE OF EMPLOYMENT OR BUSINESS: 195 Solvay   Detroit Wayne ...

Name   B. Arzoomanian (C...
NEAREST RELATIVE   Address   505 W. 41 St. New York

I AFFIRM THAT I HAVE VERIFIED ABOVE ANSWERS AND THAT THEY...
H. Arzoomanian

Card 1 (Theodore Shabshelowitz)

Form 1 - 3979 **REGISTRATION CARD** No. 62

Theodore Shabshelowitz — Age 30

1381 First Av — NY

Dec N. 1886

Naturalized citizen — Russia

Seldingin

Rabbi

Cong. Rodeph Sholem K.

348 E 82 ...

None depend...

Single — Race White

None

Because I am a Rabbi

217 / 1383

Theodore Shabsh...

Card 2 (Antonio Cepa)

REGISTRATION CARD

SERIAL NUMBER — ORDER NUMBER

1 Antonio Cepa

2 PERMANENT HOME ADDRESS: Mescalero

Age in Years 44 — Date of Birth

RACE

| White | Negro | Oriental | | Citizen | Indian |

U.S. CITIZEN

| Native Born | Naturalized | Citizen by Father's Naturalization Before Registrant's Majority | | Declarant | Non-declarant | ALIEN |

PRESENT OCCUPATION — EMPLOYER'S NAME

Farmer — Self

PLACE OF EMPLOYMENT OR BUSINESS

Mescalero, N.M.

NEAREST RELATIVE — Antonette Apache

Mescalero, N.M.

Antonio Cepa

Witness: S. Kornsfield, Mescalero N.M.

Card 3 (Vladimir Nikolaevitch Bashkiroff)

REGISTRATION CARD

SERIAL 1687 — ORDER NUMBER 2 1613

1 Vladimir Nikolaevitch Bashkiroff

2 PERMANENT HOME ADDRESS: 730 Park Ave

New-York — 929 Park avenue app 4

Age in Years 33 — Date of Birth July 25th 1885

RACE

| White | Negra | Oriental | | Citizen | Indian | Noncitizen |
| Yes | Non | Non | | Non | Non | |

U.S. CITIZEN

| Native Born | Naturalized | Citizen by Father's Naturalization Before Registrant's Majority | Declarant | Non-declarant | ALIEN |
| Non | Non | Non | | | Russian |

PRESENT OCCUPATION — EMPLOYER'S NAME

Russian Vice minister of supplies — Russian provisional government (by J. Kerensky)

929 Park Ave (Head office) Fuller Bldg. 5 ave 23d (office)

NEAREST RELATIVE: My wife Elisabeth Bashkiroff — Samara, Russia

Vladimir Bashkiroff

Card 4 (Namba)

REGISTRATION CARD

SERIAL 1949 — ORDER NUMBER

Namba

PERMANENT HOME ADDRESS: Carlisle Grays Harbor Wn

Age in Years 9 — Date of Birth Jan 5 1878

RACE

| | Negra | Oriental | | Citizen | Indian |
| | | ✓ | | | |

U.S. CITIZEN

| | Naturalized | Citizen by Father's Naturalization Before Registrant's Majority | | Declarant | Non-declarant | ALIEN |
| | | | | | ✓ |

Japan

COPALIS LUMBER CO.

Carlisle Grays Harbor Wn

Carlisle Grays Harbor Wn

Card 5 (Joseph)

REGISTRATION CARD

SERIAL 3572 — ORDER NUMBER

Joseph

PERMANENT HOME ADDRESS: 12th St — Chicago Co

Date of Birth July

RACE

| | Negro | Oriental | | Citizen | Indian | Noncitizen |

U.S. CITIZEN

| Native Born | Naturalized | Citizen by Father's Naturalization Before Registrant's Majority | | Declarant | Non-declarant |
| | ✓ | | | | |

China

PRESENT OCCUPATION — EMPLOYER

Joseph — Chicago

N. 12th St.

NEAREST RELATIVE: Lena Rec..., 846 W. 12th Chicago

Card 6 (Kichirobe Tatsuda)

REGISTRATION CARD

SERIAL NUMBER 118 — ORDER NUMBER

1 Kichirobe Tatsuda

2 PERMANENT HOME ADDRESS: Box 452 — KETCHIKAN, ALASKA

Age in Years 34 — Date of Birth March 2 1884

RACE

| White | Negro | Oriental | | Indian |
| | | ✓ | | |

U.S. CITIZEN — **ALIEN**

| Native Born | Naturalized | Citizen by Father's Naturalization Before Registrant's Majority | | Declarant | Non-declarant |

Japan

PRESENT OCCUPATION — EMPLOYER'S NAME

Merchant — Self

PLACE OF EMPLOYMENT OR BUSINESS

KETCHIKAN, ALASKA

NEAREST RELATIVE: Mrs. S. Tatsuda (wife)

KETCHIKAN, ALASKA

Kichirobe Tatsuda

Form No. 1 (Red)

Card 7 (Yung Ching Li)

Form 1 73182 **REGISTRATION CARD** No. 217

Order No. — Yung Ching Li — Age 23

Hofie, China

Date of birth Oct 20 1894

4 Are you (1) a natural-born citizen, (2) a naturalized citizen, (3) an alien, (4) or have you declared your intention — alien

5 Where were you born? Hofie, Anhui, China

6 If not a citizen, of what country are you a citizen or subject? China

7 What is your present trade, occupation or office? student

8 By whom employed? — Where employed? Massachusetts Institute of Technology, Cambridge, Mass.

9 Have you a father, mother, wife, child under 12...? No

10 Married or single? single — Race Mongolian

11 What military service have you had? Rank No — branch

12 Do you claim exemption from draft? Yes, alien

Yung Ching Li

36810

Card 8 (Diles Baylor)

REGISTRATION CARD

SERIAL NUMBER — ORDER NUMBER

Diles — Baylor — Leslie Kef...

2 PERMANENT HOME ADDRESS: Helton

Age in Years 40 — Date of Birth May 1878

RACE

| White | Negra | Oriental | | Citizen | Indian | Noncitizen |

U.S. CITIZEN — **ALIEN**

| Native Born | Naturalized | Citizen by Father's Naturalization Before Registrant's Majority | | Declarant | Non-declarant |
| ✓ | | | | | |

PRESENT OCCUPATION — EMPLOYER'S NAME

Prisoner — U.S. Penitentiary, Atlanta, Ga.

PLACE OF EMPLOYMENT OR BUSINESS — U.S. Penitentiary, Atlanta, Ga.

NEAREST RELATIVE: Hettie Baylor — Helton Leslie Ke...

Diles Baylor

Card 9 (Lee)

9-127-C **REGISTRATION CARD** ORDER NUMBER 1657

SERIAL 3500 — Den

Lee

PERMANENT HOME ADDRESS: ...Lane N.Y. N.Y. N.Y.

1872

Age in Years 45 — Date of Birth Sept. 16

RACE

| White | Negro | Oriental | | Citizen | Indian | Noncitizen |
| | | ✓ | | | |

U.S. CITIZEN — **ALIEN**

| Native Born | Naturalized | Citizen by Father's Naturalization Before Registrant's Majority | | Declarant | Non-declarant |

China

PRESENT OCCUPATION — EMPLOYER'S NAME

Cook — Lee Du

PLACE OF EMPLOYMENT OR BUSINESS: 7565 Broadway N.Y. N.Y.

NEAREST RELATIVE: Gem She (wife) — Canton China

Card 10 (Kills Them In House)

Form 1 49 **REGISTRATION CARD** No. 60

1 Name in full: KILLS THEM IN HOUSE — Age 28

2 Home address: Poplar, Montana

3 Date of birth 1889

4 Are you (1) a natural-born citizen, (2) a naturalized citizen, (3) an alien, (4) or have you declared your intention? natural born

5 Where were you born? Montana, U.S.A.

6 If not a citizen, of what country are you a citizen or subject?

7 What is your present trade, occupation or office? none

8 By whom employed? not employed — Where employed?

9 Have you a father, mother, wife, child under 12, or a sister or brother under 12...? dependent

10 Married or single? single — Race Indian

11 What military service have you had? Rank none — branch

12 Do you claim exemption from draft? blind

I affirm that I have verified above answers...

KILLS THEM IN HOUSE

Card 11 (Ramon Gil Samaniego)

1127 **REGISTRATION CARD**

SERIAL NUMBER — ORDER NUMBER

RAMON GIL SAMANIEGO

2 PERMANENT HOME ADDRESS: 2323 So Hope St — LOS ANGELES

Age in Years 19 — Date of Birth February 6th

RACE

| White | Negro | Oriental | | Citizen | Indian |

U.S. CITIZEN — **ALIEN**

| Native Born | Naturalized | Citizen by Father's Naturalization Before Registrant's Majority | | Declarant | Non-declarant |
| | | | | | ✓ |

MEXICO

PRESENT OCCUPATION — EMPLOYER'S NAME

Teacher of Piano — none

PLACE OF EMPLOYMENT OR BUSINESS: 2323 So Hope St Los Angeles Cal

NEAREST RELATIVE: MARIANO N. SAMANIEGO — 2323 So Hope St

Ramon Gil Samaniego

Company H, 347th Infantry, American Expeditionary Force, Camp Dix, New Jersey, 1919.

Boat exercises, Naval Training Station, Hampton Roads, Virginia, September 19, 1918.

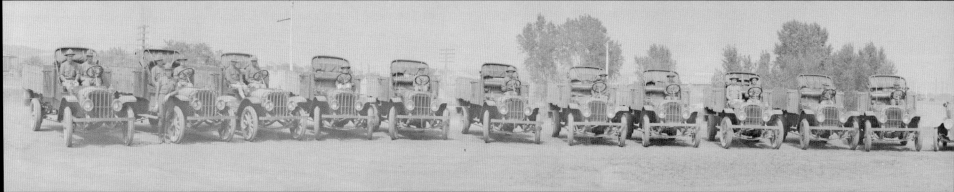

White Motor Company trucks in service at Fort Riley, Kansas, ca. 1917–1918.

"347th Inf.
Mobley Com'g
itionary Forces
N.J. Jan 1919

Photo
F.C.L
MJ H

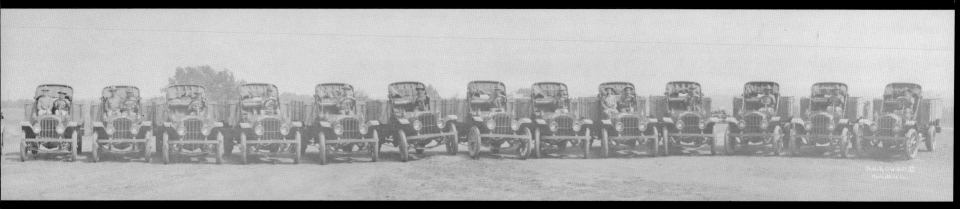

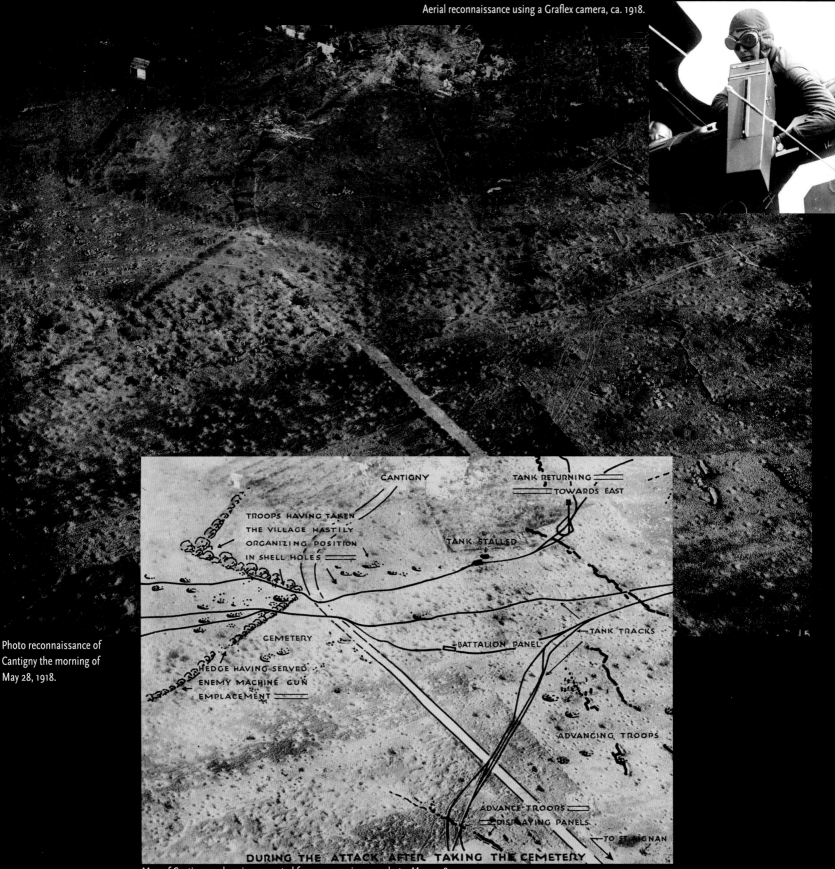

Aerial reconnaissance using a Graflex camera, ca. 1918.

Photo reconnaissance of Cantigny the morning of May 28, 1918.

CANTIGNY

TANK RETURNING

TOWARDS EAST

TROOPS HAVING TAKEN
THE VILLAGE HASTILY
ORGANIZING POSITION
IN SHELL HOLES

TANK STALLED

TANK TRACKS

CEMETERY

BATTALION PANEL

HEDGE HAVING SERVED
ENEMY MACHINE GUN
EMPLACEMENT

ADVANCING TROOPS

ADVANCE TROOPS

DISPLAYING PANELS

TO ST AIGNAN

DURING THE ATTACK AFTER TAKING THE CEMETERY

MPs bring German prisoners captured in 1st Division drive through deserted French village.

Wounded man being carried away on rolling stretcher near Cantigny, May 28, 1918.

French tank that broke down in the attack on Cantigny, May 31, 1918.

Note to General Wright accompanying "Report of Operations against Cantigny," July 9, 1918.

Report of capture of Cantigny and consolidation of position, June, 2, 1918.

Letter from the 28th Infantry commander thanking the Red Cross for lemons and chocolate, June 25, 1918.

My dear Gen. Wright—
The enclosed being an
account of first American
attack, I thought you might
be interested.
Yours very truly
N E Ely

Gen. W. M. Wright

HEADQUARTERS 28TH INFANTRY,
France, 2 June, 1918.

Report of capture of CANTIGNY and consolidation of position.

1. OBJECT OF THE OPERATION.

    To cut out an akward salient in the enemy's line at the village of CANTIGNY, which salient would give the enemy an excellent jumping off place in case of an offensive on his part and give him an extensive field of observation to the West and Northwest. General line to be reached as prescribed 18.23 corner of orchard, 24.19 East of blockhouses, 26.13-25.08, then liaison on West of 18.23 with 9th A.C. For this operation the 28th Infantry was designated. A large amount of artillery shown in Appendix marked "A" was assigned to its support, a group of 12 tanks, a platoon of Schilt Units (flame throwers), Company "D" 1st U.S.Engineers, Certain Aviation Units. An artillery diversion was made on the front of the 60th Division.

2. INFORMATION CONCERNING THE ENEMY.

    The front of the sector to be attacked was held by the 271 and 272 Reg. German Reserve Infantry. The strength of Companys in these Regiments about 160. Regiments graded as 2 on a scale of 4, showing somewhat better than average German troops. Patrols from the 28th Infantry obtained accurate information of descriptions in front of that Regiment. Intelligence reports and excellent aeroplane photographs taken immediately before the operation gave accurate information of many of the enemy's dispositions.

3. ARTILLERY.

    Total number of guns used in the preliminary preparation and during the action amounted to about 250, including calibers up to 280 mm. (See exhibit marked "A") From daylight on J day to H-1 hour the artillery obtained accurate registration and caused a certain amount of destruction without indicating serious offensive action to the enemy. From H-1 hour to H hour the artillery fire for destruction and counter battery was tremendous and most effective. Gas and smoke clouds were used at H hour minus 5 minutes. The rolling barrage was put down (See exhibit "D", Barrage and Time Table). The rolling barrage was extremely accurate, enabling the Infantry to follow at less than 50 yards in general and keeping practically all ... defense under cover and depriving them of ... objective was obtained the ... interdiction for 1-1/2 ... of the position, getting ... trong points, etc. without ... its fire and ceased.

HEADQUARTERS 28TH INFANTRY
France.

25 June 1918

From: The Commanding Officer, 28th Infantry

To : To American Red Cross Association.
     (Thru Chief Surgeon, 1st Div., A.E.F.)

1. I wish to express my thanks, with that of all members of the 28th Infantry, for the 3000 lemons and 1500 pounds of chocolate furnished to this command before the action on Cantigny.

2. They were very acceptable, the chocolate acted as a reserve ration and the lemons prevented thirst and exhaustion when it was impossible to get water to the men.

3. The efforts of the Red Cross and the quick delivery at this time are highly appreciated.

about 11:30 P.M. and pur-
... areas, each element tak-
... mpany front had been pre-
... ith not more than 5 casual-
... aisance. At 4:57 A.M.
... position for attack. All
... ion of Infantry in the
... ed "C". In addition to
... ere in support position
... "). These companies
... , 28th Infantry in case
... lines closing to 50
... in 2 minutes. The 2nd
... t should be 200 yards
... ng time it took the
... The Infantry proceeded
... ls was at H plus 1

N.E.ELY:
Colonel 28th Infantry
Commanding

Women of Boston help in the drive for peach stones, used
by the Government in the production of gas masks during
World War I, September 23, 1918.

World War I poster.

FRUIT STONES
AND
NUT SHELLS
WILL SAVE SOLDIERS' LIVES
LEAVE THEM HERE

ONLY THE FOLLOWING CAN BE USED

Prune Pits	THE SHELLS
Peach Stones	of
Apricot Pits	
Plum Pits	
Beach Plum Pits	Hickory Nuts
Date Seeds	Walnuts
Olive Pits	Butternuts and
Cherry Pits	Brazil Nuts

SAVE EVERY ONE OF THESE YOU POSSIBLY CAN

"APPROXIMATELY FIVE THOUSAND MEN HAVE RECEIVED PROPSYLATIC [sic] INFLUENZA VACCINE...THIS STATION...TWELVE THOUSAND..."

Influenza Epidemic | **1918**

Street car conductor refuses passenger not wearing mask, Seattle.

Nurse wears gauze mask to prevent spreading influenza.

Letter carrier wears mask for protection, New York City.

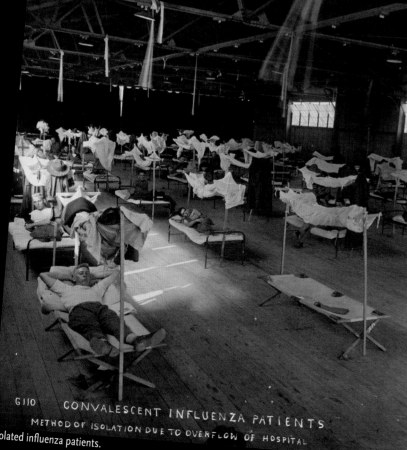
Isolated influenza patients.

Telegram from Parris Island, South Carolina, stating there are not enough vaccines, October 16, 1918.

Woman picketing the White House with suffragette banner, ca. 1917.

KAISER WILSON

HAVE YOU FORGOTTEN
YOUR SYMPATHY WITH
THE POOR GERMANS
BECAUSE THEY WERE NOT
SELF-GOVERNED?

20,000,000
AMERICAN WOMEN ARE NOT
SELF-GOVERNED.

TAKE THE BEAM
OUT OF YOUR OWN EYE.

H. J. Res. I.

5

Sixty-sixth Congress of the United States of America;

At the First Session,

Begun and held at the City of Washington on Monday, the nineteenth day of May, one thousand nine hundred and nineteen.

JOINT RESOLUTION

Proposing an amendment to the Constitution extending the right of suffrage to women.

Resolved by the Senate and House of Representatives of the United States of America in Congress assembled (two-thirds of each House concurring therein), That the following article is proposed as an amendment to the Constitution, which shall be valid to all intents and purposes as part of the Constitution when ratified by the legislatures of three-fourths of the several States.

"ARTICLE ————.

"The right of citizens of the United States to vote shall not be denied or abridged by the United States or by any State on account of sex.

"Congress shall have power to enforce this article by appropriate legislation."

F. H. Gillett

Speaker of the House of Representatives.

Thos. R. Marshall

Vice President of the United States and
President of the Senate.

19th Amendment, May 19, 1919.

CLASS OF SERVICE DESIRED		
Telegram		
Day Letter		
Night Message		
Night Letter		

Patrons should mark an X opposite the class of service desired; OTHERWISE THE MESSAGE WILL BE TRANSMITTED AS A FULL-RATE TELEGRAM

WESTERN UNION
WESTERN UNION
TELEGRAM

NEWCOMB CARLTON, PRESIDENT   GEORGE W. E. ATKINS, FIRST VICE-PRESIDENT

Receiver's No.
Check
Time Filed

Send the following message, subject to the terms
on back hereof, which are hereby agreed to

Paid.   Boston, Mass.   August 11, 1920.

Warden,

        Charles Ponzi a financial wizard confessed here today

that he served two years in federal prison at Atlanta for

smuggling man across Canadian border would greatly appreciate

if you will inform us from what place he was sentenced and when

            Dunn City Editor Boston Post.

						Class	4	Age	28
Height	1 m 57.5	Head lgth.	18.0	..ot	24.5	Areola	dk	Apparent Age	
Eng. Hgt.	5-2	Head Width	10.0	L. Mid. F	11.2	Periph	"	Nativity	Italy
Out A.	1 m 53	Cheek Width	13.4	L Lit F	8.8	Pecul		Occupation	Bookkeeper
Trunk	84.0	R Ear lgth	5.6	L Cubit	41.8				

Remarks relative
to Measurements

3113

Sup Bor mil dok ch Hair   Beard

Boston Post telegram to the
warden of the Atlanta Federal
Penitentiary, 1920.

Charles Ponzi's inmate card
from the Atlanta Federal
Penitentiary, 1910.

estation, Miller County, Arkansas

"Many complaints came to us that rats were doing great damage..."

1928

11

MILLER COUNTY, ARKANSAS 1928

·RODENTS

Early last year we found that the rat population of the
county was larger than it had been for several years. Many
complaints came to us that rats were doing great damage to
stored grain and supplies of all kinds and also that they were
eating the corn that was planted in the fields thereby ruin-
ing the stand. We decided to put on a rat killing campaign
through the schools. The U. S. Bureau of Biological Survey
was asked to send a man here ~tart us off and did so. His
first suggest was that we ge   ~o be offered to
the school accounting for th   individual
boys and girls. This matter
Commerce and they kindly ag
were as follows: Schools,
2nd prize $45.00 victrola;
equipment. Boys, 1st prize
rifle; 2nd trip to Farmers
.22 rifle. Girls, 1st $25
Week;. 3rd $15.00 cedar che
campaign were made out and
All schools in the county
campaign explained to the
Letters and instructions
in which instructions wei
The rats were killed by
carried to school where
to us each week the tota
were sent out each week
interest. When the camp
found that 50 schools h
reporting 95,849 rats

Narrative report of county
extension workers, Miller
County, Arkansas.

This school killed
7574 rats.

Ina Vaughn killed
2135 rats, won 1st
prize for girls.

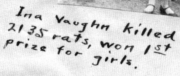

Basil Spruell killed
3082 rats, won 1st
prize for boys.

These boys killed nearly
3000 rats with "flips" or
"slingshots".

República Argentina ~~Uruguay~~ *Speeches*

Ministerio de Marina [# 965]   Dec. 16th, 1928.

MR. PRESIDENT:

   I wish to thank you for the eloquent expression you have given of your sentiments toward myself and of the friendship of the people of Uruguay toward my country.   I know that these expressions and this hospitality and this reception will meet a response in the hearts of the people of the United States.

   Your Excellency, I sometimes think that relations between nations can be compared in an humble way to the relations between neighbors. In a busy life crowded with domestic problems, we know but little of our neighbors; we hear in the press of sensational accidents; we know the gossip of unworthy members of their families; we read descriptions of their homes.   But we know little of the finer qualities of their home life; their deep affections; their sorrows; their self-denials; their courage and their idealism. So it is with nations.   Their national accomplishments, the flower of thought, and the great intangibles of natural character and ideals can come only with contact. From these contacts comes that respect and friendship that desire for helpfulness which must be the true basis of international relations.   I have hoped that I might by this visit symbolize the courtesy of a call from one good neighbor to another, that I might convey the respect, esteem and desire for spiritual contact which forms so important a part in the private life among individuals.

   Your Excellency has spoken of our common ideals of justice not only in our international relations, but in our systems of government.   Justice is not only an ideal, it is a science. In the contributions of the leaders of Uruguay to the science of jurisprudence both in the national and the international field, she

President Herbert Hoover's motorcade in Quayaquil, Ecuador, 1928.

President Hoover and Argentine President Juan Hipólito Yrigoyen.

President Hoover with Brazilian President Washington Luís Pereira de Sousa.

Draft of President Hoover's speech in Uruguay.

Departmental Reorganization—

~~There has~~
This subject has been under consideration for over 20 years, it has been repeatedly examined ~~and reported upon~~ by Commissions both congressional and executive
Their conclusions have been unanimous that reorganization is a necessity ~~for~~ of sound administration, of economy ~~in government~~, ~~and~~ of ~~better~~ more effective ~~direction~~ to governmental

Selected pages.

policies and in relief to the citizen from unnecessary harassing in his relations with government departments.
But when any detailed plan is presented it at once ~~arouses~~ enlivens opposition from every official whose authority may be curtailed or who fears such a result, of ~~their~~ departments, esp. spirit, to maintain their ~~[illegible]~~ among their activities. ~~both offices~~ or ~~citizens in no organized~~ of citizens and their organizations who are ~~curious~~ selfishly appropriately interested, or ~~those~~ who are

Women show off their caning projects, Maryland.

Postman delivering mail, rural mail route, Maine, August 26, 1930.

Farm family listening to their radio, Michigan, August 15, 1930.

Customer at Auburn Savings Bank, Auburn, Maine, 1929.

Selling pecans at roadside, Byron, Georgia.

Home garden, Florida.

Children playing baseball, Michigan.

1930
1932

Al Capone

"We...wish to protest against any action that you...might take to release Al Capone from confinement..."

Al Capone mug shot, 1930.

RESPECTFULLY REFERRED
FOR CONSIDERATION,

~Lawrence Richey~
Secy. to the President

THE WHITE HOUSE
APR 30 1932
RECEIVED

Mitchell, S. Dak.,
April 26, 1932

Honorable Herbert Hoover,

President of the United States,

The White House,

Washington, D. C.

OFFICE OF THE
RECEIVED
MAY 2- 1932
ATTORNEY GENERAL

Dear Sir:

We, as citizens of the state of South Dakota, hereby
wish to protest against any action that you, as chief executive
of our nation, might take to release Al Capone from confinement
because of his reported willingness to aid in the search for the
kidnaped son of Mr. and Mrs. Charles A. Lindberg.

While our sympathy goes out to Mr. and Mrs. Lindberg
in their loss, we feel that presidential action to free this
notori...   ...n temporarily, to assist individuals,
...ake. We believe that it would encourage
...ng violence from gangsters, and that
...e.

Most respectfully yours,

W. E. M.

MAY — 1932 A.M.
OF JUSTICE

MAY 4 1932

IN THE DISTRICT COURT OF THE UNITED STATES
FOR THE NORTHERN DISTRICT OF ILLINOIS
EASTERN DIVISION.

UNITED STATES

VS

ALPHONSE CAPONE

} NOS. 22852
   23232 } Consolidated.

We, the Jury find the Defendant NOT
GUILTY as charged in Indictment No. 22852 and we find the
Defendant GUILTY on Counts *one-five-nine-thirteen-eighteen*
and NOT GUILTY on Counts *2-3-4-6-7-8-10-11-12-14-15-16-17-19-20-21-22*
Indictment No. 23232.

~J. Walter~
~L. D. Weidling~
~Alfred G. Maehr~
~A. C. Smart~

Petition protesting the possible release
of Al Capone, April 26, 1932.

Verdict in the tax evasion case
of Al Capone, October 17, 1931.

World War I veterans block the steps of the Capitol during the Bonus March, July 5, 1932.

"Bonus Marchers" and police battle in Washington, DC, July 1932. Courtesy of AP Images.

Shacks put up by the Bonus Army on the Anacostia flats, Washington, DC, 1932.

Children at a Bonus March camp set up to criticize President Hoover's policies, July 1932.

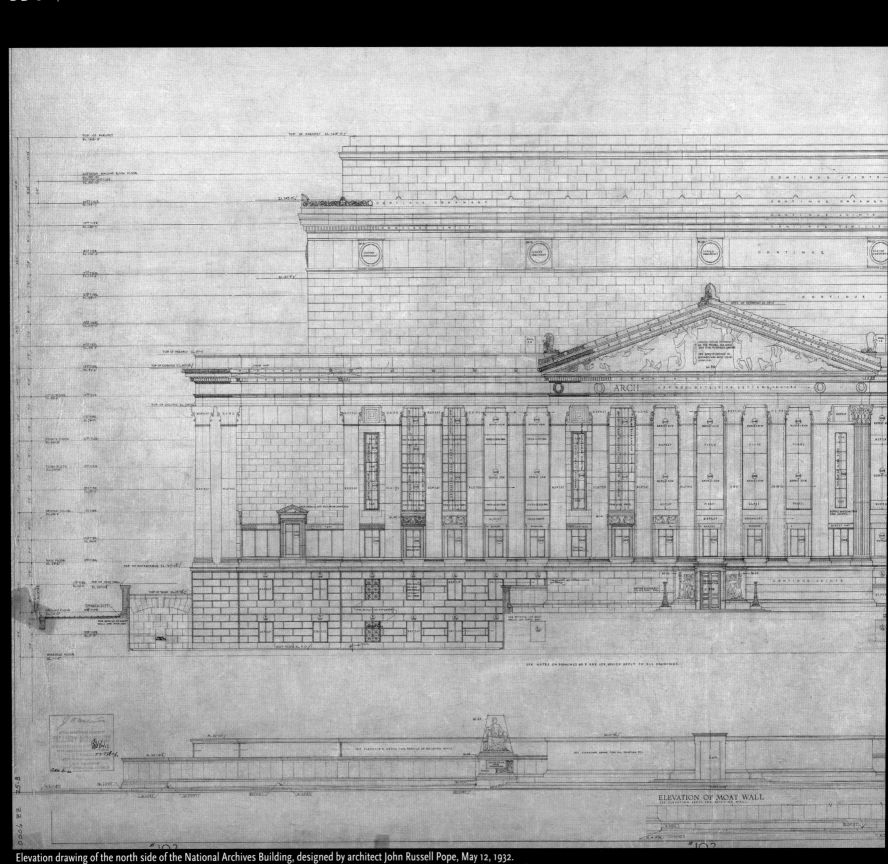

Elevation drawing of the north side of the National Archives Building, designed by architect John Russell Pope, May 12, 1932.

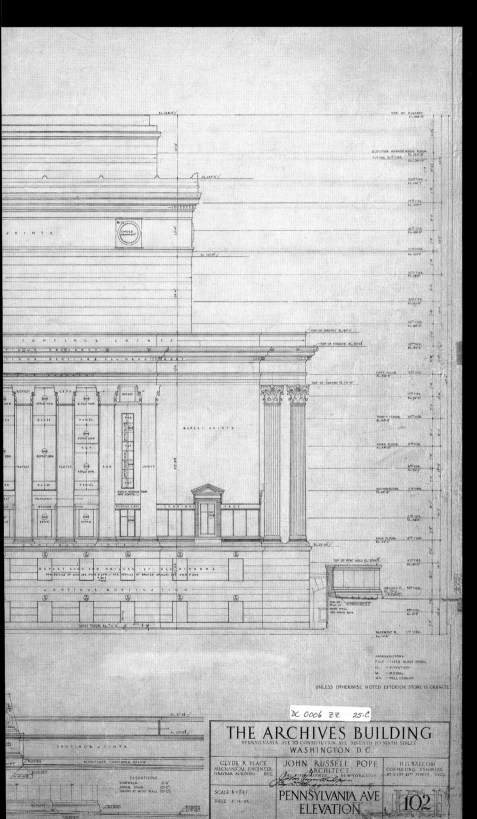

The building takes shape as the support columns are erected, September 5, 1933.

The exterior of the building nears completion, June 1, 1934.

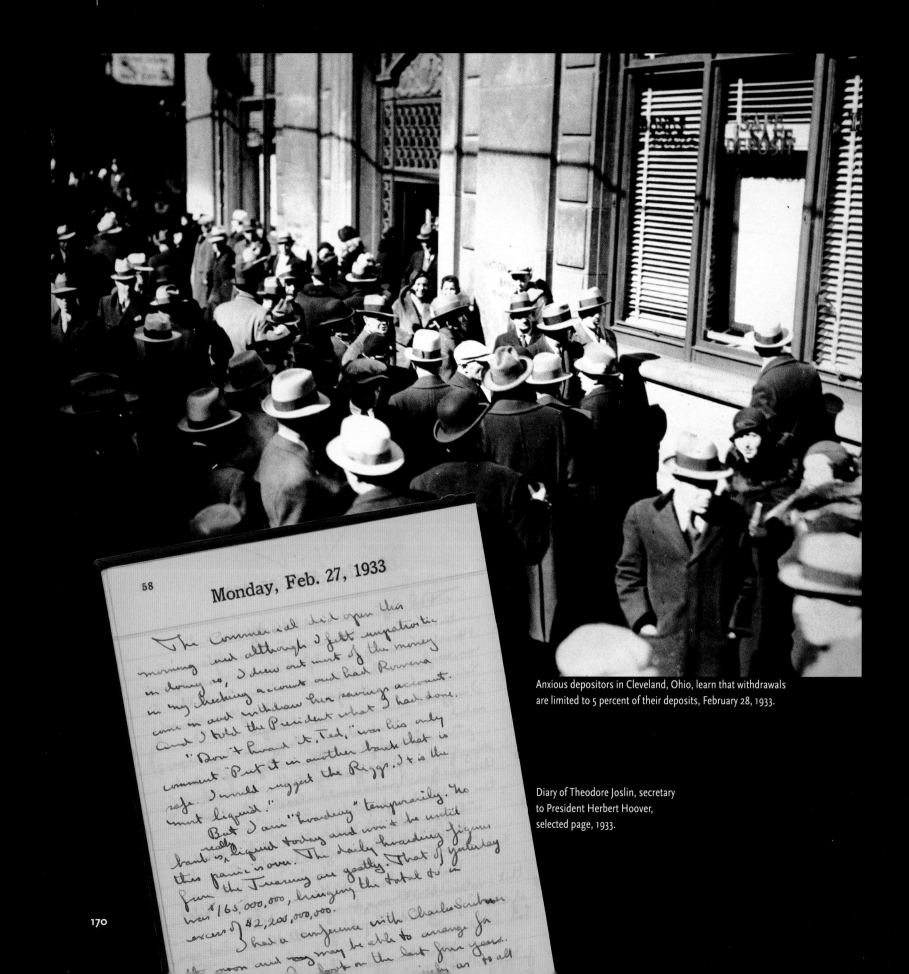

Anxious depositors in Cleveland, Ohio, learn that withdrawals are limited to 5 percent of their deposits, February 28, 1933.

Diary of Theodore Joslin, secretary to President Herbert Hoover, selected page, 1933.

58   Monday, Feb. 27, 1933

INAUGURAL ADDRESS OF

PRESIDENT FRANKLIN D. ROOSEVELT

MARCH 4, 1933.

This is a day of consecration.

I am certain that my fellow Americans expect that on my induction

into the Presidency I will address them with a candor and a decision which

the present situation of our nation impels.   This is preeminently the

time to speak the truth, the whole truth, frankly and boldly.   Nor need

we shrink from honestly facing conditions in our country today.   This

great nation will endure as it has endured, will revive and will prosper.

So first of all let me assert my firm belief that the only thing we have

to fear is fear itself, - nameless, unreasoning, unjustified terror which

paralyzes needed efforts to convert retreat into advance.   In every dark

hour of our national life a leadership of frankness and vigor has met with

that understanding and support of the people themselves which is essential

to victory.   I am convinced that you will again give that support to

leadership in these critical days.

In such a spirit on my part and on yours we face our common difficulties.

They concern, thank God, only material things.   Values have shrunken to

fantastic levels; taxes have risen; our ability to pay has fallen;

government of all kinds is faced by serious curtailment of income;   the

Dust storm in South Dakota, May 5, 1936.

President Roosevelt delivering a fireside chat, April 28, 1935.

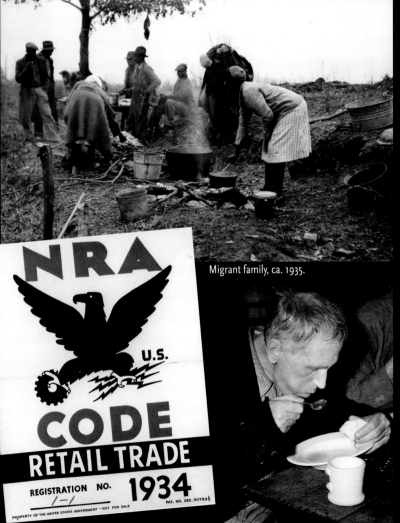
Migrant family, ca. 1935.

Farm foreclosure sale, ca. 1933.

Family leaving South Dakota, ca. 1935.

National Recovery Administration
Blue Eagle poster, ca. 1934.

Unemployed man eating in Volunteers of
America Soup Kitchen, June 1936.

Works Progress Administration worker receiving his paycheck, January 1939.

Group of CCC boys from Idaho arriving in camp near Andersonville, Tennessee, October 20, 1933.

CCC crew working on Boise Project main canal, January 25, 1940.

CCC enrollee crew planting, August 1940.

CCC Camp BR-3 and 82 Carlsbad Project, New Mexico, May 20, 1940.

CCC timber worker on plank, ca. 1935.

The Chinese Pagoda, "Big Room," detail, Carlsbad Caverns National Park, New Mexico, 1941–1942.

Natural formations at Carlsbad Caverns National Park, New Mexico, 1941–1942.

Paradise Valley, Kings River Canyon, California, ca. 1936.

Film strips from the
documentary film
*The Plow That Broke
the Plains*.

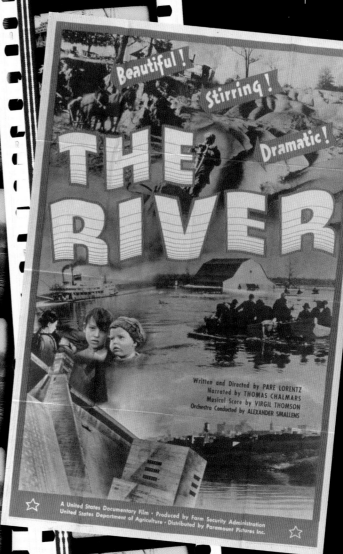

Publicity poster
for *The River*.

Film strips from the
documentary film
The River.

quatter community of 52 camps, Olivehurst, California, February 20, 1940.

rivate auto camp, Bakersfield, California, April 11, 1940.

Migratory cotton picker rests at the scales before returning to work, near Coolidge, Arizona, November 1940.

Charles Boyer.

Jean Renoir.

Maria Magdalene Sieber (Marlene Dietrich).

Albert Einstein.

Apolonia Mdivani (Pola Negri).

Ladislav Lowenstein (Peter Lorre).

UNITED STATES OF AMERICA — DECLARATION OF INTENTION

TRIPLICATE (To be given to declarant) — No. 89452

(Invalid for all purposes seven years after the date hereof)

UNITED STATES OF AMERICA, SOUTHERN DISTRICT OF CALIFORNIA, COUNTY OF LOS ANGELES

I, **ERROL LESLIE FLYNN**, now residing at 601 No. Linden Drive, Beverly Hills, California, occupation Actor-author, aged 29 years... Sex Male, color White, complexion Fair, color of eyes Grey, color of hair Brown, height 6 feet 2 inches, weight 185 pounds... race Irish, nationality British. I was born in Hobart, Australia on June 20, 1909. I am married. The name of my wife is Lilliane Marie Madeleine... we were married on May 5, 1935... Errol Leslie Flynn. No. 129952.

Errol Leslie Flynn.

TRIPLICATE (To be given to declarant) — No. 98722

UNITED STATES OF AMERICA, SOUTHERN DISTRICT CALIFORNIA

I, **EVA GABOR R. DRIMMER**, now residing at 141-A So. Canon Dr., Los Angeles, Los Angeles, California, occupation Actress, aged 21 years... Sex Female, color White, complexion Light, color of hair Light Brown, height 5 feet 2 inches, weight 106 pounds... race Hungarian, nationality Swedish. I was born in Budapest, Hungary. I am married. The name of my husband is Eric... we were married on February 11, 1939... born at Co Gavleborg, Sweden on April 19, 1910 at London, England. Eva Drimmer. SS "Ile de France" August 22, 1939. No. 439422.

Eva Gabor R. Drimmer.

UNITED STATES OF AMERICA — DECLARATION OF INTENTION

No. 9887

United States of America, District of Vermont, U.S. District, the United States, Burlington, Vermont

(1) My full, true, and correct name is **MARIA AUGUSTA VonTRAPP**. (2) My present place of residence is Stowe, Lamoille, Vermont. (3) My occupation is Singer. (4) I am 39 years old. (5) I was born in Vienna, Austria. color White, complexion Fair, color of eyes Blue, color of hair Brown, height 5 feet 7 inches, weight 160 pounds. Female. Austrian. I was born January 26, 1905. (9) My husband's name is George... married at Salzburg, Austria on December 30, 1948. Children: Rosemarie, Female, Feb. 8, 1929; Eleanore... Johannes, Male, Jan. 17, 1939 at Philadelphia, Pa.; all three now reside at Stowe, Vermont. Departed from United States. Maria Augusta von Trapp. January 21, 1944. AUSTIN H. NOBLE.

Maria Augusta von Trapp.

TRIPLICATE (To be given to declarant) — No. 93001

UNITED STATES OF AMERICA, SOUTHERN DISTRICT OF CALIFORNIA, COUNTY OF LOS ANGELES

I, **OLIVIA MARY DE HAVILLAND**, now residing at 2337 Nella Vista Ave., Hollywood, Los Angeles County, Calif., occupation Actress, aged 23 years... Sex Female, color White, complexion Fair, color of hair Light brown, height 5 feet 4½ inches, weight 107 pounds... race English, nationality British. I was born in Tokyo, Japan on July 1, 1916. I am not married... I have no children... my last foreign residence was Tokyo, Japan. I emigrated to the United States of America from Yokohama, Japan... San Francisco, California, under the name of Olivia Mary de Havilland on March 1, 1919 on the vessel SS "SIBERIA MARU". Olivia Mary de Havilland. No. 407001.

Olivia Mary de Havilland.

TRIPLICATE — No. 104751

UNITED STATES OF AMERICA — DECLARATION OF INTENTION

UNITED STATES OF AMERICA, SOUTHERN DISTRICT OF CALIFORNIA

(1) My full, true, and correct name is **IGOR STRAVINSKY**. (2) My present place of residence is 8221 Sunset Blvd., Hollywood, Calif. (3) Occupation Composer and Conductor. (4) I am 58 years old. I was born June 18, 1882 in Oranienbaum, Russia. color of hair Lt. Brown, color of eyes Hazel, complexion Light, Male, White, Russian. (6) I am married. Name of wife Vera... married on 3-9-1940 at Bedford, Mass.... St. Petersburg, Russia. Children: Theodore (M) 3/24/1907 St. Petersburg, Russia, Paris, France; Sviatoslav (M) 9/23/1910 Lausanne, Switzerland, Lausanne, Switzerland; Milene (F) 1/15/1914 ditto, ditto. My last foreign residence was Mexico City, Mexico. I emigrated to the United States from Nogales, Ariz. on Aug. 8, 1940 under the name of Igor Strawinsky by train. Igor Stravinsky. John A. Childress.

Igor Stravinsky.

TRIPLICATE — No. 133227

UNITED STATES OF AMERICA — DECLARATION OF INTENTION

IN THE UNITED STATES, SOUTHERN DISTRICT OF CAL.

(1) My full, true, and correct name is **GRETA LOVISA GARBO**. (2) My present place of residence is 904 N. Bedford Dr., Beverly Hills (L.A.) California. (3) Occupation Actress. (4) I am 42 years old. I was born in Stockholm, Sweden. color White, complexion light, color of eyes blue, color of hair lt. brn., height 5 feet 6½ inches, weight 122 pounds, Female, White, Swedish. born 9/18/1905. (7) I am not married. (8) I have no children. My place of foreign residence was Stockholm, Sweden. I emigrated from Gothenburg, Sweden... San Diego, Cal. 4/30/1933 under the name Greta Lovisa Garbo, SS Annie Johnson. Departed: New York, June '35, SS Gripsholm; Dec. '37, SS Kungsholm. Returned: New York, 5/3/36 SS Gripsholm; Oct. '38, SS Gripsholm; 10/29/40 U.S. No. 102407. Greta Lovisa Garbo.

Greta Lovisa Garbo.

hreshing wheat by machine, Canyon, December 1941.

Children line up for books when the Taos County project bookmobile visits school, Prado.

Native woodcarver Patrocina Barela, December 1941.

Patrocina Barela's daughter, December 1941.

Children at the Canyon school play a game of Broadcast

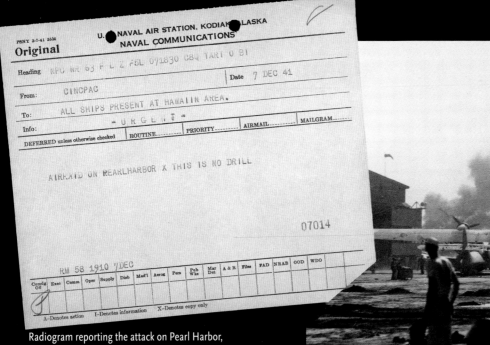

Radiogram reporting the attack on Pearl Harbor, December 7, 1941.

Damage at the Pearl Harbor Naval Air Station, Hawaii, from Japanese attack, December 7, 1941.

Aerial photograph of the naval base at Pearl Harbor, Oahu, Hawaii, January 17, 1941.

The colors still fly from the stern of the sunken battleship USS *West Virginia* after the attack on Pearl Harbor, December 7, 1941.

The USS *Arizona* burning after the attack on Pearl Harbor, December 7, 1941.

DRAFT No. 1   December 7, 1941.

PROPOSED MESSAGE TO THE CONGRESS

Yesterday, December 7, 1941, a date which will live in ~~world history~~ *infamy*

the United States of America was ~~simultaneously~~ *suddenly* and deliberately attacked

by naval and air forces of the Empire of Japan.

The United States was at the moment at peace with that nation and was

still in ~~continuing the~~ conversation with its Government and its Emperor looking

toward the maintenance of peace in the Pacific. Indeed, one hour after

Japanese air squadrons had commenced bombing in *Oahu* ~~Hawaii and the Philippines~~

the Japanese Ambassador to the United States and his colleague delivered

to the Secretary of State a formal reply to a ~~former~~ *recent American* message. ~~from the~~

~~Secretary.~~ *While* This reply ~~contained a statement~~ *stated* that diplomatic negotiations

~~must be considered at an end.~~ *it* ~~But~~ it contained no threat ~~and no~~ hint of ~~an~~ *or war or*

armed attack.

It will be recorded that the distance ~~of Hawaii, and especially~~ of

Hawaii, from Japan makes it obvious that the attack ~~were~~ *was* deliberately

planned many days ago. *or even weeks* During the intervening time the Japanese Govern-

ment has deliberately sought to deceive the United States by false

statements and expressions of hope for continued peace.

President Franklin D. Roosevelt signs the Declaration of War with Japan, December 8, 1941.

Annotated draft of President Roosevelt's "Day of Infamy" speech, page one, December 7, 1941.

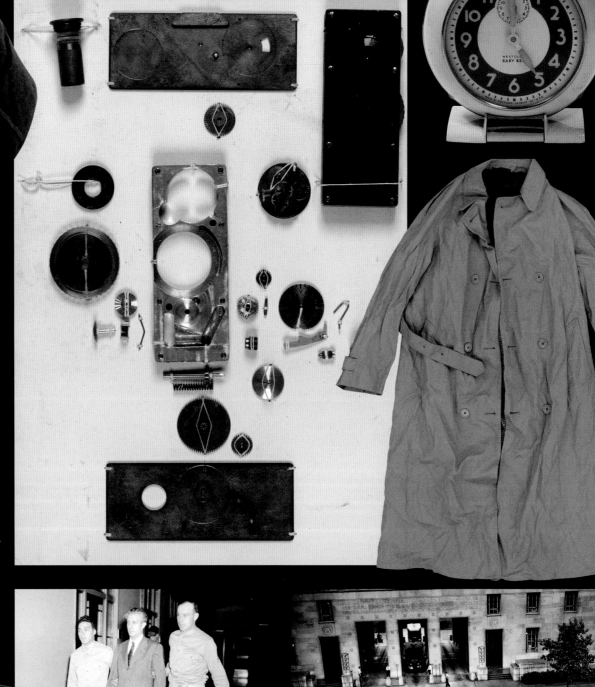

FBI officials found equipment and supplies, including this timing device and shovel, buried in the sand near drop-off points on New York and Florida beaches. These items, along with confiscated personal possessions, were used as evidence in the military tribunal against the saboteurs.

One of the saboteurs, Richard Quirin, entering the court, July 9, 1942.

Armored car and two prisoner vans leaving the Department of Justice Building, July 9, 1942.

Denying Certain Enemies Access to the Courts of the United States | **1942**

"...all persons...charged with committing...sabotage...shall be subject to the law of war and to the jurisdiction of military tribunals..."

DENYING CERTAIN ENEMIES ACCESS TO THE COURTS
OF THE UNITED STATES

BY THE PRESIDENT OF THE UNITED STATES OF AMERICA

A PROCLAMATION

WHEREAS the safety of the United States demands that all enemies who have entered upon the territory of the United States as part of an invasion or predatory incursion, or who have entered in order to commit sabotage, espionage or other hostile or warlike acts, should be promptly tried in accordance with the law of war;

NOW, THEREFORE, I, FRANKLIN D. ROOSEVELT, President of the United States of America and Commander in Chief of the Army and Navy of the United States, by virtue of the authority vested in me by the Constitution and the statutes of the United States, do hereby proclaim that all persons who are subjects, citizens or residents of any nation at war with the United States or who give obedience to or act under the direction of any such nation, and who during time of war enter or attempt to enter the United States or any territory or possession thereof, through coastal or boundary defenses, and are charged with committing or attempting or preparing to commit sabotage, espionage, hostile or warlike acts, or violations of the law of war, shall be subject to the law of war and to the jurisdiction of military tribunals; and that such persons shall not be privileged to seek any remedy or maintain any proceeding, directly or indirectly, or to have any such remedy or proceeding sought on their behalf, in the

- 2 -

United States, or of its States, territories, s, except under such regulations as the l, with the approval of the Secretary of ime to time prescribe.

WHEREOF I have hereunto set my hand and of the United States of America to be

City of Washington this 2xd day of July, in the
year of our Lord
nineteen hundred
and forty-two,
and of the
Independence
of the United
States of America
the one hundred and
sixty-sixth.

Franklin D. Roosevelt

Presidential Proclamation 2561, July 2, 1942.

"Roster of Residents" at Manzanar, California,
relocation camp, June 1, 1942–December 31, 1944.

Copy of "Conference with General De Witt" at Office
of Commanding General, page one, January 4, 1942.

HEADQUARTERS WESTERN DEFENSE COMMAND AND FOURTH ARMY
PRESIDIO OF SAN FRANCISCO, CALIFORNIA

OFFICE OF THE COMMANDING GENERAL

Conference in Office of General DeWitt: 4 January 1942

General, it wasn't so much telling you, as the Attorney General
come out here to see what we could do. I thought we could just talk about the
general problems - - -

Well, here's the situation. I might say that we are at war and this area—
8 states—has been designated as the theatre of operations. I have approximately 240,000
men at my disposal including Alaska. Of course, my Command extends from Dutch Harbor
to the Mexican border. There are two threats that we have to fact, and they are
serious threats. First, the presence of approximately 288,000 enemy aliens — or
alien enmies — which we have to watch. Of the two threats, I am concerned with
their seriousness to the large number of very important defense installations and
factories on the coast. Not necessarily the Navy yards, but primarily the aircraft
factories — Boeing up north, and a large number in the San Diego and Los Angeles
area. We are holding a large number of troops for the protection of those
installations. The threat is a constant one, and it is getting to be more dangerous
all the time. I have little confidence that the enemy aliens are law-abiding or
loyal in any sense of the word. Some of them, yes; many, no. Particularly the
Japanese. I have no confidence in their loyalty whatsoever. I am speaking now of
the native born Japanese—117,000—and 42,000 in California alone. In order to
meet that threat, we have got to do two things. We have got to be able to enter their
homes and premises, search and seize immediately without waiting for normal processes
of the law—obtaining a search warrant to make an arrest. So much of the President's
Proclamation, Paragraph 65?, Section 5 has been implemented only so far as pertains
to radios and cameras. What I want, Mr. Rowe, are two things: The centralization of
authority . . . . under the President's Proclamation. . . . . .the centralization
of authority in the FBI, to search, enter, and arrest without going to the United
States Attorney for a warrant every time. . . . . . In other words, blanket authority.

That is something I didn't know about. It is beyond my power to say that. That
is a legal problem that would have to be a matter of policy with the Attorney General.

. . . . .and full implementation of the President's Proclamation. . .
locate—the FCC or ourselves through our Intelligence . . . . we want to act at once
receiving set, we want to act at once
registration.

"All Japanese persons, both alien and non-alien, will be evacuated from the above designated area by 12:00 o'clock noon Tuesday, April 7, 1942."

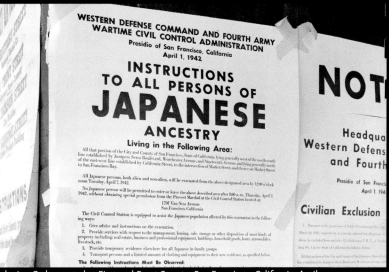

Relief map showing the location of Manzanar relocation camp, April 2, 1942.

Residents of Japanese ancestry at the Wartime Civil Control Administration Station, April 4, 1942.

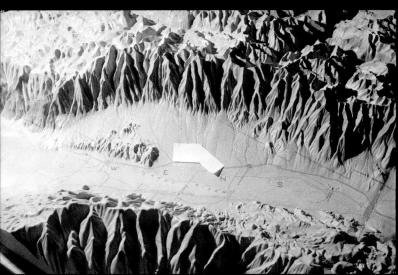

Exclusion Order posted at First and Front Streets, San Francisco, California, April 11, 1942.

Evacuees of Japanese ancestry entraining for Manzanar, California, ca. 1942–1945.

Memorial Day services at Manzanar, May 31, 1942.

View of barrack homes at Manzanar, June 30, 1942.

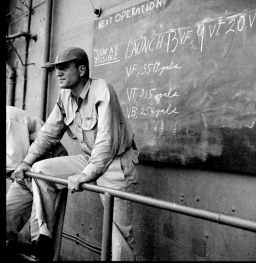

On board the USS *Saratoga* at dawn, November 1943.

Cdr. Roland Steiler oversees the launch of a raid on Rabaul.

Looking up at bridge from forward elevator.

Pilots walking toward their planes for Rabaul Raid.

Plane handlers.

Enlisted men with 30-caliber ammunition.

Lieutenant Besco gives starting signal.

Scout Bomber Douglas (SBD) leaving the deck of the carrier.

Planes flying in formation for raid on Rabaul.

Radar plot room.

Enlisted men listen to report on raid.

Giving cut signal to a torpedo bomber.

Cdr. J. C. Clifton just after he returned from raid.

Pilots report to the ACI officer after the mission.

SBD badly damaged by Japanese shell.

Wounded air crewman lifted out of aircraft.

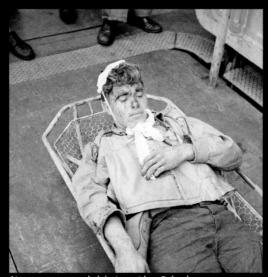
Air crewman wounded during raid on Rabaul.

Funeral services for two enlisted men.

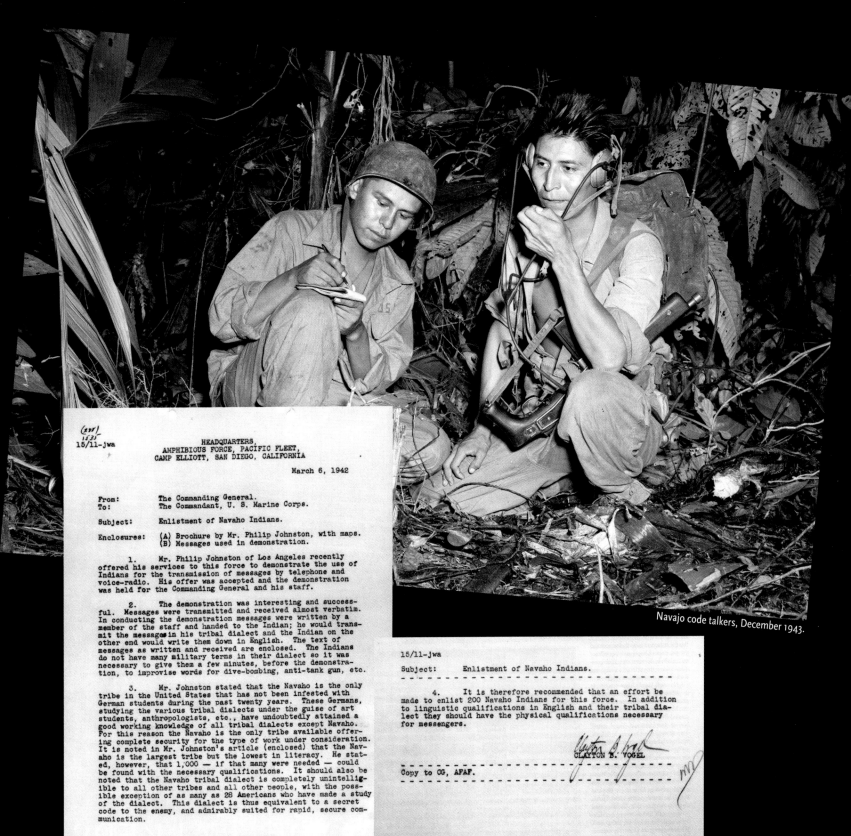

Navajo code talkers, December 1943.

(XXX)
15/11-jwa

HEADQUARTERS,
AMPHIBIOUS FORCE, PACIFIC FLEET,
CAMP ELLIOTT, SAN DIEGO, CALIFORNIA

March 6, 1942

From: The Commanding General.
To: The Commandant, U. S. Marine Corps.

Subject: Enlistment of Navaho Indians.

Enclosures: (A) Brochure by Mr. Philip Johnston, with maps.
            (B) Messages used in demonstration.

1. Mr. Philip Johnston of Los Angeles recently offered his services to this force to demonstrate the use of Indians for the transmission of messages by telephone and voice-radio. His offer was accepted and the demonstration was held for the Commanding General and his staff.

2. The demonstration was interesting and successful. Messages were transmitted and received almost verbatim. In conducting the demonstration messages were written by a member of the staff and handed to the Indian; he would transmit the messages in his tribal dialect and the Indian on the other end would write them down in English. The text of messages as written and received are enclosed. The Indians do not have many military terms in their dialect so it was necessary to give them a few minutes, before the demonstration, to improvise words for dive-bombing, anti-tank gun, etc.

3. Mr. Johnston stated that the Navaho is the only tribe in the United States that has not been infested with German students during the past twenty years. These Germans, studying the various tribal dialects under the guise of art students, anthropologists, etc., have undoubtedly attained a good working knowledge of all tribal dialects except Navaho. For this reason the Navaho is the only tribe available offering complete security for the type of work under consideration. It is noted in Mr. Johnston's article (enclosed) that the Navaho is the largest tribe but the lowest in literacy. He stated, however, that 1,000 — if that many were needed — could be found with the necessary qualifications. It should also be noted that the Navaho tribal dialect is completely unintelligible to all other tribes and all other people, with the possible exception of as many as 28 Americans who have made a study of the dialect. This dialect is thus equivalent to a secret code to the enemy, and admirably suited for rapid, secure communication.

15/11-jwa

Subject: Enlistment of Navaho Indians.

- -

4. It is therefore recommended that an effort be made to enlist 200 Navaho Indians for this force. In addition to linguistic qualifications in English and their tribal dialect they should have the physical qualifications necessary for messengers.

CLAYTON B. VOGEL

Copy to CG, AFAF.

Memorandum from General Vogel to commandant, USMC, March 6, 1942.

Officer gives pilots their "target for to-day" at a base in Italy, September 1944.

Pilots talk over the day's exploits, February 1944.

Armorer checks ammunition belts for a P-51 Mustang fighter plane, ca. September 1944.

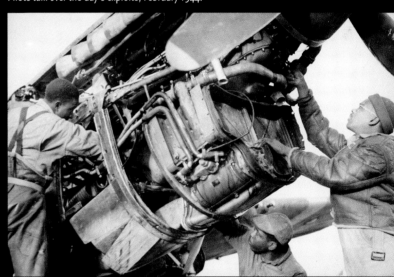
Mechanics of the 99th Fighter Squadron, ca. February 1944.

Signing in.

Mealtime in the cafeteria.

At work on a shell.

Payday.

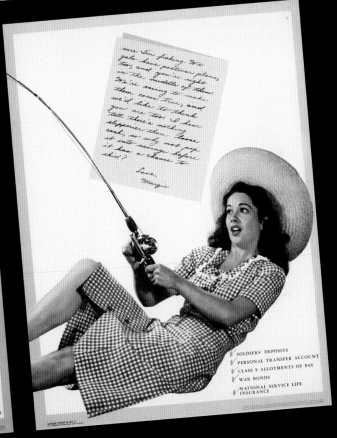

1944   **D-day**

"...saw a great portion of a United States airborne division...The enthusiasm, toughness and obvious fitness of every single man were high..."

Gen. Dwight Eisenhower speaks to U.S. paratroopers before the invasion, June 5, 1944.

U.S. troops wading through water and Nazi gunfire, June 6, 1944.

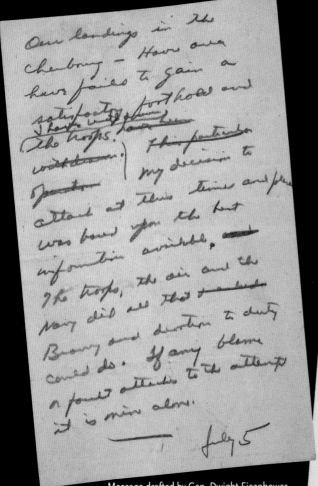

Message drafted by Gen. Dwight Eisenhower
in case the D-day invasion failed, June 5, 1944.

Cable to Gen. George C. Marshall regarding
D-day landings, June 6, 1944.

XTOP SECRET

SHAEF
STAFF MESSAGE CONTROL
INCOMING MESSAGE

XTOP SECRET

EYES ONLY

SHAEF CP

Filed 060800B June

SHAEF 83/06

TOR 060930B June

U R G E N T

FROM : SHAEF COMMAND POST, PERSONAL FROM GENERAL EISENHOWER

TO : AGWAR-TO GENERAL MARSHALL FOR HIS EYES ONLY; SHAEF FOR INFORMATION

REF NO : 90016, 6 June 1944

Local time is now 8 in the morning.

I have as yet no information concerning the actual landings nor of
our progress through beach obstacles. Communique will not be issued until we
have word that leading ground troops are actually ashore.

All preliminary reports are satisfactory. Airborne formations apparently landed in good order with losses out of approximately 1250 airplanes
participating about 30. Preliminary bombings by air went off as scheduled.
Navy reports sweeping some mines, but so far as is known channels are clear
and operation proceeding as planned. In early morning hours reaction from
shore batteries was sufficiently light that some of the naval spotting planes
have returned awaiting call.

The weather yesterday which was original date selected was impossible all along the target coast. Today conditions are vastly improved both by
sea and air and we have the prospect of at least reasonably favorable weather
for the next several days.

Yesterday, I visited British troops about to embark and last night
saw a great portion of a United States airborne division just prior to its
takeoff. The enthusiasm, toughness and obvious fitness of every single man
were high and the light of battle was in their eyes.

I will keep you informed.

DISTRIBUTION:

1. SUPREME COMMANDER

2. CHIEF OF STAFF

3. SGS

4. Gen. Strong (G-2)

DECLASSIFIED
DOD DIR. 5200.10, June 29, 1960
NE by WGL date 6-29-17

U.S. 1st Army observer on east bank of the Rhine looks down on Remagen Bridge, March 15, 1945.

First Lt. E. M. Borsuk (right) and Sgt. Gary Cronan prepare broadcast on Remagen Bridge.

Engineers putting down rails four hours before bridge collapsed into the Rhine, March 17, 1945.

East end of bridge, where several hundred engineers spilled into the Rhine when it collapsed.

Sketch of the Bridge at Remagen by Sgt. Eugene Dorland, 1945.

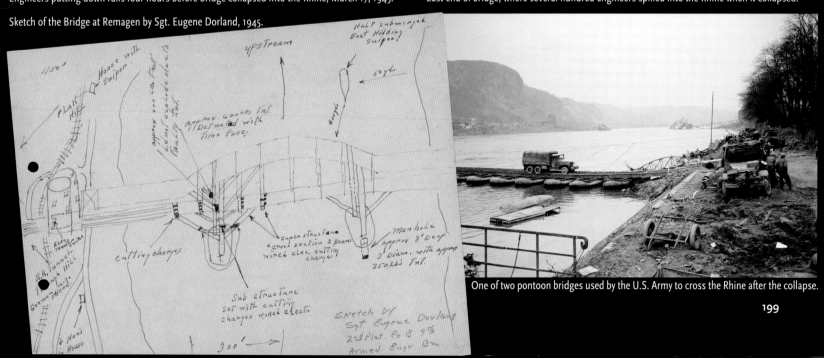

One of two pontoon bridges used by the U.S. Army to cross the Rhine after the collapse.

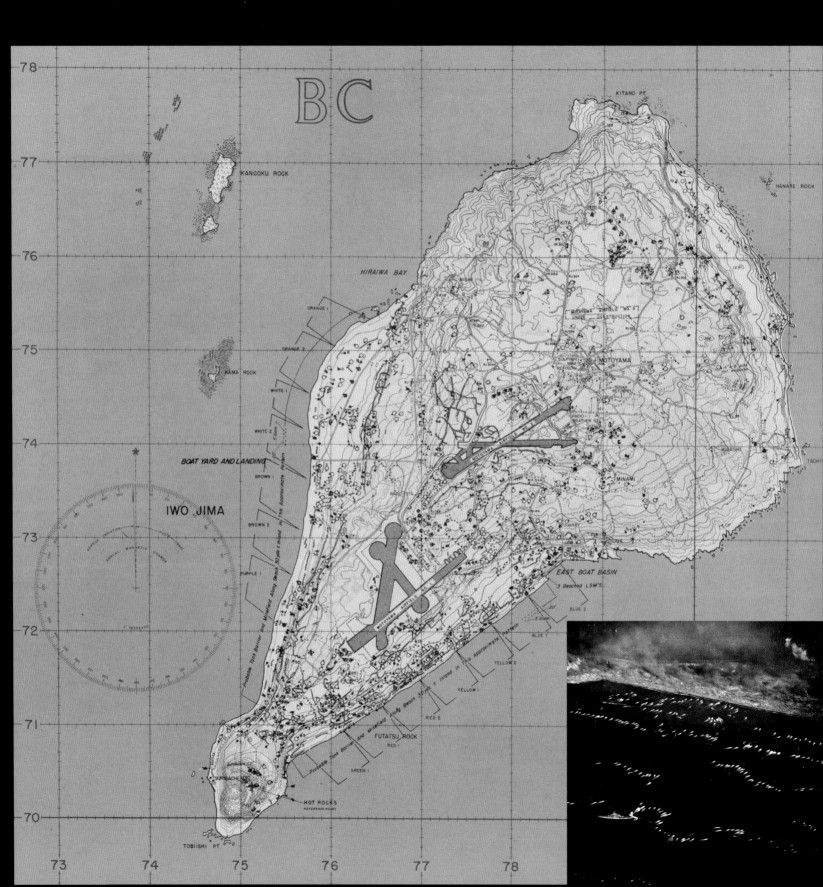

Map of Iwo Jima.

Aerial photo of Iwo Jima landing.

Marines of the 5th Division inch their way up a slope on Red Beach No.1, February 19, 1945.

Observer spots a machine gun nest and sends the information to artillery or mortars.

Capt. Edward J. Steichen, head of the Navy Photographic Unit, flies over Iwo Jima, March 1945.

Hand of Japanese soldier killed by a bomb blast on the island, March 1945.

Pvt. 1st class Rez P. Hester, 7th War Dog Platoon, naps while his war dog stands guard.

Marines shell Japanese positions.

U.S. flag waves in triumph over Iwo Jima.

Former prisoner of Buchenwald, Weimar, Germany.

American troops at the main entrance to Buchenwald.

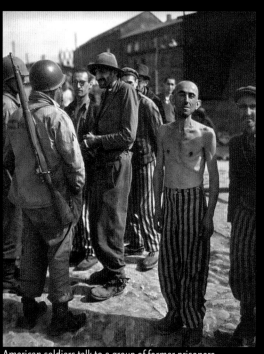

American soldiers talk to a group of former prisoners.

Former prisoner holds a human bone from crematory.

"The attached list...is said to be a complete list of all persons...who have balances with S.G.S...."

"Saphor Torahs" (Sacred Scrolls) found in a cellar of the
Race Institute in Frankfurt, Germany, July 6, 1945.

Rubens painting found in an underground cave in Siegen, Germany, 1945.

Report identifying mainly
Jewish depositors at a Swiss
financial institution and
listing their assets down
to the penny, pages one
and four, 1945.

USG-SWI-105

Bern, Switzerland

Reference: SH No. 74
Date: July 12, 1945

SECRET

No. 12100

SAFEHAVEN REPORT

Subject: Supplementary Report on Funds
Held for Others by Societe
General de Surveillance S.A.,
Geneva.

Reference is made to SAFEHAVEN Report No. 4 of April 9, 1945.
Attached hereto is a list of balances held by Societe General de
Surveillance S.A., Geneva for nationals who are also residents
of Rumania, Hungary, Bulgaria, Croatia, Moravia, Slovakia, France,
Holland, and Denmark. It will be seen from the attached list that
the balances held for nationals who are also residents of the
named countries total:

Swiss Francs	9,506,073.62
French Francs	250,000.00
Belgian Francs	31,282.08
Francs Gold (no further	
description	182,100.00
	17,739-4-17
British Sterling	291.68
Canadian Dollars	119,020.64
U.S. Dollars	599.22
Florin	5,162.60
Slovakia Cr.	1,400,000.00
Rumania Nom. Lei	500,000.00
Greek Drachmas	10,069.00
Kuna	

and one safety deposit box for which no
value can be attributed at this time.

The attached list represents certain amendments to the
list appended to SAFEHAVEN Report No. 4 suggested by our
informants, and also includes additional information in regard
to other balances not heretofore reported. The attached list,
which contains more detailed information relative to the property
held than the earlier one, is said to be a complete list of all
persons who are nationals and also residents of the countries named
who have balances with S.G.S., except that for practical reasons
later compilations omit balances below Swiss francs 10,000.
Furthermore, it may be noted that we are advised that we now have
a complete list of all accounts held by S.G.S. for all persons who are
nationals and residents of countries which are of interest except
Germany.

While./

USG-SWI-105

COPY
eb

Enclosure No. 1 to Despatch No. 12100 (SH No. 74)
dated July 12, 1945, from the American Legation Bern.

ROUMANIE

		Soldes crediteurs
M. Adler, Bucarest		
Mondy Agent, Bucarest	FrS	22,018.35
Agraproduct, Bucarest c/bloque (vente		44,219.70
432 T. pois par W. Lundig & Co.		
Zurich		
Agraproduct, Bucarest c/financier	"	330,110.00
Leo Alpern, Bucarest	"	493,095.67
Arion Samuel, Bucarest	"	14,123.00
Mihail Atias, Bucarest	"	20,703.90
Mme. Cocutza M. Bach, Bucarest	"	5,000.00
Leon Balian, Bucarest	"	43,989.10
Leon Balian, Bucarest	¥	1,591.75
Leon Balian, Constantza (actions	FrS	400.55 (debit)
Selecta SAR, Bucarest)		
Balian & Co. S.A. Bucarest	Nom.Lei	1,400,000.00
Balian & Co. S.A. Bucarest	Frs	4,557.40
Anil Neumann Borcovici, Braila	Fbg	31,282.08
Arikor Bouhartzian, Bucarest	FrS	15,772.05
Alexandru P. Bratuloscu, Bucarest	"	9,993.30
Serban Salviny Cappon, Bucarest	"	9,992.80
Jancu Chitzos, Bucarest	"	3,000.00
Jancu Chitzos, Bucarest	¥	5,953.05
Ing. Andrei V. Chrissogholos No.567	FrS	3,013.66
Ing. Andrei V. Chrissogholos No.936	"	54,850.50
Companie Cific S.A. Bucarest	"	579,263.50
H. Cohl, Bucarest	"	36,780.53
D. Constantinoscu, Bucarest	"	9,974.60
D. Constantinoscu, Bucarest c/Depot Francs OR		7,580.00
Ernst Ozollen, Bucarest	Frs	205,312.25
Ernst Ozollen, Bucarest	¥	3,800.00
Const. A. Dimitropol, Bucarest	FrS	1,270.36
Eug. Dornholm, Timisoara	"	8,100.00
"Ergedo" Radu G. Dumitroscu, Bucarest	"	35,000.00
S.A.R. de Transporturi Egor, Bucarest	"	3,272.65
S.A.R. de Transporturi Egor, Bucarest		258,381.05
c/bloque	"	
S.A.R. de Transporturi Egor, Bucarest		10,500.00
(en billets de banque)		
Adolph J. Ellenbogen, Bucarest	Ffrs	250,000.00
Extorna. S.A., Bucarest	FrS	5,925.80
Constantin Foltoianu, Bucarest	"	1,600.00
Mme Adela Foldman, Bucarest	"	523,919.14
Isaac Feldstein, Bucarest c/927	"	25,000.00
Isaac Feldstein, Bucarest c/bloque	¥	736,792.60
Isaac Feldstein, Bucarest	"	19,444.38
Isaac Feldstein, Bucarest		130.00

203

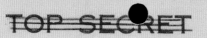 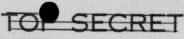

SHAEF FORWARD

STAFF MESSAGE CONTROL

OUTGOING MESSAGE

T O P   S E C R E T

U R G E N T

TO	: AGWAR FOR COMBINED CHIEFS OF STAFF, AMSSO FOR BRITISH CHIEFS OF STAFF
FROM	: SHAEF FORWARD, SIGNED EISENHOWER
REF NO	: FWD-20798 TOO: 070325B

SCAF 355

The mission of this Allied Force was fulfilled at 0241, local time, May 7th, 1945.

EISENHOWER.

ORIGINATOR   : SUPREME COMMANDER   AUTHENTICATION: J B MOORE, Lt Colonel

INFORMATION   : TO ALL GENERAL AND SPECIAL STAFF DIVISIONS

SGS Dist	COPY No.
Sc	1/2
DSC	3
GS	
DCS	
CAO	
DCS AIR	
SGS	4
COOR	5
M	6
	7
	8/9
M	10

FS OUT 3674   7 MAY 1945   0324B   JOB/jg   REF NO: FWD-20798
TOO: 070325B
COPY NO.

THE MAKING OF AN EXACT COPY OF THIS MESSAGE IS FORBIDDEN

General Eisenhower's telegram to Allied chiefs of staff, declaring the end of war in Europe, May 7, 1945.

Smoke billows over Hiroshima, August 6, 1945.

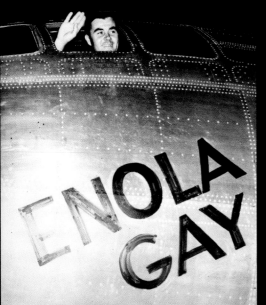

Col. Paul W. Tibbetts, Jr., pilot of the *Enola Gay*, August 6, 1945.

WHITE HOUSE
MAP ROOM

~~TOP SECRET~~   6 August 1945

FROM: ADMIRAL EDWARDS
TO : ADMIRAL LEAHY (EYES ONLY)
NR : 334

        Following information regarding MANHATTAN received:

        "Hiroshima bombed visually with only 1-10th cover at 052315Z. There was no fighter opposition and no flak. Parsons reports fifteen minutes after drop as follows:

        'Results clear cut successful in all respects. Visible effects greater than any test. Conditions normal in airplane following delivery.'"

RECD: 061445Z

Telegram reporting the
dropping of the atomic
bomb on Hiroshima,
August 6, 1945.

One of the two green
safety plugs used on
the Nagasaki bomb,
August 9, 1945.

10 Aug 45
Tinian Island
    I certify that this
is one of the two Green
Safety Plugs used on F-33
at Nagasaki, Japan on
9 August 1945. This was
the second Atomic Bomb
dropped on the Empire.

F L Ashworth
Cdr. USN.

Philip M. Barnes

Railroad tracks running past the houses and company store, Welch, West Virginia, August 13, 1946.

Children playing among typical houses, Gilliam, West Virginia, August 13, 1946.

Miners at the wash house ready for work, Gary, West Virginia, August 16, 1946.

The mantrip going into the mine, Gilliam, West Virginia, August 16, 1946.

S.2202, a bill to promote the general welfare, national interest, and foreign policy of the United States, February 26, 1948.

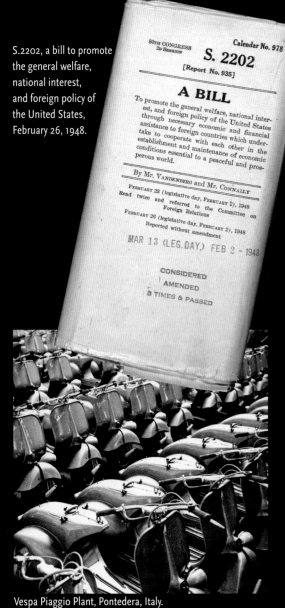

Discussing the Marshall Plan, November 29, 1948.

Worker in West Berlin, Germany.

Vespa Piaggio Plant, Pontedera, Italy.

Consett Steel Plant, Consett, England.

Shipping bauxite, Greece.

Harbor at Marseille, France.

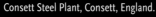

Producing a new car, known as the "Marshall Plan Baby," Italy.

Thomson-Houston Factory, London, England.

Reclaiming the Zuider Zee, Netherlands.

A hydro-electric project under construction, Portugal.

Coal import, Denmark.

Fishing industry, Ostende, Belgium.

Austin A. 40s, Longbridge works, Birmingham, England.

New housing, Greece.

Textile plant, Portugal.

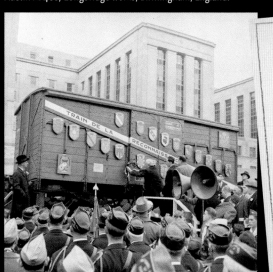

"Merci train," a gift from France, February 6, 1949.

Letter of thanks from German school children, 1948.

Ronald Regan

RONALD REAGAN:

    This individual is presently President of the Screen Actors
Guild. He has no fear of any one, is a nice talker, well informed
on the subject, and will make a spendid witness. He is of course
reticent to testify, because he states that he is a New Deal Liberal,
and does not agree with a number of individuals in the Motion Picture
Alliance. I believe we straightened out a number of his differences,
in that he felt Menjou and some of the others referred to him, Reagan,
as a man who had been a Leftist and then reformed. Reagan resents
this very much, as he states he never was a Leftist, that actually
he got tangled up with a few committees that he thought were all right,

but it took him some time to learn that they were not. As soon
as he discovered that fact, he got out of them.

    I think that that is absolutely correct. I happen to have
been raised in the same town with Reagan, and know him very well,
and because of that fact he opened up and talked to me very freely,
and he will go to Washington if we request him to do so. I think
we should have him there.

    We will have to be very careful about instances like this,
however, as when we talked to Reagan, he felt that Jim McGuinness is
a professional Red-baiter. However, when we explained McGuinness'
position to him, he admitted he was probably wrong, that he did not
personally know Mr. McGuinness, and had just drawn erroneous conclusions from promiscuous statements made by other individuals.

FROM / REPORT OF SMITH

SEPT 2, 1947

Capt. Charles E. Yeager, Pilot's Notes, 9th Powered Flight, October 14, 1947

"Acceleration was rapid and speed increased to .98 Mach1."

1947

C O P Y

P I L O T S   N O T E S   ~~SECRET~~

DECLASSIFIED

Date: 14 October 1947

Pilot: Capt. Charles E. Yeager   003057

Time: 14 Minutes

　　　　9th Powered Flight

1. After normal pilot entry and the subsequent climb, the XS 1 was dropped from the B 29 at 20,000' and at 250 MPH IAS. This was slower than desired.

2. Immediately after drop, all four cylinders were turned on in rapid sequence, their operation stabilizing at the chamber and line pressures reported in the last flight. The ensuing climb was made at .85-.88 Mach$_1$, and, as usual, it was necessary to change the stabilizer setting to 2 degrees nose down from its pre drop setting of 1 degree nose down. Two cylinders were turned off between 35,000' and 40,000' but speed had increased to .92 Mach$_1$ as the airplane was leveled off at 42,000'. Incidentally, during the slight push over at this altitude, the lox line pressure dropped perhaps 40 psi and the resultant rich mixture caused the chamber pressures to decrease slightly. The effect was only momentary, occurring at .6 G's and all pressures returned to normal at 1 G.

3. In anticipation of the decrease in elevator effectiveness at speeds above .93 Mach$_1$, longitudinal control by means of the stabilizer was tried during the climb at .83, .88, and .92 Mach$_1$. The stabilizer was moved in increments of 1/4 - 1/3 degree and proved to be very effective; also, no change in effectiveness was noticed at the different speeds.

4. At 42,000' in approximately level flight, a third cylinder was turned on. Acceleration was rapid and speed increased to .98 Mach$_1$. The needle of the machmeter fluctuated at this reading momentarily, then passed off the scale. Assuming that the off scale reading remained linear, it is estimated that 1.05 Mach$_1$ was attained at this time. Approximately 30% of fuel and lox remained when this speed was reached and the motor was turned off.

5. While the usual light buffet and instability characteristics were encountered in the .88-90 Mach$_1$ range, and elevator effectiveness was very greatly decreased at .94 Mach$_1$, stability about all three axes was good as speed increased and elevator effectiveness was regained above .97 Mach$_1$. As speed decreased after turning off the motor, the various phenomena occurred in reverse sequence at the usual speeds, and in addition, a slight longitudinal porpoising was noticed from .98-96 Mach$_1$ which controllable by the elevators alone. Incidentally, the stabilizer setting was not changed from its 2 degrees nose down position after trial at .92 Mach$_1$.

6. After jettisoning the remaining fuel and lox a 1 G stall was performed at 45,000'. The flight was concluded by the subsequent glide and a normal landing on the lake bed.

　　　　　　　　　　　/s/

Copied 11/14/50   CHARLES E. YEAGER
File 1 copy XS 1 pilot's notes   Capt., Air Corps.
　　1 copy Computers

Capt. Charles Yeager's pilot's notes for the first flight
to break the sound barrier, October 14, 1947.

Captain Yeager in the cockpit of the Bell X-1, May 1948.

anding craft loaded with U.S. Marines head for the smoking beach of Inchon, September 15, 1950.

Marines in landing crafts with scaling ladders head for the seawall at Inchon.

n Inchon beach.

Flag raised at U.S. consulate in Seoul, as fighting for the city raged, September 27, 1950.

Marines move forward after close-air support has flushed out the enemy, Hagaru-ri, December 1950.

Marines near Chosin Reservoir, withdraw after hurling back a Chinese onslaught, December 1950.

U.S. Marines pay their respects to the fallen, 1st Marine Division cemetery, Hamhung, Korea.

PROPOSED ORDER TO GENERAL MacARTHUR TO BE SIGNED BY THE PRESIDENT

I deeply regret that it becomes my duty as President and Commander in Chief of the United States military forces to replace you as Supreme Commander, Allied Powers; Commander in Chief, United Nations Command; Commander in Chief, Far East; and Commanding General, U. S. Army, Far East.

You will turn over your commands, effective at once, to Lt. Gen. Matthew B. Ridgway. You are authorized to have issued such orders as are necessary to complete desired travel to such place as you select.

My reasons for your replacement, ~~which~~ will be made public concurrently with the delivery to you of the foregoing order, ~~will be communicated to you by Secretary Pace.~~ and are *contained in the next following message.*

Harry Truman

PROPOSED STATEMENT BY THE PRESIDENT

With deep regret I have concluded that General of the Army Douglas MacArthur is unable to give his wholehearted support to the policies of the United States Government and of the United Nations in matters pertaining to his official duties. In view of the specific responsibilities imposed upon me by the Constitution of the United States and the added responsibility which has been entrusted to me by the United Nations, I have decided that I must make a change of command in the Far East. I have, therefore, relieved General MacArthur of his commands and have designated Lt. Gen. Matthew B. Ridgway as his successor.

Full and vigorous debate on matters of national policy is a vital element in the constitutional system of our free democracy. It is fundamental, however, that military commanders must be governed by the policies and directives issued to them in the manner provided by our laws and Constitution. In time of crisis, this consideration is particularly compelling.

General MacArthur's place in history as one of our greatest commanders is fully established. The nation owes him a debt of gratitude for the distinguished and exceptional service which he has rendered his country in posts of great responsibility. For that reason I repeat my regret at the necessity for the action I feel compelled to take in his case.

HST

Proposed order to General MacArthur, April 1951.

Proposed statement by the President, April 1951.

Former President Harry Truman in the reproduction of the Oval Office at the Truman Library, ca. July 1959.

"The Buck Stops Here" sign.

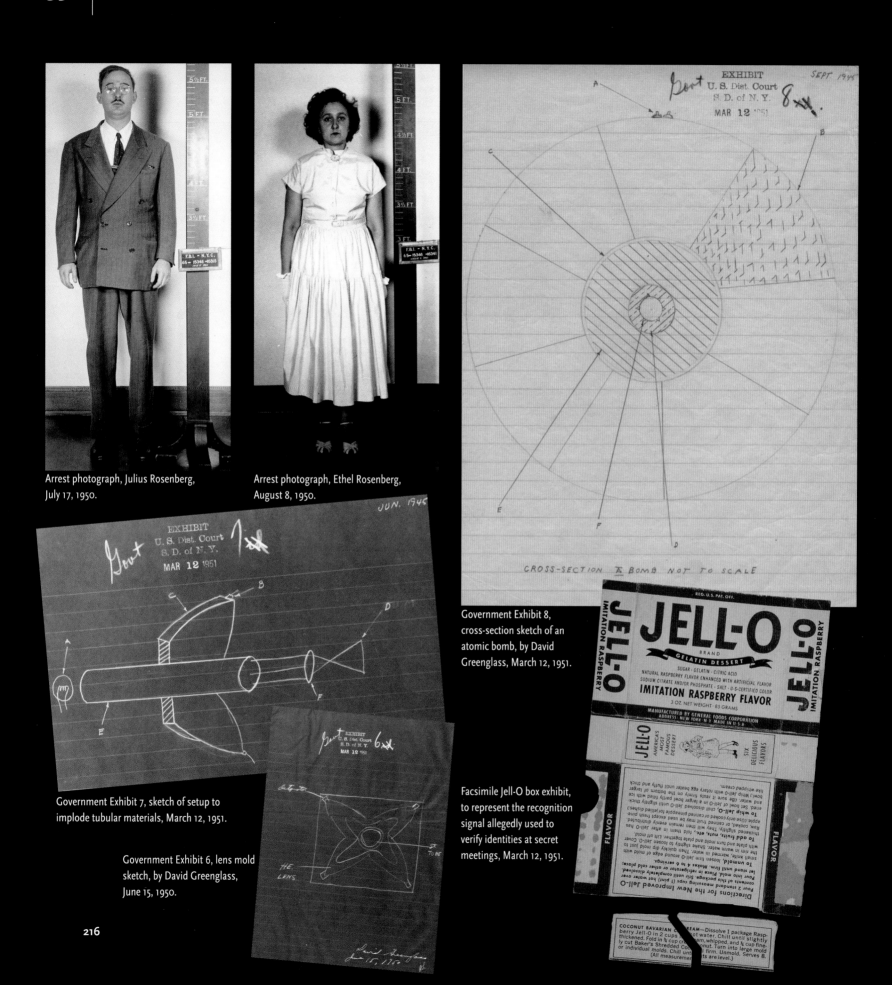

Arrest photograph, Julius Rosenberg, July 17, 1950.

Arrest photograph, Ethel Rosenberg, August 8, 1950.

Government Exhibit 8, cross-section sketch of an atomic bomb, by David Greenglass, March 12, 1951.

Government Exhibit 7, sketch of setup to implode tubular materials, March 12, 1951.

Government Exhibit 6, lens mold sketch, by David Greenglass, June 15, 1950.

Facsimile Jell-O box exhibit, to represent the recognition signal allegedly used to verify identities at secret meetings, March 12, 1951.

UNCLASSIFIED

CONFIDENTIAL

8. IF you saw the object at NIGHT, TWILIGHT, or DAWN, what did you notice concerning the STARS and MOON?

8.1 STARS (Circle One):
- a. None
- b. A few
- c. Many
- d. Don't remember

8.2 MOON (Circle One):
- a. Bright moonlight
- b. Dull moonlight
- c. No moonlight — pitch dark
- d. Don't remember

9. Was the object brighter than the background of the sky?

(Circle One):   a. Yes   b. No   c. Don't remember

10. IF it was BRIGHTER THAN the sky background, was the brightness like that of an automobile headlight?:

(Circle One) a. A mile or more away (a distant car)?
b. Several blocks away?
c. A block away?
d. Several yards away?
e. Other _____

11. Did the object: (Circle One for each question)

a. Appear to stand still at any time?	Yes	No	Don't Know
b. Suddenly speed up and rush away at any time?	Yes	No	Don't Know
c. Break up into parts or explode?	Yes	No	Don't Know
d. Give off smoke?	Yes	No	Don't Know
e. Change brightness?	Yes	No	Don't Know
f. Change shape?	Yes	No	Don't Know
j. Flicker, throb, or pulsate?	Yes	No	Don't Know

12. Did the object move behind something at anytime, particularly a cloud?

(Circle One):   Yes   No   Don't Know.   IF you answered YES, then tell what
it moved behind: _____

13. Did the object move in front of something at anytime, particularly a cloud?

(Circle One):   Yes   No   Don't Know.   IF you answered YES, than tell what
it moved in front of: _____

14. Did the object appear:

15. Did you observe
- a. Eyeglass
- b. Sun glass
- c. Windshie
- d. Window g

Project Blue Book Status
Report Number Eight,
selected pages,
December 31, 1952.

DECLASSIFIED
NND 923007
____ NARA, Date 5/7/03

CONFIDENTIAL

UNCLASSIFIED

Category	No. Reports	% Total
D. September		
Unknown		
Insufficient Data	22	27.85
Aircraft	20	25.32
Balloons	7	8.86
Astronomical	12	15.19
Other	12	15.19
	6	7.59
	79	100.00%
E. Cumulative total for June, July, August, and September		
Unknown		
Insufficient Data	206	23.25
Aircraft	216	24.38
Balloons	101	11.39
Astronomical	211	23.81
Other	113	12.75
	39	4.40
	886	100.00%

: No breakdown for the month of October 1952 is included since at the
this report was written all October reports had not been evaluated.)

PECIAL REPORT ON CONFERENCE WITH 44 PROFESSIONAL ASTRONOMERS

uring the past summer a professional astronomer, under contract with
a consultant on Project Blue Book, held conferences with 44 profes-
astronomers in the U.S.A. and submitted a report of his findings.
eople were either contacted on trips or at professional society meet-
f these, 5 had observed objects or phenomena they could not readily
The feelings of the 44 astronomers toward the investigation of un-
d flying objects were as follows:

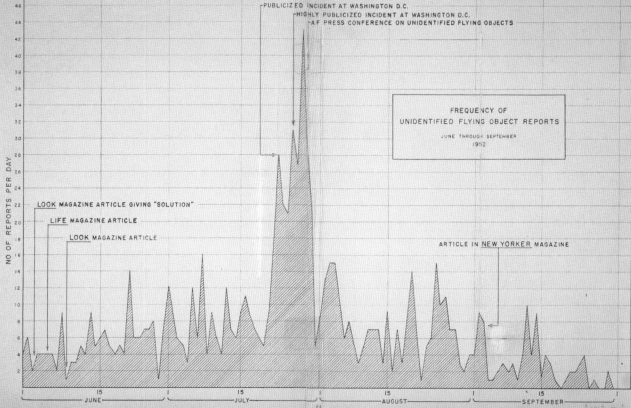

PUBLICIZED INCIDENT AT WASHINGTON D.C.

HIGHLY PUBLICIZED INCIDENT AT WASHINGTON D.C.

AF PRESS CONFERENCE ON UNIDENTIFIED FLYING OBJECTS

FREQUENCY OF
UNIDENTIFIED FLYING OBJECT REPORTS
JUNE THROUGH SEPTEMBER
1952

LOOK MAGAZINE ARTICLE GIVING "SOLUTION"

LIFE MAGAZINE ARTICLE

LOOK MAGAZINE ARTICLE

ARTICLE IN NEW YORKER MAGAZINE

NO OF REPORTS PER DAY

JUNE   JULY   AUGUST   SEPTEMBER

Appendix I to Project Blue Book Status Report Number Eight, 1952.

The Declaration of Independence and the Constitution arrive at the National Archives, December 13, 1952.

President Harry Truman and other dignitaries at the dedication of the new display of the Charters of Freedom, December 15, 1952.

JUVENILE DELINQUENCY
(COMIC BOOKS)

HEARINGS
BEFORE THE
SUBCOMMITTEE TO INVESTIGATE
JUVENILE DELINQUENCY
OF THE
COMMITTEE ON THE JUDICIARY
UNITED STATES SENATE
EIGHTY-THIRD CONGRESS
SECOND SESSION
PURSUANT TO

S. 190

INVESTIGATION OF JUVENILE DELINQUENCY IN THE
UNITED STATES

APRIL 21, 22, AND JUNE 4, 1954

Printed for the use of the Committee on the Judiciary

UNITED STATES
GOVERNMENT PRINTING OFFICE
WASHINGTON : 1954

---

44   JUVENILE DELINQUENCY

CRITERIA FOR EVALUATING COMIC BOOKS

I. CULTURAL AREA

No objection
1. Good art work, printing, and color arrangement.
2. Good diction.
3. The overall effect pleasing.
4. Any situation that does not offend good taste from the viewpoint of art or mechanics.

Some objection
1. Poor art work, printing, and color arrangement.
2. Mechanical setup injurious to children's eyes; print too small; art work crowded.
3. Poor grammar and underworld slang.
4. Undermining in any way traditional American folkways.

Objectionable
1. Propaganda against or belittling traditional American institutions.
2. Obscenity, vulgarity, profanity, or the language of the underworld.
3. Prejudice against class, race, creed, or nationality.
4. Divorce treated humorously or as glamorous.
5. Sympathy with crime and the criminal as against law and justice.
6. Criminals and criminal acts made attractive.

Very objectionable
1. An exaggerated degree of any of the above-mentioned acts or scenes.

II. MORAL AREA

No objection
1. An uplifting plot.
2. Wholesome characters.
3. Characters dressed properly for the situation.
4. If crime, when it enters the plot, is incidental.
5. Any situation that does not compromise good morals.

Some objection
1. Criminal acts or moral violations even if given legal punishment.
2. The presence of criminals, even if they are not shown as enjoying their crimes.

Objectionable
1. Women as gun molls, criminals, and the wielders of weapons.
2. Any situation having a sexy implication.
3. Persons dressed indecently or unduly exposed (costumes not appropriate to the occasion).
4. Crime stories, even if they purport to show that crime does not pay.
5. Stories that glamorize criminals.
6. Situations that glamorize unconventional behavior.
7. The details or methods of crime, especially if enacted by children.
8. Thwarted justice.
9. Law-enforcement officials portrayed as stupid or ineffective.

Very objectionable
1. An exaggerated degree of any of the above-mentioned acts or scenes.

III. MORBID EMOTIONALITY

No objection
1. Any situation that does not arouse morbid emotionality in children.

Some objection
1. Overrealistic portrayal of death of villains.
2. Grotesque, fantastic, unnatural creatures.
3. Imminent death of a hero or heroine.

Objectionable
1. The kidnaping of women or children, or the implication of it.
2. Characters shown bleeding, particularly from the face or mouth.

Picture Progress
FEBRUARY 1954

Comic books evaluated for their suitability for children as part of the U.S. Senate investigation.

Hernandez v. Texas

"...all persons were excluded who are of Mexican or Latin American descent..."

Supreme Court Petition
for Writ of Certiorari in
Pete Hernandez v.
The State of Texas,
October Term, 1952.

THE SUPREME COURT OF THE UNITED STATES

OCTOBER TERM, 1952

406

NO. ~~346-Misc.~~

RECEIVED
JAN 21 1953
OFFICE OF THE CLERK
SUPREME COURT, U.S.

PETE HERNANDEZ, Petitioner

Vs.

THE STATE OF TEXAS, Respondent

Cross examination in "Motion to
Quash Jury Panel," *State of Texas* v.
Pete Hernandez, October 1951.

"Motion to Quash Jury Panel" in
State of Texas v. *Pete Hernandez,*
October 1951.

1608

CERTIORARI TO
OF THE STATE

NO. 2091

IN THE DISTRICT COURT
OF JACKSON COUNTY,
TEXAS

THE STATE OF TEXAS
VS.
PETE HERNANDEZ

MOTION TO QUASH JURY PANEL *filed october 4, 1951*

Now comes PETE HERNANDEZ, Defendant in the above-styled and
numbered cause and files this, his motion to quash the entire panel
of petit jurors selected by the Jury Commissioners for the following reasons:

Motion to
Quash Jury
Panel
Filed Oct.
4, 1951 at
9:45 A. M.

I.

The said panel was improperly selected in that from said Grand
Jury Commissioners all persons were excluded who are of Mexican
or Latin American descent or belonging to a class known as
"Mexicans". That the Defendant herein is of Mexican descent and
that persons of his national origin or class have been systematically, intentionally and deliberately excluded from Jury Commissions and Grand Juries. That there are persons of the
Defendant's national origin or class who are citizens of Jackson
County, Texas and are qualified to serve as Jury Commissioners
but they have never been given an opportunity to do so and that
the Defendant has been denied and is being denied the equal protection of the laws.

II.

In support of the foregoing Defendant would snow the Court that
people of his national origin or class are, on the whole, of a low
economic level and considered members of a distinct race, separate
and apart from the other citizens of Jackson County and that by
reason of this fact Defendant is not afforded a trial by jury of his
peers, and is deprived of his constitutional rights guaranteed by
the Fourteenth Amendment to the Federal Constitution.

III.

Defendant would further show the Court that not only are persons of Mexican descent excluded from the Jury Commission but that
they are otherwise treated as members of an inferior race, are
denied services in many public places in Jackson County and for

7

48

Mexican or Latin American descent?

A We did not.

CROSS EXAMINATION

Questions by Mr. Garcia:

Q You are a native of this County?

A I have been here almost 33 years.

Q You know, of course, there is a certain percentage of people
of Mexican or Latin American descent that are residents of
Jackson County?

A Yes, sir.

Q By the same token matters that come before the Grand Jury often
they affect people of Mexican or Latin American descent?

A As I said, we find all nationalities have misdemeanors or
felonies and disobey the law.

Q No particular racial or nationality group has a monopoly?

A That is right.

Q However, because of the fact that Spanish is the native tongue
of these people wouldn't it occur to you that possibly having
a person who speaks Spanish on the Grand Jury would be of benefit?

A Well, to my knowledge, that was not discussed.

Q You do know, of course, there are many people of Mexican or
Latin American descent in this County who don't speak any
English at all?

A Yes, sir. In fact, I know quite a few myself that don't under-

85

Supreme Court of the United States

No. 1 ——— , *October Term, 19* 54

Oliver Brown, Mrs. Richard Lawton, Mrs. Sadie Emmanuel et al.,

Appellants,

vs.

Board of Education of Topeka, Shawnee County, Kansas, et al.

Appeal from *the United States District Court for the* ————————————
District of Kansas.

This cause *came on to be heard on the transcript of the record from the United States*
District Court for the ————————— *District of* Kansas, ——————————
and was argued by counsel.

On consideration whereof, *It is ordered and adjudged by this Court that the judgment*
of the said District ————————— *Court in this cause be, and the same is*
hereby, reversed with costs; and that this cause be, and the same
is hereby, remanded to the said District Court to take such
proceedings and enter such orders and decrees consistent with
the opinions of this Court as are necessary and proper to admit
to public schools on a racially nondiscriminatory basis with all
deliberate speed the parties to this case.

Per Mr. Chief Justice Warren,

May 31, 1955.

Supreme Court Judgment, May 31, 1955.

British and Canadian observers, Nevada test site, April 15, 1955.

Two-story wooden frame house, Operation Cue, May 5, 1955.

The frame house after the Operation Cue blast, May 5, 1955.

Mannequins after a thermal radiation test for Operation Cue.

Troops of the U.S. Army 11th Airborne Division watch a plume of radioactive smoke after an atomic bomb test at Yucca Flats, May 1, 1952.

Fallout shelter built by Louis Severance adjacent to his home near Akron, Michigan, ca. 1960.

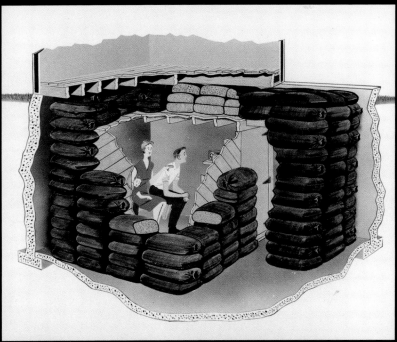

Artist's rendition of a temporary basement fallout shelter, ca. 1957.

Civil defense poster, 1953.

Students learn the theory of radiation and the use of
monitoring instruments, Davenport, Iowa, ca. 1960.

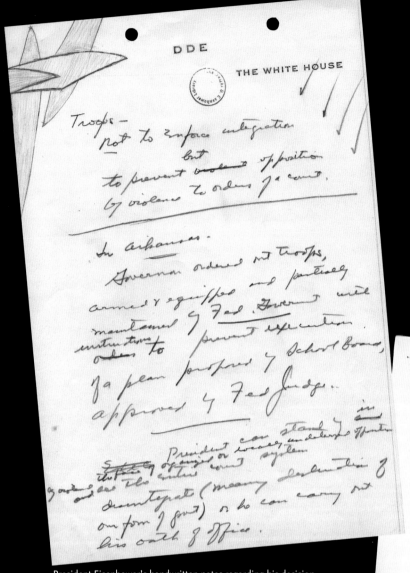

President Eisenhower's handwritten notes regarding his decision to send Federal troops into Little Rock, Arkansas, September 1957.

President Eisenhower speaking to the nation, September 24, 1957.

Draft of President Dwight D. Eisenhower's speech during the Little Rock crisis, page one, September 24, 1957.

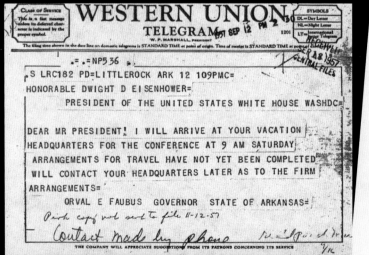

Telegram from Governor Orval Faubus to President Eisenhower, September 12, 1957.

"...your action in safe guarding their rights have strengthened our faith in democracy."

President Eisenhower at a White House meeting to discuss civil rights issues, June 23, 1958.

RECEIVED
OCT - 7 1957
The White CENTRAL FILES
Washington

WA037 NL PD

LITTLE ROCK ARK SEP 30   1957 OCT 1   AM 7 43

THE PRESIDENT

THE WHITE HOUSE

WE THE PARENTS OF NINE NEGRO CHILDREN ENROLLED AT LITTLE
ROCK CENTRAL HIGH SCHOOL WANT YOU TO KNOW THAT YOUR
ACTION IN SAFE GUARDING THEIR RIGHTS HAVE STRENGTHENED
OUR FAITH IN DEMOCRACY STOP NOW AS NEVER BEFORE WE HAVE
AN ABIDING FEELING OF BELONGING AND PURPOSEFULNESS STOP
WE BELIEVE THAT FREEDOM AND EQUALITY WITH WHICH ALL MEN

ARE ENDOWED AT BIRTH CAN BE MAINTAINED ONLY THROUGH
FREEDOM AND EQUALITY OF OPPORTUNITY FOR SELF DEVELOPMENT
GROWTH AND PURPOSEFUL CITIZENSHIP STOP WE BELIEVE THAT
THE DEGREE TO WHICH PEOPLE EVERYWHERE REALIZE AND ACCEPT
THIS CONCEPT WILL DETERMINE IN A LARGE MEASURE AMERICAS
TRUE GROWTH AND TRUE GREATNESS STOP YOU HAVE DEMONSTRATED
ADMIRABLY TO US THE NATION AND THE WORLD HOW PROFOUNDLY
YOU BELIEVE IN THIS CONCEPT STOP FOR THIS WE ARE DEEPLY
GRATEFUL AND RESPECTFULLY EXTEND TO YOU OUR HEARTFELT
AND LASTING THANKS STOP MAY THE ALMIGHTY AND ALL WISE

Three-page telegram to President Eisenhower
from the parents of the nine Little Rock African
American students, October 1, 1957.

FATHER OF US ALL BLESS GUIDE AND KEEP YOU ALWASY
OSCAR ECKFORD JR 4405 WEST 18TH LOTHAIRE S GREEN 1224
WEST 21ST ST JUANITA WALLS 1500 VALENTINE W B BROWN
1117 RINGO LOIS M PATTILLO 1121 CROSS H C RAY 2111
CROSS ELLIS THOMAS 1214 WEST 20TH W L ROBERTS 2301
HOWARD H L MOTHERSHED 1313 CHESTER.

"First, may I say that the neutrality laws are among the oldest laws in our statute books."

Department of Justice

OFFICE OF THE
RECEIVED
APR 24 1961
ATTORNEY GENERAL

April 20, 1961

Statement by Attorney General Robert F. Kennedy

There have been a number of inquiries from the press about our present neutrality laws and the possibility of their application in connection with the struggle for freedom in Cuba.

First, may I say that the neutrality laws are among the oldest laws in our statute books. Most of the provisions date from the first years of our independence and, with only minor revisions, have continued in force since the 18th Century. Clearly they were not designed for the kind of situation which exists in the world today.

Second, the neutrality laws were never designed to prevent individuals from leaving the United States to fight for a cause in which they believed. There is nothing in the neutrality laws which prevents refugees from Cuba from returning to that country to engage in the fight for freedom. Nor is an individual prohibited from departing from the United States, with others of like belief, to join still others in a second country for an expedition against a third country.

There is nothing criminal in an individual leaving the United States with the intent of joining an insurgent group. There is nothing criminal in his urging others to do so. There is nothing criminal in several persons departing at the same time.

What the law does prohibit is a group organised as a military expedition from departing from the United States to take action as a military force against a nation with whom the United States is at peace.

There are also provisions of early origin forbidding foreign states to recruit mercenaries in this country. No activities engaged in by Cuban patriots which have been brought to our attention appear to be violations of our neutrality laws.

Robert F. Kennedy's statement on Cuba and neutrality laws, April 20, 1961.

MRBM LAUNCH SITE 2
SAN CRISTOBAL
1 NOVEMBER 1962

MISSILE-READY TENT

FUEL TRAILERS

FORMER LAUNCH POSITIONS

FORMER LOCATION OF MISSILE-READY TENTS

Prime Minister Fidel Castro, April 1959.

Map showing potential missile range.

Medium-Range Ballistic Missile Field Launch Site, San Cristobal No.1, October 14, 1962.

President John F. Kennedy meeting with the Soviet Minister of Foreign Affairs, October 18, 1962.

"Within the past week, unmistakable evidence has established the fact that a series of offensive missile sites is now in preparation..."

Good evening, my fellow citizens:

This Government, as promised, has maintained the closest surveillance of the Soviet military build-up on the island of Cuba. Within the past week, unmistakable evidence has established the fact that a series of offensive missile sites is now in preparation on that imprisoned island. The purpose of these bases can be none other than to provide a nuclear strike capability against the Western Hemisphere. Upon receiving the first preliminary hard information of this nature last Tuesday morning at 9 a.m.,

Radio and television report to the American people on the Soviet arms buildup, page one, October 22, 1962.

President John F. Kennedy at the White House, October 24, 1961.

Military bases in Cuba being dismantled, November 1, 1962.

TOP SECRET
October 24, 1962

MEMORANDUM FOR THE PRESIDENT

FROM THE ATTORNEY GENERAL

I met with Ambassador Dobrynin last evening on the third floor of the Russian Embassy and/made the following points:
as you suggested

I told him first that I was there on my own and not on the instructions of the President. I said that I wanted to give him some background on the decision of the United States Government and wanted him to know that the duplicity of the Russians had been a major contributing factor. When I had met with him some six weeks before, I said, he had told me that the Russians had not placed any long-range missiles in Cuba and had no intention to do so in the future. He interrupted at that point and confirmed this statement and said he specifically told me they would not put missiles in Cuba which would be able to reach the continental United States.

I said based on that statement which I had related to the President plus independent intelligence information at that time, the President had gone to the American people and assured them that the weapons being furnished by the Communists to Cuba wer

TOP SECRET

Memorandum on Cuba for President Kennedy, page one, October 24, 1962.

President Kennedy's doodles from a meeting on the Cuban Missile Crisis, October 25, 1962.

The Soviet Ship *Ansov* departs from Cuba during the Cuban Missile Crisis, November 6, 1962.

Eleanor Roosevelt's Wallet
"He worked as if he would live forever; He lived as if he would die tomorrow."

He worked as if he would live forever;
He lived as if he would die tomorrow.

Mrs. Roosevelt

St. Christopher Be My Guide

NAME _____
STREET _____
CITY _____

GRAYMOOR, GARRISON, N. Y.

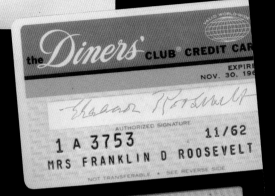

the Diners' CLUB CREDIT CARD

EXPIRE
NOV. 30, 196

Eleanor Roosevelt
AUTHORIZED SIGNATURE

1 A 3753   11/62

MRS FRANKLIN D ROOSEVELT

NOT TRANSFERABLE · SEE REVERSE SIDE

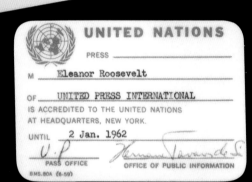

UNITED NATIONS

PRESS _____

M   Eleanor Roosevelt

OF   UNITED PRESS INTERNATIONAL

IS ACCREDITED TO THE UNITED NATIONS
AT HEADQUARTERS, NEW YORK.

UNTIL   2 Jan. 1962

U.P.
PASS OFFICE   OFFICE OF PUBLIC INFORMATION

BMS.80A (6-59)

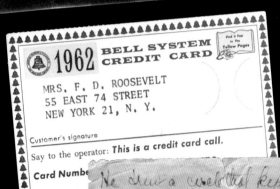

1962 **BELL SYSTEM
CREDIT CARD**

Find it Fast
in The
Yellow Pages

MRS. F. D. ROOSEVELT
55 EAST 74 STREET
NEW YORK 21, N. Y.

Customer's signature

Say to the operator: **This is a credit card call.**

Card Number

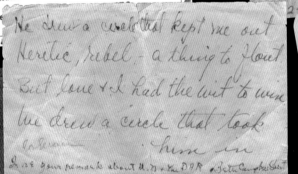

He drew a circle that kept me out
Heretic, rebel — a thing to flout.
But love & I had the wit to win
We drew a circle that took
him in

IDENTIFICATION SIGNATURE
Eleanor Roosevelt

Luckey, Platt and Company

MRS F D ROOSEVELT
HYDE PARK
NEW YORK

1961
1962 **Sheraton Hotels
GUEST CARD**

CHARGE PRIVILEGES IN ALL SHERATON HOTELS
AND AVIS RENT-A-CAR AGENCIES.

Mrs. F. D. Roosevelt
55 East 74th St.
New York 21, N. Y.

8 A A 2 0 1

SIGNATURE _____

AIR TRAVEL CARD
(INTERNATIONAL)

ROOSEVELT

CHARGES AGAINST THIS CARD PAYABLE IN UNITED STATES CU
CARD NO.

A 21677   *Eleanor Roosevelt*
CARD HOLDER'S SIGNATURE

USE OF THIS CARD IS SUBJECT TO APPLICABLE TARIFFS

PRINTED IN U. S. A.

ELEANOR ROOSEVELT

Upon presentation of this card
to the Skipper at the Admirals
Club, the privileges and courtesies
of the Club will be extended to

Mrs. Franklin D. Roosevelt, Sr.

C. R. Speers, Sr. Vice Pres.—Sales

introduced by _____

AMERICAN AIRLINES, Inc.

★ ★ ★ ★ ★ ★ ★ ★ ★ ★

Mrs Eleanor Roosevelt

Der Mensch braucht ein Plätzchen
Und wär's noch so klein
Von dem er kann sagen
Siehe hier, das ist mein
Hier lebe Ich, hier liebe Ich
Hier ruhe Ich aus
Hier ist meine Heimat, hier bin Ich zuhaus

THE METROPOLITAN MUSEUM OF ART
MEMBERSHIP CARD

MRS. FRANKLIN D. ROOSEVELT

is an Annual Member for the year ending **MAR. 31, 1963**

with the full privileges as stated on the reverse side.

Dudley T. Easby Jr.   *Roland L. Redmond*
SECRETARY   PRESIDENT

PERMISSION TO DONATE EYES ✻

I, *Son*
(RELATIONSHIP) of *Eleanor Roosevelt*
DO HEREBY GIVE PERMISSION TO HAVE HIS OR HER EYES
DONATED TO THE EYE-BANK FOR SIGHT RESTORATION, INC.
AND/OR
AT TIME OF DEMISE _____ HOSPITAL

SIGNATURE *Franklin Roosevelt Jr*
TEL. *Mu 8-3200* ADDRESS *598 Madison Ave N.Y.*
DATE *26 Feb '57* WITNESS *Lillian de Sala*

✻ TO BE GIVEN BY NEXT-OF-KIN OR WHOEVER LEGALLY RESPONSIBLE.

MO-72-24-19

Membership Card
Expires June 30, 1963
NATIONAL FEDERATION OF BUSINESS AND
PROFESSIONAL WOMEN'S CLUBS, INC.
2012 Massachusetts Ave., N. W., Washington 6, D. C.

MRS. FRANKLIN DELANO ROOSEVELT
Name of Member

NEW YORK LEAGUE OF B. & P. W., Inc.
Name of Club

Katherine Peden   *signature*
National President   Club Treasurer

Signature of Member: *Eleanor Roosevelt*

MEMBER AT LARGE
The National Federation
of Press Women, Inc.

MRS. FRANKLIN D. ROOSEVELT

COLUMNIST
CLASSIFICATION AND POSITION

NEW YORK CITY   NEW YORK
CITY   STATE

signature   *Bessie A. Ryan*
NATIONAL PRESIDENT   NATIONAL TREASURER

ASSOCIATED HOSPITAL SERVICE OF NEW YORK   **UNITED MEDICAL SERVICE, INC.**
80 Lexington Ave., New York 16, N. Y.   2 Park Avenue, New York 16, N. Y.
MUrray Hill 9-2000   ORegon 9-1400

ROOSEVELT ANNA E
HYDE PARK
N Y N Y

11095462	K10	4	1 6
CERTIFICATE NUMBER	SUFFIX		EFFECTIVE DATE

AHS → (Blue Cross) $ 1800   AHS RATE   TYPE OF CONTRACT   IND.   FAMILY
UMS → (Blue Shield) $ UMS RATE   IND.   H. & W.   FAM.   †UMS BEN.

The contract(s) you hold are identified by code numbers in the boxes "PLAN", "AHS BEN." and "UMS BEN." above. These code numbers are explained on the reverse side.

CARD OF MEMBERSHIP
...ORE ROOSEVELT ASSOCIATION
...East 20th Street, New York 3, N.Y.

1958-1959-

Dean Straus PRESIDENT

THIS CARD EXPIRES
JANUARY 31, 1961

NEWSPAPER GUILD
PRESS CLUB OF N.Y., INC.

133 WEST 44th STREET, NEW YORK 36, N.Y.

Signature _____
Is entitled to all privileges of the Club   425

Our Father, who hast set a restlessness after that which we can never fully find; forbid us to be satisfied with what we make of life. Draw us from base content, and set tasks too hard for us, that we may be driven to Thee for strength. Deliver us from fretfulness and self-pity; make us sure of the goal we cannot see, and of the hidden good in the world. Open our eyes to simple beauty all around us, and our hearts to the loveliness men hid from us because we do not try enough to understand them. Save us from ourselves, and show us a vision of a world made new. May thy Spirit of peace and illumination so enlighten our minds that all life shall glow with new meaning and new purpose; through Jesus Christ our Lord. Amen.

Prayer
For All Those Who Work or Fight in the War

Lord have pity upon all men.
To those who are in darkness
Be their Light.
To those who are in despair
Be their Hope.
To those who are suffering
Be their Healing.
To those who are fearful
Be their Courage.
To those who are defeated
Be their Victory.
To those who are dying
Be their Life.

This Permit Not Valid in the City of New York

C. **8043**
Date **August 5, 1957**
STATE OF NEW YORK
County of Dutchess
License to Carry Pistol is Hereby Granted

To **Eleanor Roosevelt**
Address **Valkill Cottage, Hyde Park**
Occupation **Writer & Lecturer**
Employed by **Self**
Nationality **U.S.A.**
Age **72** Height **5'10"** Weight **144**

signature
Judge or Justice of County Court

(Signature of Holder) *Eleanor Roosevelt*

This license is issued under the following conditions:
1. It is revocable at any time.
2. It expires December 31st of the year issued. **until revoked.**

PISTOL (WEAPON) REVOLVER

Make	Calibre	Number

THUMB-PRINT

MO 72-24-41

We may live without poetry, music and art:
We may live without conscience, and live without heart:
We may live without friends: we may live without books:
But civilized man cannot live without cooks.
He may live without books, what is knowledge but grieving?
He may live without hope, what is hope but deceiving?
He may live without love, what is passion but pining?
But where is the man that can live without dining?"
     Meredith (Lord Lytton) Lucile. Pt. I, Canto II.

President Kennedy speaks in Berlin, June 26, 1963.

President Kennedy's speech card with
German phrases written phonetically,
June 26, 1963.

View of marchers along the Mall in Washington, DC, August 28, 1963.

MARCH ON WASHINGTON FOR JOBS AND FREEDOM
AUGUST 28, 1963

LINCOLN MEMORIAL PROGRAM

1.	The National Anthem	*Led by Marian Anderson.*
2.	Invocation	The Very Rev. Patrick O'Boyle, *Archbishop of Washington.*
3.	Opening Remarks	A. Philip Randolph, *Director March on Washington for Jobs and Freedom.*
4.	Remarks	Dr. Eugene Carson Blake, *Stated Clerk, United Presbyterian Church of the U.S.A.; Vice Chairman, Commission on Race Relations of the National Council of Churches of Christ in America.*
5.	Tribute to Negro Women Fighters for Freedom Daisy Bates Diane Nash Bevel Mrs. Medgar Evers Mrs. Herbert Lee Rosa Parks Gloria Richardson	Mrs. Medgar Evers
6.	Remarks	John Lewis, *National Chairman, Student Nonviolent Coordinating Committee.*
7.	Remarks	Walter Reuther, *President, United Automobile, Aerospace and Agricultural Implement Wokers of America, AFL-CIO; Chairman, Industrial Union Department, AFL-CIO.*
8.	Remarks	James Farmer, *National Director, Congress of Racial Equality.*
9.	Selection	Eva Jessye Choir
10.	Prayer	Rabbi Uri Miller, *President Synagogue Council of America.*
11.	Remarks	Whitney M. Young, Jr., *Executive Director, National Urban League.*
12.	Remarks	Mathew Ahmann, *Executive Director, National Catholic Conference for Interracial Justice.*
13.	Remarks	Roy Wilkins, *Executive Secretary, National Association for the Advancement of Colored People.*
14.	Selection	Miss Mahalia Jackson
15.	Remarks	Rabbi Joachim Prinz, *President American Jewish Congress.*
16.	Remarks	The Rev. Dr. Martin Luther King, Jr., *President, Southern Christian Leadership Conference.*
17.	The Pledge	A Philip Randolph
18.	Benediction	Dr. Benjamin E. Mays, *President, Morehouse College.*

"WE SHALL OVERCOME"

March on Washington program at the Lincoln Memorial.

A young civil rights demonstrator at the March on Washington, August 28, 1963.

Mary for many years had been in charge of altering the clothes which I purchased at a Dallas store.

Transcript from Mrs. Johnson's tapes of November 22, 1963

(relating to)

It all began so beautifully. After a drizzle in the morning, the sun came out bright and beautiful. We were going into Dallas. In the lead car, President and Mrs. Kennedy, John and Nellie, and then a Secret Service car full of men, and then our car - Lyndon and me and Senator Yarborough. The streets were lined with people - lots and lots of people - the children all smiling, placards, confetti, people waving from windows. One last happy moment I had was looking up and seeing Mary Griffith leaning out of a window waving at me. Then almost at the edge of town, on our way to the Trade Mart where we were going to have the luncheon, we were rounding a curve, going down a hill and suddenly there was a sharp loud report - a shot. It seemed to me to come from the right above my shoulder from a building. Then a moment and then two more shots in rapid succession. There had been such a gala air that I thought it must be firecrackers or some sort of celebration. Then in the lead car, the Secret Service men were suddenly down. I heard over the radio system, "Let's get out of here," and our ~~Secret Service~~ man who was with us, Ruf Youngblood, I believe it was, vaulted over the front seat on top of Lyndon, threw him to the floor, and said, "Get down." Senator Yarborough and I ducked our heads. The car ~~excelerated~~ *accelerated* terrifically fast - faster and faster. Then suddenly they put on the brakes so hard that I wondered if they were going to make it as ~~the~~ *very sharp* wheel left ~~as we~~ went around the corner. We pulled up to a building. I looked up and saw it said "Hospital." Only then did I believe that this might be what it was. Yarborough kept on saying in an excited voice, "Have they shot the President?" I said something like, "No, it can't be." As we ground to a halt - we were still the third car -- Secret Service men began to pull, lead, guide and hustle us out. I cast one last look over my shoulder and saw *in Nellie's lap, I believe* a bundle of pink just like a drift of blossoms, lying on the back seat. I think it was Mrs.

Page Two

Kennedy lying over the President's body. They led us to the right, the left and onward into a quiet room in the hospital -- a very small room. It was lined with white sheets, I believe. People came and went -- Kenny O'Donnell, Congressman Thornberry, Congressman Jack Brooks. Always there was Ruf right there, Emory Roberts, Jerry Kivett, Lem Johns and Woody Taylor. There was talk about where we would go -- back to Washington, to the plane, to our house. People spoke of how widespread this may be. Through it all, Lyndon was remarkably calm and quiet. ~~He said we had better move the plane to another part of the field. He spoke of going back out to the plane in black cars.~~ Every face that came in, you searched for the answers you must know. I think the face I kept seeing it on was the face of Kenny O'Donnell who loved him so much. It was Lyndon as usual who thought of it ~~first~~ ~~a~~ Although I wasn't going to leave without doing it. He said, "You had better try to see if you can see Jackie and Nellie." We didn't know what had happened to John. I asked the Secret Service men if I could be taken to them. They began to lead me up one corridor, back stairs and down another. Suddenly I found myself face to face with Jackie in a small hall. I think it was right outside the operating room. You always think of her - or someone like her as being insulated, protected -- she was quite alone. I don't think I ever saw anyone so much alone in my life. I went up to her, put my arms around her and said something to her. I'm sure it was something like, "God, help us all," because my feelings for her were too tumultuous to put into words. And then I went in to see Nellie. There it was different, because Nellie and I have gone through so many things together, since 1938. I hugged her tight and we both cried and I said, "Nellie, it's going to be alright." ~~There has been enough bad that has already happened."~~ It ~~wasn't the President I was thinking about. It was Kathleen, of course.~~ And Nellie said, "Yes, John's going to be alright." Among her many other fine qualities, she is also tough. Then I turned and went

It was Lyndon who said we should go to the plane in unmarked ~~black~~ cars.

Page Three

back to the small white room where Lyndon was. Mr. Kilduff and Kenny O'Donnell were coming and going. I think it was from Kenny's face and Kenny's voice that I first heard the words, "The President is dead." Mr. Kilduff entered and said to Lyndon, "Mr. President." It was decided that we would go immeditaely to the airport. Quick plans were made about how to get to the car. ~~Who to ride in what.~~ Getting out of the hospital into the cars was one of the swiftest walks I have ever made. We got in. Lyndon said to stop the sirens. We drove along as fast as we could. I looked up at a building and there already was a flag at half-mast. I think that is when the enormity of what had happened first struck me. When we got to the airplane, we entered airplane # 1 for the first time. There was a T. V. set on and the commentator was saying "Lyndon B. Johnson, now President of the United States." They were saying they had a suspect. They were not sure he was the assassin. The President had been shot with a 30-30 rifle. On the plane, all the shades were lowered. ~~We heard~~ that we were going to wait for Mrs. Kennedy and the coffin. There was discussion about when Lyndon should be sworn in as President. There was a telephone call to Washington - I believe to the Attorney General. It was decided that he should be sworn in in Dallas as quickly as possible because of ~~national~~ *international* implications, and because we did not know how widespread this incident was as to intended victims. Judge Sarah Hughes, a Federal Judge in Dallas -- and I am glad it was she -- was called to come in a hurry. We ~~borrowed~~ a Bible. Mrs. Kennedy had arrived by this time and the coffin, and there in the very narrow confines of the plane with Jackie on his left with her hair falling in her face, but very composed, and then Lyndon, and I was on his right, Judge Hughes with the bible in front of him and a cluster of Secret Service people and Congressmen we had known for a long time, Lyndon took the oath of office. It's odd at a time like that the little things that come to your mind

Lyndon said

Lyndon Baines Johnson takes the oath of office after the assassination of John F. Kennedy, November 22, 1963.

said "no, no" and immediately

Page Four

and a moment of deep compassion you have for people who are really not at the center of the tragedy. I heard a Secret Service man say in the most desolate voice and I hurt for him -- "We never lost a President in the Service," and then Police Chief Curry of Dallas came on the plane and said to Mrs. Kennedy, "Mrs. Kennedy, believe me, we did everything we possibly could." God, that was a brave thing for that man to do. We all sat around the plane. We had at first been quickly ushered into the main private presidential cabin on the plane -- out of which we very quickly got when we saw where we were because that is where Mrs. Kennedy should be. The casket was in the hall. I went in to see Mrs. Kennedy and though it was a very hard thing to do, she made it as easy as possible. She said things like, "Oh, Lady Bird, it's always good. We've liked you two so much." She said, "Oh, what if I had not been there. I'm so glad I was there." I remember things I said. I looked at her. Mrs. Kennedy's dress was stained with blood. One leg was almost entirely covered with it and her right glove was caked -- that immaculate woman -- it was caked with blood - her husband's blood. She always wore gloves like she was used to them. I never could. Somehow that was one of the most poignant sights -- exquisitely dressed and caked in blood. I asked her if I couldn't get someone in to help her change and she said, "Oh, no. Perhaps later I'll ask Mary Gallagher but not right now." And then with something -- if, with a person that gentle, that dignified, you can say had an element of fierceness, she said, "I want them to see what they have done to Jack." She said a lot of other things like, "What if I had not been there, Oh, I'm so glad I was there." and a lot of other things that made it so much easier for us. "Oh, Lady Bird, we've always liked you both so much." I tried to express something of how we felt. I said, "Oh, Mrs. Kennedy, you know we never even wanted to be Vice President and now, dear God, it's come to this." I would have done anything to

Page Five

help her, but there was nothing I could do to help her, so rather quickly I left and went back to the main part of the airplane where everyone was seated. The ride to Washington was silent, strained -- each with his own thoughts. One of mine was something I had said about Lyndon a long time ago -- that he's a good man in a tight spot. I even remember one little thing he said in that hospital room - "Tell the children to get a Secret Service man with them." Finally we got to Washington with a cluster of people watching. Many bright lights. The casket went off first, then Mrs. Kennedy. The family had come to join them and then we followed. Lyndon made a very simple, very brief and I think strong talk to the folks there. Only about 4 sentences I think. We got in cars, we dropped him off at the White House and I came home.

# # #

235

President Lyndon Johnson signs the Civil Rights Act, July 2, 1964.

Eighty-eighth Congress of the United States of America

AT THE SECOND SESSION

Begun and held at the City of Washington on Tuesday, the seventh day of January, one thousand nine hundred and sixty-four

An Act

To enforce the constitutional right to vote, to confer jurisdiction upon the district courts of the United States to provide injunctive relief against discrimination in public accommodations, to authorize the Attorney General to institute suits to protect constitutional rights in public facilities and public education, to extend the Commission on Civil Rights, to prevent discrimination in federally assisted programs, to establish a Commission on Equal Employment Opportunity, and for other purposes.

Be it enacted by the Senate and House of Representatives of the United States of America in Congress assembled, That this Act may be cited as the "Civil Rights Act of 1964".

TITLE I—VOTING RIGHTS

SEC. 101. Section 2004 of the Revised Statutes (42 U.S.C. 1971), as amended by section 131 of the Civil Rights Act of 1957 (71 Stat. 637), and as further amended by section 601 of the Civil Rights Act of 1960 (74 Stat. 90), is further amended as follows:

(a) Insert "1" after "(a)" in subsection (a) and add at the end of subsection (a) the following new paragraphs:

"(2) No person acting under color of law shall—

"(A) in determining whether any individual is qualified under State law or laws to vote in any Federal election, apply any standard, practice, or procedure different from the standards, practices, or procedures applied under such law or laws to other individuals within the same county, parish, or similar political subdivision who have been found by State officials to be qualified to vote;

"(B) deny the right of any individual to vote in any Federal election because of an error or omission on any record or paper relating to any application, registration, or other act requisite to voting, if such error or omission is not material in determining whether such individual is qualified under State law to vote in such election; or

"(C) employ any literacy test as a qualification for voting in any Federal election unless (i) such test is administered to each individual and is conducted wholly in writing, and (ii) a certified copy of the test and of the answers given by the individual is furnished to him within twenty-five days of the submission of his request made within the period of time during which records and papers are required to be retained and preserved pursuant to title III of the Civil Rights Act of 1960 (42 U.S.C. 1974–74e; 74 Stat. 88): *Provided, however,* That the Attorney General may enter into agreements with appropriate State or local authorities that preparation, conduct, and maintenance of such tests in accordance with the provisions of applicable State or local law, including such special provisions as are necessary in the preparation, conduct, and maintenance of such tests for persons who are blind or otherwise physically handicapped, meet the purposes of this subparagraph and constitute compliance therewith.

"(3) For purposes of this subsection—

"(A) the term 'vote' shall have the same meaning as in subsection (e) of this section;

"(B) the phrase 'literacy test' includes any test of the ability to read, write, understand, or interpret any matter."

(b) Insert immediately following the period at the end of the first sentence of subsection (c) the following new sentence: "If in any such proceeding literacy is a relevant fact there shall be a rebuttable

Civil Rights Act of 1964, page one, July 2, 1964.

CLOTURE Motion

We, the undersigned Senators, in accordance with the provisions of rule XXII of the Standing Rules of the Senate, hereby move to bring to a close the debate upon the bill (H.R. 7152), an act to enforce the constitutional right to vote, to confer jurisdiction upon the district courts of the United States to provide injunctive relief against discrimination in public accommodations, to authorize the Attorney General to institute suits to protect constitutional rights in public facilities and public education, to extend the Commission on Civil Rights, to prevent discrimination in federally assisted programs, to establish a Commission on Equal Employment Opportunity, and for other purposes.

1. *Everett Dirksen*
2. *Mike Mansfield*
3. *Thomas H. Kuchel*
4. *Hubert H. Humphrey*
5. *Clifford P. Case*
6. *Daniel Brewster*
7. *Jennings Randolph*
8. *Hiram L. Fong*
9. *Edmund Muskie*
10. *Joseph S. Clark*
11. *Kenneth B. Keating*
12. *Pat McNamara*
13. *Abraham Ribicoff*
14. *J. Glenn Beall*
15. *Gordon Allott*
16. *Daniel Inouye*
17. *Lee Metcalf*
18. *Paul H. Douglas*
19. *Edward Kennedy*
20. *Stephen M. Young*
21. *Thomas J. Dodd*
22. *Philip Hart*
23. *John Williams*
24. *Lee Metcalf*
25. *Vance Hartke*
26. *Frank E. Moss*
27. *Wayne Morse*
28. *Henry M. Jackson*
29. *Thomas McIntyre*
30. *John O. Pastore*
31. *Claiborne Pell*
32. *Gaylord Nelson*
33. *Maurine Neuberger*
34. *Harrison Williams*
35. *Birch Bayh*
36. *Hugh Scott*
37. *Thruston Morton*
38. *Frank J. Lausche*
39. *Eugene J. McCarthy*
40. *George McGovern*

Cloture motion that ended a filibuster by southern senators of the civil rights bill, June 10, 1964.

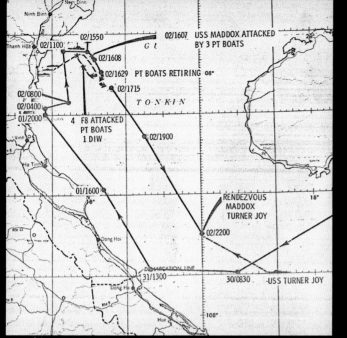

Map of the USS *Maddox* incident, August 10, 1964.

Cable regarding the attack on the USS *Maddox* in
the Gulf of Tonkin, page one, August 4, 1964.

Action viewed from the USS *Maddox* during
the Gulf of Tonkin incident, August 8, 1964.

President Lyndon Johnson's "Midnight
Address" on the second Gulf of Tonkin
incident, August 4, 1964.

INCOMING MESSAGE THE JOINT CHIEFS OF STAFF   SECRET

PRECEDENCE (ACTION)   PRECEDENCE (INFO)

FLASH   FLASH

                                                NOFORN

Z 042158Z

FM CTG 72.1

TO AIG 181

INFO RUMFZK/J8RM/CTG 77.5
RUMFZN/H3WX/CTG 77.6   DECLASSIFIED
RUEPCR/DIRSNA   Authority OSD ltr 3/15/77
RUMGCR/NENB/USS TURNER JOY   By rmg , NARS, Date 4/6/77
RUMGCR/NHHK/USS MADDOX
RUMSMA/COMUSMACV

SECRET   NORFORN
ATTACK ON DESOTO FINAL SITREP (S)

1. CHRONOLOGICAL SEQUENCE OF EVENTS:
AT 041215Z RCVD INFO THAT DRV INTENDED ATTACK. MY POSITION 19-10.7N
107-99E. PROCEED 255775 (AS RECVD) AT THIRTY KNOTS TO BUY TIME
FOR AIR COVER. REQUESTED COVER FROM CTG 77.5. AT 1$1 ?)$ (AS RECVD)
DETECTED THREE TO FIVE CONTACTS 40-2 MILES TO EAST AND IN INZXDED
SIGHT STEAM AREA. THESE CONTACTS APPEARED TO ATTEMPT PURSUIT BUT
BROKE OFF AFTER ABOUT TEN MINUTES AT RANGE 40 MILES. REQUESTED
AIR SUPPORT FROM CTG 77.5 AT 041325Z. AT 041408Z THREE CONTACTS
DETECTED 090, 14 MILES ON COURSE 130, SPEED 30 KTS. FIRST
HELD BY BOTH SHIPS. AT 1419Z CONTACTS CHANGED TO 155, 40 KTS. THIS CONTACT
CAP OVER HEAD 1410Z. AT 1439Z DESOTO UNITS COMMENCED FIRE ON LEAD
CONTACT WHICH HAD TURNED TO INTERCEPT. PROBABLE TORPEDO DETECTED
ON SONAR. FROM THIS TPW UNTIL 1635Z DESOTO UNITS OPERATED
INDEPENDENTLY ALKKVFQTPOW (AS RECVD) EVASION AND FIRING AT TARGETS
OF OPPORTUNITY. ACTION CEASED AT APPROX 1635Z WITH NO FURTHER
DETECTIONS. DESOTO UNITS PROCEEDED TO VIC 17-30N, 18-00E TO AWAIT
DECISION ON POSSIBLE LOGISTICS ARRANGEMENTS. AT 2045Z SE COURSE
FOR FIVE AUGUST PATROL AREA IAW INSTRUCTIONS FROM COMSEVENTHFLT.

2. AIR COVER FROM TICO WAS IN AREA CONTINUOSLY FROM 1410Z UNTIL
STEERED AT 1750Z AIR COVER FROM CONSTELLATION STATION FROM AFSINR
1615Z UNTIL STEER AT 1750Z. DUE TO WEATHER, LIMITED VISIBILITY
AND LACK OF EFFECTIVE ILLUMINATION, AIR SUPPORT NOT SUCESSFUL
IN LOCATING TARGETS.

INFO.....CJCS-2 DJS-1 SJCS-1 J3-2 NMCC-2 JRG-2 CSA-2 CSAF-2 (CMC-2
OSD- 8 (WHITE HOUSE)-3 (STATE)(CIA) FILE-1(28)
ADV COPIES FURN CJCS, NMCC, JRG & OSD
GARBLED PORTIONS ARE BEING SERVICED, COMPLETED TEXT WILL BE FURNISHED

DUTY OFFICER   TWC   PAGE OF PAGES   CITE NO.   DTG
                             1   3   042158Z AUG 64
                                                         SECRET

88th CONGRESS
2nd SESSION   S. J. RES. 189

                    RUSH 9 am 7 A.M.   (NOTE.—Fill in all blank lines ex-
                                         cept those provided for the date
                                         and number of resolution.)

Set Endorsement

            IN THE SENATE OF THE UNITED STATES
                                    AUG 5 - 1964
Fulbright Hickenlooper, Mr. Russell, Saltonstall

Mr. _____ introduced the following joint resolution; which was
read twice and referred to the Committee on FOREIGN RELATIONS
                               AND ARMED SERVICES JOINTLY.

            JOINT RESOLUTION   7 a.m.
To promote the maintenance of international peace
            (Insert title of joint resolution here)
            and security in Southeast Asia.

1   Resolved by the Senate and House of Representatives of the United
2   States of America in Congress assembled, That

    WHEREAS naval units of the Communist regime in Vietnam,
in violation of the principles of the Charter of the United Nations and
of international law, have deliberately and repeatedly attacked United
States naval vessels lawfully present in international waters, and have
thereby created a serious threat to international peace; and

    WHEREAS these attacks are part of a deliberate and systematic
campaign of aggression that the Communist regime in North Vietnam
has been waging against its neighbors and the nations joined with them
in the collective defense of their freedom; and

    WHEREAS the United States is assisting the peoples of
Southeast Asia to protect their freedom and has no territorial, military
or political ambitions in that area, but desires only that these peoples should
be left in peace to work out their own destinies in their own way:

Now, therefore, BE IT

Senate draft of
the Gulf of Tonkin
Resolution,
August 4, 1964.

RUSH 9 a.m. 7 A.m.   7 a.m.

1806 South Jackson
El Dorado, Arkansas
April 3, 1964

U. S. Labor Dept.
Washington D. C.

Gentlemen:
I can only hope and pray this letter will be read. I and three other girls were so upset we couldn't go to school today because of an aticle in the paper saying the Beatles can not return to the U. S. until the government gives their approval. Maybe they didn't follow the law of immigration clearance order, but you must all agree the teenagers of the U.S. want them back. Its none of my business but they've just got to return soon, please.

I sincerly hope you can
(& can't spell, I'm very upset)

give me some kind of reply to this letter. Please, if you can, answer if and when they will or wont, & return.

Very truly yours,
Janelle Blackwell

P.S.
This is no laughing matter to me or any other fan of the Beatles. Please reply a letter back to me. This is a business letter and should be treated as such, Mr. Willard Wirtz, sir or whoever is reading this. This letter I know is not in good form of any kind. But I feel terrible.
I'm 15 and I feel like 80.

Appearance Bond (Rev. 7-59)   Cr. Form No. 17

United States District Court
FOR THE
WESTERN DISTRICT OF TEXAS
EL PASO DIVISION

OCT 5 - 1965

MAXEY HART, Clerk
BY _Elizabeth J. Buckle_
DEPUTY

UNITED STATES OF AMERICA

v.

John R. Cash
w/m/

No. 2-592

APPEARANCE BOND
FOR
John R. Cash

We, the undersigned, jointly and severally acknowledge that we and our personal representatives are bound to pay to the United States of America the sum of **Fifteen Hundred** dollars ($ 1,500.00).

The conditions of this bond are that the defendant **John R. Cash** is to appear before **Colbert Coldwell**, United States Commissioner for the **Western** District of **Texas**, at' El Paso, Texas, INSTANTER, and in the United States District Court for the **Western** District of **Texas** at **El Paso, Texas, INSTANTER**, and at such other places as the defendant may be required to appear, in accordance with any and all orders and directions relating to the defendant's appearance in the above entitled matter as may be given or issued by the commissioner or by the United States District Court for the **Western** District of **Texas** or any other United States District Court to which the defendant may be removed or the cause transferred; that the defendant is not to depart the **Western** District of **Texas** _Ventura County, Calif. + where his work takes him_, or the jurisdiction of any other United States District Court to which the defendant may be removed or the cause transferred after he has appeared in such other district pursuant to the terms of this bond, except in accordance with such orders or warrants as may be issued by the Commissioner or the United States District Court for the **Western** _within the Continental U.S._ District of **Texas** or the United States District Court for such other district; that the defendant is to abide any judgment entered in such matter by surrendering himself to serve any sentence imposed and obeying any order or direction in connection with such judgment as the court imposing it may prescribe.

If the defendant appears as ordered and otherwise obeys and performs the foregoing conditions of this bond, then this bond is to be void, but if the defendant fails to obey or perform any of these conditions, payment of the amount of this bond shall be due forthwith. Forfeiture of this bond for any breach of its conditions may be declared by any United States District Court having cognizance of the above entitled matter at the time of such breach and if the bond is forfeited and if the forfeiture is not set aside or remitted, judgment may be entered upon motion in such United States District Court against each debtor jointly and severally for the amount above stated, together with interest and costs, and execution may be issued and payment secured as provided by the Federal Rules of Criminal Procedure and by other laws of the United States.

It is agreed and understood that this is a continuing bond which shall continue in full force and effect until such time as the undersigned are duly exonerated.

This bond is signed on this **5th** day of **October** 19 **65**

at **El Paso, Texas**

Name of Defendant. _John R Cash_ Address. _P.O. Box 44, Casitas Springs, Calif._

Name of Surety. UNITED BOND INSURANCE COMPA... Address. _105 S Kansas_

Name of Surety. BY _____ ATTORNEY IN FACT Address.

Signed and acknowledged before me this **5th** day of **October** 19 **65**.

Colbert Coldwell

Approved: _Colbert Coldwell_

Insert place

Woodrow Bean, Atty.

Vietnamese Air Force helicopter in flight, August 1971.

Infantryman lowered into tunnel on reconnaissance mission, Quang Ngai Province, April 24, 1967.

A Marine medic treats the wounded at Hue City, February 6, 1968.

Viet Cong base camp being burned in My Tho, April 5, 1968.

Aircraft from the USS *America* and USS *Midway* drop bombs during a strike mission, March 1973.

Demonstrator offers a flower to military police, October 21, 1967.

Napalm bombs explode on Viet Cong structures south of Saigon, 1965.

U.S. Marshals remove anti-Vietnam protestor at Pentagon demonstration, October 22, 1967.

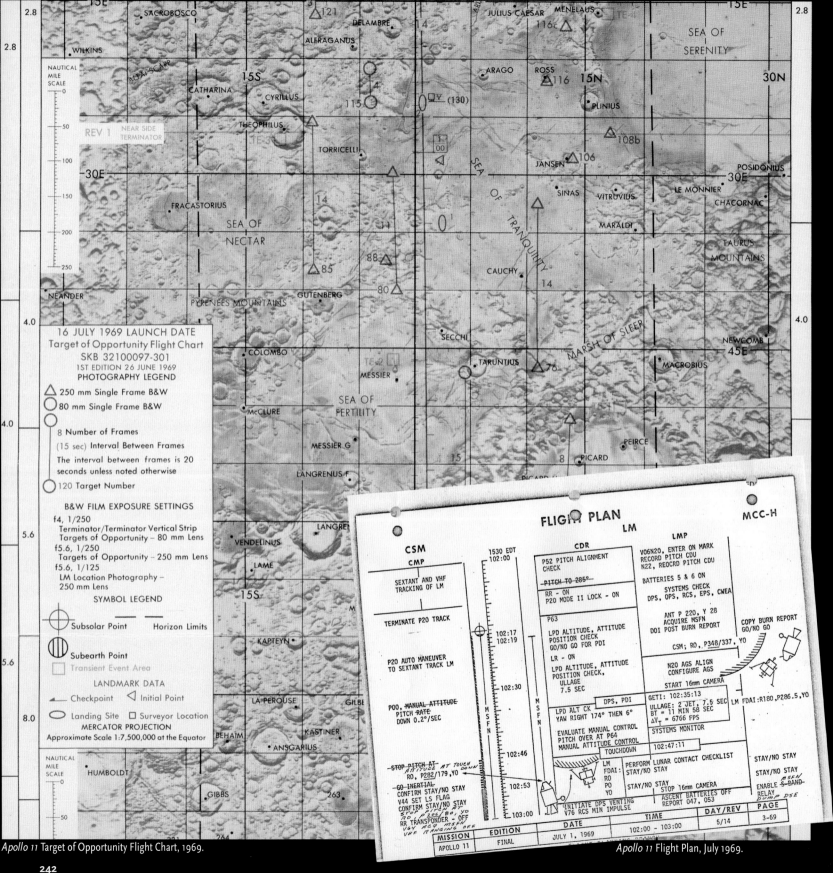

Apollo 11 Target of Opportunity Flight Chart, 1969.

Apollo 11 Flight Plan, July 1969.

Astronaut's leg, foot, and footprint in the lunar soil, July 20, 1969.

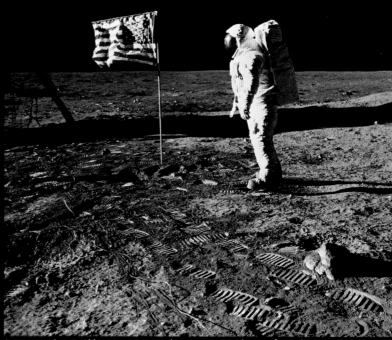

Astronaut Edwin E. Aldrin, Jr., posing on the Moon next to the U.S. flag, July 20, 1969.

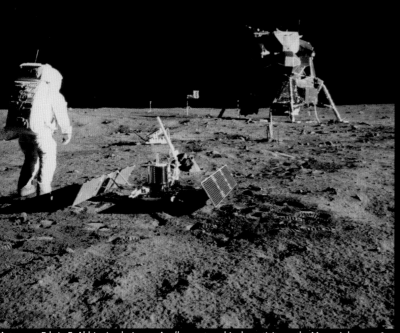

Astronaut Edwin E. Aldrin, Jr., during an *Apollo 11* extravehicular activity on the Moon, July 20, 1969.

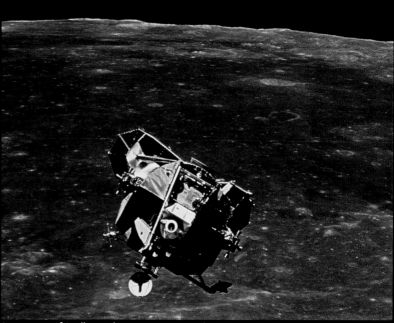

Ascent stage of *Apollo 11*, July 21, 1969.

Air Force One arrives in Beijing, February 21, 1972.

President Nixon having tea with Premier Zhou Enlai, February 21, 1972.

Mr. Prime Minister:

On behalf of all of your American guests I wish to thank you for the incomparable hospitality for which the Chinese people are justly famous throughout the world.

1. I thank you for your gracious and eloquent remarks.

At this moment, through the wonders of telecommunications, more people are seeing and hearing what we say than on any other such occasion in the history of the world.

1. Yet what we say here will not be long remembered.

2. What we do here can change the world.

As you said in your toast welcoming Dr. Kissinger to Peking in October, the Chinese people are a great people, the American people are a great people.

1. If our two great peoples are enemies, the future of the world is dark indeed.

2. If we can find common ground to work together, the chance for world peace is immeasurably greater.

Nixon's remarks to Premier Zhou Enlai, February 21, 1972.

- 2 -

In the spirit of frankness which I hope will characterize our talks this week, let us recognize at the outset these points:

1. We have at times been enemies in the past.

2. We have great differences today.

3. What brings us together is that we have common interests which transcend those differences.

As we discuss our differences neither of us will compromise our principles.

1. But while we cannot close the gulf between us, we can try to bridge it so that we can talk across that bridge.

Let us, in these next five days, start a long march together not in lock step -- but on different roads leading to the same goal -- the goal of building a world structure of peace and justice in which all may stand together with equal dignity, and in which each nation, large or small, has a right to determine its own form of government, free of outside domination or interference.

- 3 -

The world watches; the world listens; the world waits to see what we will do.

1. What is the world?

(1) In a personal sense, I think of my eldest daughter whose birthday is today and, as I think of her, I think of all children in the world -- in Asia, Africa, Europe and in the Americas -- most of whom were born since the date of the foundation of the Peoples' Republic of China.

1. What legacy shall we leave our children?

(1) Are they destined to die for the hatreds which have plagued the old world or are they destined to live because we had the vision to build a new world?

There is no reason for us to be enemies.

1. Neither of us seeks the territory of the other.

2. Neither of us seeks domination over the other.

3. Neither of us seeks to reach our hands out and rule the world.

"This is the hour, this is the day for our two peoples to rise to the heights of greatness which can build a new and better world."

MENU

Hors d'Oeuvre

Four Treasures of Duck

Fried Giblets

Roast Duck

Mushrooms and Sprouts

Duck Bone Soup

Lotus Seeds Sweet Porridge

Fruits

Menu from a dinner given during President
Nixon's visit to Beijing, February 25, 1972.

President and Mrs. Nixon tour the Great Wall
of China, February 24, 1972.

Drawing of President Nixon holding
two pandas, February 23, 1973.

Memorandum of conversation between President Nixon
and Chairman Mao Zedong, February 21, 1972.

- 4 -

As Chairman Mao has written:

1. " So many deeds cry out to be done - and always urgently.

　(1) "The world rolls on.

　(2) "Time passes.

　(3) "Ten thousand years are too long.

　　1. "Seize the day;

　　2. "Seize the hour."

This is the hour, this is the day for our two peoples to rise to
the heights of greatness which can build a new and better world.

1. In that spirit, I ask all of those present to raise
your glass to Chairman Mao, Prime Minister Chou
and to the friendship of the Chinese and American
people which can lead to friendship and peace for
the people of the world.

# # # # # # # #

MEMORANDUM

DECLASSIFIED
E.O. 12958, Sec. 3.6

THE WHITE HOUSE
WASHINGTON

By ____ Date 6/9/06

TOP SECRET/SENSITIVE/
EXCLUSIVELY EYES ONLY

February 21, 1972

MEMORANDUM OF CONVERSATION

PARTICIPANTS:　　Chairman Mao Tsetung
　　　　Prime Minister Chou En-lai
　　　　Wang Hai-jung, Deputy Chief of Protocol
　　　　of the Foreign Ministry
　　　　Tang Wen-sheng, Interpreter

　　　　President Nixon
　　　　Henry A. Kissinger, Assistant to the President
　　　　for National Security Affairs
　　　　Winston Lord, National Security Council Staff
　　　　(Notetaker)

DATE AND TIME:　　Monday, February 21, 1972 - 2:50-3:55 p.m.

PLACE:　　Chairman Mao's Residence, Peking

(There were opening greetings during which the Chairman
welcomed President Nixon, and the President expressed his great
pleasure at meeting the Chairman.)

President Nixon: You read a great deal. The Prime Minister
said that you read more than he does.

Chairman Mao: Yesterday in the airplane you put forward a very
difficult problem for us. You said that what it is required to talk about
are philosophic problems.

President Nixon: I said that because I have read the Chairman's
poems and speeches, and I knew he was a professional philosopher.
(Chinese laugh.)

Garfield County Fair parade, Colorado, September 1973.

Albuquerque Speedway Park, New Mexico, May 1972.

Central Expressway, Dallas, Texas, May 1972.

View west toward Worthington Glacier and Thompson Pass, Alaska, August 1974.

Lake Lyndon Johnson, Texas, May 1972.

"Weeding sugar beets for $2.00," near Fort Collins, Colorado, June 1972.

Folk singer at South Street Seaport, New York, June 1973.

Aluminum cans await use in experimental house near Taos, New Mexico, August 1974.

School children testing water, Arkansas, May 1972.

Farmer harvests maple syrup, Vermont, 1974.

Highway sign for new speed limit, Oregon, 1973.

Construction worker at the Navajo Generating Plant, Arizona, May 1972.

Boston's Haymarket Square. Public protest prevented it from becoming a highway, May 1973.

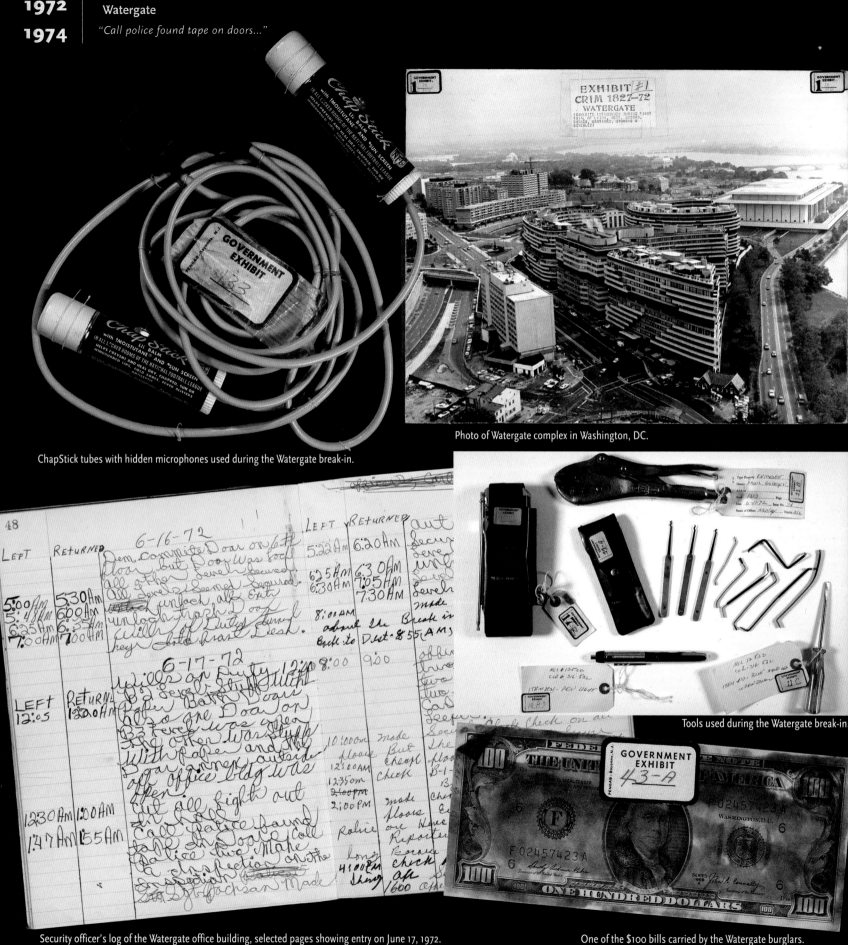

ChapStick tubes with hidden microphones used during the Watergate break-in.

Photo of Watergate complex in Washington, DC.

Security officer's log of the Watergate office building, selected pages showing entry on June 17, 1972.

Tools used during the Watergate break-in.

One of the $100 bills carried by the Watergate burglars.

248

"Schedule of Documents or Objects to be Produced by or on Behalf of Richard M. Nixon: 1. All tapes..."

Watergate | 1972 1974

President Richard Nixon at a press conference, October 26, 1973.

President Nixon releases selected transcripts of his taped conversations, April 29, 1974.

Grand Jury Subpoena ordering Richard Nixon to produce the audio tapes created by the Nixon White House tape system, July 24, 1973.

Government Exhibit 60: Uher 5000 Reel-to-Reel Tape Recorder.

Notes by White House aide Gordon Strachan from a meeting with deputy campaign manager Jeb Stuart Magruder, noting the approval of Gordon Liddy's political intelligence operations, selected page.

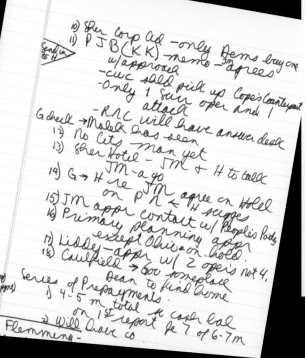

UNITED STATES DISTRICT COURT
FOR THE DISTRICT OF COLUMBIA

GRAND JURY
SUBPOENA DUCES TECUM
Dated July 23, 1973

Schedule of Documents or   Misc. # 47-73   FILED
Objects to be Produced by   JUL 24 1973
or on Behalf of Richard
M. Nixon: JAMES F. DAVEY, Clerk

1. All tapes and other electronic and/or mechanical
recordings or reproductions, and any memoranda, papers,
transcripts or other writings, relating to:

(a) Meeting of June 20, 1972, in the President's
Executive Office Building ("EOB") Office involving Richard
Nixon, John Ehrlichman and H. R. Haldeman from 10:30 a.m.
to noon (time approximate).

(b) Telephone conversation of June 20, 1972,
between Richard Nixon and John N. Mitchell from 6:08 to
6:12 p.m.

(c) Meeting of June 30, 1972, in the President's
EOB Office, involving Messrs. Nixon, Haldeman and Mitchell
from 12:55 to 2:10 p.m.

(d) Meeting of September 15, 1972, in the President's Oval Office involving Mr. Nixon, Mr. Haldeman, and
John W. Dean III from 5:27 to 6:17 p.m.

(e) Meeting of March 13, 1973, in the President's
Oval Office involving Messrs. Nixon, Dean and Haldeman
from 12:42 to 2:00 p.m.

(f) Meeting of March 21, 1973, in the President's
Oval Office involving Messrs. Nixon, Dean, and Haldeman
from 10:12 to 11:55 a.m.

(g) Meeting of March 21, 1973, in the President's
EOB Office from 5:20 to 6:01 p.m. involving Messrs. Nixon,

THE WHITE HOUSE

WASHINGTON

August 9, 1974

Dear Mr. Secretary:

I hereby resign the Office of President of the
United States.

Sincerely,

Richard Nixon

11.35 AM

The Honorable Henry A. Kissinger
The Secretary of State
Washington, D.C. 20520

HK

"...the tranquility to which this nation has been restored...could be irreparably lost by the prospects of bringing to trial a former President..."

GRANTING PARDON TO RICHARD NIXON

BY THE PRESIDENT OF THE UNITED STATES OF AMERICA

A PROCLAMATION

Richard Nixon became the thirty-seventh President of the United States on January 20, 1969 and was reelected in 1972 for a second term by the electors of forty-nine of the fifty states. His term in office continued until his resignation on August 9, 1974.

Pursuant to resolutions of the House of Representatives, its Committee on the Judiciary conducted an inquiry and investigation on the impeachment of the President extending over more than eight months. The hearings of the Committee and its deliberations, which received wide national publicity over television, radio, and in printed media, resulted in votes adverse to Richard Nixon on recommended Articles of Impeachment.

As a result of certain acts or omissions occurring before his resignation from the Office of President, Richard Nixon has become liable to possible indictment and trial for offenses against the United States. Whether or not he shall be so prosecuted depends on findings of the appropriate grand jury and on the discretion of the authorized prosecutor. Should an indictment ensue, the accused shall then be entitled to a fair trial by an impartial jury, as guaranteed to every individual by the Constitution.

It is believed that a trial of Richard Nixon, if it became necessary, could not fairly begin until a year or more has elapsed. In the meantime, the tranquility to which this nation has been restored by the events of recent weeks could be irreparably lost by the prospects of bringing to trial a former President of the United States. The prospects of such

2

trial will cause prolonged and divisive debate over the propriety of exposing to further punishment and degradation a man who has already paid the unprecedented penalty of relinquishing the highest elective office of the United States.

NOW, THEREFORE, I, Gerald R. Ford, President of the United States, pursuant to the pardon power conferred upon me by Article II, Section 2, of the Constitution, have granted and by these presents do grant a full, free, and absolute pardon unto Richard Nixon for all offenses against the United States which he, Richard Nixon, has committed or may have committed or taken part in during the period from January 20, 1969 through August 9, 1974.

IN WITNESS WHEREOF, I have hereunto set my hand this eighth day of September, in the year of our Lord nineteen hundred and seventy-four, and of the Independence of the United States of America the one hundred and ninety-ninth.

Gerald R. Ford

4311

Page 3

MR. SLAYTON: Tom just repeated it for me, sir.

Yes, I have a lot of advice for young people, but I guess probably one of the most important bits is to, number one, decide what you really want to do and then, secondly, never give up until you have done it.

THE PRESIDENT: You are a darn good example, Deke, of never giving up and continuing. I know it is a great feeling of success from your point of view to have made this flight and to be on board with your four associates.

MR. SLAYTON: Yes, sir.

THE PRESIDENT: Vance Brand, I know that you are still in the Apollo and holding the fort there. It has been my observation that the crews on both sides have worked very hard to learn either Russian on the one hand or English on the other.

Has this training period, which is so important, stood the test in the complicated procedures that all of you must execute in this very delicate mission?

MR. BRAND: Mr. President, I believe it really has. I think in a way our project and, in particular, the training that we have undergone has been sort of a model for future similar projects.

I think it has been a real pleasant experience to work on learning Russian and to be able to work with the cosmonauts, and I think we will have some ideas that would probably help people in the future on similar paths.

THE PRESIDENT: Thank you very much, Vance.

I might like to say a word or two to Valeriy Kubasov, the other member of the cosmonaut crew. I might say to him, as well as Colonel Leonov, I remember both of you on that enjoyable Saturday last September when both crews visited the White House and joined me in a picnic over in Virgina.

We flew from the White House over to this picnic just across the river. We had some crab specialties that I enjoyed, and I think you did.

I am sure you are having a little different menu, somewhat different food on this occasion. What are you having over there out in space?

MORE

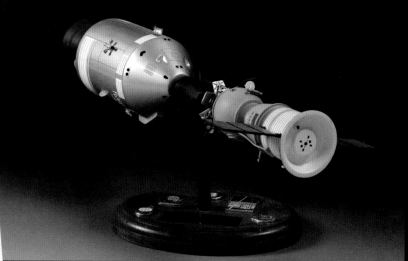

A ⅟₅₀ scale model of the *Apollo-Soyuz* spacecraft flown in the *Apollo-Soyuz* mission.

Page 4

MR. LEONOV: We get good space food. There is no Russian food, no Russian music, some juice, some coffee, and a lot of water, no beer.

THE PRESIDENT: Let me say in conclusion we look forward to your safe return. It has been a tremendous demonstration of cooperation between our scientists, our technicians and, of course, our astronauts and their counterparts, the cosmonauts from the Soviet Union.

I congratulate everybody connected with the flight, and particularly the five of you who are setting this outstanding example of what we have to do in the future to make it a better world.

May I say in signing off, here is to a soft landing.

MR. KUBASOV: Thank you very much.

MR. STAFFORD: Thank you, Mr. President. It certainly has been an honor to serve the country and work here.

THE PRESIDENT: We will see you when you get back.

MR. STAFFORD: Yes, sir.

END   (AT 3:45 P.M. EDT)

Transcript of telephone conversation between President Gerald Ford and astronauts/cosmonauts aboard *Apollo-Soyuz*, pages three and four, July 17, 1975.

"We face the future with renewed dedication to the principles embodied in our Declaration of Independence..."

President Ford and Queen Elizabeth dance at the State Dinner held in honor of the Queen and Prince Philip, July 7, 1976.

The Bicentennial Jewel, created by Pierre Touraine, is made of white gold, diamonds, rubies, and sapphires and is in the shape of the official 1976 Bicentennial symbol.

President Gerald Ford boards a covered wagon at the Bicentennial Wagon Train Pilgrimage encampment, Valley Forge, Pennsylvania, July 4, 1976.

Ceremonial copy of the Presidential Proclamation for Bicentennial Independence Day.

Bicentennial Independence Day

By the President of the United States of America

A Proclamation

The Continental Congress by resolution adopted July 2, 1776, declared that thirteen American colonies were free and independent states. Two days later, on the fourth of July, the Congress adopted a Declaration of Independence which proclaimed to the world the birth of the United States of America.

In the two centuries that have passed, we have matured as a nation and as a people. We have gained the wisdom that age and experience bring, yet we have kept the strength and idealism of youth.

In this year of our Nation's Bicentennial, we enter our third century with the knowledge that we have achieved greatness as a nation and have contributed to the good of mankind. We face the future with renewed dedication to the principles embodied in our Declaration of Independence, and with renewed gratitude for those who pledged their lives, their fortunes and their sacred honor to preserve individual liberty for us.

In recognition of the two hundredth anniversary of the great historic events of 1776, and in keeping with the wishes of the Congress, I ask that all Americans join in an extended period of celebration, thanksgiving and prayer on the second, third, fourth and fifth days of July of our Bicentennial year—so that people of all faiths, in their own way, may give thanks for the protection of divine Providence through 200 years, and pray for the future safety and happiness of our Nation.

To commemorate the adoption of the Declaration of Independence, the Congress, by concurrent resolution adopted June 26, 1963 (77 Stat. 944), declared that its anniversary be observed by the ringing of bells throughout the United States.

NOW, THEREFORE, I, GERALD R. FORD, President of the United States of America, do hereby proclaim that the two hundredth anniversary of the adoption of the Declaration of Independence be observed by the simultaneous ringing of bells throughout the United States at the hour of two o'clock, eastern daylight time, on the afternoon of the Fourth of July, 1976, our Bicentennial Independence Day, for a period of two minutes, signifying our two centuries of independence.

I call upon civic, religious, and other community leaders to encourage public participation in this historic observance. I call upon all Americans, here and abroad, including all United States flag ships at sea, to join in this salute.

As the bells ring in our third century, as millions of free men and women pray, let every American resolve that this Nation, under God, will meet the future with the same courage and dedication Americans showed the world two centuries ago. In perpetuation of the joyous ringing of the Liberty Bell in Philadelphia, let us again "Proclaim Liberty throughout all the Land unto all the Inhabitants thereof."

IN WITNESS WHEREOF, I have hereunto set my hand this twenty-ninth day of June in the year of our Lord nineteen hundred seventy-six, and of the Independence of the United States of America the two hundredth.

Gerald R. Ford

President Jimmy Carter meets with Israeli Prime Minister Menachem Begin (left) and Egyptian President Anwar Sadat (right) at Camp David, September 7, 1978.

Presidents Carter and Sadat and Prime Minister Begin join hands in celebration of the Egyptian-Israeli Peace Treaty, March 26, 1979.

President Carter's draft of what became the "Framework for the Conclusion of a Peace Treaty Between Egypt and Israel," selected pages.

#2 1-

Framework for a Settlement in Sinai

In order to achieve peace between them, Israel and Egypt agree to negotiate in good faith with a goal of concluding within three months of the signing of this framework a peace treaty between them. [There are no preconditions to the commencement of the negotiations.]

All of the principles of U.N. Resolution 242 will apply in this resolution of the dispute between Israel and Egypt. PEACE TREATY

Unless otherwise mutually

2-

between two and three years after the peace treaty is signed.

In the peace treaty ∧ the issues of: a) the full exercise of Egyptian sovereignty up to the internationally recognized border between Egypt and mandated Palestine; b) the time of withdrawal of Israeli personnel from the Sinai; c) the use of airfields near [El Arish] [Rafah] [Ras en Nagb] [Sharm el Sheikh] ∧ by Israel & other nations through the Strait of Tiran, the Gulf of Suez and Suez Canal, e)

ANNOUNCEMENT/RESCUE MISSION TERMINATION   4/25/80   [Original Speech text]

1. LATE YESTERDAY I CANCELLED A CAREFULLY PLANNED OPERATION
2. WHICH WAS UNDERWAY IN IRAN TO POSITION OUR TEAM
3. FOR A ^(LATER) RESCUE OF THE AMERICAN HOSTAGES
4. WHO HAVE BEEN HELD CAPTIVE THERE SINCE NOVEMBER 4.
5. EQUIPMENT FAILURE IN THE RESCUE HELICOPTERS
6. MADE IT NECESSARY TO END THE MISSION.
7. AS OUR TEAM WAS WITHDRAWING,
8. TWO OF OUR AIRCRAFT COLLIDED ON THE GROUND
         IN A REMOTE DESERT LOCATION IN IRAN. (REFUELING)

                                    OTHER INFO WHEN
                                    APPROPRIATE

9. THERE WAS NO FIGHTING & NO COMBAT.
10. BUT TO MY DEEP REGRET, 8 OF THE CREWMEN ON THE 2 AIRCRAFT WERE KILLED,
11. AND SEVERAL OTHER AMERICANS WERE HURT IN THE ACCIDENT.
12. OUR PEOPLE WERE IMMEDIATELY AIRLIFTED OUT OF IRAN,
13. THOSE WHO WERE INJURED ARE GETTING MEDICAL TREATMENT,
14. AND ALL OF THEM ARE EXPECTED TO RECOVER.

          KNOWLEDGE
NO DETECTION BY IRANIAN AUTHORITIES
UNTIL SEVERAL HOURS AFTER
          WITHDRAWAL.

President Jimmy Carter's annotated statement on the failed hostage rescue mission, page one, April 25, 1980.

-101-

DECEMBER 9, 1980: (402ND DAY) -
WAS TOLD AGAIN THIS MORNING THERE WOULD BE NO HOT WATER
TODAY - POSSIBLY TOMORROW - BECAUSE THERE WAS NO OIL. IT
APPEARS THAT IRAN IS SUFFERING FROM A SHORTAGE OF THE
KEROSENE THEY NEED FOR HEATING LIKE THEY WERE A YEAR OR TWO
AGO WHEN THE U.S. GAVE THEM SOMETHING LIKE TWO MILLION GALLONS
AS A "GOODWILL GESTURE" AND NOW WE SEE THE "THANKS" WE GOT!
IF I COULD BE SURE IRAN IS REALLY HURTING, I'LL BE GLAD TO DO
WITHOUT HOT WATER! SO THIS MORNING I SHAVED AS USUAL IN COLD
WATER, THEN SHAMPOOED AND TOOK A SPONGE BATH. SURELY WAS
COLD, HOWEVER! THEN WASHED MY SHEETS AND PILLOWCASE AS IT HAS
BEEN 18 DAYS SINCE THE TERRORISTS DID THEM FOR US. - YESTERDAY
I SENT A WRITTEN REQUEST FOR A DECENT MATTRESS LIKE WE
HAD OVER AT THE CHANCERY AS THIS FOAM RUBBER SLAB WE HAVE
HERE IS GIVING ME A BACKACHE. ALSO COMPLAINED ABOUT THE
LACK OF PROPER SUPPLIES IN THE TOILETS SUCH AS SAFETY RAZORS,
SHAVING SOAP, TOILET SOAP, AND DETERGENT FOR DISHES. CONDITION
KEEP GOING FROM BAD TO WORSE, THIS MORNING WE WERE GIVEN
PIE FILLING AGAIN IN PLACE OF JAM AND YESTERDAY GOT THE
"WALLPAPER" TYPE BREAD IN PLACE OF THE USUAL "BARBARI" WHICH
ITSELF IS NOT AS GOOD AS IT USED TO BE. WHEN WE WERE MOVED
TO THIS "PRISON" DUMP ON OCT. 30 WE WERE TOLD WE WOULD HAVE
"TO ADAPT" TO THE NEW QUARTERS "FOR A FEW DAYS" AND THEN "MAYBE"
WE WOULD BE GOING HOME, AHMAHD WAS RIGHT ON THE "MAYBE"
AS WE ARE STILL "ADAPTING" AS WE HAVE BEEN IN THIS DUMP FOR
41 DAYS AND ABSOLUTLY NO SIGN OF GOING HOME! LATER IN THE
MORNING THEY DID GET SOME KEROSENE SO LIT THE TANK AND I GOT A HOT
SHOWER AND WASHED MY UNDERWEAR IN HOT WATER. DON HOHMAN IS VERY
SICK - HAS TERRIBLE PAINS NEAR HIS LEFT EYE AND LEFT EAR - SO BAD IT
MADE HIM VOMIT BOTH HIS BREAKFAST AND LUNCH. HAS HAD A TERRIFIC
HEADACHE PAST FOUR DAYS AND HAS BEEN EATING TYLENOL LIKE CANDY
BUT WITH NO EFFECT IN RELIEVING THE PAIN. THIS AFTERNOON WE
ASKED ABBAS TO GET A DOCTOR FOR HIM BUT WILL SEE IF THEY DO AND
HOW LONG IT WILL TAKE. I'M AFRAID IT PROBABLY IS AN INTERNAL EYE OR EAR
CLEAR UP THE PAIN AS IT PROBABLY IS AN INTERNAL EYE OR EAR
INFECTION OF SOME SORT. HOPE IT ISN'T TOO SERIOUS, BUT SURELY
SEEMS SO RIGHT NOW. NO MAIL AGAIN TODAY.

DECEMBER 10, 1980: (403RD DAY - ALSO MY 65TH BIRTHDAY.!!)
HAD HOPED I MIGHT GET A BIRTHDAY PRESENT WITH NEWS THAT
WE WERE BEING RELEASED, BUT NO SUCH LUCK! GOT INTO THE
WASHROOM EARLY AND WHILE THE TANK WASN'T LIT THERE WAS
STILL ENOUGH IN THE TANK FOR ANOTHER HOT SHOWER, SO TOOK ONE.
THERE WERE TWO SAFETY RAZORS THERE THIS MORNING - TRIED
BOTH BUT BOTH WERE DULL! SOME IMPROVEMENT. I USED ONE ANYWAY
AS I'M TRYING TO SAVE THE ONE PLASTIC "THROWAWAY" I HAVE IN
CASE WE DON'T GET ANYMORE. (THE "ASTRA" AND A COUPLE OF OTHERS
I WAS SAVING WHEN WE WERE IN THE CHANCERY WERE CONFISCATED
THE NIGHT WE WERE MOVED OVER HERE TO OUR PRESENT
INTENDED TO IGNORE MY BIRTHDA...
IT TO D...

Entry in the diary of hostage Robert Ode (402nd Day), December 9, 1980.

Mount St. Helens erupts, May 18, 1980.

Mount St. Helens before eruption.

Mount St. Helens after eruption.

President Jimmy Carter's statement following his inspection of the volcano, May 22, 1980.

Miles of fallen timber above the Touttle River, 1980.

Draft #1
LDaft 5/22/80

Talking Points for
Statement Following Volcano Inspection

1. I first want to commend the citizens and the elected leaders of the Northwest for the calm, cooperative, resourceful way they have performed over the past few days in coping with a natural disaster of such unprecedented dimensions. Your pioneering and community spirit have shown through.

2. I have just returned from viewing area around Mount St. Helens, Gifford Pinchot National Forest, what used to be Spirit Lake, and from talking with people at the Cascade Middle School Relief and Evacuation Center, people who were directly affected by this awesome phenomena. We also surveyed the effects on the Cowlitz TOUTLE and Columbia Rivers and the Portland harbor. (Here you might want to recount your impressions of viewing the site.)

3. At the request of Governor Ray, I granted a major disaster declaration for the State of Washington yesterday, before leaving the White House. Federal agency representatives, led by Bob Stevens of the Federal Emergency Management Agency, are at the site of the disaster now. They will work closely with State and local officials to see that needed assistance is quickly provided.

4. A wide range of assistance will be made available to individuals, businesses and communities. We are in the process of inventorying those needs at this hour. Debris removal will be a big part of that effort. It is

"We had agreed to speak frankly, and we did."

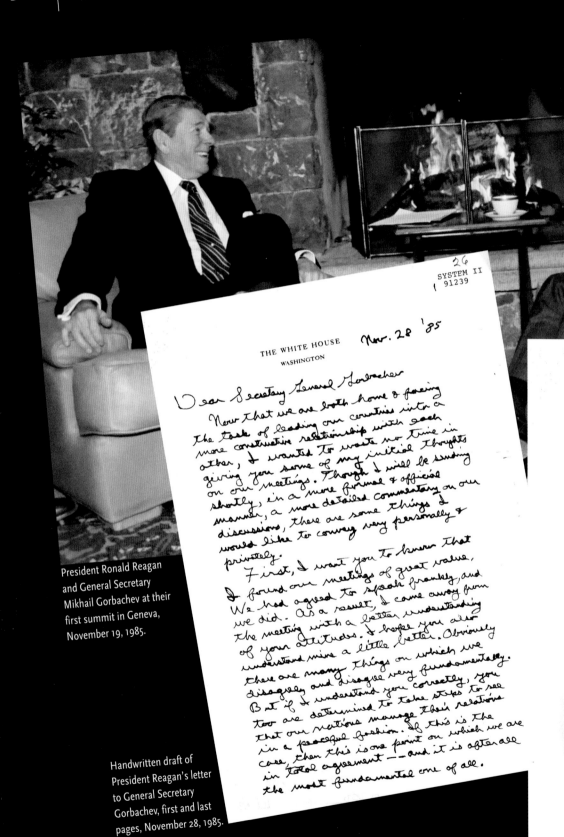

President Ronald Reagan and General Secretary Mikhail Gorbachev at their first summit in Geneva, November 19, 1985.

Handwritten draft of President Reagan's letter to General Secretary Gorbachev, first and last pages, November 28, 1985.

President Ronald Reagan speaks at the Brandenburg Gate, Berlin, June 12, 1987

A speech card from
President Reagan's
remarks, June 12, 1987.

- 10 -

THERE IS ONE SIGN THE SOVIETS CAN MAKE THAT
WOULD BE UNMISTAKABLE./THAT WOULD ADVANCE
DRAMATICALLY THE CAUSE OF FREEDOM AND PEACE.

GENERAL SECRETARY GORBACHEV, IF YOU
SEEK PEACE /- IF YOU SEEK PROSPERITY FOR
THE SOVIET UNION AND EASTERN EUROPE /-
IF YOU SEEK LIBERALIZATION/ COME HERE,
TO THIS GATE.

MR. GORBACHEV, OPEN THIS GATE.

MR. GORBACHEV, TEAR DOWN THIS WALL.

I UNDERSTAND THE FEAR OF WAR AND THE
PAIN OF DIVISION THAT AFFLICT THIS
CONTINENT /- AND I PLEDGE TO YOU MY
COUNTRY'S EFFORTS TO HELP OVERCOME THESE
BURDENS. TO BE SURE, WE IN THE WEST MUST
RESIST SOVIET EXPANSION. SO WE MUST
MAINTAIN DEFENSES OF UNASSAILABLE STRENGTH.
YET WE SEEK PEACE. SO WE MUST STRIVE TO
REDUCE ARMS ON BOTH SIDES.

THE WHITE HOUSE
WASHINGTON

7876

MEMORANDUM OF TELEPHONE CONVERSATION

SUBJECT: Telephone Call to Chancellor Helmut Kohl of
                         Germany

PARTICIPANTS: The President
                         Helmut Kohl, Chancellor
                         Notetaker: Robert Hutchings, NSC Staff
                         Interpreter: Gisela Marcuse

DATE, TIME   October 3, 1990, 9:56 - 9:59 a.m.
AND PLACE: The Oval Office

The President: Helmut! I am sitting in a meeting with members
of our Congress and am calling at the end of this historic day to
wish you well.

Chancellor Kohl: Things are going very, very well. I am in
Berlin. There were one million people here last night at the
very spot where the Wall used to stand -- and where President
Reagan called on Mr. Gorbachev to open this gate. Words can't
describe the feeling. The weather is very nice and warm,
fortunately. There were large crowds of young people. Eighty
percent were under thirty. It was fantastic.

A short time ago there was enormous applause when our President
said that our gratitude was owed especially to our Allied friends
and above all our American friends. I share that view. When the
parliamentary declaration is made, it will say that all American
Presidents from Harry Truman all the way up to our friend George
Bush made this possible. I would like to thank you again for all
your support for us.

The President: It was covered widely on American television.
America is proud to have stood with you through these
negotiations, and we identify with the hopes of the German
people. I have to run to another meeting, but I wanted you to
know what pride we have in standing by the German people.

Chancellor Kohl: Thank you very much.

The President: Good-bye, my friend.

Chancellor Kohl: Tell your Congressmen good wishes and thanks.

                    -- End of Conversation --

President Bush phones Chancellor Kohl, October 3, 1990.

In 1993, the German people presented George H.W. Bush with a 2½-ton piece of the Berlin Wall.

Memorandum of telephone conversation between President George H.W. Bush and Chancellor Helmut Kohl of Germany, October 3, 1990.

Dec. 31, 1990

Dear George, Jeb, Neil, Marvin, Doro.

I am writing this letter on the last day of 1991./

First, I can't begin to tell you how great it was to have you here
at Camp David. I loved the games (the Marines are still smarting
over their 1 and 2 record), I loved Christams Day, marred only by the absence
of Sam and Ellie. I loved the movies- some of 'em- I loved
the laughs. Most of all, I loved seeing you together. We are a family blessed; and this
Christmas simply reinforced all that.

I hope I didn't seem moody. I tried not to.

When I came into this job I vowed that I would never ring my hands
and talk about "the loneliest job in the world"
or ring my hands about the "pressures or the trials".

Having said that I have been concerned about what lies ahead.
There is no 'loneliness' though because I am backed by a first rate
team of knowledgeable and committed people. No President has been more
blessed in this regard..

I have thought long and hard about what might have to be done.
As I write this letter at Year's end, there is still some hope
that Iraq's dictator will pull out of Kuwait. I vary on this . Sometimes
I think he might, at others I think he simply is too unrealistic- too
ignorant of what he might face. I have the peace of mind that comes from knowing
that we have tried hard for peace. We have gone to the uN ;we have formed an historic
coalition; there have been diplomatic initiatives from country after country.
And so here we are a scant 16 days from a very important

date- the date set by the uN for his total compliance with all UN resolutions

including getting out of Kuwait- totally.

I guess what I want you to know as a father is this:

Every Human life is precious. When the question is asked "How many lives
are you willing to sacrifice"- it tears at my heart. The answer ,of course, is
none- none at all. We have waited to give sanctions a chance, we have moved
a tremendous force so as to reduce the risk to every American soldier
if force has to be used; but of loss of life the question still lingers and plagues the heart.

My mind goes back to history:

How many lives might have been saved if appeasement had given way to force
earlier on in the late '30's or earliest '40's? How many Jews might have been
sapred the gas chambers, or how many Polish patriots might be alive today?
I look at todays crisis as "good vs."evil".... yes, it is that clear.

I know my stance must cause you a little grief from time to time;and this
hurts me; but here at 'years end' I just wanted you to know that I feel:

- every human life is precious.. the little Iraqi kids' too.

- Principle must be adhered to- Saddam cannot profit in any
way at all from his aggression and from his brutalizing the people of Kuwait.

- and sometimes in life you have to act as you think best-you
can't compromise, you can't give in....even if your critics are loud and numerous.

Letter from George H.W. Bush to his children, December 31, 1990.

President George H.W. Bush shares Thanksgiving dinner while
visiting U.S. troops in Saudi Arabia, November 22, 1990.

-2-

So, dear kids- batten down the hatches.
Senator Inouye of HAwaii told me : " Mr. President, do what you have to do.
If it is quick and successful everyone can take the credit. If it is drawn
out , then be prepared for some in Congress to file impeachment papers
against you"... that's what he said, and he's 100% correct.
ANd so I shall say a few more prayers, mainly for our kids in the Gulf,
and I shall do what must be done, and I shall be strengthened every day
by our family love which lifts me up every single day of my life.
I am the luckiest Dad in the whole wide world.
I love you, Happy New Year and May God Bless
every one of you and all of your family

Devotedly

Dad

President Bill Clinton signs the North American Free Trade Agreement (NAFTA).

T-shirts sent to President Clinton expressing sentiments about NAFTA.

"This bombing in Oklahoma City...was an act of cowardice."

OA 22058   40-7-6-2

THE PRESIDENT HAS SEEN
4/19/95

I want the people of Oklahoma City to know that my
~~The prayers of all Americans are wt~~
thoughts are with you all. To you, to the innocent

victims of this brutal attack, and to the friends and
The people of Oklahoma City
families of the dead and wounded; We are praying for

~~you.~~

Okla City
This bombing was ~~an act of cowardice~~
~~Most of all, I want all the people of this country and I~~
an attack on defenseless children and innocent
~~want people around the world to know this: The United~~
~~citizens~~ → It was an act of cowardice. And it
~~States of America does not, and will never, tolerate~~ acts
was evil. The U.S. will not tolerate it. I will
~~of terror against our people.~~
not allow the people of this country to be
intimidated by sick cowards.

met w/ our   The
I have just ~~received a briefing from~~ a federal friendly
~~We~~   Deputy of the Witt's
~~interagency~~ team. I have taken the following steps to

the strongest
ensure ~~a total maximum~~ response to this situation:

President Clinton meets with heads of search and rescue teams and is briefed on the situation.

have declared   Okla City
2. I ~~am declaring~~ an emergency in the ~~State of~~

~~Oklahoma.~~ At my direction, James Lee Witt, the

Director of the Federal Emergency Management
Agency
~~Administration~~ is on his way to Oklahoma City.

We will do everything in our power to help the

people of Oklahoma deal with this tragedy.

1. I have deployed a crisis management ~~investigative~~

team under the leadership of the FBI, working with

the Department of Justice, the Bureau of Alcohol,

Tobacco, and Firearms, military, and local

authorities. We are sending the finest investigators
John Q. Public's
in the world to ~~get to the bottom of this.~~

2

[If any of those killed were federal employees, then

under the Crime Bill signed last year, the penalty for

this crime could be death.]

I ask all Americans to be conscious of the precautions

they must take at this time. I know that this situation

may mean certain inconveniences in the short run. But

working together, we will get through this.

Finally,
~~Meanwhile,~~ I ask all Americans to
pray tonight for the innocent victims
of this brutal attack —
                    for the friends + families
                    buried
of the dead + ~~wounded~~
                    + for the people of Okla. City.
             + grieving
May God ~~bless them~~ ~~these~~ —

4

President Bill Clinton's statement regarding the Oklahoma City
bombing, pages one, two, and four, April 19, 1995.

Manhattan on the morning of September 11, 2001.

AMERICAN AIRLINES FLIGHT #11
(Boeing 767)

- Pilot: Mohammed Atta (8D)
- Abdul Aziz al Omari (8G)
- Waleed al Shehri (2A)
- Wail al Shehri (2B)
- Satam al Suqami (10B)

Location of terrorists on American Airlines Flight #11.

UNITED AIRLINES FLIGHT #175
(Boeing 767)

- Pilot: Marwan al Shehhi (6C)
- Mohand al Shehri (2B)
- Hamza al Ghamdi (9C)
- Fayez Banihammad (2A)
- Ahmed al Ghamdi (9D)

Location of terrorists on United Airlines Flight #175.

Exterior of the crash site after the attack on the Pentagon, Arlington, Virginia, September 12, 2001.

AMERICAN AIRLINES FLIGHT #77
(Boeing 757)

- Pilot: Hani Hanjour (1B)
- Khalid al Mihdhar (12B)
- Nawaf al Hazmi (5E)
- Salem al Hazmi (5F)
- Majed Moqed (12A)

Location of terrorists on American Airlines Flight #77.

UNITED AIRLINES FLIGHT #93
(Boeing 757)

- Pilot: Ziad Samir Jarrah (1B)
- Saeed al Ghamdi (3D)
- Ahmed al Nami (3C)
- Ahmad al Haznawi (6B)

Location of terrorists on United Airlines Flight #93.

04/APR.10.2004 7: 5:11PM   NO.824   P.3
APR 10 '04 05:04PM

Declassified and Approved
for Release, 10 April 2004

Bin Ladin Determined To Strike in US

Clandestine, foreign government, and media reports indicate Bin Ladin since 1997 has wanted to conduct terrorist attacks in the US. Bin Ladin implied in US television interviews in 1997 and 1998 that his followers would follow the example of World Trade Center bomber Ramzi Yousef and "bring the fighting to America."

— After US missile strikes on his base in Afghanistan in 1998, Bin Ladin told followers he wanted to retaliate in Washington, according to a ▮▮▮▮▮ service.

— An Egyptian Islamic Jihad (EIJ) operative told an ▮▮▮ service at the same time that Bin Ladin was planning to exploit the operative's access to the US to mount a terrorist strike.

The millennium plotting in Canada in 1999 may have been part of Bin Ladin's first serious attempt to implement a terrorist strike in the US. Convicted plotter Ahmed Ressam has told the FBI that he conceived the idea to attack Los Angeles International Airport himself, but that Bin Ladin lieutenant Abu Zubaydah encouraged him and helped facilitate the operation. Ressam also said that in 1998 Abu Zubaydah was planning his own US attack.

— Ressam says Bin Ladin was aware of the Los Angeles operation.

Although Bin Ladin has not succeeded, his attacks against the US Embassies in Kenya and Tanzania in 1998 demonstrate that he prepares operations years in advance and is not deterred by setbacks. Bin Ladin associates surveilled our Embassies in Nairobi and Dar es Salaam as early as 1993, and some members of the Nairobi cell planning the bombings were arrested and deported in 1997.

Al-Qa'ida members—including some who are US citizens—have resided in or traveled to the US for years, and the group apparently maintains a support structure that could aid attacks. Two al-Qa'ida members found guilty in the conspiracy to bomb our Embassies in East Africa were US citizens, and a senior EIJ member lived in California in the mid-1990s.

— A clandestine source said in 1998 that a Bin Ladin cell in New York was recruiting Muslim-American youth for attacks.

We have not been able to corroborate some of the more sensational threat reporting, such as that from a ▮▮▮▮▮ service in 1998 saying that Bin Ladin wanted to hijack a US aircraft to gain the release of "Blind Shaykh" 'Umar 'Abd al-Rahman and other US-held extremists.

continued...

For the President Only   ▮▮▮▮   Declassified and Approved
6 August 2001   for Release, 10 April 2004

APR 10 '04

Declassified and Approved
for Release, 10 April 2004

04/APR.10.2004 7: 5:11PM

— Nevertheless, FBI information since that time indicates patterns of suspicious activity in this country consistent with preparations for hijackings or other types of attacks, including recent surveillance of federal buildings in New York.

— The FBI is conducting approximately 70 full field investigations throughout the US that it considers Bin Ladin–related. CIA and the FBI are investigating a call to our Embassy in the UAE in May saying that a group of Bin Ladin supporters was in the US planning attacks with explosives.

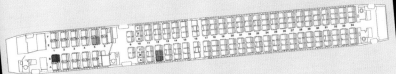

Declassified President's Daily Brief titled "Bin Ladin Determined to Strike in US," August 6, 2001.

processes as the President may establish, the Director of the Federal Emergency Management Agency also shall assist in the implementation of and management of those processes as the President may establish. The Director of the Federal Emergency Management Agency also shall assist in the implementation of national security emergency preparedness policy by coordinating with the other Federal departments and agencies and with State and local governments, and by providing periodic reports to the National Security Council and the Homeland Security Council on implementation of national security emergency preparedness policy."

(f) Section 201(7) is amended by inserting the words "and the Homeland Security Council" after the words "National Security Council."

(g) Section 206 is amended by inserting the words "and the Homeland Security Council" after the words "National Security Council."

(h) Section 208 is amended by inserting the words "or the Homeland Security Council" after the words "National Security Council."

THE WHITE HOUSE,
October 8, 2001.

Presidential Documents

Executive Order 13228 of October 8, 2001

Establishing the Office of Homeland Security and the Homeland Security Council

By the authority vested in me as President by the Constitution and the laws of the United States of America, it is hereby ordered as follows:

Section 1. *Establishment.* I hereby establish within the Executive Office of the President an Office of Homeland Security (the "Office") to be headed by the Assistant to the President for Homeland Security.

Sec. 2. *Mission.* The mission of the Office shall be to develop and coordinate the implementation of a comprehensive national strategy to secure the United States from terrorist threats or attacks. The Office shall perform the functions necessary to carry out this mission, including the functions specified in section 3 of this order.

Sec. 3. *Functions.* The functions of the Office shall be to coordinate the executive branch's efforts to detect, prepare for, prevent, protect against, respond to, and recover from terrorist attacks within the United States.

(a) *National Strategy.* The Office shall work with executive departments and agencies, State and local governments, and private entities to ensure the adequacy of the national strategy for detecting, preparing for, preventing, protecting against, responding to, and recovering from terrorist threats or attacks within the United States and shall periodically review and coordinate revisions to that strategy as necessary.

(b) *Detection.* The Office shall identify priorities and coordinate efforts for collection and analysis of information within the United States regarding threats of terrorism against the United States and activities of terrorists or terrorist groups within the United States. The Office also shall identify, in coordination with the Assistant to the President for National Security Affairs, priorities for collection of intelligence outside the United States regarding threats of terrorism within the United States.

(i) In performing these functions, the Office shall work with Federal, State, and local agencies, as appropriate, to:

(A) facilitate collection from State and local governments and private entities of information pertaining to terrorist threats or activities within the United States;

(B) coordinate and prioritize the requirements for foreign intelligence relating to terrorism within the United States of executive departments and agencies responsible for homeland security and provide these requirements and priorities to the Director of Central Intelligence and other agencies responsible for collection of foreign intelligence;

(C) coordinate efforts to ensure that all executive departments and agencies that have intelligence collection responsibilities have sufficient technological capabilities and resources to collect intelligence and data relating to terrorist activities or possible terrorist acts within the United States, working with the Assistant to the President for National Security Affairs, as appropriate;

(D) coordinate development of monitoring protocols and equipment for use in detecting the release of biological, chemical, and radiological hazards; and

"Uniting and Strengthening America by Providing Appropriate Tools Required to Intercept and Obstruct Terrorism..."

USA PATRIOT Act

2001

PUBLIC LAW 107-56

H. R. 3162

11/6

One Hundred Seventh Congress
of the
United States of America

AT THE FIRST SESSION

Begun and held at the City of Washington on Wednesday,
the third day of January, two thousand and one

An Act

To deter and punish terrorist acts in the United States and around the world,
to enhance law enforcement investigatory tools, and for other purposes.

Be it enacted by the Senate and House of Representatives of
the United States of America in Congress assembled,

SECTION 1. SHORT TITLE AND TABLE OF CONTENTS.

(a) SHORT TITLE.—This Act may be cited as the "Uniting and
Strengthening America by Providing Appropriate Tools Required
to Intercept and Obstruct Terrorism (USA PATRIOT ACT) Act
of 2001".

(b) TABLE OF CONTENTS.— ... of contents for this Act
is as follows:

THE WHITE HOUSE RECEIVED OCT 2 5 2001

OFFICE OF THE FEDERAL REGISTER NATIONAL ARCHIVES AND RECORDS ADMINISTRATION OCT 26 2001

H. R. 3162—131

(f) AUTHORIZATION OF APPROPRIATIONS.—There is hereby
authorized for the Department of Defense for fiscal year 2002,
$20,000,000 for the Defense Threat Reduction Agency for activities
of the National Infrastructure Simulation and Analysis Center
under this section in that fiscal year.

Speaker of the House of Representatives.

Vice President of the United States and
President of the Senate pro tempore.

APPROVED
OCT 2 6 2001

2009 | Official Tally from the Joint Session of Congress for the Counting of the Electoral Votes for President and Vice President of the United States

"...for the term beginning on the twentieth day of January, two thousand and nine."

Rob A Brady
PA 1

JOINT SESSION OF CONGRESS FOR THE
COUNTING OF THE ELECTORAL VOTES FOR PRESIDENT
AND VICE PRESIDENT OF THE UNITED STATES
OFFICIAL TALLY

The undersigned, Charles Schumer and Robert F. Bennett tellers on the part of the Senate, Robert A. Brady and Daniel E. Lungren tellers on the part of the House of Representatives, report the following as the result of the ascertainment and counting of the electoral vote for President and Vice President of the United States for the term beginning on the twentieth day of January, two thousand and nine.

Electoral Votes of each State	STATES	FOR PRESIDENT		FOR VICE PRESIDENT	
		Barack Obama	John McCain	Joseph Biden	Sarah Palin
9	ALABAMA		9		9
3	ALASKA		3		3
10	ARIZONA		10		10
6	ARKANSAS		6		6
55	CALIFORNIA	55		55	
9	COLORADO	9		9	
7	CONNECTICUT	7		7	
3	DELAWARE	3		3	
3	DISTRICT OF COLUMBIA	3		3	
27	FLORIDA	27		27	
15	GEORGIA		15		15
4	HAWAII	4		4	
4	IDAHO		4		4
21	ILLINOIS	21		21	
11	INDIANA	11		11	
7	IOWA	7		7	
6	KANSAS		6		6
8	KENTUCKY		8		8
9	LOUISIANA		9		9
4	MAINE	4		4	
10	MARYLAND	10		10	
12	MASSACHUSETTS	12		12	
17	MICHIGAN	17		17	
10	MINNESOTA	10		10	
6	MISSISSIPPI		6		6
11	MISSOURI		11		11
3	MONTANA		3		3
5	NEBRASKA	1	4	1	4
5	NEVADA	5		5	
4	NEW HAMPSHIRE	4		4	
15	NEW JERSEY	15		15	
5	NEW MEXICO	5		5	
31	NEW YORK	31		31	
15	NORTH CAROLINA	15		15	
3	NORTH DAKOTA		3		3
20	OHIO	20		20	
7	OKLAHOMA		7		7
7	OREGON	7		7	
21	PENNSYLVANIA	21		21	
4	RHODE ISLAND	4		4	
8	SOUTH CAROLINA		8		8
3	SOUTH DAKOTA		3		3
11	TENNESSEE		11		11
34	TEXAS		34		34
5	UTAH		5		5
3	VERMONT	3		3	
13	VIRGINIA	13		13	
11	WASHINGTON	11		11	
5	WEST VIRGINIA		5		5
10	WISCONSIN	10		10	
3	WYOMING		3		3
538					

Tellers on the part of the Senate.

Tellers on the part of the House of Representatives.

The state of the vote for President of the United States, as delivered to the President of the Senate, is as follows:

The whole number of the electors appointed to vote for President of the United States is 538, of which a majority is 270.

Barack Obama, of the State of Illinois, has received for President of the United States 365 votes;

John McCain, of the State of Arizona, has received 173 votes;

The state of the vote for Vice President of the United States, as delivered to the President of the

RECORD DESCRIPTIONS

ca. 1762 | PAGES 24–25

Annotated Map of the British Colonies in North America

Signers to the 1783 Treaty of Paris, which formally ended the American War for Independence, used this Mitchell Map of the former British colonies. This second English edition, revised by John Mitchell and probably issued before 1762, is annotated with a faint penciled line between the "highlands" and a point a little to the west of the northwest branch of the Connecticut River and with a penciled "X" near the portage at the north end of Ourangabena Lake. A notation, formerly on the original cloth backing and now preserved in a pocket on the back, reads "Mitchell's map. The copy used by the framers of the treaty of 1783."

RG 76, Records of Boundary and Claims Commissions and Arbitrations (Series 27, #1)

1775 | PAGE 26

Deposition of John Robins Regarding Hostilities at Lexington, April 24, 1775

In his deposition of April 24, 1775, delivered to the Massachusetts Assembly and later forwarded to the Continental Congress, John Robins gave an account of the Battle of Lexington, Massachusetts. He reported that the militia began dispersing when they were fired upon by a thousand of the King's troops being led by three mounted officers. Robins was wounded in the action.

RG 360, Records of the Continental and Confederation Congresses and the Constitutional Convention

1775 | PAGE 27

Boston, Its Environs and Harbour, with the Rebels Works Raised Against That Town in 1775

This British map depicting Boston and Boston Harbor during the Revolutionary War shows colonial military defenses and fortifications, such as Bunker Hill. The map was printed in London in 1778 but is based on firsthand British military observations. It came into the hands of the Corps of Engineers in the War Department in 1839.

RG 77, Records of the Office of the Chief Engineers (Fortification File, Drawer 19, Sheet 5)

1775 | PAGE 28

A Proclamation by the King for Suppressing Rebellion and Sedition, August 23, 1775

Following the outbreak of armed conflict at Lexington and Concord in the spring of 1775, King George III of England issued this proclamation on August 23, 1775. It stated that the colonies stood in open rebellion to his authority and were subject to severe penalty, as was any British subject who failed to report the knowledge of rebellion or conspiracy. This document literally transformed loyal subjects into traitorous rebels.

RG 360, Records of the Continental and Confederation Congresses and the Constitutional Convention

1775 | PAGE 29

The Agreement of Secrecy, November 9, 1775

Three months after King George III declared every rebel a traitor, and with a reward posted for the capture of certain prominent rebel leaders, delegates to the Continental Congress adopted these strict rules of secrecy to protect the cause of American liberty and their own lives. The agreement bears the signatures of 87 delegates; 39 signed on November 9, and the other delegates signed as they reported to Congress.

RG 360, Records of the Continental and Confederation Congresses and the Constitutional Convention

1776 | PAGE 30

Lee Resolution, July 2, 1776

In June 1776, Richard Henry Lee of Virginia introduced this resolution in the Second Continental Congress proposing independence for the American colonies. The Lee Resolution contained three parts: a declaration of independence, a call to form foreign alliances, and "a plan for confederation." Because many members of the Congress believed seeking independence would be premature or wanted instructions from their colonies before voting, approval was deferred until the following month, when Congress adopted the first part, the Declaration of Independence.

RG 360, Records of the Continental and Confederation Congresses and the Constitutional Convention

1776 | PAGE 31

Declaration of Independence, August 2, 1776

Thomas Jefferson, one of five members of the committee appointed by Congress to draft a statement of independence for the colonies, wrote the Declaration between June 11 and 28, 1776. He submitted a version to John Adams and Benjamin Franklin. They made some changes. The draft was then presented to Congress following the July 2 adoption of the independence section of the Lee Resolution. The congressional revision process took all of July 3 and most of July 4. Finally, on the afternoon of July 4, the Declaration was adopted. This engrossed copy of the Declaration, August 2, 1776, bears the bold signature of John Hancock, president of the Congress, and 55 other signers.

RG 360, Records of the Continental and Confederation Congresses and Constitutional Convention

1778 | PAGE 32

Oaths of Allegiance

During the War for Independence, military officers swore oaths of allegiance, declaring their loyalty to the United States. George Washington, Alexander Hamilton, and Marquis de Lafayette signed oaths of allegiance, as did Benedict Arnold, an American hero who would defect to join the British Army in 1780.

RG 93, War Department Collection of Revolutionary War Records

1781 | PAGE 33

Articles of Confederation, Adopted by Congress on November 15, 1777, and Ratified by the States on March 1, 1781

The first attempt at a formal, written constitution for the United States was the Articles of Confederation. With fear of a strong national government, the authors of the Articles denied Congress many important powers. Ultimately, the Articles proved unwieldy and inadequate to resolve the issues that faced the United States in its earliest years; but in granting any Federal powers to a central authority— Congress—this document marked a crucial step toward nationhood. The engrossed Articles of Confederation were presented to Congress on July 9, 1778; with Maryland's ratification, the Articles went into effect on March 1, 1781.

RG 360, Records of the Continental and Confederation Congresses and the Constitutional Convention

1781 | PAGE 34

Plan of the Attacks of York in Virginia by the Allied Armies of America and France

This is an original 1781 manuscript map of the Battle of Yorktown, the culminating battle of the Revolutionary War. The map shows the besieged British Army in Yorktown commanded by Lt. Gen. Earl Cornwallis, as well as American and French trench works around the town. The map also includes a brief chronology of the siege.

RG 360, Records of the Continental and Confederation Congresses and the Constitutional Convention

1781 | PAGE 35

Sarah Benjamin's Eyewitness Account of the Surrender at Yorktown, November 20, 1837

Sarah Osborn followed her first husband, Aaron, a commissary sergeant with the 3rd New York Regiment, during the Revolutionary War. She submitted this deposition to support her claim for a pension based upon her husband's service. These pages record her exploration of Yorktown the day Cornwallis surrendered, October 19, 1781, her meeting with Governor Nelson, and her subsequent trip back north. After the birth of their second child, Aaron abandoned the family and married another woman. Sarah later married John Benjamin.

RG 15, Records of the Department of Veterans Affairs

ca. 1782–ca. 1835 | PAGES 36–37

Frakturs, Proof of Birth and Family Heritage of Revolutionary War Veterans

Revolutionary War veterans and their families submitted hundreds of documents, including birth and marriage records, to support claims for pensions based on their service to the nation. Even family trees were saved as evidence. Some of these family histories are beautifully illustrated with decorative elements, whether printed or hand-drawn. One type of illustrated family record, commonly bearing bird and leaf motifs, is the *fraktur*. Created by and for members of the Pennsylvania Dutch culture, *frakturs* typically were written in German.

RG 15, Records of the Department of Veterans Affairs

1783 | PAGE 38

Treaty of Paris, September 3, 1783

The Treaty of Paris, sent to Congress by the American negotiators, John Adams, Benjamin Franklin, and John Jay, formally ended the Revolutionary War. Ratified on January 14, 1784, it is one of the most advantageous treaties ever negotiated for the United States. Two crucial provisions of the treaty were British recognition of U.S. independence and the delineation of boundaries that would allow for American western expansion.

RG 11, General Records of the U.S. Government

1785 | PAGE 39

Letter from John Adams, Minister to Britain, to John Jay, Secretary of State, Reporting on His Audience with King George III, June 2, 1785

On May 26, 1785, John Adams arrived in London to assume the post of the first United States Minister Plenipotentiary to Britain. Less than one week later, King George formally received John Adams, representative of the fledgling nation that had dealt the British Empire a bitter defeat. This letter is Adams's official report on that extraordinary meeting. It includes the remarks that Adams made in a speech and, as best as he could remember, the words spoken by the King in reply.

RG 360, Records of the Continental and Confederation Congresses and the Constitutional Convention

1786 | PAGE 40

Seven Ranges, Township No. IX, Second Range (Township 9 North, Range 2 West)

Designed to link up with the western terminus of the Mason-Dixon Line, the Seven Ranges were the first land surveys conducted by the Federal Government through the General Land Office. They would later extend all the way westward across the United States and account for why almost all land in the West is divided by right angles. The U.S. Government hoped to use profits from the land sales in the Seven Ranges to pay off debts from the Revolutionary War. But land sales were very slow. Eventually, the Government began to sell large tracts of land to investors and speculators, leaving them the task of finding buyers. This map shows the original survey for Township 9 North, Range 2 West.

RG 49, Records of the Bureau of Land Management (Township Plats; Ohio, Seven Ranges, T9N, R2W)

1787 | PAGE 41

Northwest Ordinance, July 13, 1787

The Northwest Ordinance, adopted July 13, 1787, by the Second Continental Congress, chartered a Government for the Northwest Territory, provided a method for admitting new states to the Union from the territory, and listed a bill of rights guaranteed in the territory. Following the principles outlined by Thomas Jefferson in the Ordinance of 1784, the authors of the Northwest Ordinance spelled out a plan that was used as the country expanded to the Pacific Ocean.

RG 360, Records of the Continental and Confederation Congresses and the Constitutional Convention

1787 | PAGE 42

George Washington's Annotated Copy of the First Printed Draft of the U.S. Constitution, August 6, 1787

George Washington, a delegate from Virginia who had served as commander in chief of the American forces during the War for Independence, presided over the Constitutional Convention in Philadelphia in the summer of 1787. Working in secret, delegates representing 12 of the 13 states abandoned the Articles of Confederation that had joined the states together during the American Revolution but had failed to create a cohesive nation. This is Washington's draft of the new Constitution, showing his handwritten notes. The draft was passed on to the Committee of Style to adjust the wording for the final text.

RG 360, Records of the Continental and Confederation Congresses and the Constitutional Convention

1787 | PAGE 43

Constitution of the United States, September 17, 1787

Delegates meeting in Philadelphia in May 1787 to revise the Articles of Confederation soon decided they would draft an entirely new frame of Government. This new constitution established a stronger central Government whose powers would be split among three branches—executive, legislative, and judicial—each with the authority to check and balance the other two. They also balanced the powers of big states and small states and made clear that the real power rested with the people. The work of many minds, the Constitution stands as a model of cooperative statesmanship and the art of compromise.

RG 11, General Records of the U.S. Government

1789 | PAGE 44

**President George Washington's
First Inaugural Address, April 30, 1789**

George Washington, hero of the American Revolution, was unanimously elected to serve as the first President of the United States. At his inauguration at Federal Hall in New York City on April 30, 1789, Washington accepted the Presidency and spoke of "the sacred fire of liberty" being "entrusted to the hands of the American people." All eight pages of the speech delivered to Congress are in Washington's own clear and distinctive handwriting.

RG 46, Records of the U.S. Senate

1789 | PAGE 45

**The Bill of Rights As Passed by the Senate,
September 9, 1789**

On June 8, 1789, Representative James Madison of Virginia introduced a series of proposed amendments to the newly ratified U.S. Constitution. That summer, the House of Representatives debated the issue and on August 24 passed 17 proposed constitutional amendments. The Senate then took up the matter and altered and consolidated the House amendments into 12. This printed document reflects the Senate's changes as passed on September 9, 1789. The line-outs on the first, third, and eighth articles indicate wording that had been amended in conference committee on September 24, 1789. Twelve articles of amendment were then sent to the states. Articles 3 through 12 were ratified and became the Bill of Rights in 1791.

RG 46, Records of the U.S. Senate

1790 | PAGE 46

Petition from the Pennsylvania Society for Promoting the Abolition of Slavery, Signed by Benjamin Franklin, President of the Society, February 3, 1790

Benjamin Franklin became a vocal opponent of slavery late in his long life. After the ratification of the Constitution in 1789, he wrote and published several essays supporting the end of slavery. His last public act was to send to Congress a petition on behalf of the Pennsylvania Society for Promoting the Abolition of Slavery. The petition, signed on February 3, 1790, asked the first Congress, then meeting in New York City, to "devise means for removing the Inconsistency from the

Character of the American People" and to "promote mercy and justice toward this distressed Race."

RG 46, Records of the U.S. Senate

1791 | PAGE 47

Memorial from Hannah Stephens Requesting the Release of Her Husband from Prison in Algiers, December 9, 1791

Hannah Stevens of Massachusetts sent this petition to Congress after the crew of her husband's ship was taken hostage by pirates in Algeria. Unable to keep up with payments on the house her husband had mortgaged before he left, Mrs. Stevens and her children had "been turned out of doors." She pleaded with Congress to ransom her husband from captivity and also to "make some provision for the subsistence of herself and her Children, in order that she may have some Alleviation of her accumulated Load of human Woe." After years of negotiations by the American Government, Isaac Stevens was among the hostages released in the summer of 1796.

RG 46, Records of the U.S. Senate

1794 | PAGE 48

Eli Whitney's Cotton Gin Patent Drawing, March 14, 1794

One of the earliest patents in the holdings of the National Archives, Eli Whitney's cotton gin was designed to separate cotton fiber from seed. Such machines had been around for centuries, but Whitney's design in 1794 was the first to clean short-staple cotton. A single cotton gin could produce up to 50 pounds of cleaned cotton in a day, making cotton a profitable crop for the first time. Cotton yields doubled each decade after 1800.

RG 241, Records of the Patent and Trademark Office
(Restored Patent Drawings, #72X)

1795 | PAGE 49

Design for the Hulls of the USS *Constellation* and the USS *Congress*

Built to protect American merchant shipping from attacks at sea, the USS *Constellation* and the USS *Congress* were two of the first six frigates authorized by Congress on March 27, 1794. The *Constellation* was built at the Sterrett Shipyard in Baltimore, Maryland, and launched in September 1797; the *Congress*, built in Portsmouth, New Hampshire, was launched in August 1799.

RG 19, Records of the Bureau of Ships (Dash File, 40-7-11)

Treaty of Greenville, Ratified Indian Treaty #23, August 3, 1795

Signed by Gen. "Mad" Anthony Wayne and several Indian tribes, the Treaty of Greenville ended the Indian War on the Northwestern Frontier, commonly called "Wayne's War," in 1795. The treaty, in which the Native Americans turned over to the United States much of present-day Ohio and Indiana, was signed by the Wyandot, Delaware, Shawnee, Ottawa, Chippewa, Potawatomi, Miami, Eel River, Wea, Kickapoo, Piankashaw, and Kaskaskia.

RG 11, General Records of the U.S. Government

Thomas Cooper's Violation of the Sedition Act

President John Adams and the Federalists, fearful of dissent at home while embroiled in conflict with France, sought to reduce opposition through the enactment of a series of laws by Congress known as the Alien and Sedition Acts. Under the Sedition Act of 1798, it was illegal to criticize the Government of the United States under penalty of fines and/or imprisonment. Thomas Cooper, a lawyer and newspaper editor in Sunbury, Pennsylvania, was indicted, prosecuted, and convicted of violating the Sedition Act after he published a broadside that was sharply critical of Adams. The Sedition Act was repealed after Thomas Jefferson won the Presidency.

National Archives at Philadelphia, RG 21, Records of District Courts of the United States

Congress Moves to Washington

The day before adjourning for the last time in Philadelphia on May 14, 1800, Congress passed this bill setting the time and place of its next session—the City of Washington on the third Monday in November 1800.

Top, RG 46, Records of the U.S. Senate; Bottom, RG 23, Records of the Coast and Geodetic Survey (Library & Archives, 859-1800)

Tally of Electoral Votes for the 1800 Presidential Election, February 11, 1801

Because the Constitution did not distinguish between President and Vice President in the votes cast by the Electoral College, both Thomas Jefferson and his running mate Aaron Burr received 73 votes in the election of 1800. The House of Representatives cast 35 ballots over five days to break the tie, but neither candidate received a majority. Finally, on February 17, 1801, on the 36th ballot, the House elected Thomas Jefferson to be President. In 1804, the 12th Amendment was passed, providing for separate Electoral College votes for President and Vice President.

RG 46, Records of the U.S. Senate

Louisiana Purchase

In what has been described as the greatest real estate deal in history, treaties were signed in April 1803 in Paris for the transfer of the Louisiana Territory to the United States for $15 million. The lands acquired stretched from the Mississippi River to the Rocky Mountains and from the Gulf of Mexico to the Canadian border, nearly doubling the size of the United States and making it one of the largest nations in the world. In October and November 1803, Congress considered the treaties and legislation to implement them. President Thomas Jefferson's message to Congress reported on the progress of the transfer and recognized the need for congressional action as "some important conditions cannot be carried into execution but with the aid of the legislative."

On December 20, 1803, Louisiana was officially transferred from France to the United States. On that day, William C.C. Claiborne, governor of the Mississippi Territory and one of the commissioners appointed to take possession of Louisiana, participated in the ceremonial exchange of land from Spain to France to the United States. Claiborne issued this proclamation to inform the residents of New Orleans that they now lived in the United States and owed allegiance to the new Government. The proclamation is written in English, French, and Spanish.

Top, RG 46, Records of the U.S. Senate; bottom, RG 233, Records of the U.S. House of Representatives

1803 | PAGE 55

Lewis and Clark Expedition

In January 1803, in a confidential message to Congress concerning trade with Native Americans, President Thomas Jefferson proposed to send the Federal Government's first exploration party west of the Mississippi River "to explore the whole line...to the Western Ocean." Congress acquiesced and provided an initial appropriation to support the endeavor. Jefferson selected his personal secretary Meriwether Lewis to lead the expedition, and, at Lewis's suggestion, William Clark shared the command. One of Jefferson's stated goals for the Lewis and Clark expedition was to make contact and establish trade relations with the Native American societies they encountered. To that end, the expedition was outfitted with a variety of Indian presents including "white glass beads," "calico shirts," and "small cheap looking glasses."

Top, RG 233, Records of the U.S. House of Representatives; bottom, RG 92, Records of the Office of the Quartermaster General

1804 | PAGE 56

Mediterranean Passport Guaranteeing Safe Passage for the Vessel *Mount Hope*, September 6, 1804

This 1804 passport, signed by President Thomas Jefferson, allowed U.S.-owned ships to sail the Mediterranean Sea without fear of interference by Barbary pirates.

National Archives at Boston, RG 36, Records of the U.S. Customs Service

1806 | PAGE 57

Zebulon Pike's Notebook of Maps, Traverse Tables, and Meteorological Observations

On July 15, 1806, U.S. soldier and explorer Zebulon Pike launched his expedition to map the southwestern portion of the Louisiana Purchase. Pike never successfully reached the summit of the famous peak in the Colorado Rocky Mountains that bears his name. He attempted it in November 1806 but turned back during a blizzard after having gone almost two days without food.

RG 94, Records of the Adjutant General's Office

1814–1815 | PAGES 58–59

Defense of Fort McHenry

In the War of 1812, 1,000 American soldiers defended the star-shaped Fort McHenry against the British during the Battle of Baltimore, September 13–14, 1814. Francis Scott Key, a young lawyer, witnessed the bombardment of Fort McHenry while under British guard on an American truce ship in the Patapsco River. Seeing his country's flag still flying over the fort the next morning, he was moved to write a poem, which became the U.S. national anthem in 1931.

Page 58: RG 107, Records of the Office of the Secretary of War. Page 59: RG 77, Records of the Office of the Chief Engineer (Civil Works Map file, G4-12)

1818 | PAGE 60

Patent Drawing of a Raft, February 14, 1818

As Americans pushed westward, they made full use of the Mississippi River system to explore new territory and to move agricultural products to market. This patent, granted to David Gordon on February 14, 1818, introduced innovations for a sturdier raft. The original drawing for this patent was destroyed by a fire in the Patent Office in 1836. This drawing is a restoration created in 1837 or shortly thereafter.

RG 241, Records of the Patent and Trademark Office (Restored Patent Drawings; #2912X)

1820 | PAGE 61

Conference Committee Report on the Missouri Compromise Bill, March 1, 1820

The Missouri Compromise admitted Missouri to the union as a slave state and Maine as a non-slave state to preserve the balance between free and slave states nationwide. It also outlawed slavery above the 36° 30´ latitude line in the remainder of the Louisiana Territory. This provision held for 34 years, until it was repealed by the Kansas-Nebraska Act of 1854.

RG 128, Records of Joint Committees of Congress

1830 | PAGE 62

Congressman Davy Crockett's Resolutions to Abolish West Point, February 25, 1830

In 1830, the frontiersman and soldier Davy Crockett was a young member of the House of Representatives from Tennessee. In these resolutions, Crockett attempted to abolish the Military Academy at West Point because he thought it was too elitist.

RG 233, Records of the U.S. House of Representatives

1831 | PAGE 63

Trial of Cadet Edgar Allan Poe, January 28, 1831

Edgar Allan Poe entered West Point in June 1830. He was a good student but wanted to leave because of money problems and continuing quarrels with his foster father. A parent's signature was required to withdraw from the military academy. When permission was refused, Poe decided to get himself court-martialed by ignoring his studies and failing to report for duty. These papers from the trial list charges against him of gross neglect of duty and absence from his "academical duties." On March 6, 1831, he was dismissed from West Point by sentence of court-martial.

RG 153, Records of the Office of the Judge Advocate General (Army)

1834 | PAGE 64

Register of Cherokee Indians Who Have Emigrated to the West of the Mississippi, 1834

In the Indian Removal Act of 1830, President Andrew Jackson called for the movement of native populations from lands east of the Mississippi River to make way for settlement by U.S. citizens. The tribes occupied portions of what are now the states of North and South Carolina, Florida, Georgia, Alabama, Tennessee, and Mississippi. Members of at least five tribes—the Cherokees, Choctaws, Chickasaws, Creeks, and Seminoles—were forced to move. No one really knows how many people were involved, or how many died, but there are a few types of records such as muster rolls and this register that give names and dates. This register recorded census-like data on Cherokee Indian family groups who were part of one migration.

RG 75, Records of the Bureau of Indian Affairs

ca. 1834 | PAGE 65

Map of Lands Assigned to Indians, Western Territory, ca. 1834

As the United States expanded westward, President Andrew Jackson promoted the removal of Indians to lands west of the Mississippi River. This map of the Western Territory, dating to the early 1830s, was prepared by the War Department at the request of the U.S. House Committee on Indian Affairs. It shows where different Indian tribes would be forcibly resettled.

RG 233, Records of the U.S. House of Representatives

1836–1837 | PAGE 66

Gag Rule

In 1836 under the gag rule resolution in the House of Representatives, antislavery petitions were prohibited from being read or debated on the floor, referred to a committee, or printed. The resolution was renewed in each Congress between 1837 and 1839, and in 1840, the House passed an even stricter rule, refusing to accept any antislavery petitions. Representative John Quincy Adams strongly opposed the gag rule, believing that it violated the First Amendment right to petition and that Congress was required to receive petitions even if it intended no action. When Adams's name was called to vote on the gag rule, he attempted to introduce a motion explaining his vote but was ruled out of order.

RG 233, Records of the U.S. House of Representatives

1838 | PAGE 67

Petition from the Women of Brookline, Massachusetts, Praying That the Gag Rule Be Rescinded, February 14, 1838

With the passage of the gag rule tabling all petitions relating to slavery, many more petitions were sent to Congress in protest. The petition of the women of Brookline, Massachusetts, to rescind the gag rule is an example of the hundreds of similar petitions that flooded into Congress each day. Two well-known abolitionists, Sarah and Angelina Grimké, signed this petition during their sensational speaking tour through New England. This petition was sent to Representative John Quincy Adams, the tireless opponent of the gag rule in the House of

Representatives. Unable to attack slavery directly, Adams used the gag rule to stir up discussion on the forbidden topic and to obstruct the daily legislative business of the opposition party by reading petitions on the House floor for hours each day.

RG 233, Records of the U.S. House of Representatives

1838 | PAGE 68

Gen. Winfield Scott's General Order No. 25, May 17, 1838

In 1830, President Andrew Jackson called for the relocation of eastern Native American tribes to land west of the Mississippi River in order to open new land to settlers. The most infamous of the Indian removals took place in 1838, two years after Jackson left the White House, as military forces under Gen. Winfield Scott forcibly removed the Cherokee. Their journey west became known as the "Trail of Tears" because of the thousands who were deliberately killed or who died from the brutal conditions and treatment along the way.

RG 393, Records of the U.S. Army Continental Commands

1838–1841 | PAGE 69

Financial Account of John Ross for Transporting a Detachment of Emigrant Cherokee by Steamboat to Indian Territory in Late 1838 and 1839, September 8, 1841

John Ross, principal chief of the Cherokee Nation, sent this eight-page letter to the War Department in September 1841, providing a rough estimate of the cost of transporting Cherokee emigrants to their new lands west of the Mississippi River under the Indian Removal Act. In the letter, Ross explained changes in the emigration plan, forcing them to go by water as the roads were impassable. After leaving his own sick family to check on the progress, Ross reported that his wife had died. His personal tragedy was followed by disputes over the cost of the Indians' forced relocation, sparking two congressional investigations. Ross's figures did not agree with those of the Army, leading many to believe that he had padded the number of people involved and the supplies needed to make a profit for his brother, who acted as a contractor for part of the emigration.

RG 217, Records of the Accounting Officers of the Department of the Treasury

1839–1841 | PAGES 70–71

The *Amistad* Case

The *Amistad* was a Cuban ship illegally transporting 53 Africans who had been abducted from Sierra Leone by Portuguese slave hunters and sold in Havana to Spanish planters. On July 1, 1839, the Africans, who were being sent to work on a Caribbean plantation, seized control of the ship, killed the captain and the cook, and ordered the planters to sail to Africa. On August 24, the *Amistad* was seized off of Long Island by the U.S. brig *Washington*. The planters were freed, and the Africans were imprisoned in New Haven, Connecticut, on charges of murder. Although the murder charges were dismissed, the Africans continued to be held as the commander of the U.S. vessel that seized the *Amistad* sought salvage of the schooner and its cargo, which he valued at $40,000 for the cargo and $25,000 for the Africans as slaves.

Claims to the *Amistad* Africans by the planters, the Government of Spain, and the captain of the brig that seized the vessel in U.S. waters led the case to trial in the Federal Circuit and District Courts in Connecticut. The court ruled that the case fell within Federal jurisdiction and that the claims to the Africans as property were not legitimate because they were illegally held as slaves. The case went to the Supreme Court in January 1841 with former President John Quincy Adams arguing that the Africans had the right to fight to regain their freedom. The Supreme Court decided in their favor, and 35 of them were returned to their homeland. The others died at sea or in prison awaiting trial.

National Archives at Boston, RG 21, Records of District Courts of the United States

1839 | PAGE 72

U.S. Ex. Ex. Expedition, Seagull Harbour, Gretton Bay, Wollaston Island, Tierra del Fuego

The U.S. Exploring Expedition, 1838–1842, was the first Government-sponsored naval voyage to discover and chart remote areas of the globe. Under the eccentric command of Lt. Charles Wilkes, six vessels traveled more than 87,000 miles, succeeding in surveying hundreds of islands and vast stretches of the Pacific Ocean and its coastlines.

RG 37, Records of the Hydrographic Office (Archives Section, 1838–1908, #272.24-18)

1847 | PAGE 73

Plan of the Battle Ground of Contreras and its Defenses, August 19–20, 1847

The Battle of Contreras, fought on the outskirts of Mexico City toward the end of the Mexican-American War of 1846–1848, was a lopsided victory for the American Army under Maj. Gen. Winfield Scott. The war resulted in a large portion of Mexican territory being ceded to the United States. This map was surveyed by R[obert]. E. Lee and George McClellan, future commanders of the Confederate and Union Armies, respectively, during the American Civil War. At the time of the battle, both were working for the U.S. Corps of Engineers. The map also includes Lee's signature.

RG 77, Records of the Office of the Chief of Engineers
(Fortification File; Drawer 112, Sheet 57)

1848 | PAGE 74

Electromagnetic Telegraph Patent

Samuel F.B. Morse, inventor of the Morse code, changed the course of history and revolutionized long-distance communications with his invention of the telegraph. Morse was issued a patent for the electromagnetic telegraph on June 20, 1840. The U.S. Patent Office certificate was submitted as an exhibit in the case *Samuel F.B. Morse, et al. v. Henry O'Reilly, et al.* The patent was reissued in 1848.

Top, 111-B-2591; National Archives at Atlanta, RG 21, Records of District Courts of the United States; Bottom, RG 241, Records of the Patent and Trademark Office (Reissued Patent Drawings, # RE117)

1848 | PAGE 75

Gold Rush, July 20, 1848

This map shows Sutter's Mill in Coloma, California, the sawmill owned by John Sutter where the first flakes of gold were spotted—a discovery that would trigger the California Gold Rush in 1848. Over the next seven years, 300,000 people headed to California to seek their fortunes. The map bears a simple hand-written notation: "Gold first discovered here."

RG 77, Civil Works Map File, W8-1

1848–1850 | PAGES 76–77

Westward Expansion and the Debate over Slavery

By 1850, disagreements over slavery threatened the bond between the North and South. Tensions escalated when Congress considered whether slavery would be permitted in the western territories acquired after the Mexican War. The issue was further complicated by the pending admission of California to the Union as a free state, jeopardizing the long-standing balance of free and slave states. Senator Henry Clay of Kentucky proposed a series of resolutions in the attempt to reach a compromise solution. Clay's resolutions ultimately failed, but after months of debate, Congress approved a compromise. The key provisions of the Compromise of 1850 admitted California as a free state, established a stricter Fugitive Slave Act, and outlawed the slave trade in the District of Columbia.

Left, RG 233, Records of the U.S. House of Representatives; right, RG 46, Records of the U.S. Senate

ca. 1851–ca. 1860 | PAGES 78–79

Lighthouse Plans for Minot's Ledge, Massachusetts

The National Archives holds more than 20,000 lighthouse plans, including more than 80 drawings of the Minot's Ledge Lighthouse, located one mile off the coast of the towns of Cohasset and Scituate, Massachusetts. In response to numerous shipwrecks along the rocky coast between 1832 and 1841, the original lighthouse was completed in 1849 but was destroyed in a storm within two years. It was understood that the new lighthouse would have to be built much stronger. The U.S. Army Corps of Topographical Engineers was given responsibility for the construction and work was completed by the end of the 1850s. The sturdier stone tower went into service in 1860. In the 1890s, the lighthouse's rotating light flashed in a 1-4-3 pattern, reminding those at sea and on land of the words "I love you." This lighthouse is still active today.

RG 26, Records of the U.S. Coast Guard [MA, Minot's Ledge #65 (page 78, top left), #4 (page 78, right), #11 (page 78, bottom left), #12 (page 79, left), #20 (page 79, right)]

1852 | PAGE 80

Diseño of Land Claim of Tomas Sanchez

The Mexican Cession of 1848 transferred 529,017 square miles of territory to the United States along with jurisdiction over a legal battle over land left by Vicente Sanchez, who died in 1846. This hand-drawn map of his ranch, "Cienega O'Paso de la Tjera," along with a claim appealing the division of the land, was filed in 1852 with the California Land Commission (PLC Docket 417), which eventually confirmed the division of the land between Sanchez's widow and Tomas Sanchez.

RG 49, Records of the Bureau of Land Management

1857–1862 | PAGE 81

Northwest Boundary Survey, Landscape Views by James Madison Alden

These landscapes are part of a series of watercolor sketches of the northwest boundary of the United States between the Rocky Mountains and the Pacific Ocean, commissioned by an act of Congress on August 11, 1856. The sketches were created by James Madison Alden between 1857 and 1862. They were produced as visual documentation of the work of the U.S. and British Commission in surveying and marking this boundary.

RG 76, Records of Boundary and Claims Commissions and Arbitrations (Series 70, #1, 2, 3, 4, 4.5, 5)

ca. 1860–ca. 1865 | PAGES 82–83

Mathew Brady, Photographs of Civil War–Era Personalities

After achieving success with his photographic portraits in New York, Mathew Brady opened a Washington studio in 1856, stating his obligation "to my country to preserve the faces of its historic men and mothers." Before turning his attention to documenting the Civil War, Brady's lens captured the politicians, diplomats, officers, actors, society matrons, and children of the capital city. The National Archives has more than 6,000 Brady images in its holdings.

Page 82: top, 111-B-1617; 111-B-1599; 111-B-1719; 111-B-2585; middle, 111-B-1716; 111-B-1742; 111-B-1616; 111-B-1673; bottom, 111-B-2381; 111-B-2302; 111-B-2276; 111-B-5864. Page 83: top,111-B-2245; 111-B-4521; 111-B-3791; 111-B-4256; middle, 111-B-1074; 111-B-2627; 111-B-4621; 111-B-2303; bottom, 111-B-5140; 111-B-6218; 111-B-3251; 111-B-3546

1861 | PAGE 84

Fort Sumter

Decades of strife between the North and South erupted in Civil War on April 12, 1861, when Confederate artillery opened fire on Fort Sumter, a Federal fort in Charleston Harbor. After 34 hours of fighting, the Union surrendered the fort. In February 1865, Confederate forces abandoned Fort Sumter when they evacuated Charleston due to Gen. William Sherman's advance through South Carolina.

Top, 121-B-A914A; bottom, 111-B-72; RG 94, Records of the Adjutant General's Office

1861 | PAGE 85

Ordinance of Secession of the Commonwealth of Virginia, April 17, 1861

On April 17, 1861, delegates to a special convention of the Commonwealth of Virginia voted to repeal its ratification of the United States Constitution. The Ordinance of Secession also dissolved Virginia's union with other states under the Constitution and declared it a free and independent state. Virginia was among the 11 states that seceded from the Union to form the Confederate States of America. After Virginia joined the Confederacy, the new Government moved its capital to Richmond.

RG 59, General Records of the Department of State

1861–1865 | PAGE 86

Confederate Currency

On the eve of the Civil War, the Confederate States of America created its own currency. The Confederate dollar bill was first issued in April 1861. At first, the currency was widely accepted throughout the South, but as confidence in the Confederates' chances of success waned and inflation rose, it became practically worthless. Individual states, cities, and banks also issued their own notes.

RG 39, Records of the Bureau of Accounts (Treasury)

1861 | PAGE 87

**Confederate States of America Court Record,
September 19, 1861**

The short-lived Confederate courts continued to use the
Federal court record books of the pre-secession period.
With a bit of crucial editing, forms from these record books
allowed "foreigners" from Rhode Island, New York, and
other "foreign homelands" to declare their intention to
become citizens of the Confederate States of America.

National Archives at Atlanta, RG 21, Records of District Courts of the United States

ca. 1860–ca. 1865 | PAGES 88–89

Mathew Brady, Photographs of the Civil War

In addition to the formal portraits of military men, Mathew
Brady and his associates—most notably Alexander Gardner,
George Barnard, and Timothy O'Sullivan—photographed
many battlefields, camps, towns, and people during the
Civil War. Their images present many aspects of war,
including camp life, routines, preparations, moments just
prior to battle, and the aftermath of battle. Battle scenes are
missing, however, because the photographic technology of
the time required that subjects be still at the moment the
camera's shutter snapped.

Page 88: top row, 111-B-2193; 111-B-4372; 111-B-1782; 111-B-4468; second row, 111-B-5249;
111-B-5123; 111-B-2514; 111-B-1867; third row, 111-B-4358; 111-B-2775; 111-B-5274; 111-B-4077;
bottom row, 111-B-2520; 111-B-5128; 111-B-4624; 111-B-2368. Page 89: top row, 111-B-3351;
111-B-5067; middle, 111-B-5071; 111-B-6355; bottom, 111-B-487; 111-B-2009

1862 | PAGES 90–91

After the Battle of Fredericksburg

Though the technology of the time prevented Mathew
Brady and his photographers from depicting the movement
and chaos of battle, they did capture the terrible aftermath.
Brady's photos of battlefield corpses shocked the public
when first displayed in 1862. In this poignant pairing
taken after the Battle of Fredericksburg, the survivors pose
for the camera while the vanquished await burial.

Page 90, 111-B-168. Page 91, 111-B-514

1863 | PAGE 92

Emancipation Proclamation, Presidential Proclamation 95

Initially, the Civil War was fought by the North to prevent
the secession of Southern states and preserve the Union.
Even though sectional conflicts over slavery had been a
major cause of the war, ending slavery was not a stated
goal of the war. That changed on September 22, 1862,
when President Abraham Lincoln issued his Preliminary
Emancipation Proclamation, stating that slaves in those
states still in rebellion as of January 1, 1863, would be
declared free. One hundred days later, the President issued
the Emancipation Proclamation declaring that slaves within
the rebellious areas "shall be then, thenceforward, and
forever free."

RG 11, General Records of the U.S. Government

ca. 1860–ca. 1865 | PAGE 93

Contraband Camps

Before the Emancipation Proclamation was issued in 1863,
slaves who escaped into Union territory were referred to as
"contraband," or prizes of war, as a way to sidestep the issue
of returning them to their owners. Slaves who escaped from
plantations and sought help from the Union Army were
placed in contraband camps, like this one in Arlington,
Virginia. The Bureau of Refugees, Freedmen, and Abandoned
Lands was established on March 3, 1865, to aid former
slaves. Organized in the War Department, the Freedmen's
Bureau provided food and clothing, operated hospitals and
dispensaries, helped reunite families, promoted education,
and assisted freedmen in legalizing marriages.

Top, 111-B-5240; bottom, 92-PR-MAP110(5)

1863–1864 | PAGES 94–95

Black Soldiers in the Civil War

Though free black men were turned away early in the Civil
War, the declining number of white volunteers, the growing
number of former slaves, and the increasing personnel
needs of the Union Army pushed the Government to
reconsider the ban. When the Emancipation Proclamation
was announced, black leaders such as Frederick Douglass
encouraged black men to become soldiers to ensure

eventual citizenship. Volunteers responded, and in May 1863 the Government established the Bureau of Colored Troops. Two of Douglass's sons joined the 54th Regiment of Massachusetts Volunteers, which lost two-thirds of its officers and half of its troops in the July 1863 assault on Fort Wagner, South Carolina.

RG 94, Records of the Adjutant General's Office, 1780s–1917

ca. 1861– ca. 1865 | PAGE 96
Cipher Device

Albert J. Myer was an Army surgeon whose interest in communication across long distances led him to invent a single flag code known as wig-wag signaling. After field-testing the device, Myer was appointed to organize and command the new U.S. Army Signal Corps in 1860. In an effort to improve the security of his system, Myer created this cipher disk, for which he later received a patent. The outer ring used only the numbers one through eight, while the movable inner ring placed the alphabet at random.

RG 111, Records of the Office of the Chief Signal Officer

1864–1865 | PAGE 97
President Abraham Lincoln's Telegrams

Patented by Samuel Morse in 1848, telegraphy was in its infancy when the Civil War broke out. The telegraph not only revolutionized the speed of communication but also affected the way battles were planned. Aided by field telegraph wagons, commanders could send and receive battle information. President Abraham Lincoln immediately grasped the advantage of electronic communication and was the first national leader to use the new device as a way to gather information and provide advice.

Top, left and right, and bottom right, RG 107, Records of the Office of the Secretary of War; bottom left, 165-SB-73

1864–1865 | PAGES 98–99
The End of the Civil War

Though temporarily set back by Gen. Robert E. Lee's last victory at the Battle of Cold Harbor in 1864, Gen. Ulysses S. Grant's strategy of attrition finally took its toll on the Confederate forces. The long Union siege of Petersburg severed supply lines and led to the fall of Richmond in April 1865. The two men most responsible for determining the

course of the Civil War met in a parlor at Appomattox Court House, Virginia, on the morning of April 9 to discuss the formalities of surrendering the Army of Northern Virginia. On April 12, 1865, the war that had lasted four years and cost 623,000 lives effectively ended when Confederate soldiers stacked their arms in a surrender ceremony.

Page 98: 111-B-36. Page 100, 111-B-1564

1865 | PAGES 100–101
The Assassination of President Abraham Lincoln

On April 14, 1865, John Wilkes Booth, a prominent American actor, snuck up behind President Abraham Lincoln as he watched a play at Ford's Theater and shot him in the back of the head at point-blank range. The President was carried across the street to a private home where he was attended to by several doctors throughout the night, including his family physician Dr. Robert King Stone. Lincoln died early the following morning. Booth, pursued by Union soldiers for 12 days through southern Maryland and Virginia, died of a gunshot wound on April 26 after refusing to surrender to Federal troops.

Page 100, top, RG 153, Records of the Office of the Judge Advocate General (Army); 64-M-19; middle, RG 60, General Records of the Department of Justice; bottom, RG 94, Records of the Adjutant General's Office; 111-B-3475. Page 101, top, RG 153, Records of the Office of the Judge Advocate General (Army); bottom, 111-B-5927

1865–1866 | PAGES 102–103
Freedmen's Bureau Marriage Records

Established in the years following the Civil War, the War Department's Bureau of Refugees, Freedmen, and Abandoned Lands—generally known as the Freedmen's Bureau—provided assistance to tens of thousands of former slaves making the transition to freedom. While many slave couples formed lasting bonds during their enslavement, slave marriages had no legal foundation or protection. The abolishment of slavery not only meant citizenship but also the ability to have legally recognized marriages without fear of the loss of a spouse through sale. The Bureau helped facilitate and record marriages.

RG 105, Records of the Bureau of Refugees, Freedmen, and Abandoned Lands

1866 | PAGE 104

A Petition for Universal Suffrage, January 1866

The end of slavery raised more questions than it answered regarding the future of freed women and men. Proposals for a 14th Amendment to define and protect the rights of black men quickly followed the ratification of the 13th Amendment abolishing slavery in 1865. Suffragists Elizabeth Cady Stanton and Susan B. Anthony were determined to include women in any constitutional changes being considered in Congress. The two organized a small group of women's rights advocates and former abolitionists to launch a campaign for "universal suffrage"—unrestricted voting rights for all male and female citizens. This campaign marked the first national petition drive to feature woman suffrage among its demands.

RG 233, Records of the U.S. House of Representatives

1866 | PAGE 105

H.J. Res. 127. Joint Resolution Proposing an Amendment to the Constitution of the United States, Passed on June 13, 1866

The 14th Amendment to the U.S. Constitution, passed by Congress on June 13, 1866, and ratified by the states on July 9, 1868, is one of the post-Civil War amendments (known as the Reconstruction Amendments) first intended to secure rights for former slaves. It includes the Due Process and Equal Protection Clauses, among others.

RG 46, Records of the U.S. Senate

1867–1869 | PAGES 106–107

Timothy O'Sullivan, Photographs for the 40th Parallel Survey

Orders for the Government-sponsored Geological Exploration of the 40th Parallel, begun in 1867, called for a comprehensive survey "to examine and describe the geological structure, geographical condition and natural resources...along the 40th parallel of latitude" and to include the line of the projected Union and Central Pacific railroads. Under the direction of Clarence King, the survey mapped the area from western Nevada to eastern Wyoming and also examined mines and collected geological, botanical, and zoological specimens. Timothy O'Sullivan, who had helped Mathew

Brady photograph the Civil War, was chosen to accompany the survey. His photographs present a record of the vast landscape as well as the first encroachments of civilization.

Page 106: top, 77-KS-3460; 77-KN-125; middle, 77-KN-134; 77-KN-95; bottom, 77-KN-20; 77-KN-21; 77-KN-17; 77-KN-19. Page 107: top row, 77-KW-117; 77-KW-133; second row, 77-KW-139; 77-KW-141; third row, 77-KW-166; 77-KW-207; bottom, 77-KW-34; 77-KW-35

1868 | PAGE 108

Impeachment of President Andrew Johnson

When the Civil War ended, President Andrew Johnson and Congress were divided on how to rebuild the former Confederacy. The President saw Reconstruction as an executive responsibility and vetoed all congressional initiatives. Tensions between the President and the Radical Republicans in Congress reached the boiling point when Johnson fired Secretary of War Edwin Stanton, violating the Tenure of Office Act. The outraged House voted immediately to impeach the President. The Senate trial began in March and concluded on May 26, 1868, with Johnson escaping removal from office by one vote.

Left and right, RG 46, Records of the U.S. Senate; top, 111-B-4279; center, RG 233, Records of the U.S. House of Representatives; bottom, 111-B-5929

1868 | PAGE 109

Alaska Purchase

In 1866, the Russian Government offered to sell the territory of Alaska to the United States. Secretary of State William H. Seward, enthusiastic about the prospects of American expansion, negotiated to pay Russia $7.2 million for the territory. Though disparaged at the time as "Seward's Folly," the purchase brought the United States 600,000 mineral-rich acres for less than 2 cents an acre. The Treaty of Cession, signed in 1868 by the Russian Czar Alexander II, formally concluded the transaction.

Left, RG 11, General Records of the U.S. Government; right, 111-B-4305; bottom, RG 217, Records of the Accounting Officers of the Department of the Treasury

1869 | PAGES 110–111

Joining the Tracks for the First Transcontinental Railroad, Promontory, Utah Territory

On May 10, 1869, the Union Pacific and Central Pacific railroads met at Promontory Summit, Utah Territory. In a ceremony that featured the driving of a golden spike, the companies joined 1,776 miles of track to complete the nation's first transcontinental railway.

Page 110: 30-N-36-2994. Page 111: RG 77, Civil Works Map File, W123

1871–1874 | PAGES 112–113

Timothy O'Sullivan, Photographs for the Wheeler Survey

In 1871, Lt. George Wheeler was sent to explore the U.S. territory lying south of the Central Pacific Railroad in an expedition directed by the Army Corps of Engineers. This exploration ultimately grew into a four-year series of expeditions covering areas west of the 100th meridian, including portions of present-day California, Nevada, Arizona, Utah, New Mexico, Colorado, and Idaho. Along with mapping, the Wheeler Survey was expected to collect information about mineral resources, geology, and agricultural prospects. Timothy O'Sullivan, who also accompanied Clarence King on the Geological Exploration of the 40th Parallel, photographed extensively for the 1871, 1873, and 1874 Wheeler expeditions, while William Bell served as the lead photographer for the 1872 Wheeler expedition. O'Sullivan's images show the harsh landscape and the people, natives, and newcomers, who populated it.

Page 112: top, 77-WF-51; 77-WF-39; middle, 106-WA-159; 106-WA-384; bottom, 106-WA-122; 106-WA-387. Page 113: 106-WB-343

1876 | PAGE 114

Battle of Little Bighorn

Despite the 1868 treaty recognizing the Black Hills as part of the Great Sioux Reservation, Gen. George A. Custer led an expedition there in 1874, accompanied by miners seeking gold. Once gold was discovered, miners started moving into the Sioux hunting grounds, demanding protection from the U.S. Army. The Army was ordered to move against wandering bands of Sioux, though the Indians were hunting there in accordance with their treaty rights. In 1876, Custer, leading an Army detachment, encountered an encampment of Sioux and Cheyenne at the Little Bighorn River. Custer's detachment was annihilated, but the United States would continue its battle against the Sioux in the Black Hills until the Government confiscated the land in 1877.

Top and bottom left, RG 94, Records of the Adjutant General's Office; top right, 77-HQ-264-847; bottom right, 111-SC-82966

1876 | PAGE 115

Deadwood, Dakota Territory

Deadwood sprang up in the Dakota Territory in 1876 as a result of the gold rush into the Black Hills. The population grew quickly, and the town developed a reputation for lawlessness. Deadwood was the scene of the notorious murder of Wild Bill Hickok.

165-FF-2F-10; 165-FF-2F-15

1879–1884 | PAGE 116

Homestead Applications

Laura Ingalls Wilder, beloved author of *Little House on the Prairie* and other books about growing up on the frontier, shared her first home with her husband, Almanzo Wilder, in Dakota Territory. The 1884 final certificate demonstrates that they had "proved up" or built a house, improved the land, and lived on it for five years. Eliza Wilder, Almanzo's sister, also filed a homestead application on August 21, 1879. Homesteaders would often display the patent in their home to honor their hard work.

RG 49, Records of the Bureau of Land Management

1886 | PAGE 117

Family with Their Covered Wagon during the Great Western Migration, Loup Valley, Nebraska

As Americans pushed westward to make their homes and seek their fortunes, settlers traveled and lived aboard covered wagons. They formed wagon trains with other homesteaders for protection through the difficult and dangerous frontier.

69-N-13606C

1889–1894 | PAGE 118

Oklahoma Territory

The state of Oklahoma was settled in 1889 with the first land run to assign ownership of unoccupied land. At noon on April 22, 1889, an estimated 50,000 people lined up in a race to stake their claims. Under the Homestead Act of 1862, settlers could claim lots of up to 160 acres and could eventually receive the title to the land by living on it and improving it. Settlers could also make claim under the Preemption Act of 1841, and after 14 years, they could purchase the land from the General Land Office for as little as $1.25 an acre.

Top, 111-SC-87337; second row, 233-TRP-64; 49-AR-19b; third row, 49-AR-7; 49-AR-32; bottom, 48-RST-7B-79; 33-TRP-47

1894 | PAGE 119

Hopi (Moqui) Petition Asking the Federal Government to Give Them Title to Their Lands, March 27–28, 1894

After 1870, Federal policy toward native people shifted away from treaties and the establishment of reservations to granting individual land allotments and encouraging farming. The Dawes Act of 1887 allowed the President to break up reservations, which tribes held in common, into small parcels for individual tribal members. In many cases, this was disastrous for the Indians because land was often unsuitable for agriculture and farming differed from their traditional way of life. The chiefs and headmen of the Moqui Villages of Arizona sent this 1894 petition to the Federal Government, asking for title to their lands instead of allotting parcels to individuals. This document is unique in that every family in the tribe is represented by their "totem signatures."

RG 75, Records of the Bureau of Indian Affairs

1895 | PAGE 120

Death of Secretary of State Walter Q. Gresham, May 28, 1895

Walter Q. Gresham, a general in the Union Army during the Civil War, served as U.S. postmaster general, a Federal appellate court judge, and secretary of the treasury before becoming President Grover Cleveland's secretary of state in 1893. He died in office two years later and was given a military funeral in the East Room of the White House. A sculptor was called in to make a death mask of the Cabinet officer shortly after his death so that monuments in bronze or marble could be made in his honor.

RG 59, General Records of the Department of State

1895 | PAGE 121

Patent Drawing for the Duryea Road Vehicle, June 11, 1895

This patent was granted to Charles Duryea on June 11, 1895, for improvements in road vehicles that he and his brother Frank had developed. The Duryeas produced the first successful American gasoline-powered automobile and later went on to help found the Duryea Motor Wagon Company, which manufactured 13 automobiles in 1896.

RG 241, Records of the Patent and Trademark Office
(Utility Patents, #540,648, Sheet 1 of 4)

1896 | PAGE 122

Wong Kim Ark

The Chinese Exclusion Act of 1882, renewed in 1892, provided an absolute moratorium on Chinese labor immigration although Chinese merchants, students, teachers, and clergy were allowed to enter the United States. San Francisco–born Wong Kim Ark visited China in 1894. When he returned to the United States in 1895, he was denied entry on the claim that he was not a U.S. citizen and was not a member of one of the Chinese classes exempt from exclusion. Wong appealed and the case went all the way to the U.S. Supreme Court, which ruled that U.S.-born descendants of immigrants could not be denied citizenship, regardless of their ethnicity or the nationality of their ancestors.

National Archives at San Francisco: top left and bottom, RG 21, Records of District Courts of the United States; top right, RG 85, Records of the Immigration and Naturalization Service

1897 | PAGE 123

Petition Against the Annexation of Hawaii

In 1897 more than 21,000 native Hawaiian men and women, out of a population of less than 40,000, signed this petition asking the U.S. Senate to defeat a proposed treaty for the annexation of Hawaii to the United States. However, after America went to war with Spain in 1898, proponents of annexation argued that Hawaii was needed to support military action in the Philippines. In July 1898 Congress passed a joint resolution taking control over Hawaii's 6,450 square miles of territory.

RG 46, Records of the U.S. Senate

1899 | PAGE 124

Passenger Manifest of Immigrants on the SS *Brasilia*, January 31, 1899

Among the most useful records for genealogists at the National Archives are the passenger arrival records. This manifest contains the names of immigrants who arrived on the SS *Brasilia* from Hamburg, Germany, on January 31, 1899. In addition to standard information such as name and age, this form requests that each respondent identify who paid for the passage on the ship and whether he or she is a polygamist.

RG 85, Records of the Immigration and Naturalization Service

ca. 1900 | PAGE 125
Ellis Island

The Immigration Station at Ellis Island in New York Harbor was the major East Coast processing center for immigrants who came to the United States between 1892 and 1924. After July 1, 1924, immigrants were processed aboard ship and only went to Ellis Island if detained. It functioned primarily as a detention center from 1924 to 1955 when Ellis Island closed. An estimated 20 million individuals began their new lives in America at Ellis Island.

Top, 90-G-125-6; National Archives at New York City, RG 79, Records of the National Parks Service; middle, 90-G-125-23; 90-G-125-3; bottom, 90-G-125-17; 90-G-125-16

1900 | PAGES 126–127
Boxer Rebellion

In June 1900, a crisis erupted in China as the "Boxers," a secret society, rose up against the presence and influence of foreigners and Christians on their soil. On October 1, 1900, the U.S. Consul in Canton, China, Robert M. McWade, included examples of propaganda handbills in his dispatch to Assistant Secretary of State David J. Hill describing "The Boxer Rebellion." These colored drawings depict scenes from the Boxer Rebellion, in which the Boxers attacked foreign embassies in Peking. Diplomats, civilians from abroad, foreign sailors and marines, and some Chinese Christians held out for nearly two months in the city's Legation Quarter until an alliance of eight nations—the United States, Austria-Hungary, France, Germany, Britain, Italy, Japan, and Russia—sent in troops to rescue them.

RG 59, General Records of the Department of State

ca. 1900 | PAGES 128–129
Thomas Edison Patent Infringement Case

Thomas Edison, a prolific inventor and the holder of more than 1,000 patents, including those for the light bulb, the phonograph, and improvements to the telegraph and telephone, fought in court to defend many of his inventions. But in a 1902 decision, the U.S. Circuit Court of Appeals for the Southern District of New York ruled against him, saying that despite his work on the movie camera, he was not its official inventor.

National Archives at New York City, RG 21, Records of District Courts of the United States

1901–1902 | PAGES 130–131
Russell W. Porter Arctic Paintings

Russell Williams Porter (1871–1949) was one of several turn-of-the-century explorers to venture above the Arctic Circle in a quest to reach the North Pole. Porter made the trip six times between 1894 and 1903, leaving behind a collection of paintings, drawings, diaries, letters, and maps, many of which were donated to the National Archives by Porter's family. The National Archives officially began collecting personal papers of Polar explorers and their families in September 1967. Many explorers and their descendants donated their journals and diaries chronicling their exploits.

Collection XRWP: Russell W. Porter Papers, ca. 1889–ca. 1970

1902 | PAGE 132
Holland Submarine

Inventor John P. Holland submitted this drawing of a submarine boat to the U.S. Patent Office in support of his application for a patent, which he received on September 2, 1902. An earlier Holland submarine, *Plunger*, was an experimental steam-powered submarine launched in 1897. The boat's complex machinery proved unworkable, so it was never accepted for service by the Navy.

Top, RG 241, Records of the Patent and Trademark Office (Utility Patents, #708,553, Sheet 2 of 2); bottom, 19-N-15-26-14

1903 | PAGE 133
The Wright Brothers' Aircraft

Wilbur and Orville Wright patented the design for several unpowered gliders before making their first successful flight in a powered aircraft later in 1903. This patent oath is for one of their unpowered gliders. The Wright brothers' invention launched a revolution in transportation.

Top, 165-WW-713-6; bottom, RG 241, Records of the Patent and Trademark Office

1906 | PAGES 134–135

San Francisco Earthquake

On the morning of April 18, 1906, a massive earthquake shook San Francisco, California. Although the quake lasted less than a minute, its impact was disastrous as fires destroyed nearly 500 city blocks. Despite a quick response from San Francisco's large military population, the city was devastated. The earthquake and fires killed an estimated 3,000 people and left half of the city's 400,000 residents homeless. Aid poured in from around the country and the world, but those who survived faced weeks of hardship, sleeping in tents in city parks and the Presidio, standing in long lines for food, and doing their cooking in the street to minimize the threat of additional fires.

Page 134: top, 111-SC-95117; 111-SC-95101; middle, RG 46, Records of the U.S. Senate; bottom, 111-SC-95133; 111-SC-95176. Page 135: RG 77, Records of the Office of the Chief of Engineers (Fortification File, Drawer 215, Sheet 3-2)

ca. 1906 | PAGES 136–137

Meatpacking

In *The Jungle*, author Upton Sinclair took aim at the exploitation of workers in a Chicago meatpacking house. His descriptions of the unsafe and filthy conditions, and the threat they posed to consumers, prompted President Theodore Roosevelt to call for an investigation of the industry. In his message transmitting the investigation's findings, Roosevelt urged Congress to immediately enact legislation providing for meat inspection and ensuring sanitary meat-packing conditions. The subsequent Meat Inspection Act of 1906 established a system of meat inspection that endured for nearly a century.

Page 136: RG 16, Records of the Office of the Secretary of Agriculture; RG 233, Records of the U.S. House of Representatives. Page 137: 17-PE-10

1907 | PAGE 138

"Life on the Mississippi," by Clifford Berryman, October 2, 1907.

President Theodore Roosevelt traveled down the Mississippi River in October 1907 to show support for the creation of a deep waterway to the Gulf of Mexico. His voyage was interrupted by heavy rain and choppy river conditions. The political climate was also threatening, as Roosevelt had serious railroad issues to straighten out. In this cartoon by Pulitzer Prize winner Clifford K. Berryman, the path of the

President's ship is marked by driftwood labeled, "railroad trust" and "Harriman interests." More than 2,000 of Berryman's cartoons, which appeared on the front page of Washington newspapers from 1898 through 1949, are housed with the historical records of Congress at the National Archives.

U.S. Senate Collection, Center for Legislative Archives

1908 | PAGE 139

"The House in Session (According to the Minority Point of View)," by Clifford Berryman, April 16, 1908

Joseph G. Cannon served in the U.S. House of Representatives as a Republican from Illinois for 23 terms over the course of nearly 50 years, but he is most notable for the four terms he served as Speaker of the House (1903–1911). First elected Speaker on November 9, 1903, Cannon is regarded as one of the most powerful and colorful Speakers in U.S. history. He is depicted in this 1908 cartoon by Clifford K. Berryman, published in the *Washington Evening Star*.

U.S. Senate Collection, Center for Legislative Archives

1908–1911 | PAGES 140–141

Lewis Hine, Photographs for the National Child Labor Committee

As the demand for labor grew in the late 19th and early 20th centuries, many children were drawn into the labor force. As an investigative photographer with the National Child Labor Committee, Lewis Hine documented young workers laboring in coal mines, factories, fields, and street trades. Hine's images are unflinching, and he accompanied them with his own captions, which are sparely written but filled with facts about the children's lives.

Page 140: top, 102-LH-462; 102-LH-136; middle, 102-LH-2260; 102-LH-490; bottom, 102-LH-1377; 102-LH-947. Page 141: 102-LH-1938

1912 | PAGES 142–143

Sinking of the *Titanic*

When the British ship *Titanic* steamed out of Southampton bound for New York on April 10, 1912, it was the largest and most sumptuous luxury liner that had ever sailed. Because the ship was thought to be unsinkable, its owners and builders rejected plans calling for as many as 64 lifeboats.

Although the 20 lifeboats on the *Titanic* exceeded Government standards, the boats would only accommodate about half of the 2,228 people aboard. The *Titanic* sank on its maiden voyage, after colliding with an iceberg off the banks of Newfoundland. More than 1,500 people died. The chart was one of many produced by the Hydrographic Office to be used in the U.S. Senate Committee hearings on the *Titanic* disaster.

Page 142: National Archives at New York City, RG 21, Records of District Courts of the United States. Page 143: RG 37, Records of the Hydrographic Office (Library & Archives 1908–1924, #64563-Chart #1)

1913 | PAGE 144

Income Tax Form 1040

Passed by Congress on July 2, 1909, and ratified February 3, 1913, the 16th Amendment established Congress's right to impose a Federal income tax. In 1913, due to generous exemptions and deductions, less than 1 percent of the population paid income taxes at the rate of only 1 percent of net income.

RG 56, General Records of the Department of the Treasury

1913 | PAGE 145

Map Showing Schools and Saloons in the District of Columbia

This map shows schools and saloons in the District of Columbia in 1913. It notes that there are 47 "licensed places" along the Presidential Inaugural Parade route alone. The map was submitted with a petition in support of the Jones-Works excise law, which, among other provisions, restricted the location of saloons in the District in the lead up to the national law on Prohibition.

RG 233, Records of the U.S. House of Representatives

1914–1916 | PAGES 146–147

Public Markets

In the late 19th and early 20th centuries, in cities around the country, indoor and open-air markets became public gathering places as shoppers purchased meat, fish, produce, and other necessities of living. Records on public markets were kept by the U.S. Department of Agriculture's Bureau of Agricultural Economics, which conducted research on agricultural marketing and transportation.

Page 150: top, 83-G-3678; 83-G-3121; middle, 83-G-3716; 83-G-546; bottom, 83-G-3725; 83-G-3228. Page 151: 83-G-21

ca. 1917 | PAGES 148–149

Passport Photos

In the early part of the 20th century, Americans increased their travels around the world, as evidenced by the National Archives' vast holdings of passport photos and applications. Photos were not required for passports until December 21, 1914.

RG 59, General Records of the Department of State

ca. 1917 | PAGES 150–151

World War I Draft Cards

Almost immediately after the United States declared war in April 1917, President Woodrow Wilson authorized a draft in which 24 million men registered, and 2 million were drafted. The records are noteworthy for the range of listed occupations from the era, including "furrier," "weaver," and "vaudeville artist."

National Archives at Atlanta, RG 163, Records of the Selective Service System (World War I)

1917–1919 | PAGES 152–153

World War I Panoramas

Since the earliest days of photography, panoramic views have drawn interest for their ability to convey a wide perspective, especially in depicting landscapes and groups of people. Panoramas in the Still Pictures branch of the National Archives start around 1864, with the majority of the holdings dating from World War I.

Top, 165-PP-77-1; middle, 24-PAN-30; bottom, 92-PN-28a

1918 | PAGES 154–155

Cantigny

The Battle of Cantigny, fought in a small village north of Paris, France, was the first American-led offensive of World War I. On May 28, 1918, the 28th Infantry Regiment of the 1st Division attacked and defeated German forces and held the village against repeated counterattacks despite suffering more than 1,000 casualties. During the attack, the American troops utilized the modern tactics of combining infantry, artillery, tanks, and airplanes. Preparations for the battle were based on maps drawn from aerial reconnaissance, and the fighting was documented with ground and aerial photography.

Page 154: RG 120, Records of the Allied Expeditionary Forces (Aerial Photographs of Operations with Interpretations, Cantigny, #20, #19); 111-SC-2913. Page 155: left, top to bottom, 111-SC 13928; 111-SC-13948; 111-SC-13954; right, top to bottom, RG 120, Records of the American Expeditionary Forces (World War I)

1918 | PAGE 156

Fruit Stones for Gas Masks

A horrible new weapon emerged during World War I—poison gas. The most widely used gases were chlorine, phosgene, and mustard gas, all of which caused severe injury or death if inhaled. Gas masks became more sophisticated as the war progressed, with filter respirators being the most effective. Encouraged by wartime posters promoting fruit stone drives, people throughout the United States collected fruit stones and nut shells to manufacture charcoal filters for gas masks.

Top, 165-WW-600D(5); bottom, National Archives at Boston, RG 4, Records of the U.S. Food Administration

1918 | PAGE 157

Influenza Epidemic

The influenza pandemic of 1918 emerged without warning in late spring and was known as the "three-day fever." Most victims recovered within days, and few deaths were reported. But when the disease resurfaced that fall, it was far more severe. The deadly virus attacked one-fifth of the world's population, and within months, it had killed between 20 million and 40 million people—more than any other illness in recorded history.

Top, 165-WW-269B-11; 165-WW-269B-52; 165-WW-269B-15; bottom, 165-WW-269B-1A; RG 52, Records of the Bureau of Medicine and Surgery

1919 | PAGE 158

Women Rivet Heaters at Puget Sound Navy Yard, May 29, 1919

The Woman-In-Industry Service was established in 1918 as a war emergency service to ensure effective employment of women during World War I. Among its records are photographs of women working industrial jobs traditionally filled by men, such as these riveters at the Navy Yard in Puget Sound, Washington, posing in May 1919. This photo was taken a generation before the more famous World War II recruitment poster of "Rosie the Riveter."

RG 86, Records of the Women's Bureau

1919 | PAGE 159

19th Amendment

Passed by Congress in 1919 and ratified on August 18, 1920, the Joint Resolution Proposing an Amendment to the Constitution Extending the Right of Suffrage to Women (19th Amendment) gave women the right to vote in Federal elections. Achieving this milestone required a lengthy and difficult struggle; victory took decades of agitation and protest. Beginning in the mid-19th century, several generations of woman suffrage supporters lectured, wrote, marched, lobbied, and practiced civil disobedience to achieve what many Americans considered a radical change of the Constitution. Few early supporters lived to see the final victory.

165-WW-(600A)5; RG 11, General Records of the U.S. Government

1920 | PAGE 160

Charles Ponzi

Charles Ponzi gave his name to a scheme for defrauding investors. In a Ponzi scheme, old clients are repaid with money invested by new ones, rather than from the actual profits earned on their investments. In this way, Ponzi swindled thousands of people and made millions of dollars. Arrested in 1920, he pleaded guilty to mail fraud and was sent to prison. As this prison record attests, Ponzi had other encounters with the law. Prior to his arrest in Boston, he served two years in the Atlanta Federal Penitentiary for smuggling illegal aliens into the United States from Canada. As a result of his criminal activities, Ponzi was later deported to his homeland of Italy.

National Archives at Atlanta, RG 21, Records of District Courts of the United States

1928 | PAGE 161

Rat Infestation, Miller County, Arkansas

In 1928, several counties in Arkansas were plagued by a rat infestation that resulted in heavy losses for area farmers and businesses. The rodents damaged grain storage buildings and ruined entire fields of crops. The U.S. Bureau of Biological Survey calculated the cost of destruction per rat at $1.87 per year. Spurred by the growing losses, County Extension Services worked with local organizations, school boards, and individuals to initiate rat-killing campaigns.

National Archives at Fort Worth, RG 33, Records of the Extension Service

1928 | PAGE 162

Good Will Cruise to South America

When President Herbert Hoover was elected in 1928, U.S. relations with Latin America were at a low point following decades of American coercion and outright occupation of Latin American countries. In an effort to improve relations, Hoover set out immediately after winning the 1928 election, but before his inauguration, on a goodwill trip to Latin American capitals. Once in office, his Good Neighbor Policy reversed the United States' longtime practice of armed intervention in Latin America.

Herbert Hoover Presidential Library and Museum

1929 | PAGE 163

President Herbert Hoover's State of the Union, December 3, 1929

Herbert Hoover was the last President to write his own speeches. In this draft of his State of the Union speech on December 3, 1929, Hoover wrestled with the important issue of departmental reorganization within the Government.

Herbert Hoover Presidential Library and Museum

ca. 1930 | PAGES 164–165

George Ackerman, Photographs for the Agricultural Extension Service

During a nearly 40-year career with the Department of Agriculture, George W. Ackerman (1884–1962) took more than 50,000 photographs. Ackerman began working as a photographer for the Bureau of Plant Industry in 1910 at a salary of $900 a year. His early photos for the Extension Service capture an idyllic vision of rural America during the Great Depression.

Page 164: top, 33-SC-14909; 33-SC-14560c; middle, 33-SC-14524c; 33-SC-12790c; bottom, 33-S-13287c; 33-S-13564c. Page 165: 33-S-14546c

1930–1932 | PAGE 166

Al Capone

Al Capone, one of the most notorious gangsters of the 20th century and the man held most responsible for the bloody lawlessness of Prohibition-era Chicago, remained free despite being indicted in Federal court several times on bootlegging and smuggling charges. But in June 1930, after an exhaustive investigation by the Federal Government, Capone was indicted and tried for income tax evasion. He was convicted and sentenced to 11 years in prison and fined $80,000.

Top left, 306-NT-163820C; top right, RG 60, General Records of the Department of Justice; bottom, National Archives at Chicago, RG 21, Records of District Courts of the United States

1932 | PAGE 167

Bonus March

In the summer of 1932, in the midst of the Great Depression, World War I veterans seeking early payment of a bonus scheduled for 1945 assembled in Washington, DC, to pressure Congress and the White House. After losing their fight in the U.S. Senate, most of the protesters went home, but 10,000 members of the "Bonus Army" remained behind, camping out with their families in the Anacostia section of the city. On the morning of July 28, violence erupted between the protesters and police, and President Herbert Hoover reluctantly sent in U.S. Army troops under Maj. Gen. Douglas MacArthur. Ignoring the President's order for restraint, the flamboyant general drove the defiant protesters from the city and violently cleared their campsite.

Top left and bottom right, Herbert Hoover Presidential Library and Museum; top right, 111-SC-97560; bottom left, 111-SC-97532

1932–1934 | PAGES 168–169

Construction of the National Archives Building, Washington, DC

Noted architect John Russell Pope designed the neoclassical National Archives Building not only as a repository for Federal records but also as a national shrine where public attention is directed to the documents that mark the creation of the fundamental institutions of the Federal Government and the American experience. Located in Washington, DC, the building is halfway between the U.S. Capitol and the White House. Ground was broken in September 1931, and the first National Archives staff members moved in four years later. The building's interior courtyard, intended for future expansion, was immediately filled in with more stacks to house the onslaught of records ready for transfer. The building was completed in 1937.

Pages 168–169: RG 121, Records of the Public Buildings Service (CEDIS; DC0006ZZ, #25C). Page 169: top, 64-NAC-110; bottom, 64-NAC-146

1933 | PAGE 170

The Banking Crisis

Some of the most harrowing moments of the Great Depression came in the final weeks of President Herbert Hoover's administration with the collapse of the nation's banking system in February 1933. The imminent failure of two large banks in Michigan prompted that state's governor to declare a "banking holiday" on February 14, setting off a panic that soon infected the entire nation. The fear reached all the way to the White House, where the President's secretary, Theodore Joslin, admitted to the President that he had withdrawn money from a Washington, DC, bank that he feared was on the brink of failure. The President urged Joslin to redeposit the money in another bank.

Top, 306-NT-443H-1; bottom, Herbert Hoover Presidential Library and Museum

1933 | PAGE 171

President Franklin D. Roosevelt's First Inaugural Address, March 4, 1933

By March 4, 1933, Americans had already endured three years of the Great Depression. Banks in all 48 states were either closed or severely restricting withdrawals. One in four workers was unemployed, and millions more were working at jobs that barely provided subsistence wages. Falling crop prices and drought had decimated farming in the Great Plains and Southwest. In his inaugural address, President Franklin D. Roosevelt rallied the country, saying, "The only thing we have to fear is fear itself." He also declared his intention to expand the powers of the Federal Government to combat the effects of the Great Depression and relieve "a stricken nation."

Franklin D. Roosevelt Presidential Library and Museum

ca. 1930s | PAGE 172

President Franklin D. Roosevelt Tackles the Great Depression

To counter the effects of the Great Depression, President Franklin D. Roosevelt pushed his New Deal program through Congress with legislation creating Federal programs administered by so-called Alphabet Agencies: AAA (Agricultural Adjustment Administration) stabilized crop prices and saved farms; CCC (Civilian Conservation Corps) provided jobs to unemployed youths while improving the environment; TVA (Tennessee Valley Authority) brought jobs and electricity to the rural South; FERA (Federal Emergency Relief Administration) and the later WPA (Works Progress Administration) provided jobs to thousands of unemployed Americans in construction and arts projects across the country; and NRA (National Recovery Administration) stabilized consumer goods prices through business and labor cooperation. Roosevelt kept the public informed about the progress of his plans through radio talks known as "fireside chats."

Top left, 114-DL-SD-5066; top right, middle row, and bottom middle and right, Franklin D. Roosevelt Presidential Library and Museum; bottom left, 69-N-19626

ca. 1935 | PAGE 173

Civilian Conservation Corps (CCC)

The Civilian Conservation Corps (CCC) was created by President Franklin D. Roosevelt during his first 100 days to put unemployed men, aged 17 to 24, to work on conservation projects in healthy rural environments. They were assigned to military-style CCC camps around the nation. During its nine-year existence, the CCC employed nearly 3 million young men and became one of the New Deal's most popular public works programs. The CCC planted more than 2 billion trees, fought forest fires, built trails, campgrounds, and reservoirs, and aided soil conservation. Its legacy remains today in America's national forests and parks.

Top left, 142-H-83; top right and bottom left, National Archives at Denver, RG 115, Records of the Bureau of Reclamation; middle left, National Archives at Chicago, RG 95, Records of the Forest Service; bottom right, National Archives at Seattle, RG 95, Records of the Forest Service

1936–1942 | PAGES 174–175

Ansel Adams, Photographs for the Department of the Interior

Ansel Adams (1902–1984) is one of the most celebrated photographers of all time. His images of the American landscape are familiar to millions. Secretary of the Interior Harold Ickes commissioned Adams to make photographs of the national parks. Ickes planned to have the photos enlarged into murals for the Department of the Interior's main building. Beginning with the Carlsbad Caverns of New Mexico, Adams made hundreds of photographs for the department until 1942. The planned murals were never executed.

Page 174: 79-AAW-25; 79-AAW-15. Page 175: 79-AAH-23

1936–1938 | PAGES 176–177

The Plow That Broke the Plains and *The River*

Directed by Pare Lorentz, *The Plow That Broke the Plains* (1936) and *The River* (1938) are two of the most widely praised and studied documentaries to be produced in the United States. Commissioned for the Farm Security Administration, *The Plow* showed the devastating effects of the Dust Bowl on farming, while *The River* highlighted the results of soil erosion on flooding. Lorentz headed the short-lived United States Film Service, which produced documentaries promoting Franklin D. Roosevelt's New Deal programs.

Page 176: 96.2A. Page 177, 96.1; 96-P-1

1940 | PAGES 178–179

**Dorothea Lange, Photographs for
the Bureau of Agricultural Economics**

Photographer Dorothea Lange (1895–1965) created images of the unemployed and migratory farm workers that became synonymous with the Great Depression. This series of photographs, not as well known as her earlier work for the Farm Security Administration, was shot for an agricultural "Community Stability and Instability" study by the Bureau of Agricultural Economics. The photographs provide a record of rural life and social institutions just before World War II.

Page 178: top, 83-G 41493; 83-G-41494; bottom, 83-G-41551. Page 179: 83-G-41837

ca. 1940 | PAGES 180–181

Declarations of Intention

In the years before and during World War II, thousands of foreigners—including actors, scientists, musicians, composers, and others—filed declarations of intention in court, stating they wished to become U.S. citizens. They sought entry into the United States for various reasons, including fleeing Nazi persecution in Europe.

Page 180: top, bottom (center and right), National Archives at Riverside, RG 21, Records of District Courts of the United States; bottom left, National Archives at New York City, RG 21, Records of District Courts of the United States. Page 181: top (left and center), bottom, National Archives at Riverside, RG 21, Records of District Courts of the United States; top right, National Archives at Boston, RG 21, Records of District Courts of the United States

1941 | PAGES 182–183

Irving Rusinow, Photographs of Taos County, New Mexico, for the Bureau of Agricultural Economics

As part of a study of rural communities for the Bureau of Agricultural Economics, photographer Irving Rusinow (1914–1990) documented Hispanic farms and villages in Taos, New Mexico, on the eve of World War II.

Page 182: top, 83-G-41664; 83-G-41624; bottom, 83-G-41631; 83-G-41636; 83-G-41610. Page 183: 83-G-41682

1941 | PAGE 184

Pearl Harbor

At 7:55 a.m. on December 7, 1941, Japanese bombers and torpedo planes attacked the U.S. Pacific fleet anchored at Pearl Harbor on Oahu, Hawaii, catapulting the United States into World War II. In less than two hours, the fleet was decimated, and more than 3,500 Americans were killed or wounded.

Top left, National Archives at Anchorage, RG 181, Records of Naval Districts and Shore Establishments; top and bottom right, Franklin D. Roosevelt Presidential Library and Museum; middle left, RG 373, Records of the Defense Intelligence Agency (Aerial Photographs, Can # ON002917, Exp. M-32-30-18); bottom left, National Archives at San Francisco, RG 21, Records of District Courts of the United States

1941 | PAGE 185

Proposed Message to the Congress

At the White House on December 7, 1941, President Franklin D. Roosevelt spent the afternoon receiving reports of casualties and damage to ships, planes, and installations at Pearl Harbor and across the Pacific. He also drafted what he termed a "short" message. Delivered to a Joint Session of Congress on December 8, his message became one of the most famous speeches of the 20th century. Referring to December 7 as "a date which will live in infamy," he declared that, "the American people in their righteous might will win through to absolute victory." Immediately after the speech, Congress declared that a state of war existed with Japan.

Franklin D. Roosevelt Presidential Library and Museum; 79-AR-82

1942 | PAGE 186

Nazi Saboteurs

In June 1942, eight Nazi saboteurs, carrying money and explosives, snuck into the United States from submarine drop-off points on Long Island and Florida beaches. Their mission, code-named Operation Pastorius, was to attack economic targets such as hydroelectric and manufacturing plants. One of the leaders had second thoughts and contacted the FBI, turning in the whole team. All eight men were tried in July before a military commission comprised of seven U.S. Army officers appointed by President Franklin D. Roosevelt. All eight saboteurs were found guilty and sentenced to death. The commission and the attorney general recommended clemency for two saboteurs who had assisted the Government's case, and the President commuted their sentences to long imprisonment in a Federal penitentiary. The two were pardoned by President Harry Truman in 1948 and deported back to Germany. The other six were executed in August 1942 by electrocution.

Artifacts, RG 65, Records of the Federal Bureau of Investigation; bottom center, 111-SC-137995; bottom right, 111-SC-137991

1942 | PAGE 187

**Denying Certain Enemies Access
to the Courts of the United States**

The arrest of eight Nazi saboteurs in June 1942 presented a dilemma for the Roosevelt administration. One of the saboteurs betrayed the mission, leading to the capture of the others. Their intent to sabotage targets in the United States was clear, but questions remained about how to try them. On July 2, President Franklin Roosevelt issued a proclamation stating, "All persons who are subjects, citizens or residents of any nation at war with the United States...and are charged with committing or attempting or preparing to commit sabotage...shall be subject to the law of war and to the jurisdiction of military tribunals...." The proclamation was upheld by the Supreme Court, and the saboteurs were tried by a military commission in July 1942 in the Justice Department Building in Washington, DC.

RG 11, General Records of the U.S. Government

1942 | PAGES 188–189

Japanese Internment

The shock of Pearl Harbor fueled national security concerns and already tense race relations on the West Coast. In February 1942, President Franklin Roosevelt signed Executive Order 9066 authorizing the military to exclude "any or all persons" from areas of the United States designated as "military zones." A month later, Congress passed a law enforcing the order. Officially, EO 9066 was designed to protect the West Coast from all forms of sabotage. In practice, it was used almost exclusively to intern Americans of Japanese ancestry, not those of Italian or German heritage. By the end of 1942, more than 110,000 Japanese Americans, two-thirds of whom were native-born American citizens, were forced from their homes and moved to relocation camps across the United States, where many remained until war's end.

Page 188: top, RG 210, Records of the War Relocation Authority; bottom, National Archives at San Francisco, RG 21, Records of District Courts of the United States. Page 189: top, 210-G-B4; 210-G-A81; middle, 210-G-A39; 210-G-B16; bottom, 210-G-D538; 210-G-C845

ca. 1943 | PAGES 190–191

World War II Posters

Just as military weapons engaged the enemy during World War II, posters and other media waged a battle for the hearts and minds of American citizens. The Government launched an aggressive propaganda campaign to galvanize public support, and it recruited some of the nation's foremost writers, intellectuals, artists, and filmmakers to wage the war on the home front. Thousands of posters were produced and disseminated by the Office of War Information, War Production Board, and other Government, civilian, and military agencies to persuade the American people to support the war effort, conserve the nation's vital resources, buy savings bonds, and avoid revealing national secrets.

Page 190: top, 44-PA-2272; 44-PA-2314; 44-PA-230; 179-WP-1563; middle, 44-PA-227A; 44-PA-2376; 44-PA-124; 208-PMP-68; bottom, 208-PMP-129; 44-PA-2415; 179-WP-1386; 44-PA-380. Page 191: 208-AOP-120-119

1943 | PAGES 192–193

**Wayne Miller, Photographs of the USS *Saratoga*
for the Naval Aviation Photographic Unit**

Wayne F. Miller (b. 1918) left art school in 1942 to join the Naval Aviation Photographic Unit, headed by Cdr. Edward Steichen, to document and publicize its aviation activities.

As a combat photographer, Lieutenant Miller was assigned to document the human side of war. His photographs of action aboard the USS *Saratoga* in the Pacific convey the drudgery and the drama of wartime life at sea.

Page 192: top, 80-G-470943; 80-G-470677; 80-G-470683; middle, 80-G-470673; 80-G-470953; 80-G-470945; bottom, 80-G-470964; 80-G-470814; 80-G-470941. Page 193: top, 80-G-470970; 80-G-470948; 80-G-470962; middle, 80-G-470678; 80-G-470679; 80-G-470906; bottom, 80-G-470907; 80-G-470905; 80-G-470938

1943 | PAGE 194
Navajo Code Talkers

During World War II, the U.S. Marine Corps, in an effort to secure radio and telephone communications from Japanese intelligence, enlisted Navajos as "code talkers." The Navajo language was very complex and few people in the world could understand it. The Marines established a special code consisting of 211 words, most of which were Navajo terms that had been given new, distinctly military meanings. Approximately 400 Navajo code talkers served at Iwo Jima and other battles, providing essential communications as well as serving with distinction as Marines. The code talker program was highly classified throughout the war and remained so until 1968. An act "Honoring the Code Talkers" was signed in 2000, finally recognizing the efforts of the Navajo Marines who served in World War II.

Top, 127-MN-69889-B; bottom, RG 127, Records of the U.S. Marine Corps

1944 | PAGE 195
332nd Fighter Group

The 332nd Fighter Group, composed entirely of African American pilots and support personnel, trained at Tuskegee Institute and flew its first combat mission on June 2, 1943. The four squadrons in the group participated in the air battle against Sicily and supported the invasion of Italy. The Tuskegee Airmen flew more than 1,500 missions in Europe and destroyed more than 260 enemy planes. They never lost a bomber to enemy aircraft. Ninety-five of the group's pilots received the Distinguished Flying Cross.

Top, 208-MO-18K-32983; 208-MO-18H-22051; middle, 208-MO-18H-32984; 208-AA-49E-1-1; bottom, 208-AA-46BB-4; 208-MO-18K-32981

1944 | PAGE 196
Women in the Wartime Labor Force

During World War II approximately 3 million women worked in war plants across the United States. Women were vital to war production, as the loss of men to military service left employee shortages in many factories. The U.S. Government undertook a major public relations campaign to encourage women to work. These photographs from the Cornhusker Ordnance Plant in Grand Island, Nebraska, show a typical ordinance worker going about her day.

National Archives at Kansas City, RG 156, Records of the Office of the Chief of Ordnance

1944 | PAGE 197
Margie Posters

Among the thousands of posters produced during World War II, the "Margie" posters were intended to encourage soldiers to manage their pay through soldiers' deposits, personal transfer accounts, Class E allotments of pay, war bonds, and national service life insurance. The vivacious yet practical "Margie," a young wife pining for her soldier husband, writes letters reminding him to save for their future. The Army distributed copies throughout posts, facilities, commands, and theatres of operation.

Top, 44-PA-1334F; 44-PA-1334; bottom, 44-PA-1334A; 44-PA-1334B

1944 | PAGE 198
D-day

After the Allied military successes in North Africa and Italy in 1943, the Allies began planning Operation Overlord, the invasion of the European continent through France. Hundreds of thousands of Allied troops were assembled and trained in England, while supplies, ships, and planes were stockpiled for the complicated amphibious action against Normandy. Gen. Dwight Eisenhower, commander of the Allied Expeditionary Force, gave the final order that put the vast operation in motion in the early morning hours of June 5, as meteorologists predicted a temporary break in the stormy weather. Hours later, he wrote a note in case the operation failed. In the statement, he praised the men he commanded and accepted total responsibility for the failure the next day could bring. The only apparent hint of nerves on his part was his error in dating the note "July 5" instead of June 5. About 4,900 U.S. soldiers were killed on D-day, but 155,000 Allied troops were set ashore to continue the march inland.

Top, 111-C-194399; 26-G-2343; bottom, Dwight D. Eisenhower Presidential Library and Museum

1945 | PAGE 199

Bridge at Remagen

The Ludendorff Bridge, also known as the Bridge at Remagen, was the last standing bridge across the Rhine and the scene of a desperate battle by the 27th Armored Infantry Battalion of the 9th Armored Division to capture it in 1945. On March 7, U.S. soldiers, under heavy gunfire, prevented the Germans from blowing up the bridge by yanking out explosives only minutes before demolition was triggered. Their success was important as it allowed American units to move swiftly into Germany's industrial heartland with tanks and supplies. The Germans continued to bomb the bridge from the air as American engineers worked to strengthen it. It finally collapsed on March 17, killing 28 men and injuring dozens more. By then, the Americans had established a solid bridgehead on the other side of the river.

Top, 111-SC-202694; 111-SC-528487; middle, Franklin D. Roosevelt Presidential Library and Museum; 111-SC-207356; bottom, RG 407, Records of the Adjutant General's Office; 111-SC-234525

1945 | PAGES 200–201

Iwo Jima

The invasion of Iwo Jima, an important stepping stone to the Japanese mainland, produced some of the fiercest fighting in the Pacific campaign. The rugged island was filled with heavily fortified bunkers connected to 11 miles of twisting tunnels, where desperate Japanese troops defended their positions. Marines used flamethrowers and grenades to clear tunnels, only to find them reoccupied with enemy soldiers. In 36 days of fighting, 6,821 Allies were killed and 20,000 were wounded. Of the 22,000 Japanese fighters, more than 20,000 were killed.

Page 200: top, RG 37, Records of the Hydrographic Office (Operational Archives, Pacific–Bonin/Volcano Is. #21, Sheet 1); bottom, RG 373, Records of the Defense Intelligence Agency (Aerial Photographs; Can #ON027800, Exposure #40). Page 201: top, 127-N-110249; 127-N-109619; middle, 80-G-412474; 80-G-412532; bottom, 127-N-110104; 26-G-4122; 26-G-4140

1945 | PAGE 202

Buchenwald Concentration Camp

During the 12 years of the Third Reich (1933–45), the Nazi regime established and operated a system of concentration camps to imprison people perceived to represent a "racial" or political threat to Nazi authority. Nazi leaders identified Jews as the priority enemy of Germany and sought to annihilate them. The Germans and their Axis partners murdered approximately 6 million Jews, as well as millions of other innocent men, women, and children during the Holocaust. Buchenwald was one of the first and largest camps. Started as a work camp in 1937 near Weimar, Germany, Buchenwald was the scene of an estimated 50,000 deaths by starvation and execution. Thousands of Soviet prisoners of war were among the victims. American forces liberated the camp in April 1945.

Top, 111-C-1071; bottom, 111-C-1061; 111-C-1069; 111-C-1243

1945 | PAGE 203

Holocaust-Era Assets

As the Nazi Army moved across Europe, it looted museums, castles, religious institutions, and private homes of art, books, other valuables, and cultural artifacts. The treasures were hidden away in remote caves and mines. A different kind of looting took place with the transfer of bank accounts, gold, and other financial assets, many of them stolen from Holocaust victims. The Nazis were meticulous record keepers, and when the war was over, Allied armies salvaged many of the records and began the arduous work of finding and restoring the looted treasures.

Top, 111-SC-209154; 111-SC-204155; bottom, RG 153, Records of the Office of the Judge Advocate General (Army)

1945 | PAGE 204

End of War in Europe

Gen. Dwight Eisenhower's telegram announcing the end of World War II in Europe was short and to the point.

Dwight D. Eisenhower Presidential Library and Museum

1945 | PAGE 205

Hiroshima and Nagasaki

Developed by scientists at the Manhattan Project, the atomic bomb was tested successfully in July 1945. After consulting with the Allies, President Harry Truman issued an ultimatum threatening the Japanese with "prompt and utter destruction" if they did not surrender unconditionally. Truman approved the use of the bomb in August. The unit selected for this dangerous mission was the 509th Composite Group, commanded by Col. Paul W. Tibbets, Jr., who dropped the first bomb on Hiroshima on August 6, 1945. When the Japanese again refused to surrender, a second bomb was dropped on Nagasaki. Between 120,000 and 170,000 people were killed by the bombs. Japan surrendered on August 14, 1945.

Top left, 342-AF-58189, bottom left, 208-LU-13H-5; right (top and bottom), Harry S. Truman Presidential Library and Museum

1946 | PAGES 206–207

Russell Lee, Photographs for a Medical Survey of the Bituminous Coal Industry

In 1946, the Department of Interior and the United Mine Workers agreed to a joint survey of the medical, health, and housing conditions in coal mining communities. Survey teams under the direction of Rear Adm. Joel T. Boone went into mining areas to collect data and photographs, later compiled into a published report. Most of the photographs were taken by Russell W. Lee (1903–1986), an acclaimed documentary photographer who also created many iconic images of American social, economic, and cultural life for the Farm Security Administration during the Great Depression.

Page 206: top, 245-MS-1404-L; 245-MS-1428-L; bottom, 245-MS-1428-L; 245-MS-1464-L. Page 207: 245-MS-1437-L

1947–1955 | PAGES 208–209

Marshall Plan

Responding to the devastation, famine, and economic ruin in Europe after World War II, Secretary of State George Marshall proposed that European nations create a plan for their economic reconstruction and that the United States provide economic assistance. President Harry Truman presented Marshall's ideas for aid to Congress in December 1947. The following April, Congress overwhelmingly passed the Economic Cooperation Act of 1948, also known as the Marshall Plan. Over the next four years, Congress appropriated $13.3 billion for European recovery. This aid provided much-needed capital and materials that enabled Europeans

to rebuild the continent's economy. For the United States, the Marshall Plan provided markets for American goods, created reliable trading partners, and supported the development of stable democratic governments in Western Europe.

Page 208: top, Records of the U.S. Senate; Harry S. Truman Presidential Library and Museum; 286-ME-6(2); middle, 286-ME-9(14); 286-ME-12(4); 286-ME-7(5); bottom, 286-ME-5(4); 286-ME-9(18); 286-ME-12(1). Page 209: top, 286-ME-8(6); 286-ME-11(12); 286-ME-4(2); middle, 286-ME-3(2); 286-ME-12(6); 286-ME-7(1); bottom (left), 286-ME-11(11); bottom (center and right), Harry S. Truman Presidential Library and Museum

1947 | PAGE 210

The House Committee on Un-American Activities Report on Ronald Reagan, September 2, 1947

The House Committee on Un-American Activities was first established in the 1930s as a special committee to investigate un-American and subversive propaganda. Following World War II, the committee, now permanent, focused its investigations on potential Communist infiltration in various U.S. industries. The committee became notorious in 1947 when it summoned witnesses to testify about the Communist influence in the motion picture industry. Ronald Reagan, then president of the Screen Actors Guild, was called to testify about the Communist threat in Hollywood.

RG 233, Records of the U.S. House of Representatives

1947 | PAGE 211

Capt. Charles E. Yeager, Pilot's Notes, 9th Powered Flight, October 14, 1947

Capt. Charles "Chuck" E. Yeager, an Air Force test pilot, was the first man to fly faster than the speed of sound. In his "Pilot's Notes" from October 14, 1947, Yeager coolly describes the facts and sensations of the historic 14-minute flight in the XS-1, an experimental aircraft being tested in the California desert.

Top, National Archives at Riverside, RG 255, Records of the National Aeronautics and Space Administration; bottom, 342-C-5027(KE)

1950 | PAGES 212–213

Korean War

When Communist North Korea launched a surprise attack against South Korea on June 25, 1950, the Truman administration decided to intervene, putting its policy of Communist containment into practice. Backed by a United Nations (U.N.) resolution signed the next day, military combat forces from the United States and, ultimately, 15 other U.N. allies entered Korea. After initial difficulties, they succeeded in breaking the supply lines of the North Korean Army with an amphibious landing at Inchon in September 1950, which enabled U.S. and allied forces to drive deep into North Korean territory, toward the Yalu River and the Manchurian border. But Communist China, countering the perceived threat to its territory, sent its army across the border in October 1950. In the bitter cold and snow of November and December, Chinese forces successfully counter-attacked U.N. forces at the Chosin Reservoir, inflicting heavy casualties that forced a major U.N. withdrawal south. Names of other battles and operations during the next three years echoed across the peninsula to America—Punchbowl, Heartbreak Ridge, Old Baldy, Outpost Kelly, and Pork Chop Hill. Fighting continued until an armistice was signed in July 1953 that stopped hostilities and created a demilitarized zone between the north and the south along the 38th Parallel. A total of 1,587,040 American men and women served in Korea, and 36,568 U.S. service members died there.

Page 212: top, 127-N-A2716, 127-N-A3189; bottom, 127-N-A3191, 80-G-420027. Page 213: top, 127-N-A3386, 127-N-A5439; bottom, 127-N-A4852, 127-N-A5426

1951 | PAGE 214

President Harry Truman's Dismissal of Gen. Douglas MacArthur

In 1951, the Truman administration prepared to negotiate with the Chinese and North Koreans in an attempt to end the Korean conflict. Gen. Douglas MacArthur, commander of the U.N. forces in Korea, issued an unauthorized statement containing a veiled threat to expand the war into China if the Communists refused to come to terms. When MacArthur continued his belligerent statements, President Harry Truman, backed by the Joint Chiefs of Staff as well as the Secretaries of State and Defense, decided to replace the

general with a military commander who would conform to the administration's foreign policy. On April 11, 1951, President Truman relieved MacArthur of his command.

Harry S. Truman Presidential Library and Museum

ca. 1951 | PAGE 215

President Harry Truman

President Harry Truman liked to remind supporters and detractors alike that he took responsibility for his own decisions, and he often spoke of a sign on his desk reading "The Buck Stops Here." In his farewell address to the American people in January 1953, Truman said: "The President—whoever he is— has to decide. He can't pass the buck to anybody. No one else can do the deciding for him. That's his job."

Harry S. Truman Presidential Library and Museum

ca. 1951 | PAGE 216

U.S. v. *Julius Rosenberg, Ethel Rosenberg, et al*

Ethel and Julius Rosenberg—along with Morton Sobell, David Greenglass, and Anatoli Yakovlev—were indicted on charges of conspiracy to commit espionage by passing U.S. industrial and atomic secrets to the Soviet Union. Julius Rosenberg began furnishing the Soviets with secrets beginning in late 1942. By 1944, he had engaged his brother-in-law, David Greenglass, an army scientist working on the atomic bomb, in the spy network. During his trial testimony, Greenglass detailed how he passed on secrets he learned at the atomic laboratory at Los Alamos, New Mexico. The sketches were "offered as replicas of information given to [Harry] Gold and Rosenberg in 1945." The Rosenbergs were convicted and sentenced to death in 1951 and executed in 1953.

National Archives at New York City, RG 118, Records of U.S. Attorneys

1952 | PAGE 217

Project Blue Book

Project Blue Book was the codename for the most well known of the U.S. Air Force's investigations into Unidentified Flying Objects (UFOs). The staff created reports summarizing UFO sightings around the country. The Project Blue Book files also include reports about international sightings. From 1947 to 1969, 12,618 sightings were reported; 701 remain "unidentified."

RG 341, Records of Headquarters U.S. Air Force (Air Staff)

1952 | PAGES 218–219

Dedication of the Charters of Freedom

On December 13, 1952, the Declaration of Independence and the Constitution were transferred to the National Archives from the Library of Congress. Joining the Bill of Rights, which had been at the Archives since 1938, they became collectively known as the Charters of Freedom, the most precious documents in the historical heritage of the United States. On December 15, 1952, the formal enshrining ceremony was held, presided over by Chief Justice Fred M. Vinson, with President Harry Truman and other dignitaries in attendance.

Page 218: 64-NA-1-434; Page 219: Harry S. Truman Presidential Library and Museum

1954 | PAGES 220–221

Hearings Before the Senate Judiciary Subcommittee to Investigate Juvenile Delinquency, April 21, 1954–June 4, 1954

The Senate Judiciary Subcommittee to Investigate Juvenile Delinquency was created in 1953 to "conduct a full and complete study of juvenile delinquency in the United States." They investigated the effects of radio, television, and movies, but they gained most of their notoriety when they investigated and held televised hearings on comic books. The committee established a four-level rating system for evaluating comic books: "no objection, some objection, objectionable, and very objectionable."

Page 220: left (top and bottom), RG 287, Publications of the U.S. Government. Page 220 (right) and page 221: RG 46, Records of the U.S. Senate

1954 | PAGE 222

Hernandez v. Texas

In 1951, Pete Hernandez, a migrant cotton picker in Edna, Texas, was accused of murdering his employer. Gustavo "Gus" Garcia, an experienced civil rights lawyer, took the case for free, arguing it was impossible for Hernandez to get a fair trial in a county where no Mexican American had served on a jury in more than 25 years. Garcia used the case to challenge discrimination against Hispanics, arguing that they should not be lumped together with whites in a legal system that recognized only blacks and whites. He appealed Hernandez's conviction to the Texas Court of Criminal Appeals and lost. But the U.S. Supreme Court agreed to hear the case and decided unanimously in 1954 that Hernandez had a 14th Amendment right to be indicted and tried "by juries from which all members of his class are not systematically excluded."

RG 267, Records of the Supreme Court of the United States

1955 | PAGE 223

Brown v. Board of Education, May 31, 1955

On May 17, 1954, Chief Justice Earl Warren delivered the unanimous U.S. Supreme Court ruling in the landmark civil rights case *Brown* v. *Board of Education of Topeka*. The court ruled that separating public school children on the basis of race violated the 14th Amendment. The decision marked the end of the "separate but equal" precedent set by the Supreme Court nearly 60 years before in *Plessy* v. *Ferguson*. Although the decision is commonly known as *Brown* v. *Board of Education of Topeka*, it was actually six cases grouped together.

RG 267, Records of the Supreme Court of the United States

ca. 1955 | PAGE 224

Atomic Testing

In August 1945, the United States unleashed a new weapon of mass destruction against the Japanese at Hiroshima and Nagasaki, bringing an abrupt end to World War II. Atomic bombs killed in two ways: by the magnitude of the blast and resulting firestorm and by exposure to radioactive fallout. When the Soviet Union detonated its first atomic bomb in 1949, the arms race was on. With the Americans and the Soviets building and testing nuclear weapons, the need to develop civil defense procedures became more apparent. Operation Cue, testing conducted in Nevada in 1955, was exclusively concerned with civil defense matters. It consisted of technical tests, field exercises, observer activities, and press coverage.

Left (top to bottom), 434-RF-49(2); 304-OC-408; 304-OC-737; 304-OC-825; right, 111-SC-389297

ca. 1955 | PAGE 225

Civil Defense

As the Cold War intensified and the nuclear arms race escalated, the U.S. Government began to develop and publicize civil defense procedures to prepare for a potential Soviet attack. Americans constructed fallout shelters in public buildings and private homes, stocking them with canned food and other supplies. Where a fallout shelter was not available, virtually any barrier would have to do, even a school desk or a kitchen table. Public school students participated in "duck and cover" drills to prepare for the possibility of a nuclear attack as practicing for nuclear war became a part of life's routine in the 1950s.

Top, 397-MA-2s-159; 311-D-14(1); bottom, Dwight D. Eisenhower Presidential Library and Museum, 311-D-20(1)

1957 | PAGES 226–227

Little Rock

In September 1957, despite orderly plans to desegregate the Little Rock public high school in compliance with the Supreme Court ruling in *Brown* v. *Board of Education of Topeka*, Arkansas Governor Orval Faubus refused to comply. The night before school was to start, he called out the state's National Guard to surround Little Rock Central High School and prevent any black students from attending, claiming he was protecting citizens and property from possible violence by protesters. When nine African American students attempted to register at the school, a riot erupted and Faubus did nothing to stop it. President Dwight Eisenhower then issued an executive order placing the Arkansas National Guard under Federal control and sending an additional 1,000 Army paratroopers from the 101st Airborne Division to assist them in restoring order in Little Rock. Eisenhower's actions made clear that the Federal Government was committed to enforcing *Brown* v. *Board of Education*.

Dwight D. Eisenhower Presidential Library and Museum

1962 | PAGES 228–229

Cuban Missile Crisis

In October 1962, a U.S. spy plane photographed a Soviet nuclear missile installation under construction in Cuba. Just 90 miles off the coast of Florida, the missiles put the United States at risk of a nuclear attack that could come on very short notice. President John F. Kennedy met in secret with his advisors for several days to discuss the problem. In a televised address on October 22, 1962, he informed the American people of the presence of the Cuban missile sites and his decision to place a naval blockade around Cuba. The world watched for 13 days as tensions mounted between United States and the Soviet Union before Soviet leader Nikita Khrushchev turned his ships back. The Soviets agreed to dismantle the weapon sites, and in exchange, the United States agreed not to invade Cuba. In a separate, unpublicized deal, the United States also agreed to remove its own nuclear missiles from Turkey.

Page 234 (top left, top right, bottom center, bottom right) and page 235 (top left, top center, bottom left, bottom center): John F. Kennedy Presidential Library and Museum. Page 234: (bottom left), 306-PSA-59-2091. Page 235: (top left), 306-N-62-67; (bottom left), 306-N-62-7101

1962 | PAGES 230–231

Eleanor Roosevelt's Wallet

Eleanor Roosevelt, First Lady of the United States from 1933 to 1945, was an untiring social activist. After President Franklin Roosevelt's death in 1945, she was appointed to be a delegate to the United Nations, where she was the first chairperson of the U.N. Human Rights Commission. She resigned from her post in 1953, but briefly served again after being reappointed as a delegate by President John F. Kennedy in 1961. The contents of her wallet reflect her many causes, interests, and associations. Among the items she carried were favorite poems and words of inspiration. The photograph is of a young friend, Joseph P. Lash, who later wrote several biographies of Mrs. Roosevelt.

Franklin D. Roosevelt Presidential Library and Museum

1963 | PAGE 232

President John F. Kennedy's Visit to Berlin

On June 26, 1963, President John F. Kennedy spoke in the shadow of the Berlin Wall—a symbol of repression since its construction by the Soviets to divide east from west. He paid tribute to the stalwart spirit of Berlin's citizens, and the crowd roared with approval upon hearing the President's dramatic pronouncement, "Ich bin ein Berliner" ("I am a Berliner"). The wall fell in 1989, signaling the end of the Cold War.

John F. Kennedy Presidential Library and Museum

1963 | PAGE 233

March on Washington, August 28, 1963

On August 28, 1963, more than 250,000 demonstrators descended on the nation's capital to participate in the March on Washington for Jobs and Freedom. It was the largest demonstration for civil rights in U.S. history, and the three-hour long program at the Lincoln Memorial included speeches from prominent civil rights and religious leaders, including the Rev. Martin Luther King, Jr., who delivered his impassioned speech, "I Have a Dream." The day ended with a meeting between the leaders of the march and President John F. Kennedy at the White House.

Top, 306-SSM-4D(80)10, John F. Kennedy Presidential Library and Museum, courtesy of the Bayard Rustin Fund; bottom, 306-SSM-4A-35-6; 306-SSM-4B-61-32

1963 | PAGES 234–235

Typed Transcript of Lady Bird Johnson's Audio Diary from November 22, 1963

In the Dallas motorcade on November 22, 1963, Lady Bird Johnson was at her husband's side, two cars behind President and Mrs. Kennedy when the President was assassinated. Two or three days later, Mrs. Johnson recorded her recollections of the tragic event in her audio diary.

Page 234–235: Lyndon Baines Johnson Presidential Library and Museum.
Page 235 (right): John F. Kennedy Presidential Library and Museum

1964 | PAGE 236

Civil Rights Act of 1964

President Lyndon Johnson pressed for the adoption of a civil rights act as a tribute to the late President John F. Kennedy, who had supported it prior to his death. The subsequent Civil Rights Act of 1964 became one the most significant legislative accomplishments of Johnson's Presidency. Although southern legislators strongly opposed it, Johnson worked with his Democratic allies to maneuver the legislation through the House and Senate. The act protected voting rights; banned racially discriminatory practices in employment; and barred segregation in public places such as restaurants, swimming pools, libraries, and public schools.

Top, Lyndon Baines Johnson Presidential Library and Museum; RG 11, General Records of the U.S. Government; bottom, RG 46, Records of the U.S. Senate

1964 | PAGE 237

Gulf of Tonkin

On August 4, 1964, President Lyndon Johnson announced that U.S. ships in the Gulf of Tonkin had been attacked by the North Vietnamese. Johnson dispatched U.S. planes against the attackers and asked Congress to pass a resolution to support his actions. The joint resolution "to promote the maintenance of international peace and security in southeast Asia" passed on August 7 and became the subject of great political controversy in the course of the undeclared war that followed. President Johnson, and later President Richard Nixon, relied on the resolution as the legal basis for their military policies in Vietnam. However, in the face of growing public resistance to the war, Congress repealed the resolution in December 1970. President Nixon signed the repeal in January 1971.

Top left, top right, and bottom left, Lyndon Baines Johnson Presidential Library and Museum; top middle, 428-GX-482-N-711524; bottom right, RG 46, Records of the U.S. Senate

1964 | PAGE 238

Letter to the U.S. Department of Labor, April 3, 1964

In an effort to protect American jobs, the Department of Labor in 1964 made it more difficult for foreign musicians to enter the country. When the press reported that these new requirements would prevent the Beatles from performing in the United States, hundreds of distraught teenagers deluged President Lyndon Johnson and Secretary of Labor Willard Wirtz with letters and petitions like this one.

RG 174, General Records of the Department of Labor

1965 | PAGE 239

Bond of John R. Cash, October 5, 1965

Johnny Cash, renowned country singer and songwriter, was arrested in Texas for drug possession. This appearance bond, in which Cash put down $1,500 as a guarantee he would appear in court, includes an unusual handwritten condition allowing him to travel "where his work takes him in the Continental U.S."

National Archives at Fort Worth, RG 21, Records of the District Courts of the United States

1965–1975 | PAGES 240–241

Vietnam War

The Vietnam War was one of the longest and most controversial in U.S. history. The United States entered the war to prevent a Communist takeover of South Vietnam as part of a containment strategy. U.S. military advisors began arriving in 1950. The first U.S. casualties were in 1959, and U.S. involvement escalated in the early 1960s. Fought on the ground in jungles and rice paddies, and from the air with bombers, this unconventional war stymied the strategies of three successive Presidential administrations. Despite signing peace accords in Paris in 1973, North Vietnam resumed fighting after American combat troops left and easily captured South Vietnam in April 1975. Nearly 60,000 Americans were killed during the conflict.

Page 240: top, 342-C-KE44789; 111-CC-39781; bottom, 127-N-A371948; 111-CC-47777.
Page 241: top, 428-K-98293; 111-C-46331; bottom, 342-C-K20652; 111-CC-46391

1969 | PAGES 242–243

Apollo 11

In the late 1950s, the United States was losing the space race with the Soviet Union. President John F. Kennedy challenged NASA in 1961 to land a man on the Moon and return him safely to Earth by the end of the decade. The resulting Apollo program enlisted 20,000 companies, hundreds of thousands of individuals, and some $25.5 billion. Astronauts Neil Armstrong, Michael Collins, and Edwin "Buzz" Aldrin were launched into space aboard *Apollo 11*, and on July 20, 1969, Armstrong and Aldrin became the first humans to set foot on the Moon. Watched by millions on television, the lunar landing was a stunning achievement that commanded worldwide attention.

Page 242: National Archives at Fort Worth, RG 255, Records of the National Aeronautics and Space Administration. Page 243: top, 306-PSD-69-3133c; 306-AP-A11F-40-5875; bottom, 306-AP-A11F-AS-40-5948; 306-PSD-69-3099-c

1972 | PAGES 244–245

President Richard Nixon in China

Relations between the United States and China were ruptured in 1949 when Communist forces defeated the Nationalists and proclaimed a People's Republic. In 1971, after a series of delicate negotiations, President Richard Nixon announced he had accepted China's invitation to visit. He viewed his trip as an opportunity to improve relations and build a lasting structure of peace. President and Mrs. Nixon traveled to Beijing in February 1972, where they toured the Great Wall, posed for photographs holding pandas, and dined with top officials. Nixon spoke with Premier Zhou Enlai and met briefly with the ailing Chairman Mao Zedong. As a consequence of Nixon's initiative, the United States and China pursued normalized relations and restored full diplomatic relations in 1979.

Richard Nixon Presidential Library and Museum

1972–1977 | PAGES 246–247

DOCUMERICA

During the 1970s, the U.S. Environmental Protection Agency (EPA) assigned some 70 photographers to document subjects of environmental concern—defined broadly in social as well as physical terms—across the United States. The thousands of images that resulted provide a detailed record of life and landscape throughout the country.

Page 246: top, 412-DA-10177; 412-DA-2825; middle, 412-DA-11379; 412-DA-13211; bottom, 412-DA-10581; 412-DA-11420. Page 247: top, 412-DA-9221; 412-DA-14188; middle, 412-DA-10460; 412-DA-13072; 412-DA-12968; bottom, 412-DA-1670; 412-DA-7543

1972–1974 | PAGES 248–249

Watergate

During the night of June 17, 1972, five burglars broke into the offices of the Democratic National Committee at the Watergate office complex in Washington, DC. An investigation into the break-in exposed a trail of abuses that led to the highest levels of the Nixon administration and ultimately to President Richard Nixon himself. For two years, public revelations of wrongdoing by the White House convulsed the nation in a series of confrontations that pitted the President against the media, executive agencies, Congress, and the Supreme Court. The Watergate affair was a constitutional crisis and a national trauma that tested the rule of law. Under threat of impeachment, President Nixon resigned on August 9, 1974.

Page 248: top left and right, middle and bottom right, RG 21, Records of District Courts of the United States; bottom left, RG 460, Records of the Watergate Special Prosecution Force. Page 249: top left and right, bottom left, Richard Nixon Presidential Library and Museum; middle and bottom right, RG 21, Records of District Courts of the United States

1974 | PAGE 250

President Richard Nixon's Resignation, August 9, 1974

In July 1974, following revelations in the continuing Watergate investigation, the House Judiciary Committee approved articles of impeachment against President Richard Nixon. Forced by the Supreme Court to release additional taped conversations that demonstrated his participation in obstructing justice, Nixon's remaining support in Congress and among the public crumbled. On August 8, Nixon announced in a broadcast to the nation his decision to resign the Presidency at noon the next day. His terse letter of resignation was delivered to Secretary of State Henry Kissinger at 11:53 a.m. on August 9.

RG 59, General Records of the Department of State

1974 | PAGE 251

President Gerald Ford's Pardon of Richard Nixon, September 8, 1974

Following President Richard Nixon's resignation, Gerald Ford was sworn in as the nation's 38th President at noon on August 9, 1974. He reassured the American people that "our long national nightmare is over." In the first weeks of his Presidency, he faced many economic and foreign policy challenges, including the controversial war in Vietnam. In an effort to put the Nixon ordeal behind him, Ford made a surprise announcement to the nation on September 8, granting the former President a "full, free and absolute" pardon. Though this decision may have cost him the 1976 election, President Ford never wavered in his belief that he had done the right thing for the welfare of the country.

RG 11, General Records of the U.S. Government

1975 | PAGE 252
Apollo-Soyuz Test Project

By the mid-1970s, Americans had successfully landed on the Moon six times, and the United States and Soviet Union had each launched space stations. With the diplomatic chill thawing, it was time for a joint mission. The *Apollo-Soyuz* Test Project was the first human spaceflight mission managed jointly by the two nations. Requiring the astronauts and cosmonauts to overcome language and cultural barriers, the project tested the compatibility not only of the crews, but of rendezvous and docking systems for American and Soviet spacecraft. On July 17, 1975, a U.S. *Apollo* craft docked with a Soviet *Soyuz* craft and the Americans and Soviets shook hands in space, laying the groundwork for future cooperation in the Shuttle-Mir program and in the still-orbiting International Space Station.

Gerald R. Ford Presidential Library and Museum

1976 | PAGE 253
Bicentennial of the United States

July 4, 1976, marked the Bicentennial of the United States' independence from England, and celebrations were held throughout the nation. President Gerald Ford attended events at Valley Forge, New York City, and Philadelphia. On July 7, the President and Mrs. Ford hosted Queen Elizabeth and Prince Philip at a formal State Dinner.

Gerald R. Ford Presidential Library and Museum

1978 | PAGE 254
Camp David Summit

The historic Camp David Summit was held for 13 days in September 1978, between President Jimmy Carter, Egyptian President Anwar Sadat, and Israeli Prime Minister Menachem Begin. Carter recognized in these two men

a genuine desire to resolve the problems of the Middle East, and he hoped face-to-face meetings away from press scrutiny could bring about a new approach. The meetings ended with the Camp David Accords, a framework for a peace treaty that was concluded on the South Lawn of the White House in March 1979.

Jimmy Carter Presidential Library and Museum

1980 | PAGE 255
Iranian Hostage Crisis

On November 4, 1979, Iranian militants stormed the U.S. embassy in Tehran, taking 66 diplomatic personnel hostage. On April 30, 1980, a planned rescue mission to Iran went awry when several helicopters developed mechanical problems and one went down. President Jimmy Carter aborted the mission. As efforts to negotiate a release continued, the hostages were treated badly, often blindfolded, threatened, or neglected by their student captors. The hostages were not released until January 20, 1981, moments after Carter officially turned the Presidency over to Ronald Reagan. The crisis had lasted 444 days.

Jimmy Carter Presidential Library and Museum

1980 | PAGES 256–257
Mount St. Helens

Mount St. Helens, an active volcano in the Gifford Pinchot National Forest of Washington State, roared to life on May 18, 1980. For nine hours, the volcano erupted, destroying plant and animal life in the surrounding 230 square miles of forest. The blast of ash, rock, and steam blew across the land at speeds up to 670 miles per hour, with the ash plume reaching 15 miles high. President Jimmy Carter visited the site and declared it a disaster area. In 1982, President Ronald Reagan created the 110,000-acre National Volcanic Monument to protect the area around the volcano and give nature time to restore the environment.

Page 256: 95-JK-135-1. Page 257: top, National Archives at Seattle, RG 95, Records of the Forest Service; bottom, 311-M-30-4; Jimmy Carter Presidential Library and Museum

1985 | PAGE 258

Geneva Summit

President Ronald Reagan first met Mikhail Gorbachev, General Secretary of the Central Committee of the Communist Party of the Soviet Union, at a summit in Switzerland on November 19, 1985. Shortly afterward, he wrote a candid letter to Gorbachev, expressing his desire for a more constructive relationship.

Ronald Reagan Presidential Library and Museum

1987 | PAGE 259

Brandenburg Gate Speech, June 12, 1987

The Soviets erected the Berlin Wall in August 1961 to stop the mass exodus of people fleeing Soviet East Berlin for West Berlin and the non-Communist world. The wall, a mass of concrete, barbed wire, and stone cutting through the heart of the city, separated families and friends for more than a quarter-century. On June 12, 1987, President Ronald Reagan gave a historic speech at Berlin's famous Branden-burg Gate in which he challenged Soviet General Secretary Mikhail Gorbachev to demonstrate his commitment to change: "Mr. Gorbachev, open this gate. Mr. Gorbachev, tear down this wall." The wall finally fell in November 1989, signaling the end of the Cold War.

Ronald Reagan Presidential Library and Museum

1990 | PAGE 260

German Reunification, October 3, 1990.

On October 3, 1990, one year after the fall of the Berlin Wall, East and West Germany were officially reunified. This memo transcribes the brief telephone conversation that occurred between President George H.W. Bush and German Chancellor Helmut Kohl, who discussed the reunification celebration.

George Bush Presidential Library and Museum;
Berlin Wall image by Brian Blake

1990–1991 | PAGE 261

1991 Persian Gulf War

In August 1990, Iraq invaded neighboring Kuwait to gain possession of its rich oil fields and access to the sea. In response, the United States mounted Operation Desert Shield, condemning Iraq and gathering international support for economic embargoes. When Iraqi leader Saddam Hussein refused to retreat, President George H.W. Bush ordered the U.S. military into battle, launching Operation Desert Storm in January 1991. In a letter to his children before the fighting began, President Bush expressed his thoughts about the possibility of war with Iraq. The U.S. and NATO coalition achieved a swift victory by the end of February, and polls showed that 89 percent of Americans approved of the President's actions.

George Bush Presidential Library and Museum

1993 | PAGE 262

North American Free Trade Agreement

Though negotiations for the North American Free Trade Agreement (NAFTA) began at the end of his predecessor's term in 1991, President Bill Clinton took on the task of steering its ratification through Congress. Designed to lower tariffs and other trade restrictions between the United States, Canada, and Mexico over 15 years, the pact was opposed by many who thought it would drive manufacturing to other countries. Clinton was convinced it would create new American jobs and help keep existing jobs in the United States. The agreement was signed into law December 8, 1993.

William J. Clinton Presidential Library and Museum

1995 | PAGE 263

Oklahoma City Bombing, April 19, 1995

On April 19, 1995, Americans Timothy McVeigh and Terry Nichols used a truck bomb to destroy the Alfred P. Murrah Federal Building in Oklahoma City, killing 168 people and injuring more than 800. President Bill Clinton spoke to the American people that evening and visited the scene a few days later to deliver a eulogy. The bombers, sympathizers of an American militia movement, were tried and convicted in 1997. McVeigh was executed by lethal injection in 2001, and Nichols was sentenced to life in prison.

William J. Clinton Presidential Library and Museum

2001 | PAGES 264–265

9/11

On September 11, 2001, terrorists hijacked four U.S. commercial airliners, crashing two into the World Trade Center in New York City and one into the Pentagon in Arlington, Virginia. The fourth plane, believed to be bound for Washington, crashed into a Pennsylvania field after passengers stormed the cabin in an attempt to retake the plane. Thousands of people died in the crashes and the collapse of the two World Trade Center buildings. The National Commission on Terrorist Attacks upon the United States (known as the 9/11 Commission) was created by Congress in late 2002 to investigate the attacks and the American response. The 9/11 Commission records are now in the Center for Legislative Archives of the National Archives. The Federal Emergency Management Agency images, including the one of the Pentagon, were among the first accessions the National Archives received of digital photographs.

All of Page 264, Page 265: left center and bottom, right top and bottom, RG 148, Records of Commissions of the Legislative Branch. Page 265: top left, RG 311, Records of the Federal Emergency Management Agency [retrieved from the Access to Archival Databases (AAD)]

2001 | PAGE 266

Establishing the Office of Homeland Security, October 8, 2001

After the terrorist attacks of September 11, 2001, President George W. Bush issued an Executive Order creating the Office of Homeland Security within the Executive Office of the President to develop a comprehensive national strategy to shield the United States against terrorist threats. In November 2002, Congress established a new Cabinet department, consolidating several Executive branch agencies into the Department of Homeland Security, in one of the largest Government reorganizations in U.S. history.

Federal Register: 66 FR 51812, October 8, 2001

2001 | PAGE 267

USA PATRIOT Act, Public Law 107-56, October 26, 2001

In the aftermath of the September 11, 2001, terrorist attacks, the USA PATRIOT Act was passed by wide margins in both the House and Senate and signed into law by President George W. Bush on October 26, 2001. The acronym stands for Uniting and Strengthening America by Providing Appropriate Tools Required to Intercept and Obstruct Terrorism, but it is commonly known as the Patriot Act. Among its provisions, the law increased the surveillance and investigative powers of law enforcement agencies, allowing them to search telephone, e-mail, and other records, and expanded the definition of terrorism to include domestic terrorism.

RG 11, General Records of the U.S. Government

2009 | PAGE 268

Official Tally from the Joint Session of Congress for the Counting of the Electoral Votes for President and Vice President of the United States, January 8, 2009

After every Presidential election, the Senate and House of Representatives meet in joint session to verify the certificates and count the votes of the electors from each of the states. This is the official tally issued on January 8, 2009, confirming the historic election of Barack Obama for President and Joseph Biden for Vice President.

RG 46, Records of the U.S. Senate

NATIONAL ARCHIVES LOCATIONS

National Archives Building
Washington, DC

The National Archives Building in downtown Washington is the original National Archives, which opened its doors in 1935. It is home to the Charters of Freedom—the Declaration of Independence, the U.S. Constitution, and the Bill of Rights. In addition, the original building contains the National Archives Experience with its award-winning "Public Vaults," a permanent educational exhibition showcasing the treasured records of the Archives. The Lawrence F. O'Brien Gallery, displaying temporary and traveling exhibitions, the 294-seat William G. McGowan Theater, and the Boeing Learning Center, the flagship venue for National Archives educational outreach, are also located here.

The National Archives Building is a major research facility for historical records of all three branches of the Federal Government, including judicial records of the U.S. Supreme Court and the District of Columbia court. American Indian, old military (records of the Army before World War I and the Navy and Marine Corps before World War II), and maritime records are also found here.

Federal records of particular value to genealogical researchers are preserved in the National Archives Building. The microfilm research room contains self-service census records, passenger arrival lists, and indexes to late 18th- and 19th-century military service and pension records. American Indian, old military, and maritime records are also located here. For more information, see *www.archives.gov/genealogy/*.

The Center for Legislative Archives is the designated repository, reference center, and outreach organization for the historically valuable records of the U.S. Congress. The Center holds records dating from the First Federal Congress. The official records from the committees of the House of Representatives and the Senate—the standing, select, special, and joint committees—represent the core holdings of the Center. In addition, the Center holds records of legislative agencies, including out-of-print publications of the Government Printing Office. More information is available at *www.archives.gov/legislative*.

Established in 1934, the National Historical Publications and Records Commission (NHPRC), a statutory body affiliated with the National Archives and Records Administration (NARA), supports a wide range of activities to preserve, publish, and encourage the use of documentary sources, created in every medium—ranging from quill pen to computer—relating to the history of the United States. For more information see *www.archives.gov/nhprc/*.

In addition, the National Archives houses the Information Security Oversight Office (ISOO), which is responsible to the President for developing policies for classifying, declassifying, and safeguarding national security information generated in Government and in industry to protect information vital to U.S. national security interests. For more information, see *www.archives.gov/isoo/*.

National Archives and Records Administration
700 Pennsylvania Avenue, NW
Washington, DC 20408-0002

Web site: *www.archives.gov*
Telephone: 202-357-5000
Customer Service Center Telephone Number: 1-866-272-6272

National Archives at College Park

The National Archives at College Park, Maryland, opened for research in 1994 and was specially designed for housing archival records and supporting archival research. In addition to textual records, the National Archives at College Park contains special media records, including motion pictures, still photographs and posters, sound recordings, maps, architectural drawings, aerial photographs, and electronic records. The research complex is located on five floors, consisting of separate research rooms for textual, microform, still picture, motion picture and sound, cartographic and architectural, and electronic media.

Records of civilian agencies date from 1789 and include records of the Departments of Agriculture, Commerce, Education, Energy, Health and Human Services, Housing and Urban Development, Interior, Justice, Labor, State, Transportation, and Treasury. Also among the records are those for World War I emergency agencies, New Deal and Depression-era agencies, and the Office of Management and Budget and other components of the Executive Office of the President.

Notable bodies of investigative records include those relating to the assassination of President John F. Kennedy and those accumulated by the Watergate Special Prosecution Force and Independent Counsels.

Military holdings at College Park include records of the Army and Army Air Forces dating from World War I and Navy, Marine Corps, intelligence, defense-related, and seized enemy records dating from World War II. These records document policy making at the most senior level as carried out by the civilian service secretaries, the uniformed chiefs of services, and the Joint Chiefs of Staff. Although the College Park facility generally does not have records documenting the service and contributions of individual military personnel in the 20th century, it does hold the organizational records of a variety of military units. Documented units include World War II Army Air Forces bomb groups, World War II Marine Corps units, Navy ships, and Army units that served in World Wars I and II, Korea, and Vietnam.

National Archives and Records Administration
8601 Adelphi Road
College Park, MD 20740-6001

Web site: *www.archives.gov/dc-metro/college-park/*
Telephone: 301-837-2000
Customer Service Center Telephone Number: 1-866-272-6272

Office of the Federal Register

First published in 1936, the *Federal Register* is a daily record of the official actions of the Executive Branch of the Federal Government. The Office of the Federal Register provides access to the American people to the official text of Federal laws, Presidential documents, administrative regulations and notices of proposed rulemaking by Federal agencies, and descriptions of Federal organizations, programs, and activities. When the first edition of the *Federal Register* was printed, it was a 16-page booklet, delivered to interested citizens by mail. Today, the *Federal Register* is available on the World Wide Web, and each year, the information is compiled in the *Code of Federal Regulations*. The *Federal Register* also administers the Electoral College, which oversees the selection of U.S. Presidents and the Constitutional Amendment process.

Office of the Federal Register (NF)
National Archives and Records Administration
8601 Adelphi Road
College Park, MD 20740-6001

Web site: *www.archives.gov/federal-register/*
E-mail: *fedreg.info@nara.gov*
Telephone: 202-741-6000

Regional Archives

In addition to the National Archives Buildings in Washington, DC, and nearby College Park, Maryland, 13 National Archives locations in major metropolitan areas across the nation provide access to original documents and other records that illuminate the past. Regional archives are located from Atlanta to Anchorage, from Boston to Seattle, from New York to San Francisco, from Philadelphia to Los Angeles, and throughout the nation's heartland, encompassing Chicago, St. Louis, Kansas City, Ft. Worth, and Denver. Each is unique, focusing on a geographic area of the United States, and is a point-of-entry to the whole of the National Archives' resources and expertise.

Since 1968, these National Archives locations have been responsible for preserving and providing access to the retired records of U.S. courts and of Federal agency programs, administered by agency field offices and sometimes headquarter offices, within a certain geographic region. For example, whereas the Washington, DC, locations hold records of Federal agencies' headquarters, the Atlanta location—covering states of the American southeast—holds the archived records of Federal agency field offices for the following states: Kentucky, North Carolina, South Carolina, Tennessee, Georgia, Florida, and Alabama. The National Archives at Atlanta also houses records of agencies based primarily in the southeast, such as the Centers for Disease Control and the Tennessee Valley Authority.

How do visitors use records, and why? Through the regional archives web site, visitors use records to research their family histories, to study a favorite historical topic, whether for personal or for professional reasons, to research school projects and legal claims, and to create educational materials. Among most-often-used records are court records, which contain evidence ranging from fascinating pop culture to heartbreaking personal stories, naturalization records and ships' passenger arrival records noting immigration and citizenship details, and Federal land records important to demographics, land rights, and ecology. The greatest volume of records served at the regional archives—over one million every year—are copies of Official Military Personnel Files needed by veterans and their next-of-kin to prove eligibility for veterans' benefits. When these files reach a certain age, they become available to the public for genealogical and historical research as well.

Better than an online experience is an in-person visit to the nearest National Archives location. There is no digital substitute for the experience of holding an authentic historical record, for being on-site to learn from professionals how to search documents while discovering connections to the nation's past. Access is free—to documents, displays and exhibits, online genealogy subscription services, workshops, events, and more.

And if researchers need help when looking for an important piece of history, expert staff and volunteers will point the way.

Regional archives reach communities through partnerships with other cultural, educational, and civic organizations. Through opportunities with the Department of Education and National History Day, regional archives programs teach that the nation's records are the foundation of Government accountability, the basis of individual, legal rights, and for understanding ourselves as a people. National Archives programs in major metropolitan areas assist teachers locally and are a resource to educators in the inner city and underserved districts.

Another way the National Archives provides access to Federal records is through the Affiliated Archives program. Affiliated Archives are public or non-profit archives that hold—by written agreement with the National Archives—Federal records owned by the National Archives and Records Administration. And through Affiliated Archives, Federal records remain in unique collections, preserved for use at institutions such as the Pennsylvania State Archives, the Oklahoma Historical Society, Yellowstone National Park, West Point U.S. Military Academy Archives, the U.S. Naval Academy William J. Jeffries Memorial Archives, the Library of Congress Prints and Photographs Division, the National Park Service HABS/HAER Division, the University of North Texas Libraries, and the State Records Center and Archives, Santa Fe, New Mexico.

National Archives at Anchorage
654 West Third Avenue
Anchorage, Alaska 99501-2145
Web site: *www.archives.gov/pacific-alaska/anchorage/*
E-mail: *alaska.archives@nara.gov*
Telephone: 907-261-7820
Federal records of Alaska.

National Archives at Atlanta
5780 Jonesboro Road
Morrow, Georgia 30260
Web site: *www.archives.gov/southeast/*
E-mail: *atlanta.archives@nara.gov*
Telephone: 770-968-2100
Federal records of Alabama, Florida, Georgia, Kentucky, Mississippi, North Carolina, South Carolina, and Tennessee.

National Archives at Boston
Frederick C. Murphy Federal Center
380 Trapelo Road
Waltham, Massachusetts 02452-6399
Web site: *www.archives.gov/northeast/boston/*
E-mail: *waltham.archives@nara.gov*
Telephone: 781-663-0130
Federal records of Connecticut, Maine, Massachusetts, New Hampshire, Rhode Island, and Vermont.

National Archives at Chicago
7358 South Pulaski Road
Chicago, IL 60629-5898
Web site: *www.archives.gov/great-lakes/*
E-mail: *chicago.archives@nara.gov*
Telephone: 773-948-9001
Maintains records created or received by Federal agencies in Illinois, Minnesota, and Wisconsin, and Federal courts in Illinois, Indiana, Michigan, Minnesota, Ohio, and Wisconsin.

National Archives at Denver
Located in Denver Federal Center,
Buildings 46 and 48
P.O. Box 25307
Denver, Colorado 80225
Web site: *www.archives.gov/rocky-mountain/*
E-mail: *denver.archives@nara.gov*
Telephone: 303-407-5740
Federal records of Colorado, Montana, New Mexico, North Dakota, South Dakota, Utah, Wyoming, and other states. Please note: North and South Dakota records created before 1972 are held at the National Archives at Kansas City.

National Archives at Fort Worth
Research Room, original paper records
1400 John Burgess Drive
Fort Worth, Texas 76140
Web site: *www.archives.gov/southwest/*
E-mail: *ftworth.archives@nara.gov*
Telephone: 817-551-2000
Federal records of Louisiana, Oklahoma, and Texas.

National Archives at Kansas City
400 West Pershing Road
Kansas City, MO 64108
Web site: *www.archives.gov/central-plains/kansas-city/*
E-mail: *kansascity.archives@nara.gov*
Telephone: 816-268-8000
Federal records of Iowa, Kansas, Missouri, and Nebraska.

National Archives at New York City
201 Varick Street, 12th Floor
New York, NY 10014
Web site: *www.archives.gov/northeast/nyc/*
E-mail: *newyork.archives@nara.gov*
Telephone: 1-866-840-1752 or 212-401-1620
Federal records of New York, New Jersey, Puerto Rico, and the U.S. Virgin Islands.

National Archives at Philadelphia
900 Market Street
Philadelphia, Pennsylvania 19107-4292
Web site: *www.archives.gov/midatlantic/*
E-mail: *philadelphia.archives@nara.gov*
Telephone: 215-606-0100
Federal records of Pennsylvania, Delaware, West Virginia, Maryland, and Virginia.

Pittsfield Annex, The National Archives at Boston
Silvio O. Conte National Records Center
10 Conte Drive
Pittsfield, Massachusetts 01201-8230
Web site: *www.archives.gov/northeast/pittsfield/*
E-mail: *pittsfield.archives@nara.gov*
Telephone: 413-236-3600

National Archives at Riverside
23123 Cajalco Road
Perris, CA 92570
Web site: *www.archives.gov/pacific/riverside/*
Telephone: 951-956-2000
Federal records of Arizona, southern California, and Clark County, Nevada. (These are the holdings formerly located at the facility in Laguna Niguel.)

National Archives at San Francisco
1000 Commodore Drive
San Bruno, California 94066-2350
Web site: *www.archives.gov/pacific/san-francisco/*
E-mail: *sanbruno.archives@nara.gov*
Telephone: 650-238-3501
Federal records of northern and central California, Nevada (except Clark County), Hawaii, American Samoa, and the Trust Territory of the Pacific Islands.

National Archives at Seattle
6125 Sand Point Way, NE
Seattle, Washington 98115-7999
Web site: *www.archives.gov/pacific-alaska/seattle/*
E-mail: *seattle.archives@nara.gov*
Telephone: 206-336-5115
Federal records of Idaho, Oregon, and Washington.

Federal Records Centers

Since 1950, the National Archives has operated a nationwide network of Federal Records Centers (FRCs), which protect, preserve, and make available records of agencies of the Federal Government. The FRCs store more than 26 million cubic feet of records and process an average of 13 million reference requests per year. The FRCs include 17 facilities employing more than 1,100 Federal employees and serving 400 Federal agencies.

FRCs store and service every kind of Federal record—tax returns, claims files for military veterans, blueprints of Federal buildings and structures, cancelled checks for Social Security payments and tax refunds, bankruptcy court records, inmate files on Federal prisoners, and maps of national parks, to name just a few. FRCs hold records for citizens who have served in the military, had a Social Security number, or applied for a passport.

The records in the physical custody of FRCs legally belong to the Federal agencies that created them and generally can be requested only by authorized representatives of these agencies. However, a number of Federal records (such as military records stored at the National Personnel Records Center or certain Federal court documents) can be accessed by the public under agreement with the owning Federal agency.

In addition to storing and servicing temporary records, FRCs protect and preserve permanent records from the time they are no longer needed for daily business until they are accessioned into the National Archives. Archival control of the permanent records is assured because the records are in continuous Federal custody for their entire lifecycle. About 90 percent of textual permanent records that are accessioned into the National Archives have come through the Federal records center system.

Over the years, the holdings in FRCs have steadily increased. When funds appropriated by Congress to operate the FRC system no longer kept up with the demand from agencies for services, Public Law 106-58 established a revolving fund to operate the centers. Since October 1, 1999, the Federal Records Centers Program has been supported entirely by the fees it charges to other agencies.

Each of NARA's Federal records centers has unique capabilities to serve customer needs. Facilities in the system include traditional warehouses, climate-controlled space for permanent records, underground retrofitted limestone mines, a custom-built cold storage vault for film, high-security vaults for classified records, and state-of-the-art storage vaults for records stored on electronic media.

The FRCs are embracing new technologies to better manage and service the records in their custody. The FRC is currently developing the Archives and Records Centers Information System (ARCIS). When fully deployed at the end of 2009, ARCIS will be the online portal through which NARA's customer agencies will do business with FRCs and will automate and streamline workflow within the centers.

Atlanta, GA
NARA Southeast Region
Federal Records Center
4712 Southpark Boulevard
Ellenwood, GA 30294-3595
Web site: *www.archives.gov/southeast/agencies*
Telephone: 404-736-2820

Boston, MA
NARA Northeast Region
Waltham Federal Records Center
380 Trapelo Road
Waltham, MA 02452-6399
Web site: *www.archives.gov/northeast/boston/agencies/frc/about.html*
Telephone: 781-663-0130

Chicago, IL
NARA Great Lakes Region
Chicago Federal Records Center
7358 Pulaski Road
Chicago, IL 60629-5898
Web site: *www.archives.gov/great-lakes/contact/frc-chicago.html*
Telephone: 773-948-9000

Dayton, OH
NARA Great Lakes Region
Dayton Springboro Road Federal Records Center
3150 Springboro Road
Dayton, OH 45439-1867
Web site: *www.archives.gov/great-lakes/contact/directions-oh.html*
Telephone: 937-425-0600

Dayton-Miamisburg (Kingsridge)
NARA Great Lakes Region
Dayton Kingsridge Drive Federal Records Center
8801 Kingsridge Drive
Miamisburg, OH 45458-1617
Web site: *www.archives.gov/great-lakes/contact/directions-oh.html*
Telephone: 937-425-0601

Denver, CO
NARA Rocky Mountain Region
Federal Records Center
Building 48 -Denver Federal Center
Denver, CO 80225-0307
Web site: *www.archives.gov/rocky-mountain/frc*

Fort Worth, TX
NARA Southwest Region
Federal Records Center
1400 John Burgess Drive
Fort Worth, TX 76140-6222
Web site: *www.archives.gov/southwest/agencies/frc*
Telephone: 817-551-2000

Lee's Summit, MO
NARA Central Plains Region
Lee's Summit Federal Records Center
200 Space Center Drive
Lee's Summit, MO 64064-1182
Web site: *www.archives.gov/central-plains/lees-summit/agencies*
Telephone: 816-268-8150

Lenexa, KS
NARA Central Plains Region
Lenexa Federal Records Center
17501 W. 98th Street
Lenexa, KS 66219
Web site: *www.archives.gov/central-plains/lenexa*
Telephone: 913-563-7600

Philadelphia, PA
NARA Mid-Atlantic Region
Federal Records Center
14700 Townsend Road
Philadelphia, PA 19154-1025
Web site: *www.archives.gov/midatlantic/agencies*
Telephone: 215-305-2000

Pittsfield, MA
NARA Northeast Region
Silvio O. Conte National Records Center
10 Conte Drive
Pittsfield, MA 01201-8230
Web site: *www.archives.gov/northeast/pittsfield*
Telephone: 413-236-3600

Riverside, CA
NARA Pacific Region
Riverside Federal Records Center
23123 Cajalco Road
Perris, CA 92570-7298
Web site: *www.archives.gov/pacific/riverside*
Telephone: 951-956-2000

San Francisco, CA
NARA Pacific Region
San Francisco Federal Records Center
1000 Commodore Drive
San Bruno, CA 94066-2350
Web site: *www.archives.gov/pacific/frc/san-francisco/contacts.html*
Telephone: 650-238-3500

Seattle, WA
NARA Pacific Alaska Region
Federal Records Center
6125 Sand Point Way NE
Seattle, WA 98115-7999
Web site: *www.archives.gov/pacific-alaska/seattle/agencies*
Telephone: 206-336-5115

St. Louis, MO
NARA National Personnel Records Center
(Civilian Personnel Records)
111 Winnebago Street
St. Louis, MO 63118-4126
Web site: *www.archives.gov/st-louis/civilian-personnel/*
E-mail: *cpr.center@nara.gov*
Telephone: 314-801-0800

St. Louis, MO
National Archives at St. Louis
National Personnel Records Center
(Military Personnel Records)
9700 Page Avenue
St. Louis, MO 63132-5100
Web site: *www.archives.gov/st-louis/military-personnel/public/archival-programs.html*
E-mail: *MPR.center@nara.gov*
Status check: *mpr.status@nara.gov*
Telephone: 314-801-0800

St. Louis, MO
NARA National Personnel Records Center Annex
1411 Boulder Boulevard
Valmeyer, IL 62295

Suitland, MD
NARA Washington National Records Center
4205 Suitland Road
Suitland, MD 20746-8001
Web site: *www.archives.gov/dc-metro/suitland*
Telephone: 301-778-1600

Herbert Hoover
Presidential Library and Museum

Herbert Hoover served as President from 1929 to 1933. The library was dedicated on August 10, 1962.

The Herbert Hoover Presidential Library and Museum promotes the collection, interpretation, and preservation of historical resources relating to the life, ideas, values, and times of Herbert Hoover. The library was dedicated on Mr. Hoover's 88th birthday in 1962. In the years since, more than three million visitors have toured the museum and more than 3,000 scholars from every state in the union and a dozen foreign countries have utilized the library's eight million pages of documentary holdings and 40,000 photographs.

In recent years, the library has become a nationally recognized center for the study of 20th-century history, the American Presidency, and American life and culture. In addition to the papers of Herbert Hoover, manuscript holdings include the papers of Hoover associate and Atomic Energy Commission Chairman Lewis Strauss, U.S. Senators Gerald Nye of North Dakota and Bourke Hickenlooper of Iowa, newspaper columnists Westbrook Pegler, Walter Trohan, and Clark Mollenhoff, and writer and journalist Rose Wilder Lane, whose papers include correspondence with and manuscripts from her mother, Laura Ingalls Wilder.

The library has sponsored major exhibits featuring personal memorabilia from every U.S. President and First Lady, a pioneering look at World War I, and an unprecedented display of Presidential gifts. Other exciting exhibits have focused on the Roaring Twenties, the Civil War, the Mississippi River, Elvis Presley, Abraham Lincoln, and other subjects of broad public appeal.

The Herbert Hoover Presidential Library Association is the non-profit foundation that supports the work of the library. The library and the Library Association periodically host featured speakers or conferences pertaining to issues related to Hoover, and more broadly, to U.S. history and culture. The Library Association annually awards travel grants to researchers, hosts the annual Uncommon Student Award (a scholarship and community service program for high school juniors) and organizes Hooverfest, the annual celebration of Hoover's birthday.

Herbert Hoover Presidential Library and Museum
210 Parkside Drive
West Branch, Iowa 52358-0488

Web site: *http://hoover.archives.gov/*
E-mail for general inquiries: *hoover.library@nara.gov*
Telephone number for general inquiries: 319-643-5301

Franklin D. Roosevelt
Presidential Library and Museum

Franklin Delano Roosevelt served as President from 1933 to 1945. The library was dedicated on June 30, 1941; the Henry A. Wallace Visitor and Education Center was dedicated on November 15, 2003.

The Franklin D. Roosevelt Presidential Library and Museum is the Federal Government's first Presidential library—and the only one used by a sitting President. It was designed by FDR himself, in the Dutch colonial style, and opened during World War II. By donating his papers to the library, Roosevelt established the precedent for public ownership of Presidential papers, which became Federal law in 1978.

The Roosevelt Library is the world's premier research center for the study of the Roosevelt era. The library houses more than 17 million pages of manuscript materials in some 400 distinct collections including the 3 million page archive of Eleanor Roosevelt; 51,000 books, including FDR's personal collection of 21,000 volumes; and 150,000 photographs and audiovisual items. The library conducts one of the busiest research operations in the Presidential library system and is used by several thousand on-site and remote researchers each year.

As he planned his Presidential library, FDR took care to include space for a museum. Today's museum visitors can explore exhibits about the lives of Franklin and Eleanor Roosevelt and the dramatic events of the Great Depression and World War II.

The Roosevelt Presidential Library conducts educational programs designed for K–12 and college students, teachers, and adult learners based on the library's documentary, audiovisual, and museum collections. Programs include on- and off-site workshops, museum programs, and teacher-development seminars. The library offers an active calendar of public programs including an annual Roosevelt Reading Festival, book talks, public forums, and living history displays. The library's web site has more than 1 million visitors each year, including researchers using the digital archives and teachers and students exploring educational resources.

The Franklin and Eleanor Roosevelt Institute is dedicated to informing new generations of the ideas and achievements of Franklin and Eleanor Roosevelt and serves as the library's private sector partner. It provides essential support for the library's planned renovation, exhibit program, educational and public programs, as well as a variety of other programs.

Franklin D. Roosevelt Presidential Library and Museum
4079 Albany Post Road
Hyde Park, New York 12538

Web site: *www.fdrlibrary.marist.edu*
E-mail for general inquiries: *roosevelt.library@nara.gov*
Telephone number for general inquiries: 1-800-337-8474

Harry S. Truman
Presidential Library and Museum

Harry S. Truman served as President from 1945 to 1953.
The library was dedicated on July 6, 1957.

The Harry S. Truman Presidential Library and Museum was established to preserve the papers, books, artifacts and other historical materials of the 33rd President of the United States and make them available for purposes of research, education, and exhibition. The Truman Library was the nation's second Presidential library.

The Truman Library has 15 million pages of manuscript materials, of which about half are President Truman's papers. The library has hundreds of transcripts of oral history interviews with President Truman's family, friends, and associates available for research. It also contains an extensive audiovisual collection of still pictures, audio recordings, motion pictures, and videotape recordings. The museum's collection consists of approximately 30,000 objects—including hundreds of Truman family possessions, political memorabilia, and diplomatic gifts.

The library features the first of its kind Oval Office replica and a working office in which Harry Truman met with visiting dignitaries, handled correspondence, and directed activities of the library from 1957 until 1966.

Through its public programs, the library reaches a diverse audience of people and organizations. It sponsors conferences and research seminars, conducts special tours of the library's museum for school classes and educational groups, and creates a wide range of other activities.

The library's education department sponsors teacher workshops and prepares activities and lesson plans for elementary and secondary students. The White House Decision Center gives students a firsthand look at President Truman's decisions concerning civil rights, the Korean War, the Berlin Airlift, and the ending of the war against Japan.

The Truman Library is supported, in part, by the Harry S. Truman Library Institute, its not-for-profit partner. The Institute promotes, through educational and community programs, a greater appreciation and understanding of American politics and government, history and culture, and public service, as exemplified by Harry Truman.

Harry S. Truman Presidential Library and Museum
500 West U.S. Highway 24
Independence, Missouri 64050-1798

Web site: *www.trumanlibrary.org*
E-mail for general inquiries: *truman.library@nara.gov*
Telephone number for general inquiries: 1-800-833-1225

Dwight D. Eisenhower
Presidential Library and Museum

Dwight D. Eisenhower served as President from 1953 to 1961.
The museum was dedicated on November 11, 1954.
The library was dedicated on May 1, 1962.

The mission of the Eisenhower Presidential Library and Museum is to collect, preserve, and make available to scholars, students, teachers, and the general public, historical materials relating to the life and times of General of the Army and President of the United States Dwight D. Eisenhower.

The historical materials consist of more than 26 million pages of manuscripts, including the papers of President Eisenhower and members of his administration; 330,000 still photographs; 767,000 feet of motion picture film; 1,120 hours of audio recordings; 31,850 pages of oral history transcripts; 28,300 books; and 68,000 artifacts. The holdings include the "In case of failure" note Eisenhower wrote the night before the Normandy invasion; the platinum-, diamond-, and ruby-encrusted "Order of Victory" medallion he received from the Soviet Union; and his boyhood home. The Place of Meditation provides the final resting place for Dwight, Mamie, and Doud Eisenhower.

The Eisenhower Library and Museum is also home to the Kansas Town Hall, a forum for political debates, panel discussions on the issues of the day, cultural exchanges with foreign guests, and film series. The Town Hall program of the Eisenhower Presidential Library and Museum is the public square of Kansas and enhances the civic literacy of all visitors.

Education programs similarly increase the civic literacy of teachers and students through the use of primary source research and document analysis exercises. "Five Star Leaders" is an experiential learning program that challenges students (8th grade and up) to chart a course through military and political crises using the documents that were available to the original participants during the events under consideration.

The Eisenhower Foundation's mission is to honor President Eisenhower and to perpetuate his legacy; to support programs relating to citizenship; and to support those operations of the Eisenhower Presidential Library and Museum that are not federally funded.

Dwight D. Eisenhower Presidential Library and Museum
200 Southeast Fourth Street
Abilene, Kansas 67410-2900

Web site: *www.eisenhower.archives.gov*
E-mail for general inquiries: *Eisenhower.library@nara.gov*
Telephone number for general inquiries: 1-877-746-4453

John F. Kennedy
Presidential Library and Museum

John F. Kennedy served as President from 1961 to 1963. The library was dedicated on October 20, 1979.

The John F. Kennedy Presidential Library and Museum is dedicated to the memory of the nation's 35th President and to all those who through the art of politics seek a new and better world.

The library's purpose is to advance the study and understanding of President Kennedy's life, career, and the times in which he lived; and to promote a greater appreciation of America's political and cultural heritage, the process of governing, and the importance of public service.

The library accomplishes its mission by preserving and making accessible the records of President Kennedy and his times; promoting open discourse on current critical issues; and educating and encouraging citizens to contribute, through public and community service, to shaping our nation's future.

The library's archives contain 48 million pages of documents, 400,000 photographs, 8 million feet of film, 20,000 hours of audio and video recordings and more than 20,000 museum objects. It also includes the papers of Ernest Hemingway.

The Kennedy Library strives to share its collections and mission with the public through its permanent and changing exhibits. Its lively and diverse educational programs facilitate the way young students learn about the Kennedy era and how it relates to the world today, and encourage open discussion among citizens through a series of public forums on a wide range of topics. Since launching its new web site in March 2006, there have been more than seven million online visits.

All Kennedy Library programs are generously supported by the John F. Kennedy Library Foundation, a non-profit organization that enables the John F. Kennedy Presidential Library and Museum to expand its research and archival capacity, to undertake marketing and public information projects, to offer intern and research fellowship programs, to enhance its museum and exhibits, and to offer nationally recognized educational and public programming.

John F. Kennedy Presidential Library and Museum
Columbia Point
Boston, Massachusetts 02125-3398

Web site: *www.jfklibrary.org*
E-mail for general inquiries: *kennedy.library@nara.gov*
Telephone number for general inquiries: 1-866-535-1960

Lyndon Baines Johnson
Presidential Library and Museum

Lyndon Baines Johnson served as President from 1963 to 1969. The library was dedicated on May 22, 1971.

The Lyndon Baines Johnson Library and Museum is located at the University of Texas, Austin, and is the first Presidential library constructed on a college campus. The LBJ Library houses vast archives to be mined, a national forum for the free exchange of ideas, and a splendid museum containing the visual record of a tumultuous era.

The LBJ Library preserves and protects the historical materials in its collections and makes them readily accessible; increases public awareness of the American experience through relevant exhibitions, symposia, and educational programs; and serves as a center for intellectual activity and community leadership while meeting the challenges of a changing world. The holdings of the library include more than 45 million pages of documents, extensive audiovisual collections, over 2,500 oral history interviews, and 54,000 museum artifacts.

The Lyndon Baines Johnson Foundation supports activities of the LBJ Library and Museum not funded by the Federal Government. President Johnson was the first President to establish a foundation to provide financial support for the library's ongoing endeavors, and it has served as a model emulated by other Presidential libraries.

In accordance with President Johnson's wishes, admission to the library is free, and more than 300,000 people visit the museum exhibits each year. Many more visit the library's web site to use its educational and audiovisual materials and digitized documents, while scholars from around the world conduct research in the library.

President Johnson said that the library has the story of his administration's time "with the bark off," showing the facts whether they be joys and triumphs or sorrows and failures. He said that he hoped that visitors to the library would get a closer understanding of the Presidency and "a clearer comprehension of what this nation tried to do in an eventful period in its history."

Lyndon Baines Johnson Presidential Library and Museum
2313 Red River Street
Austin, Texas 78705-5702

Web site: *www.lbjlib.utexas.edu*
E-mail for general inquiries: *johnson.library@nara.gov*
Telephone number for general inquiries: 512-721-0200

Richard Nixon
Presidential Library and Museum

Richard Nixon served as President from 1969 to 1974. The library was opened as a Federal institution on July 11, 2007, incorporating some of the facilities of the private Richard Nixon Library & Birthplace Foundation.

The Richard Nixon Presidential Library and Museum preserves the record of the Nixon administration and materials related to Richard Nixon's life and career.

The library's holdings include the papers of the Nixon Presidential administration, the Nixon Vice Presidential and congressional materials, and a limited selection of other pre- and post-Presidential materials. Among the most noteworthy records in the collection are the approximately 3,700 hours of secretly recorded Presidential conversations—the "Nixon tapes"—which cover the period from February 1971 until July 1973. The library also has an extensive audiovisual collection that includes many contemporary television broadcasts, recordings of White House events, and still photographs of White House functions. In late 2009, more than a hundred video oral history interviews with former administration officials and others who were prominent in the era were opened to the public.

Among the highlights of the library's museum in Yorba Linda are permanent exhibits exploring President Nixon's foreign policy, the life and style of First Lady Patricia Nixon, and the Apollo space program, featuring a lunar rock. A new, multimedia, and interactive Watergate gallery was added in 2009. The library also hosts public programs in its auditorium and its new Presidential Classroom. Its web site presents digitized copies of selected Presidential documents (including the complete Presidential Daily Diary for the Nixon administration) and Nixon tapes.

The library is developing an outreach program to local schools and universities to encourage students to use the library's archival resources and develop research skills. The staff of the Nixon Library at College Park, Maryland, is preparing to move the Presidential materials currently located at the College Park location to the permanent facility in Yorba Linda in 2010.

The library has an association with the private Richard Nixon Library & Birthplace Foundation which built the Yorba Linda facility and operated it until 2007. The Foundation supports the library's public programs, events, and exhibits.

Richard Nixon Presidential Library and Museum

18001 Yorba Linda Boulevard
Yorba Linda, California 92886

Web site: *www.nixonlibrary.gov*
E-mail for general inquiries: *Nixon@nara.gov*
Telephone number for general inquiries: 714-983-9120

Gerald R. Ford
Presidential Library and Museum

Gerald R. Ford served as President from 1974 to 1977. The library was dedicated on April 27, 1981; the museum was dedicated on September 18, 1981.

The Gerald R. Ford Presidential Library and Museum collects, researches, and preserves historical materials related to the Presidency, life, and times of Gerald R. Ford. Located separately, the library and museum work together to plan and implement exhibitions that explore their holdings and the history of the United States. They also develop and make available educational components and programs to further understanding of Gerald R. Ford, the Presidency, and U.S. history.

The museum houses artifacts that document the lives and careers of Gerald and Betty Ford. Significant parts of the collection include artifacts associated with the Bicentennial celebration of America's independence, foreign and domestic gifts to the President, and dresses and gowns of the First Lady. The library collects, preserves, and makes accessible to the public a rich body of archival materials on U.S. domestic issues, foreign relations, and political affairs during the Cold War era. Current holdings include 23 million pages of historical documents and half a million audiovisual items. The 1974–77 Presidential papers of Gerald Ford and his White House staff form the core collection. These are supplemented by the pre- and post-Presidential papers of Gerald Ford, the papers of Betty Ford, collections of Federal records, and private donations from former Government officials and private individuals.

The library and museum present speakers of public and political renown whose lectures support the mission of both institutions. Educational programs as varied as teacher workshops, curriculum aids, distance learning, and musical plays are also offered. The museum regularly hosts activities for patriotic holidays, Boy Scout functions, and naturalization ceremonies.

The Gerald R. Ford Foundation, a private, non-profit corporation, underwrites much of the library and museum's public programs, including speakers, community activities, and exhibits. The Foundation also offers scholarship grants, awards for excellence in journalism, and the Gerald R. Ford Public Service Medal.

Gerald R. Ford Presidential Library

1000 Beal Avenue
Ann Arbor, Michigan 48109-2114

Gerald R. Ford Presidential Museum

303 Pearl Street, NW
Grand Rapids, Michigan 49504-5353

Web site: *www.fordlibrarymuseum.gov*
E-mail for general inquiries: Library *ford.library@nara.gov*
Museum *ford.museum@nara.gov*
Telephone numbers for general inquiries: Library 734-205-0555
Museum 616-254-0400

Jimmy Carter
Presidential Library and Museum

Jimmy Carter served as President from 1977 to 1981. The Library was dedicated on October 1, 1986.

Situated on 35 acres of beautifully landscaped grounds with two small lakes and a serene Japanese Garden, the Jimmy Carter Presidential Library and Museum is the only Presidential library in the Southeast region of the United States.

The library houses more than 27 million pages of Presidential papers, one million feet of film, 600,000 photographs, and 3,750 hours of audio- and videotapes. Among the fascinating documents available to researchers is former Chief of Staff Hamilton Jordan's 1974 campaign strategy paper. Carter credits that strategy with enabling him to successfully run for President in 1976.

There are wide-ranging collections about the Middle East including the diary hostage Robert Ode wrote during his 444-day captivity in Iran, Carter's notes on the Camp David Summit, and his handwritten letters to Egyptian President Anwar Sadat and Israel's Menachem Begin.

In addition to the White House Photographers collection documenting the day-to-day activities of President and Mrs. Carter, the First Family has donated a large personal photo collection that includes their pictures from family vacations, Carter's Navy years, his governorship, and campaign for President.

The museum has a diverse collection of artifacts, awards, and gifts, ranging from President Carter's 2002 Nobel Peace Prize to a box of ten grains of rice from India, each grain inscribed with one of the Ten Commandments.

The library presents lectures by best-selling authors and partners with the Carter Center for discussions on global issues. It hosts school groups for educational programs and has developed lesson plans in conjunction with Georgia Performance Standards.

Adjoining the library is the Carter Center, the non-profit organization founded by President and Mrs. Carter to fight disease and promote peace. Together, the Carter Presidential Library and Museum and the Carter Center strive to educate, preserve, and illuminate the past and help shape a better future.

Jimmy Carter Presidential Library and Museum

441 Freedom Parkway
Atlanta, Georgia 30307-1498

Web site: *www.jimmycarterlibrary.gov*
E-mail for general inquiries: *carter.library@nara.gov*
Telephone number for general inquiries: 404-865-7100

Ronald Reagan
Presidential Library and Museum

Ronald W. Reagan served as President from 1981 to 1989. The library was dedicated on November 4, 1991.

The Ronald Reagan Presidential Library sits on a picturesque hilltop in Simi Valley, California. Its 100-acre campus includes archives and research facilities, a museum, a café, and the Air Force One Pavilion. The manicured grounds include President Reagan's grave site, a full-size section of the Berlin Wall, and an F-14 Tomcat jet fighter. It is approximately 50 miles northwest of downtown Los Angeles and about 45 minutes from Los Angeles International Airport.

Museum highlights include a full-size replica of the Oval Office, gifts from heads of state, an 1823 engraving of the Declaration of Independence, a 1930s-style movie theater featuring film clips from Reagan's days at Warner Brothers Studio, and exhibits that trace the life and times of Ronald Reagan.

The Air Force One Pavilion features a Marine One Helicopter and the Boeing 707 that served as Air Force One to Reagan and six other Presidents. Visitors can board this "flying White House" to view the magnificent aircraft in detail.

The archives collection of some 60 million pages includes records from the Reagan White House, the Reagan Gubernatorial papers, and the 1980 Reagan Presidential campaign papers. Audiovisual collections include more than 1.6 million photographs, hundreds of thousands of feet of film and audiotape, and over 20,000 videotapes.

The library is a favorite destination for school groups, where students can participate in the Air Force One Discovery Center. This unique interactive and immersive experience features a replica of the Oval Office, the White House Press Briefing Room, and the Command Decision Center aboard the USS *Ronald Reagan*. Here students assume the role of President and his advisors, making critical Presidential decisions.

The library is supported by the Ronald Reagan Presidential Foundation, which promotes the timeless principles Ronald Reagan stood for: individual liberty, economic opportunity, global democracy, and national pride. The Foundation supports extensive public programming including temporary exhibits, the Reagan Forum and Lecture, holiday celebrations, and Colonial America Week.

Ronald Reagan Presidential Library and Museum

40 Presidential Drive
Simi Valley, California 93065-0699

Web site: *www.reagan.utexas.edu*
E-mail for general inquiries: *reagan.library@nara.gov*
Telephone number for general inquiries: 1-800-410-8354

George Bush
Presidential Library and Museum

George Bush served as President from 1989 to 1993.
The Library was dedicated on November 6, 1997.

The George Bush Presidential Library and Museum is responsible for preserving President Bush's official records, personal papers, and museum artifacts for posterity, research, and exhibit.

The library tells the story of the life and times of its namesake. On a larger scale, it also focuses on American history and the office of the President, with an emphasis upon post-World War II history. The library embraces the role it plays in helping to shape an educated, informed, sensitive, and aware citizenry.

It takes many people to accomplish this mission. The library and museum's professional staff has formed a solid partnership with a dedicated team of 200 volunteers who represent the museum and work behind the scenes in the operation of the library and its programs. Having a living President who remains very active and interested in its mission allows it to host programs that continually place College Station on the world stage.

The education department is unparalleled and annually brings in 48,000 students to explore history and learn civic literacy; and the educational programs are fully integrated with the state's education standards. It hosts an annual summer camp for school children ages 7 to 11. Area high school juniors spend a day at the museum each year touring the featured exhibit and hearing keynote addresses from such luminaries as astronauts, prominent historians, groundbreaking scientists, and cultural pioneers.

The library's involvement with the Brazos Valley is an integral part of its mission. Community programs such as the monthly Issue Forums, Classic Film Series, Easter Egg Roll, 4th of July Celebration, Halloween Night at the Museum, and Holidays in the Rotunda make the institution a part of the cultural experience of the region.

Its changing exhibition program is ambitious, covering topics as varied as the "Art of China," the "Extraordinary Journey of Barbara Bush," the "50th Anniversary of the Space Program," "Berlin and the Cold War," "100 Tall Texans," and "Fathers & Sons: Two Families, Four Presidents." More than 1.5 million visitors have come through the museum in its 11 years of operation.

George Bush Presidential Library and Museum
1000 George Bush Drive West
College Station, Texas 77845

Web site: *http://bushlibrary.tamu.edu/*
E-mail for general inquiries: *bush.library@nara.gov*
Telephone number for general inquiries: 979-691-4000

William J. Clinton
Presidential Library and Museum

William J. Clinton served as President from 1993 to 2001.
The Library was dedicated on November 18, 2004.

The William J. Clinton Presidential Library promotes the understanding of the Clinton Presidency and its effects on the world at the end of the 20th century. It provides access to Presidential papers and creates museum exhibits that teach visitors about President Clinton's life, times, and Presidency.

The library preserves, protects, and provides access to the materials of Clinton's administration. It holds the day-to-day papers (such as letters, memos, and drafts of speeches) from the President, First Lady, and White House staff members.

It has photographs and videos taken by White House photographers and videographers, and copies of all audio and video feeds from all press events recorded in the White House.

Library holdings include 18.5 million e-mails, 76.8 million pages of documents, 1.85 million photographs, 12,500 videotapes and 85,000 museum artifacts. The holdings include gifts given to the Clinton family and White House staff members. These are from heads of foreign countries, from American private citizens, and from people throughout the world. Some are objects of great age and high value; others are simple gifts made by children. All are being preserved in proper museum conditions for future generations.

The library supports research and creates interactive programs and exhibits based on the interests and themes important to President Clinton during and after his Presidency. It also creates exhibits and programming related to the American Presidency as a whole.

The Clinton Library web site showcases papers, artifacts, and exhibits which people around the world can view without leaving home. It holds public events related to exhibits, the Clinton Presidency, and other topics in U.S. history.

The Clinton Foundation works around the world on projects that are important to President Clinton. The Foundation supports and promotes the Clinton Library's temporary exhibit program and public programs and special events for the entire Clinton Center.

William J. Clinton Presidential Library and Museum
1200 President Clinton Avenue
Little Rock, Arkansas 72201

Web site: *www.clintonlibrary.gov*
E-mail for general inquiries: *clinton.library@nara.gov*
Telephone number for general inquiries: 501-374-4242

George W. Bush
Presidential Library

George W. Bush served as President from 2001 to 2009. The George W. Bush Presidential Library and Museum's permanent location will be on the campus of Southern Methodist University (SMU) in Dallas, Texas. It is temporarily located in Lewisville, Texas, and is not yet open to the public or to researchers.

The George W. Bush Presidential Library seeks to preserve, protect, and provide access to the official records and other historical materials documenting the career of America's 43rd President. In addition, the library will play an important role in its community and beyond through educational initiatives and partnerships, public programs, museum exhibitions, and state-of-the-art archives storage, processing, and research. It is also engaged in archival research and exhibit planning for the public opening of the museum in Dallas, anticipated for 2013.

To date, the library holds more than 50,000 cubic feet of Presidential material. This material includes textual records, audiovisual materials, and artifacts, all detailing the immense responsibilities of and complex issues confronted by the President, First Lady, and White House staff members.

A unique characteristic of the George W. Bush Library is the enormous size of its electronic records collection, which includes over 100 terabytes of information. The various White House electronic systems, which included e-mails, the Daily Diary, and photographs, are part of the library's archives and are being incorporated into NARA's Electronic Records Archive (ERA). Through ERA, the library intends to preserve what is a tremendous resource for researchers.

The library will be supported by the George W. Bush Presidential Foundation, which has begun planning a museum with permanent and temporary exhibition galleries. Encompassing four themes—Freedom, Opportunity, Compassion, and Individual Responsibility—the museum will exhibit Presidential domestic and foreign gifts. The library's artifact holdings include the bullhorn that President Bush used to speak to rescue personnel at the World Trade Center site shortly after the September 11, 2001, attacks.

The United States confronted many daunting challenges during the Presidency of George W. Bush. The library will document how the President made significant decisions for the country's future and how the Government addressed highly complex issues. In its archives, through its programs, and by fostering its partnership in education with Southern Methodist University and the Bush Institute, it will provide the public the opportunity to learn more about the issues, events, and people that have helped define the nation in this new century.

George W. Bush Presidential Library
1725 Lakepointe Drive
Lewisville, TX 75057

Web site: *www.georgewbushlibrary.gov*
E-mail for general inquiries: *gwbush.library@nara.gov*
Telephone number for general inquiries: 972-353-0545